STRESS AND COPING

Stress and Coping

AN ANTHOLOGY

EDITED BY ALAN MONAT & RICHARD S. LAZARUS

COLUMBIA UNIVERSITY PRESS   NEW YORK

LIBRARY OF CONGRESS CATALOGING IN PUBLICATION DATA

Main entry under title:

Stress and coping.

  Bibliography: p.
  Includes index.
  1. Stress (Psychology)   2. Adjustment (Psychology)
I. Monat, Alan, 1945–   II. Lazarus, Richard S.
BF575.S75S77   155.9   77-3264   ISBN 0-231-04013-X (cloth)
                                    ISBN 0-231-08358-0 (paperback)

~~~~~~

Columbia University Press   New York   Guildford, Surrey
Copyright © 1977 Columbia University Press
All rights reserved   Printed in the United States of America
Second cloth and fourth paperback printing

To Our Wives, Murline and Bunny, and Our Families

For many years the research literature pertaining to stress and coping has been proliferating. General interest in this body of knowledge and ideas has also increased dramatically, partially due, no doubt, to its relevance to our personal lives. Yet, paradoxically, there are few texts or readers offering a systematic presentation of the major issues or findings in this field. While many technical books containing conference papers on the topic have recently appeared, there is currently no general book of readings in the stress and coping area based upon a broad sampling of available writings, theoretical and empirical in nature, and geared primarily to the undergraduate student. Such a book would be highly appropriate not only to courses related directly to stress and coping, but also to those concerned with psychological adjustment and health. This book is designed to help remedy this omission.

Certain considerations were given prime importance in its design. First, readings dealing primarily with humans were given top priority. Although there has been much significant animal research, studies conducted with humans are generally more engaging to the student, and we believe they are ultimately the most relevant for understanding the struggles of humans to cope with the problems of living. Second, the current trend toward naturalistic studies is a healthy and strong one and also deserves emphasis. Third, because of the vast amount of available material, we decided to concentrate primarily upon articles written within the last ten years or so; however, a few earlier articles such as those by Cannon, Lindemann, Menninger, and Selye were included because of their strong and persisting impact. Fourth, while methodological issues, including those pertaining to physiological processes, are represented, they are not emphasized; these topics tend to bore or perplex most students, particularly those who are not yet prepared to grasp their significance. We think the important issues of method need to be dealt with by instructors in other ways, perhaps through lectures or organized commentaries about the readings.

The book begins with an introductory chapter, written by the editors, which systematically presents some of the major issues relevant to the concepts of stress and coping—for example, problems of definition, relationships between stress and illness, etc. This chapter does not summarize the selections in the book but rather provides the reader with a basic and fundamental background for approaching the selections.

At the start of each section of the book we have provided summaries and, often, critical evaluations of the readings. Our comments present what we see as the author's main points and in many cases clarify and elaborate upon theoretical biases, relationships with other research and, to a lesser extent, methodological problems.

The core of the book is divided into five sections, the first two dealing primarily with the concept of stress and the latter three with the nature of coping. The division of stress and coping into separate sections is of course somewhat artificial, as the concepts are intertwined. We found it useful, however, for purposes of organization and clarity of emphasis.

As might be expected, we were faced with a number of critical problems and decisions regarding the organization of this book. First of all, while many would understandably prefer rather narrow working definitions of "stress" and "coping," such a task seems to us to be unnecessarily restrictive here. Though adopting a broad perspective may preserve a certain amount of ambiguity in these terms, we believe a broad approach is more instructive for two reasons: (1) particularly valuable contributions are being made by investigators in fields as diverse as psychology, medicine, anthropology, and sociology, and (2) our understanding of the complex and urgent issues relevant to stress and coping is just only beginning to emerge. Thus, we do not try to give a restrictive definition of the field but treat stress and coping as broad rubrics. In line with this, articles examining stress and coping from many perspectives were selected. Secondly, choice of articles posed a most difficult and distressing problem because of the tremendous variety of interesting and outstanding works. We would have liked to include additional readings but this was prohibited by space limitations.

We express our appreciation to the many authors and publishers who gave us permission to reprint their works and our regrets to the many other investigators whose fine works we were unable to include. John Moore and David Diefendorf of Columbia Press have been most supportive and helpful throughout this project and we thank them sincerely for their efforts and encouragement. Also helpful have been the comments and suggestions of many colleagues and friends including Frances Cohen, Reuven Gal, Murline Monat, and Neil Weinstein. In addition, two anonymous reviewers provided valuable critiques of an earlier draft of the book but, in all fairness, we must assume full responsibility for the final product.

We hope our efforts provide the prospective reader with an accurate, representative, and exciting picture of current theory and research in the stress and coping field.

Alan Monat
Richard S. Lazarus

Hayward, California
Berkeley, California
April 1976

ACKNOWLEDGMENTS

The editors would like to thank the following publishers for permission to reprint materials used in this book. It should be noted that, to achieve uniformity, we have in some cases slightly altered the original reference and/or footnote formats to conform with the author-date method of citation used throughout this book. It was also necessary to make some minor editorial changes appropriate to an anthology of this kind.

1. "Selections from *The Stress of Life*" by Hans Selye: From *The Stress of Life* by Hans Selye. Copyright © 1956 by Hans Selye. Used with permission of McGraw-Hill Book Co.

2. "Life-change Patterns Surrounding Illness" by Richard H. Rahe and Ransom J. Arthur: From *Journal of Psychosomatic Research* 11:341–45, 1968. Used with permission of Pergamon Press.

3. "Ethology and Stress Diseases" by Nikolaas Tinbergen: From *Science* 185:20–23, 5 July 1974. Copyright © 1974 by the American Association for the Advancement of Science; Permission was also obtained from the Elsevier Scientific Publishing Company which holds the copyright distributions for the Nobel Lectures in English.

4. "On the Concept of Psychological Stress" by Mortimer H. Appley and Richard Trumbull: Mortimer H. Appley & Richard Trumbull, *Psychological Stress: Issues In Research,* © 1967, pp. 5–11. Reprinted by permission of Prentice-Hall, Inc., Englewood Cliffs, New Jersey.

5. "Settings, Measures, and Themes: An Integrative Review of Some Research on Social-Psychological Factors in Stress" by Joseph E. McGrath: From *Social and Psychological Factors in Stress* by Joseph E. McGrath. Copyright © 1970 by Holt, Rinehart and Winston, Inc. Reprinted by permission of Holt, Rinehart and Winston.

6. " 'Voodoo' Death" by Walter B. Cannon: Reproduced by permission of the American Anthropological Association from the *American Anthropologist* 44(2):169–81, 1942.

7. "Differences and Similarities" by Mark Zborowski: From *People in Pain* by Mark Zborowski. Copyright © 1969 by Jossey-Bass, Inc., Publishers. Used with permission of Jossey-Bass, Inc.

8. "The Living World" by Rene Dubos: From *Man Adapting* by Rene Dubos. Copyright © 1965 by Yale University. Used with permission of Yale University Press.

9. "The Psychological Stresses of Intensive Care Unit Nursing" by Donald Hay and Donald Oken: From *Psychosomatic Medicine* 34:109–18, 1972. Used with permission of Harper & Row, Publishers, Inc.

10. "Environmental Stress and the Adaptive Process" by David C. Glass and Jerome E. Singer: From *Urban Stress: Experiments on Noise and Social Stressors* by David C. Glass and Jerome E. Singer. Copyright © 1972 by Academic Press, Inc. Used with permission of Academic Press, Inc.

11. "Cognitive and Coping Processes in Emotion" by Richard S. Lazarus: From *Cognitive Views of Human Motivation,* edited by B. Weiner. Copyright © 1974 by Academic Press, Inc. Used with permission of Academic Press, Inc.

12. "Regulatory Devices of the Ego Under Major Stress" by Karl Menninger: From *International Journal of Psychoanalysis* 35:412–20, 1954. Used with permission of the *International Journal of Psychoanalysis.*

13. "Religious Systems as Culturally Constituted Defense Mechanisms" by Melford E. Spiro: From *Context and Meaning in Cultural Anthropology,* edited by M. E. Spiro. Copyright © 1965 by The Free Press, a Division of The Macmillan Publishing Company. Used with permission of Macmillan Publishing Co., Inc.

14. "Obsessive-Compulsive Style" by David Shapiro: From Chapter 2, "Obsessive-Compulsive Style" from *Neurotic Styles,* by David Shapiro, © 1965 by Basic Books, Inc., Publishers, New York. Used with permission of Basic Books, Inc., Publishers.

15. "The Key Cause—Type A Behavior Pattern" by Meyer Friedman and Ray H. Rosenman: From *Type A Behavior and Your Heart,* by Meyer Friedman and Ray H. Rosenman. Copyright © 1974 by Meyer Friedman. Reprinted by permission of Alfred A. Knopf, Inc. and Wildwood House Limited.

16. "Factors Influencing Adjustment of Burn Patients During Hospitalization" by N.J.C. Andreasen, Russell Noyes, Jr., and C.E. Hartford: From *Psychosomatic Medicine* 34:517–23, 1972. Used with permission of Harper & Row, Publishers, Inc.

17. "Stress, Distress, and Ego Defenses" by Jack L. Katz, Herbert Weiner, T. F. Gallagher, and Leon Hellman: Reprinted from the *Archives of General Psychiatry* 23:131–42, 1970. Copyright © 1970, American Medical Association.

18. "Some Modes of Adaptation: Defense" by David Mechanic: From *Students Under Stress: A Study in the Social Psychology of Adaptation* by David Mechanic. Copyright © 1962 by The Free Press, a Division of The Macmillan Company. Used with permission of David Mechanic.

19. "The Management of Abhorrent Behavior—Survival Period" by Rex A. Lucas: From Chapter 6, "The Management of Abhorrent Behavior—Survival Period," from *Men in Crisis: A Study of a Mine Disaster,* by Rex A. Lucas, © 1969 by Basic Books, Inc., Publishers, New York. Used with permission of Basic Books, Inc., Publishers.

20. "Adaptive Personality Changes" by Irving L. Janis: From Part I, "Stress and Frustration" by Irving L. Janis in *Personality: Dynamics, Development, and Assessment* by Janis, Mahl, Kagan, and Holt, copyright © 1969 by Harcourt Brace Jovanovich, Inc., and reprinted with their permission.

21. "Dehumanization: A Composite Psychological Defense in Relation to Modern War" by Viola W. Bernard, Perry Ottenberg, and Fritz Redl: Reprinted by

permission of the editor and the publisher from V. W. Bernard, P. Ottenberg, & F. Redl, "Dehumanization: A composite Psychological defense in relation to modern war." In M. Schwebel (ed.), *Behavioral Science and Human Survival*. Palo Alto, California: Science and Behavior Books, 1965.

22. "The Terror of Death" by Ernest Becker: From *The Denial of Death* by Ernest Becker. Copyright © 1973 by The Free Press, a Division of The Macmillan Publishing Company. Used with permission of Macmillan Publishing Co., Inc.

23. "Reactions to the Imminence of Death" by Thomas P. Hackett and Avery D. Weisman: Reprinted from *The Threat of Impending Disasters*, edited by G. H. Grosser, H. Wechsler, & M. Greenblatt, by permission of The M.I.T. Press, Cambridge, Massachusetts. Copyright © 1964 by The Massachusetts Institute of Technology.

24. "Symptomatology and Management of Acute Grief" by Erich Lindemann: From *American Journal of Psychiatry* 101:141–48, 1944. Copyright © 1944, the American Psychiatric Association. Reprinted by permission.

25. "Behavioral Observations on Parents Anticipating the Death of a Child" by Stanford B. Friedman, Paul Chodoff, John W. Mason, and David A. Hamburg: From *Pediatrics* 32:610–25, 1963. Used with permission of the American Academy of Pediatrics.

26. "Grieving for a Lost Home" by Marc Fried: From Chapter 12, "Grieving for a Lost Home," by Marc Fried, from *The Urban Condition: People and Policy in the Metropolis*, edited by Leonard J. Duhl, M.D., with the assistance of John Powell, © 1963 by Basic Books, Inc., Publishers, New York. Used with permission of Basic Books, Inc., Publishers.

CONTENTS

STRESS AND COPING

Stress and Coping—Some Current Issues and Controversies

War, pollution, unemployment, natural disasters, divorce, "getting ahead," and illness all make us painfully aware of our daily struggles with adversities. Whether we master these stresses and prosper or become their victim, there is little question that they provide the scientist (and layman) with vital and abundant material for observation and systematic study of human adaptation.

Interest in the stresses and strains of "modern" life and how we cope with them has increased in recent years. The tremendous popularity of the stress and coping field can be seen by the relatively current outpouring of theoretical and empirical reports (e.g., Appley & Trumbull, 1967b; Coelho, Hamburg, & Adams, 1974; Dohrenwend & Dohrenwend, 1974; Janis, 1974; Lazarus, 1966; Levine & Scotch, 1970; McGrath, 1970b; Spielberger, 1972, to mention some of the best known), and of relevant books for the general public (e.g., Friedman & Rosenman, 1974; Toffler, 1970). Because of the vast amount of writings on stress and coping, it is time to pull together and organize representative studies to give the interested reader a sound and basic introduction to contemporary thought in a field relevant to everyone's concerns about successful living.

In this introductory chapter we provide an overall perspective for viewing and understanding some of the major theoretical issues and controversies in the field of stress and coping. A summary and evaluation of each of the readings included in this book can be found in the section introductions.

THE CONCEPT OF "STRESS"

Definitions. There has been a tendency to distinguish three basic types of stress: systemic or physiological, psychological, and social. Systemic stress is concerned primarily with the disturbances of tissue systems (e.g., Cannon, 1929; Selye, 1956), psychological stress with cognitive factors leading to the evaluation of threat (e.g., Lazarus, 1966), and social stress with the disruption of a social unit or system (e.g., Smelser, 1963). While many believe the three types of stress are related, the nature of this relationship is far from clear (Mason, 1975a). Perhaps most surprising (and confusing) is the lack of agreement on a definition of "stress" among those researchers closest to the field. As Mason (1975b) recently stated:

Whatever the soundness of logic may be in the various approaches to defining "stress," however, the general picture in the field can still only be described as one of confusion. The disenchantment felt by many scientists with the stress field is certainly understandable when one views two decades in which the term "stress" has been used variously to refer to "stimulus" by some workers, "response" by some workers, "interaction" by others, and more comprehensive combinations of the above factors by still other workers. Some authorities in the field are rather doubtful that this confusion over terminology is correctable in the near future. (p. 29)

The reasons investigators have been unable to reach any general agreement on a definition of "stress" are undoubtedly complex but revolve largely around the problems inherent in defining any intricate phenomenon. For example, a response-based definition of stress (e.g., one that looks at increased autonomic activity as an indicator of stress) suffers from, among other things, the fact that the same response pattern (such as increased blood pressure or heart rate) may arise from entirely different stimulus conditions, for example, from heavy exercise or extreme fright. And, of course, the psychological meanings of these conditions are typically quite different (McGrath, 1970b). Likewise, stimulus-based definitions are incomplete because any situation may or may not be stressful, depending on characteristics of the individual and the meaning of the situation for him or her.

Because of these problems some have suggested abandoning the term "stress" (Hinkle, 1974; Mason, 1975b) while others have argued for using "stress" as a general label for a large, complex, interdisciplinary area of interest and study (Lazarus, 1966):

It seems wise to use "stress" as a generic term for the whole area of problems that includes the stimuli producing stress reactions, the reactions themselves, and the various intervening processes. Thus, we can speak of the field of stress, and mean the physiological, sociological, and psychological phenomena and their respective concepts. It could then include research and theory on group or individual disaster, physiological assault on tissues and the effects of this assault, disturbances or facilitation of adaptive functioning produced by conditions of deprivation, thwarting or the prospects of this, and the field of negatively toned emotions such as fear, anger, depression, despair, hopelessness, and guilt. *Stress is not any one of these things; nor is it stimulus, response, or intervening variable, but rather a collective term for an area of study.* (p. 27)

To amplify this, the arena that the stress area refers to consists of any event in which environmental demands, internal demands, or both *tax* or *exceed* the adaptive resources of an individual, social system, or tissue system. However one chooses to define stress, to avoid confusion it seems mandatory that the concepts and procedures employed in their specific study be made explicit—i.e., the antecedent conditions used to induce "stress," the response patterns measured as indices of "stress," and, finally, the intervening processes believed responsible for the nature of the responses must be indicated.

Other stress-related concepts. When one thinks of stress, other concepts often come to mind and these need to be distinguished from stress and from each other. *Frustration* or psychological harm refers to blockage or delay in progress toward some goal. It implies something that is ongoing or has already happened. *Threat,* like frustration, also involves a harm of some kind, only it is one that has not yet happened. The harm is anticipated, however, on the basis of present cues. The person recognizes, somehow, or believes that future harm portends. The reason this distinction between past or present harm and anticipated harm is so important is that these two types of stress situations require different forms of coping. Harm that has already happened cannot be prevented, so it allows the person only to try to compensate for the damage, make restitution for it, tolerate or accept it, or give up his investment in what he has lost (as in the readjustments taking place in grief). On the other hand, future harm might be prevented or prepared for, so threat provides a warning that invites the person to take preventive steps or to do what he or she can to mitigate the impending harm.

Empirically, the importance of anticipation of harm in the production of stress reactions (physiological and psychological) is well supported. For instance, Shannon and Isbell (1963) have demonstrated that anticipation of a dental anesthetic injection results in the same amount of physiological stress reaction (increases in serum hydrocortisone) as the actual physical injection. Epstein (1967) has indicated that sport parachutists exhibit marked physiological and psychological stress reactions prior to a jump. In the laboratory, Birnbaum (1964) and Nomikos et al. (1968) have shown that unpleasant motion pictures elicit anticipatory physiological stress reactions. Moreover, considerable research has been done on antecedent conditions which may affect the appraisal of threat and the resulting stress reactions such as past experience (Epstein, 1967), availability of response options (Averill & Rosenn, 1972; Elliott, 1965; Pervin, 1963), personality dispositions (Hodges & Spielberger, 1966; Lazarus & Alfert, 1964), and uncertainty (D'Amato & Gumenik, 1960; Monat, Averill, & Lazarus, 1972).

It might be noted, as an aside, that accurate assessment of harm and threat is, of course, crucial to the study of psychological stress and typically four classes of response variables are used to infer their presence (Lazarus, 1966): negatively toned affect, motor-behavioral reactions, alterations of adaptive functioning, and/or physiological reactions. Unfortunately, each response class is characterized by inherent limitations and problems and, hence, it is desirable to rely upon the simultaneous measurement of several indices of threat (e.g., within and/or between response modalities) whenever feasible. (For a review of many of these measurement problems, the reader should consult Averill & Opton, 1968; Brown, 1967; Lacey et al., 1963; Sternbach, 1966; Venables & Martin, 1967; and Weinstein et al., 1968.)

Finally, *conflict* involves the presence simultaneously of two incompatible goals or action tendencies, and so in conflict, frustration or threat of some sort is virtually inevitable. This makes it of great importance in human adaptation. Goals or action tendencies may be incompatible because the behavior and attitudes necessary to reach one such goal are contrary to those necessary to reach the other. If one spends now for enjoyment, saving up for future pleasure is negated. If one goal is attained, the other must be frustrated. Hence, conflict is a major source of psychological stress in human affairs and is a lifelong problem requiring much adaptive effort if one is to achieve a successful and rewarding life.

The excitement many find in the study of stress is often attributable to an interest in the biological, psychological, and sociological stress factors believed to contribute to the development of physical and mental disorders. Although the issues and literature in this area are far too vast to cover here (see Cohen, 1975; Coleman, 1976), we would like to point out some basic theoretical positions relating stress and physical illnesses.

Possible links between stress and illness. There are three main ways in which stress might lead to somatic illness. The first is by the disruption of tissue function through neurohumoral influences under stress. In other words, under stress there are major outpourings of powerful hormones creating dramatic alterations in bodily processes many of which we sense as in the case of a pounding heart, sweating, trembling, fatigue, etc. A second way is by engaging in coping activities that are damaging to health, for example, by trying to advance occupationally or socially by means of a pressured style of life, by taking minimal rest, by poor diet, heavy use of tobacco or alcohol, etc. Intrinsically noxious styles of living can increase the likelihood of disease by damaging the tissues of the body. A third way stress might lead to disease is by psychological and/or sociological factors which consistently lead the person to minimize the significance of various symptoms. That is, a person may frequently interpret pain or illness symptoms in such a way as to neglect to seek medical aid when it is crucial. Avoidance of doctors or of medical regimens can come about as a defense mechanism, for example, denial, or merely because the individual is a member of a culture or subculture that values stoicism (Mechanic, 1974; Zborowski, 1969). Such avoidance can be fatal in certain instances, as in the case of heart attack victims who delay seeking medical attention, thereby decreasing their chances of survival (Hackett & Cassem, 1975).

The issue of generality versus specificity. The way in which stress produces somatic illness via hormonal secretions that alter tissue function has been of tremendous recent interest. This interest has no doubt received its greatest impetus from the work of Hans Selye (e.g., 1956). In his studies, Selye has attempted to demonstrate how physical and psychological "stressors" may lead to "diseases of adaptation" via a series of "nonspecific" biological responses, called the "General Adaptation Syndrome" (GAS). The GAS is the defensive physiological reaction of the organism which is set in motion by any noxious stimulus. Its characteristic pattern includes three stages: an alarm reaction, a stage of resistance, and a stage of exhaustion. This sequence is invariant, although it need not be carried to completion if the stressor is terminated early enough, and involves increased secretions of the pituitary gland. These secretions in turn stimulate the production of hormones by the cortex or outer shell of the adrenal glands. If the stressor (e.g., heat, cold, exercise, psychological threat) persists or is severe, diseases of adaptation, such as stomach or intestinal ulcers, increased susceptibility to infection, etc., will occur and eventually, if the stressor is unabated, the organism dies.

Until the last decade or so, Selye's work was widely accepted and largely unchallenged. Recently, however, several researchers (e.g., Lazarus, 1974b; Mason, 1971, 1975a, 1975b) have criticized aspects of Selye's position, particularly his total commitment to the concept of the physiological nonspecificity of the stress response. Selye distinguishes

between the *specific* effects induced by a stressor agent and the effects induced by such stimulation which are *not* specific to it. Thus he observes that whereas one stimulus (e.g., cold) may produce a vasoconstriction and a second stimulus (e.g., heat) a vasodilation, both (or either), if applied intensely or long enough, produce(s) *effects in common* and therefore not specific to either stimulus. These common changes, taken together, constitute the stereotypical response pattern of systemic stress. Selye "operationally" defines stress as *"a state manifested by a syndrome which consists of all nonspecifically induced changes in a biologic system."* (Cofer & Appley, 1964, p. 442)

Mason and Lazarus have offered theoretical viewpoints and presented empirical evidence which strongly suggest Selye has overstated the role of nonspecificity in the production of illness. Mason (1975b) suggests that the pituitary-adrenal cortical system is remarkably sensitive and responds easily to emotional stimuli. This is important, for many laboratory situations designed to study physical stressors very often elicit discomfort or pain. Therefore, what would happen to the GAS if psychological factors were minimized?

When special precautions are taken, however, to minimize psychological reactions in the study of physical stimuli, such as heat, fasting, and moderate exercise, it now appears that the pituitary-adrenal cortical system is *not* stimulated in nonspecific fashion by these stimuli which are generally regarded as "noxious," "demanding," or as appreciably disturbing to homeostatic equilibrium. . . . [In] heat studies with both human and monkey subjects, it appears heat *per se* either does not change or actually *suppresses* adrenal cortical hormone levels when measures are taken to avoid such factors as novelty or extremely sudden or severe temperature changes. (Mason, 1975b, p. 24)

These findings are important, for they imply that somatic illness may depend on quite specific reactions to specific stressors. As Lazarus (1974b) points out, the role of specificity in illness creates more varied options, since

the nature and severity of the stress disorder could depend on at least three factors: (1) the formal characteristics of the environmental demands, (2) the quality of the emotional response generated by the demands, or in particular individuals facing these demands, and (3) the processes of coping mobilized by the stressful commerce. (p. 327)

It may be too early to evaluate adequately the role(s) of nonspecific and specific factors in the etiology of illness, but clearly there is a growing belief in the importance of the latter.

Summary. The concept of stress has received considerable theoretical and empirical attention in recent years, yet much "confusion and controversy" remain. Major problems have to do not only with definitions of stress but also with proposed relationships between psychological stress and somatic illness. Early research on somatic illness minimized the etiological significance of psychological stress factors and, instead, emphasized the role of stereotypic bodily reactions (i.e., adrenal cortical hormones) to *any* tissue assault in increasing susceptibility to all illnesses. Recently, however, sentiment has been expressed that bodily assaults must first be appraised as threatening before the various hormonal adjustments are set into motion and, furthermore, that these adjustments are specific to specific threats. In other words, there may be specific as well as general causes of distinct stress-related disease patterns.

In our discussion so far, we have not yet dealt with a very significant and intimately related aspect of stress—i.e., the concept of coping. Once a stimulus is judged as harmful, coping processes to undo the harm or to get the person out of jeopardy are set into motion. Therefore, let us turn to some of the research issues pertaining to the psychology of coping.

Definitions and classification systems. While much is known about the damaging effects of stress, less systematic attention has been devoted to the ways in which humans respond to stress positively. More recently, however, there has been a rapid growth of curiosity and concern among researchers about coping and "adaptation" (e.g., Coelho, Hamburg, & Adams, 1974; Moos, 1976).

Perhaps because of its common lay usage (there is even a drug named "Cope"), the term "coping" has accrued a variety of meanings. Nevertheless, there seems to be growing agreement among professionals (e.g., Lazarus, Averill, & Opton, 1974; Murphy, 1962, 1974; White, 1974) that coping refers to efforts to master conditions of harm, threat, or challenge when a routine or automatic response is not readily available. Here, environmental demands must be met with new behavioral solutions or old ones must be adapted to meet the current stress. As White (1974) notes:

It is clear that we tend to speak of coping when we have in mind a fairly drastic change or problem that defies familiar ways of behaving, requires the production of new behavior, and very likely gives rise to uncomfortable affects like anxiety, despair, guilt, shame, or grief, the relief of which forms part of the needed adaptation. Coping refers to adaptation under relatively difficult conditions. (pp. 48–49)

An adequate system for classifying coping processes has yet to be proposed, although initial efforts along these lines have been made (Haan, 1969; Hamburg, Coelho, & Adams, 1974; Lazarus, 1966, 1975; Mechanic, 1962; Menninger, 1963; Murphy, 1974). For example, Lazarus (1975) has suggested a taxonomy of coping which emphasizes two major categories, direct actions and palliative modes. *Direct actions* are behaviors, such as fight or flight, which are designed to alter a troubled relationship with one's social or physical environment. *Palliative modes* of coping refer to thoughts or actions whose goal is to relieve the emotional impact of stress (i.e., bodily or psychological disturbances). The term "palliative" is used because these methods do not actually alter the threatening or damaging events but make the person feel better. Some kinds of palliative methods are intrapsychic in nature, such as defense mechanisms (e.g., denial) or the deployment of attention from the stressful circumstances (e.g., thinking about last summer's romance rather than studying for the "big" exam), while others are somatically oriented (e.g., the use of tranquilizers, biofeedback, and relaxation).

The above classification in no way implies that we use one kind of coping process or another exclusively. Rather, all of us employ complex combinations of direct actions and palliative methods to cope with stress. The conditions determining our coping methods in particular situations are undoubtedly complex and largely unknown at this time but likely depend upon the conditions being faced, the options available to us, and our personality.

Coping outcomes. An issue that frequently emerges in discussions of coping is whether some coping processes are more effective than others. Unfortunately, any answer to this problem must be prefaced with a long string of qualifiers due to inherent value questions (Smith, 1961), levels of analysis (i.e., physiological, psychological, or sociological), points in time (i.e., short- vs. long-run), and particular situations (Cohen, 1975). For instance, behavior which might be effective from, say, the physiological perspective might have devastating consequences for the psychological or sociological domains. Moreover, within any one domain, what is an optimal response in one situation at a particular point in time may be damaging in some other situation or at a different point in time. For example, denial may be effective (in the physiological domain in terms of lowered secretions of stress-related hormones) for parents of terminally ill children prior to the child's death (Wolff et al., 1964) but may prove ineffective after the child dies, i.e., stress-related hormones then increase dramatically (see Hofer et al., 1972). It is clear that what is considered to be an optimal or beneficial response is highly dependent upon one's perspective and judgments.

Traditionally, palliative modes of coping (particularly defense mechanisms such as denial) have been viewed as pathological or maladaptive. This view is often supported in studies where defensive behaviors (such as denial that a suspicious lump in the breast might be cancerous) have actually endangered the lives of individuals (e.g., Katz et al., 1970b). On the other hand, denial can initially serve a positive function (cf. Hamburg & Adams, 1967) in preventing a person from being overwhelmed by a threatening situation where the possibilities for direct actions are limited and/or of little use (e.g., the person who has suffered severe burns or polio). Cohen (1975) states the matter as follows:

Thus we see that denial has been found a useful defense in many situations, lowering physiological response levels and helping the person avoid being overwhelmed by negative life circumstances. However, its usefulness seems most apparent on a short-term basis, in particular situations (such as situations where the person would be otherwise overwhelmed by the unpleasant reality, where the likelihood of threats occurring is small, where there is nothing the individual can do to prepare for the potential threatening event, or where a hopeful attitude prevents feelings of giving up). Further studies must be done to determine the usefulness of denial in other situations and determinations of both long- and short-run consequences of this behavior must be made. (pp. 14–15)

In general, then, palliative modes of coping may be damaging when they prevent essential direct actions but may also be extremely useful in helping a person maintain a sense of well-being, integration, or hope under conditions otherwise likely to encourage psychological disintegration.

Coping dispositions versus strategies. Two different approaches to the study of coping have been pursued by various investigators. On the one hand, some (e.g., Byrne, 1964; Goldstein, 1973) have emphasized general coping traits, styles, or dispositions, while others (e.g., Cohen & Lazarus, 1973; Katz et al., 1970b; Wolff et al., 1964) have preferred to study active, ongoing coping strategies in particular stress situations. The former approach, often used by researchers interested in the study of personality, assumes that an individual will utilize the same type of coping (such as repression or sensitization) in most stressful situations. It is for him or her a stable pattern or style. A person's coping style or disposition is typically assessed by personality tests, not by actual observation of what the person says or does in a particular stress situation. Whether the person actually behaves under stress as predicted by the test depends largely on the adequacy of the personality assessment, the generality of the trait being measured, and the myriad internal and external factors affecting the person's actions and reactions in any given situation. It should be noted that many psychological traits, including coping styles, show very limited generality (cf. Cohen & Lazarus, 1973; Mischel, 1968) and, hence, are poor predictors of behavior in any given situation.

In contrast, those concentrating on active coping strategies prefer to observe an individual's behavior as it occurs in a stressful situation and then proceed to infer the particular coping processes implied by the behaviors. This approach has been largely neglected in the study of coping. We think that assessing coping processes, while time-consuming and often costly, will produce valuable information often unobtainable with the dispositional emphasis.

Summary. While the concept of coping is intimately tied to that of stress, it has been largely neglected by researchers until rather recently. Today much more interest is being expressed in the classification and measurement of coping processes, and the study of their causes and effects. A highly pertinent issue is the "adaptive" value of various coping processes—i.e., are some processes more effective or ineffective than others? There is a growing conviction that all coping processes, including those traditionally considered undesirable (i.e., defense mechanisms), have both positive and negative consequences for an individual, and that any evaluation of coping and adaptation must take into account diverse levels of analysis (physiological, psychological, sociological), the short- versus long-term consequences, and the specific nature of the situation in question. Our understanding of how people cope with specific stress situations will probably be advanced further by assessing coping *in vivo* as well as by generalized trait measurements. With increased interest in the psychology of coping, we shall, no doubt, see rapid advances in our understanding of how people cope with the stresses of living, how their coping patterns are shaped by situational and personality factors, and how these patterns change during the course of development.

section I

STRESS AND SOME OF ITS EFFECTS

The readings in Section I present divergent and controversial view-points about the stress concept, emphasizing its physiological, psychological, and sociological dimensions. The first three articles look at the interdependency of stress and illness. A bit of Selye's (1956) writings on stress, which we have discussed critically in the Introduction, is highlighted here because of his pioneering influence on research and thought in this field. He writes with great charm of his frustrations with medical tradition and of his excitement over the "discovery" of the General Adaptation Syndrome. The selection provides the reader with excellent insights into various processes of scientific investigation, at least as experienced by one outstanding medical researcher.

Probably no recent and ongoing program of research on stress and illness has had the degree of impact on psychosomatic medicine as the one initiated by Holmes and Rahe (1967), despite some methodological and theoretical weaknesses that continue to provoke controversy and debate. They and their colleagues have reported evidence that illnesses of all kinds increase following periods of "stressful" life changes because of the major coping activities such changes require. Both positive and negative changes, such as marriage and divorce, are considered to be stressful by Holmes and Rahe because they all presumably demand adjustments by the individual to a new life style or pattern. To measure these life changes, Holmes and Rahe developed a self-administered questionnaire, the Schedule of Recent Experiences (SRE), which the person uses to report the number of times the indicated life changes have occurred during the past few months or years (usually the preceding one or two-year period). Each change is assigned a Life Change Unit (LCU) score and a total LCU score for each person is then obtained. Numerous studies (e.g., Rahe, 1972; Rahe, McKean, & Arthur, 1967; see reviews by Holmes & Masuda, 1974, and Rahe, 1974) have demonstrated that the likelihood of illness is greater if a person has experienced considerable life change. The paper by Rahe and Arthur (1968) which we have selected to represent this research supports the above viewpoint and, furthermore, its findings suggest that life changes not only lead to but also result from illness.

While empirical findings from Holmes and Rahe's approach have been rather consistent in showing a small relationship between stressful life changes and illness, there has also been much concern over theoretical and methodological weaknesses (e.g., Dohrenwend & Dohrenwend, 1974; Sarason, de Monchaux, & Hunt, 1975). For example, individual differences in illness susceptibility, due to biochemical agents, psychological coping factors, and/or social supports, are largely ignored, yet may prove vital when one notes that many people undergo severe life changes without developing illness (e.g., Gore, 1973; Hinkle, 1974). In addition, the reliability of the SRE is considered low (Sarason, de Monchaux, & Hunt, 1975) and the self-report and retrospective nature of the SRE (and some of the illness measures) creates the possibility of subjectivity and bias affecting the relationships. One could argue too that relatively "minor" but continuous day-to-day hassles (like family quarrels, making ends meet, disagreements at work, etc.) might be just as important in increasing the risk of illness as stresses tied to major life changes, though this possibility has not yet been examined in research.

Only rarely does an "outsider" contribute valuable observations and fresh interpretations of data in a field other than his own. In our next selection, Nikolaas Tinbergen's 1974 Nobel Prize acceptance speech, the noted ethologist makes such contributions to the study of stress disorders. Tinbergen reminds us of the value of frequently stepping back and observing behavior, whether in animals or humans. To watch and to wonder, he says, must come before theoretical interpretation. To illustrate the importance of such open-minded observation, Tinbergen describes efforts by himself and his wife to evaluate the possible causes and treatments of autism, sometimes called childhood schizophenia. Based upon their observations of "normal" and autistic children, Tinbergen firmly believes many normal children also exhibit autisticlike behaviors on occasions (e.g., in approach-avoidance situations), and that a careful "taming procedure" could eliminate such behaviors in both the normal and autistic child. Tinbergen argues against a genetically based abnormality and maintains that autism is caused by environmental stresses. While this view of autism is somewhat unorthodox, it has recently gained increasing support. All in all, Tinbergen has provided stress workers with a fascinating series of observations and a healthy reminder of the importance of first simply "seeing" what is there.

The final two selections in this section emphasize the psychological and, to some extent, sociological aspects of the stress concept. Appley and Trumbull (1967a) concentrate primarily on the various problems associated with defining "psychological stress" with particular concern for the fact of individual differences. The authors note that, with few exceptions, no stimulus is a stressor to all people—in other words, stress must be perceived or appraised as such. This is a viewpoint emphasized in recent years by Arnold (1960), Lazarus (1966), and others and reflects a currently increasing orientation in psychology toward the role of cognitive processes. Appley and Trumbull prefer to define stress as a response state rather than an event in the environment; and in order to predict which conditions are to be stressful for a particular person, these writers argue that his or her motivational structure and prior history must be taken into account.

Based upon an extensive review of the stress literature, Joseph McGrath (1970a) discusses five general principles, or themes, which have received substantial empirical support: (1) the cognitive appraisal theme; (2) the experience theme; (3) the negative experience theme; (4) the inverted-U theme; and, (5) the social-interaction theme. In some respects, these themes are variations on the individual differences principle emphasized by Appley and Trumbull. Note that McGrath discusses the problem of circularity which is inherent in some of the principles (e.g., the inverted-U theme), a problem resulting from our current inability to calibrate systematically, to any extent, either degrees of stress or degrees of stimulus intensity. For example, if one does not find the "expected" inverted-U relationship between stimulus intensity and performance effectiveness, one might argue that the "optimal" intensity (that intensity which results in superior performance, with higher or lower intensities leading to inferior efforts) was simply missed, by too much or too little, thus making the principle virtually infallible! Until we can predict with considerable accuracy what will be perceived as stressful by particular individuals, a certain amount of circularity will continue to plague the stress field.

1

Selections from *The Stress of Life*

MY FIRST GLIMPSE OF STRESS

A Young Medical Student's First Impressions of Medicine

In 1925 I was a student at the Medical School of the ancient German University of Prague. I had just completed my courses in anatomy, physiology, biochemistry, and the other preclinical subjects which were required as a preparation before we saw a patient. I had stuffed myself full of theoretical knowledge to the limit of my abilities and was burning with enthusiasm for the art of healing; but I had only vague ideas about how clinical medicine worked in practice. Then came the great day, which I shall never forget, when we were to hear our first lecture in internal medicine and see how one examines a patient.

It so happened that, on that day, by way of an introduction, we were shown several cases in the earliest stages of various infectious diseases. As each patient was brought into the lecture room, the professor carefully questioned and examined him. It turned out that each of these patients felt and looked ill, had a coated tongue, complained of more or less diffuse aches and pains in the joints, and of intestinal disturbances with loss of appetite. Most of them also had fever (sometimes with mental confusion), an enlarged spleen or liver, inflamed tonsils, a skin rash, and so forth. All this was quite evident, but the professor attached very little significance to any of it.

Then, he enumerated a few "characteristic" signs which might help in the diagnosis of the disease. These I could not see. They were absent or, at least, so inconspicuous that I could not distinguish them; yet these, we were told, were the important changes to which we would have to give all our attention. At present, our teacher said, most of the characteristic signs happened to be absent, but until they appeared, not much could be done; without them it was impossible to know precisely what the patient suffered from; and hence it was obviously impossible to recommend any efficient treatment against the disease. It was clear that the many features of disease which were already manifest did not interest our teacher very much because they were "nonspecific," and hence "of no use" to the physician.

Since these were my first patients, I was still capable of looking at them without being biased by current medical thought. Had I known more I would never have asked questions, because everything was handled "just the way it should be," that is, "just the way every good physician does it." Had I known more, I would certainly have been stopped by the biggest of all blocks to improvement: the certainty of being right. But I did not know what was right.

I could understand that our professor had to find specific disease manifestations in order to identify the particular cause of disease in each of these patients. This, I clearly realized, was necessary so that suitable drugs might be prescribed, medicines having the specific effect of killing the germs or neutralizing the poisons that made these people sick.

I could see this all right; but what impressed me, the novice, much more was that apparently only a few signs and symptoms are actually characteristic of any one disease; most of the disturbances are apparently common to many, or perhaps even to all, diseases.

Why is it, I asked myself, that such widely different disease-producing agents as those which cause measles, scarlet fever, or the flu, share with a number of drugs, allergens, etc., the property of evoking the nonspecific manifestations which have just been mentioned? Yet evidently they do share them; indeed, they share them to such an extent that, at an early stage, it might be quite impossible, even for our eminent professor, to distinguish between various diseases because they all look alike.

The "Syndrome of Just Being Sick"

Even now—thirty years later—I still remember vividly the profound impression these considerations made upon me at the time. I could not understand why, ever since the dawn of medical history, physicians should have attempted to concentrate all their efforts upon the recognition of *individual* diseases and the discovery of *specific* remedies for them, without giving any attention to the much more obvious "syndrome of just being sick." I knew that a syndrome is usually defined as "a group of signs and symptoms that occur together and characterize a disease." Well, the patients we had just seen had a syndrome, but this seemed to be the syndrome that characterized disease as such, not any one disease.

Surely, if it is important to find remedies which help against one disease or another, it would be even more important to learn something about the mechanism of being sick and the means of treating this "general syndrome of sickness," which is apparently superimposed upon all individual diseases!!

As an apology for the two exclamation marks, let me point out that I was only eighteen years old at that time. Because of the confusion created in Central Europe by the aftermath of World War I, I was allowed to complete my premedical studies as fast as I could pass the exams, and, with the help of an excellent private tutor, I got to Medical School at an unusually impressionable age.

In view of this I might perhaps also be forgiven for having thought that I could solve all these problems in a jiffy by applying classical research techniques to my problem. For several days, I intended asking our profesor of physiology for some lab space, so that I might analyze the "general syndrome of being sick" with the techniques of physiology, biochemistry, and histology which we had learned in our courses. If these methods could be used to clarify such specific things as the normal mechanisms of blood circulation or nervous conduction, I saw no reason why they could not be used with equal success to analyze the "general syndrome of disease" which interested me so much.

My immediate plans to dissect the general from the specific did not materialize, however. I was soon confronted with a problem which did not have the same general importance, but was more urgent specifically for me—the necessity of passing exams. Besides, I never did dare to present my proposition to the profesor of physiology for fear of being laughed at. After all, I really had no precise plan; I had no blueprint to guide the work I wanted to do.

Then, as time went by, this whole problem lost its meaning for me. As I learned more and more about medicine, the many specific problems of diagnosis and treatment began to blur my vision for the nonspecific. The former gradually assumed an ever-increasing importance and pushed the "syndrome of just being sick," the question "what is disease in general?" out of my consciousness into that hazy category of the purely abstract arguments which are not worth bothering about.

HOW TO QUESTION NATURE

The Urge to Learn

What is disease—not any one disease, just disease in general? This question lingered on in my mind, as it undoubtedly has in the minds of most physicians of all nations throughout history. But there was no hope of an early answer, for nature—the source of all knowledge—rarely replies to questions unless they are put to her in the form of experiments to which she can say "yes" or "no." She is not loquacious; she merely nods in the affirmative or in the negative. "What is disease?" is not a question to which one can reply this way.

Occasionally, if we ask, "What would you do if . . . ?" or, "What is in such and such a place?" she will silently show you a picture. But she never explains. You have to work things out yourself first, aided only by instinct and the feeble powers of the human brain, until you can ask precise questions, to which nature can answer in her precise but silent sign language of nods and pictures. Understanding grows out of a mosaic of such answers. It is up to the scientist to draw a blueprint of the questions he has to ask before the mosaic makes sense.

It is curious how few laymen, or even physicians, understand this.

If you want to know whether a certain endocrine (that is, hormone-producing) gland is necessary for growth, you remove it surgically from the body of a growing young experimental animal. If growth stops, the answer is "yes." If you want to know whether a certain substance extracted from this gland is a growth-promoting hormone, you inject it into the same animal, and, if now the latter begins to grow again, the answer is "yes."

These are the nods of nature.

If you want to know what is in the fat tissue around the kidney, you dissect it and find the adrenal. If your question concerns the shape, size, or structure of this gland, just look at it; you can even examine the finest details of its appearance under a powerful microscope.

Such are the pictures of nature.

But if now you ask, "What is an adrenal?" you will get no reply. This is the wrong question; it cannot be answered by nods or pictures.

Only those blessed with the understanding that comes from a sincere and profound love of nature will, by an intuitive feeling for her ways, succeed in constructing a blueprint of the many questions that need to be asked to get even an approximate answer to such a question.

Only those cursed with a consuming, uncontrollable curiosity for nature's secrets will be able to—because they will have to—spend their lives working out patiently, one by one, the innumerable technical problems involved in performing each of the countless experiments required.

What is disease? What is stress?

I did not know how to ask the first of these questions; I did not even think of asking the second.

Not until about ten years after hearing my first lecture in internal medicine did these same problems confront me again, although now under entirely different circumstances. At the time, I was working as a young assistant in the Biochemistry Department of McGill University in Montreal, on an entirely unrelated subject: the sex hormones. Still, I must say something about this work because it led me right back to the "syndrome of being sick."

Great Hopes

Various extracts prepared from the ovaries (the female sex glands) and the placenta (the highly vascular afterbirth through which the embryo gets nourishment from the mother's womb) are very rich in female sex hormones.

A *hormone* is a specific chemical messenger-substance, made by an endocrine gland and secreted into the blood, to regulate and coordinate the functions of distant organs. Sex hormones are coordinators of sexual activities, including reproduction.

An *extract* is made by mixing tissue (say, the ovaries of cows) with solvents (water, alcohol, etc.) and taking what goes into solution. The extract is pure when it contains only the desired substance (for instance, a hormone) and impure when it also contains contaminants (for instance, unwanted and perhaps damaging ovarian substances).

Several sex hormones had already been prepared by that time (1935), but I thought there was still another one to be discovered. It would lead us too far afield if I were to explain why I thought so. (Besides, my theory was all wrong anyway, so let us not bother with it.) Still, to prove my point, I injected rats with various ovarian and placental extracts to see whether the organs of these animals would show such changes as could *not* be due to any *known* sex hormone.

Much to my satisfaction, such changes were produced in my rats even by my first and most impure extracts:

1. There was a considerable enlargement of the *adrenal cortex.*

The *adrenals* are two little endocrine glands which lie just above the kidneys, on both sides. Each of them consists of two portions, a central part, the medulla, and an outer rind, the cortex. Both of these parts produce hormones, but not the same kind. My extracts seemed to stimulate the cortex, without causing much of a change in the medulla. The cortical portion of the adrenals was not only enlarged, but it also showed the microscopic features of increased activity (such as cell-multiplication and discharge of stored secretion droplets into the blood).

2. There was an intense shrinking (or atrophy) of the thymus, the spleen, the lymph nodes, and of all other lymphatic structures in the body.

The *lymphatic structures* are made up of innumerable, small white blood cells, similar to the *lymphocytes,* which circulate in the blood. What a lymphocyte does in solid lymphatic tissue or in the blood is not yet very well known, but it seems to play some part in the defense of the organism against various types of damage. For instance, in people exposed to x-rays, the lymphocytes tend to disappear, and then resistance against all kinds of germs and poisons is much impaired.

The *lymphocytes* are made in the lymph nodes, little nodules in the groin, under the armpits, along the neck, and in various other parts of the body. Lymphocytes also make up most of the tissue in the *thymus* and *spleen:* that is why these organs are called *lymphatic tissues* or *thymicolymphatic system.* The thymus is a huge lymphatic organ just in front of the heart in the chest. In children it is very well developed but, after puberty, it tends to shrink, presumably under the influence of sex hormones.

When I saw that the lymphatic organs had so rapidly disintegrated in the rats, I naturally also examined the lymphocytes in the blood. Their number had also diminished under the influence of my tissue extracts, but while studying them I accidentally found an even more striking change in the blood picture: the almost complete disappearance of the *eosinophil cells*.

These are somewhat larger white blood cells, which have received their name because they stain very easily with a dye called *eosin*. This coloring agent is frequently used for histologic studies to make cells more visible under the microscope. The function of the eosinophils is also still debated, but they seem to be related to allergy, because their number increases remarkably when a person suffers from asthma, hay fever, or allied conditions.

3. There appeared bleeding, deep *ulcers* in the lining of the stomach, and that uppermost part of the gut, just after the stomach, which we call the duodenum.

These three types of changes formed a definite syndrome, because they were closely interdependent in some way. When I injected only a small amount of extract, all these changes were slight; when I injected much extract, they were all very pronounced. But with no extract could I ever produce one of these three changes without the others. This interdependence of lesions is precisely what makes them a syndrome. (See Fig. 1.1.)

Incidentally, a syndrome such as ours, which consists of three types of changes, is usually called a *triad*.

Now, from all this I concluded that my extracts must contain some very active substance, and having been prepared from ovaries, this was first presumed to be an ovarian hormone. In apparent agreement with this view, one major manifestation of the triad was a change in an endocrine gland, the adrenal cortex, and another was the involution of the thymicolymphatic apparatus, a type of tissue known to shrink under the influence of sex hormones.

Of course, to me, the most important thing was that no ovarian hormone or combination of ovarian hormones known at that time ever produced adrenal enlargement, thymicolymphatic involution, and ulcers in the intestinal tract. It seemed rather obvious that we were dealing with a *new* ovarian hormone.

You may well imagine my happiness! At the age of 28, I seemed

Normal   Alarmed

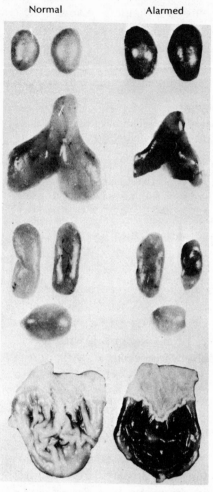

A

B

C

D

Fig. 1.1. The typical triad of the alarm reaction. A. Adrenals. B. Thymus. C. A
group of three lymph nodes. D. Inner
surface of the stomach. The organs on the
left are those of a normal rat, those on
the right of one exposed to the frustrating
psychologic stress of being forcefully im-
mobilized. Note marked enlargement and
dark discoloration of the adrenals (due to
congestion and discharge of fatty secre-
tion-granules), the intense shrinkage of
the thymus and the lymph nodes, as well
as the numerous blood-covered stomach
ulcers in the alarmed rat. (After Selye,
1952; Courtesy of Acta, Inc., Montreal)

to be already on the track of a new hormone. I even had a perfect
method with which to identify it in extracts, namely, the appearance
in rats treated with this hormone, of the triad just described. It
seemed only a matter of time now to concentrate and isolate the new
hormone in pure form.

Grave Doubts

Unfortunately, this happiness was not to last long. Not only
ovarian, but placental, extracts also produced our triad. This did not

worry me very much at first; after all, we knew that both the ovaries and the placenta can produce female sex hormones. I began to be somewhat confused, however, when it turned out subsequently that even pituitary extracts produced the same syndrome.

> The *pituitary* (or hypophysis) is a little endocrine gland embedded in the bones of the skull, just below the brain. It produces a number of hormones, but, as far as we knew, no ovarian hormones.

Yet, even this was not too disturbing, since mine was supposed to be a new hormone and (who knew?) perhaps the pituitary could manufacture this one.

But I really became puzzled when I found, a little later, that extracts of the kidney, spleen, or any other organ would produce the same triad. Was the causative factor some kind of general "tissue hormone" that could be produced by almost any cell?

Another inexplicable fact was that all efforts to purify the active extracts led to a diminution of their potency. The crudest preparations—the most impure ones—were invariably the most active. This did not seem to make sense.

The Great Disappointment

I shall never forget one particularly dark, rainy afternoon during the spring of 1936, when the great disappointment came. I was sitting in my small laboratory, brooding about the ever-increasing volume of findings which by now had made it quite improbable that my extracts could contain a new hormone, at least in the usual sense of the word. Mine could not be a specific substance of any one endocrine gland; I found about equal amounts of it everywhere. Yet the changes produced with these extracts were very real and constant. There must have been something in these preparations to account for such characteristic effects. What could it be?

It was then that a horrible thought occurred to me: for all I knew, this entire syndrome might be due merely to the toxicity of my extracts, to the fact that I did not purify them well enough.

In this case, of course, all my work meant nothing. I was not on the track of a new ovarian hormone; indeed, I was not even dealing with any specific ubiquitous "tissue hormone," but merely with damage as such.

As I thought of this, my eyes happened to fall upon a bottle of Formalin on a shelf in front of my desk.

> Formalin is an extremely toxic and irritating fluid. We use it in the preparation of tissues for microscopic study, as a fixative. Just as you use fixatives in photography, so for microscopic work, we employ certain agents to *fix* the structure of cells by instantly precipitating their constituents in the natural state.

Now, I thought, if my syndrome is really due only to tissue-damage, I should be able to reproduce it by injecting rats with a dilute Formalin solution. The cells in immediate contact with the Formalin would be precipitated and killed and considerable tissue-damage would result. This seemed to be a good way to formulate the question I wanted to ask: can even a toxic fluid not derived from any living tissue also produce my syndrome?

I immediately undertook such experiments and, within 48 hours, when I examined the organs of my animals, the answer was only too clear. In all the rats there was even more adrenocortical enlargement, thymicolymphatic atrophy, and intestinal-ulcer formation than I had ever been able to produce with any of my tissue-extracts.

I do not think I have ever been more profoundly disappointed! Suddenly all my dreams of discovering a new hormone were shattered. All the time and all the materials that went into this long study were wasted.

I tried to tell myself, "You must not let this sort of thing get you down; after all, fortunately, nothing has been published about the 'new hormone,' so no confusion has been created in the minds of others and there is nothing to retract." I tried to tell myself over and over again that such disappointments are inevitable in a scientist's life; occasionally anyone can follow a wrong track, and it is precisely the vision necessary to recognize such errors that characterizes the reliable investigator. But all this gave me little solace and, indeed, I became so depressed that for a few days I could not do any work at all. I just sat in my laboratory, brooding about how this misadventure might have been avoided and wondering what was to be done now.

Eventually I decided that, of course, the only thing to do was to pull myself together, admit my defeat, and return to some of the more orthodox endocrinological problems that had occupied my attention before I was sidetracked into this regrettable enterprise. After all, I was young and much of the road was still ahead. Yet, somehow I could not forget my triad, nor could I get hold of myself sufficiently to do anything else in the laboratory for several days.

The ensuing period of introverted contemplation turned out to be the decisive factor in my whole career; it pointed the way for all my subsequent work. But much more important than that, it revealed vistas sufficiently alluring in their promise of adventure and fulfillment to inspire that irresistible curiosity about nature's ways which was to be my delightful damnation ever after.

THE BIRTH OF THE G.A.S.

A New Point of View

As I repetitiously continued to go over my ill-fated experiments and their possible interpretation, it suddenly struck me that one could look at them from an entirely different angle. If there was such a thing as a single nonspecific reaction of the body to damage of any kind, this might be worth study for its own sake. Indeed, working out the mechanism of this kind of stereotyped "syndrome of response to injury as such" might be much more important to medicine than the discovery of yet another sex hormone.

As I repeated to myself, "a syndrome of response to injury as such," gradually, my early classroom impressions of the clinical "syndrome of just being sick" began to reappear dimly out of my subconscious, where they had been buried for over a decade. Could it be that this syndrome in man (the feeling of being ill, the diffuse pains in joints and muscles, the intestinal disturbances with loss of appetite, the loss of weight) were in some manner clinical equivalents of the experimental syndrome, the triad (adrenocortical stimulation, thymicolymphatic atrophy, intestinal ulcers) that I had produced with such a variety of toxic substances in the rat?

If This Were So . . .

If this were so, the general medical implications of the syndrome would be enormous! Some degree of nonspecific damage is undoubtedly superimposed upon the specific characteristics of any disease, upon the specific effects of any drug.

If this were so, everything we had learned about the characteristic manifestations of disease, about the specific actions of drugs, would be in need of revision. All the actually observed biological effects of any agent must represent the sum of its specific actions and of this nonspecific response to damage that is superimposed upon it.

If this were so, it would mean that my first classroom impressions about the one-sidedness of medical thinking were quite justified and by no means sterile questions without practical answers. If the "damage syndrome" is superimposed upon the specific effects of all diseases and remedies, a systematic inquiry into the mechanism of this syndrome might well furnish us with a solid scientific basis for the treatment of damage as such.

If this were so, we had been examining medicine—disease and treatment—looking only for the specific, but through glasses tinted with the color of nonspecificity. Now that we had become aware of this misleading factor, we could remove the glasses and study the properties of disease and treatment apart from the color we saw through the glasses.

It had long been learned by sheer experience that certain curative measures were nonspecific, that is, useful to patients suffering from almost any disease. Indeed, such measures had been in use for centuries. One advises the patient to go to bed and take it easy; one tells him to eat only very digestible food and to protect himself against drafts or great variations in temperature and humidity.

Furthermore, there were all these nonspecific treatments that we had learned about in medical school, such as injection of substances foreign to the body, fever therapy, shock therapy, or bloodletting. They were unquestionably useful in certain cases. The trouble was that often they did not help, and sometimes they did much harm; since one knew nothing about the mechanism of their action, using them was like taking a shot in the dark.

If we could prove that the organism had a general nonspecific reaction-pattern with which it could meet damage caused by a variety of potential disease-producers, this defensive response would lend itself to a strictly objective, truly scientific analysis. By clearing up the mechanism of the response through which nature herself fights injuries of various kinds, we might learn how to improve upon this reaction whenever it is imperfect.

A Change of Mind

I was simply fascinated by these new possibilities and immediately decided to reverse my plans for the future. Instead of dropping the stress problem and returning to classical endocrinology, I was now prepared to spend the rest of my life studying it. I have never had any reason to regret this decision.

Discouragement

It may be worth mentioning that I often had to overcome considerable mental inhibitions in my efforts to carry on with this plan. Nowadays it is perhaps difficult to appreciate just how absurd this plan seemed to most people before I had more facts to show that it worked. For example, I remember one senior investigator whom I admired very much and whose opinion meant a great deal to me. I knew he was a real friend who seriously wanted to help me with my research efforts. One day, during these busy weeks, he asked me into his office for a good heart-to-heart talk. He reminded me that for months now he had attempted to convince me that I must abandon this futile line of research. He assured me that, in his opinion, I possessed all the essential qualifications of an investigator and that I could undoubtedly contribute something to the generally recognized and accepted fields of endocrinology, so why bother with this wild goose chase?

I met these remarks with my usual outbursts of uncontrolled youthful enthusiasm for the new point of view; I outlined again the immense possibilities inherent in a study of the nonspecific damage which must accompany all diseases and all but the mildest medications.

When he saw me thus launched on yet another enraptured description of what I had observed in animals treated with this or that impure, toxic material, he looked at me with desperately sad eyes and said in obvious despair, "But, Selye, try to realize what you are doing before it is too late! You have now decided to spend your entire life studying *the pharmacology of dirt!*"

Of course, he was right. Nobody could have expressed it more poignantly; that is why it hurt so much that I still remember the phrase today, almost twenty years later. Pharmacology is the science which explores the actions of specific drugs or poisons and I was going to study nothing but their undesired, incidental, that is, nonspecific effects. But to me, "the pharmacology of dirt" seemed the most promising subject in medicine.

Yet I could not say that I never wavered; as time went by, I often doubted the wisdom of my decision. Few among the recognized, experienced investigators, whose judgment one could usually trust, agreed with my views; and, after all, was it not silly and pretentious for a beginner to contradict them? Perhaps I had just developed a warped viewpoint. Was I, perhaps, merely wasting my time?

Encouragement

In such moments of doubt I derived considerable strength and courage from the fact that, right from the beginning, one of the most respected Canadian scientists, Sir Frederick Banting, was manifestly interested in my plans. At that time, he frequently visited university laboratories throughout Canada, since he acted as an adviser to the Canadian National Research Council. When in Montreal, he often dropped quite informally into my somewhat overcrowded little laboratory. There was not much space and he usually settled down on top of the desk, listening attentively to my daydreaming about the "syndrome of being sick."

Nothing could have done me more good! He also helped to secure the first modest financial aid for this kind of research, but that was comparatively unimportant. More than anything in the world, I needed his moral support, the reassuring feeling that the discoverer of insulin took me seriously.

I often wonder whether I could have stuck to my guns without his encouragement.

Plans for Future Research

The next point to decide was how to go about studying *the new syndrome*. Right from the start a multitude of questions arose:

1. To what extent is this syndrome *really nonspecific?*

2. Apart from those already observed, what *other manifestations* are part of it?

3. *How does it develop in time?* Is the degree of its manifestations

merely proportional to the magnitude of the damage at all times, or does the syndrome—like many infectious diseases—go through distinct stages in a certain chronological order?

4. To what extent are the manifestations of the nonspecific syndrome *influenced by the specific actions* of the agents which elicit it? All germs, poisons, and allergens have special characteristics which distinguish their effects from those of all other agents. Yet, when any substance acts upon the body, it automatically mobilizes the nonspecific mechanism also. Hence, the resulting picture would have to be a composite one, consisting of both specific and of nonspecific actions. Could these be separated?

5. What could we find out about the *mechanism,* the "dynamics" of this reaction; that is, the pathways through which the various organ-changes are produced?

These and many other questions not only presented themselves quite spontaneously, but became immediately accessible to objective scientific analysis, as soon as the concept of the "nonspecific syndrome" had crystallized. Now it was only a matter of time to find the answers to all these questions which could not even have been asked before the theory of a single "stereotyped response to damage" had taken a precise form.

What is the Scope of This Approach?

I thought that our first question should be, "Just how nonspecific is this syndrome?" Up to now, I had elicited it only by injecting foreign substances (tissue-extracts, Formalin). Subsequent experiments showed that one can produce essentially the same syndrome with purified hormones, for instance, with adrenaline (a hormone of the adrenal medulla), or with insulin (a hormone of the pancreas). One can also produce it with physical agents, such as cold, heat, x-rays, or mechanical trauma; one can produce it with hemorrhage, pain, or forced muscular exercise; indeed, *I could find no noxious agent that did not elicit the syndrome.* The scope of this approach appeared to have no limits.

The First Semantic Difficulties

At this point I first became painfully aware of the purely linguistic difficulties arising out of new viewpoints in medical research. Novel concepts require new terms with which to describe them. Yet most of us dislike neologisms, perhaps because—especially in referring to clinical syndromes and signs—new names are so often proposed merely to give a semblance of a new discovery. Of course, a new designation, if badly chosen or superfluous, can confuse more than clarify. However, now I clearly needed terms for two things: first, for the nonspecific syndrome itself, and second, for that which produced it. I could not think of any good name for either.

The First Publication on the Stress Syndrome

My first paper, in which I endeavored to show that the syndrome of stress can be studied independently of all specific changes, happened to come out on American Independence Day, July 4, in 1936. It was published as a brief note of only 74 lines in a single column of the British journal *Nature,* under the title, "A Syndrome Produced by Diverse Nocuous Agents."

Although in conversation and in lectures I had previously often used the term *biologic stress,* in referring to what caused this syndrome, by the time the first formal paper was published—yielding to violently adverse public opinion—I had temporarily given up this term. There was too much criticism of my use of the word *stress* in reference to bodily reactions, because in everyday English it generally implied nervous strain. I did not want to obscure the real issues by such squabbles over words and hoped that the word *noxious* (especially after being refined to *nocuous* by the British editor) would be considered less obnoxious than *stress.*

The Three Stages

In this same paper I also suggested the name *alarm reaction* for the initial response—that is, in the previously mentioned triad—because I thought that this syndrome probably represented the bodily expression of a generalized call to arms of the defensive forces in the organism.

But this alarm reaction was evidently not the whole response. My very first experiments showed that upon continued exposure to any noxious agent capable of eliciting this alarm reaction (unless it killed immediately), a stage of adaptation or resistance followed. In other words, no living organism can be maintained continuously in a state of alarm. If the body is confronted with an agent so damaging that continuous exposure to it is incompatible with life, then death ensues during the alarm reaction within the first hours or days. If survival is possible at all, this alarm reaction is necessarily followed by a second stage, which I called the *stage of resistance.*

The manifestations of this second stage were quite different from, and in many instances the exact opposite of, those which characterized the alarm reaction. For instance, during the alarm reaction, the cells of the adrenal cortex discharged their miscroscopically visible granules of secretion (which contain the hormone) into the blood stream. Consequently, the stores of the gland were depleted. Conversely, in the stage of resistance, the cortex accumulated an abundant reserve of secretory granules. In the alarm reaction, the blood became concentrated and there was a marked loss of bodyweight; but during the stage of resistance, the blood was diluted and the body-weight returned toward normal. Many similar examples could be cited, but these suffice to illustrate the way one can objectively follow resistance-changes in various organs.

Curiously, after still more prolonged exposure to any of the noxious agents I used, this acquired adaptation was eventually lost. The animal entered into a third phase, the *stage of exhaustion,* the symptoms of which were, in many respects, strikingly similar to those of the initial alarm reaction. At the end of a life under stress, this was a kind of premature aging due to wear and tear, a sort of second childhood which, in some ways, resembled the first.

All these findings made it necessary to coin an additional all-embracing name for the entire syndrome. Since the latter appeared to be so evidently related to adaptation, I called the entire nonspecific response the *general adaptation syndrome.* This is usually abbreviated as G.A.S. This whole syndrome then evolves in time through the three stages which I have just mentioned, namely: (1) the alarm reaction (A.R.), (2) the stage of resistance (S.R.), (3) the stage of exhaustion (S.E.).

I call this syndrome *general,* because it is produced only by agents which have a general effect upon large portions of the body. I call it *adaptive* because it stimulates defense and thereby helps the acquisition and maintenance of a stage of inurement. I call it a *syndrome* because its individual manifestations are coordinated and even partly dependent upon each other.

We have seen that the idea of stress goes back to the *pónos* of Greek medicine and that even certain nonspecific effects of drugs had long been known. The practical use of stress-producing measures of treatment had been repeatedly hailed as a panacea, each time only to be rejected a few years later as superstition and charlatanism. The parts of this concept were too elusive to be connected and grasped as a whole, hence it could not be analyzed and understood.

Significantly, in English, we use the word *grasp* as synonymous with *understanding,* precisely because it means "to hold or grasp a physical object with our hands." To *understand* is to "lay hold of with the mind." You can physically grasp something only if you manage to get hold of it between other things, for instance, your fingers, over which you have control.

Understanding is quite similar. It is not a totally new mental experience, essentially different from observation, any more than physical grasping is essentially different from touching. Understanding merely represents the solid fixation of a thing relative to the rest of our knowledge.

Throughout recorded medical history, parts of the stress concept have floated about aimlessly, as loose logs on the sea, periodically rising high on the crests of waves of popularity, then sinking low into the troughs of disgrace and oblivion. First we had to bind the loose logs (observed facts) together by solid cables (workable theories) and then, secure the resulting raft (G.A.S.) by mooring it to generally accepted, solid supports (classical medicine) before we could make use of the timber.

That is what I had in mind when I spoke about the essence of discovery. *To discover does not mean to see, but to uncover sufficiently that many can see and continue to see forever.*

As regards the G.A.S., the process of grasping and attaching it to the rest of our knowledge has progressed by this time in two dimensions: (1) *In space,* three fixed points have been established as being part of a coordinated syndrome: the adrenal, the thymicolymphatic, and the intestinal changes. These have been described as a triad. (2) *In time,* it had been shown that the G.A.S. goes through three distinct changes: the alarm reaction, the stage of resistance, and the stage of exhaustion. It thus follows a predictable path of evolution.

This picture was woefully sketchy and incomplete. Much had been known before about *pónos*. Much more has been written since on the many additional changes subsequently recognized as belonging to the G.A.S. or the *stress syndrome,* as it is also called now. The only important thing about our fixed points in space and time was that they just sufficed to get a hold on stress; they were just strong enough to prevent the concept from ever slipping through our fingers again; they made it amenable to a precise scientific analysis. We could now draw a blueprint for a systematic plan of research on stress. . . . Just to take an example, we could now devise experiments to see whether the effect of stress on lymphatic tissue depends upon adrenal activity. To establish this, we only had to verify whether the thymicolymphatic tissue of experimental animals shrinks during stress even after removal of the adrenals. We could not have formulated such precise questions about the mechanism of stress before our fixed points were established.

    •   •   •   •

2

Life-Change Patterns Surrounding Illness Experience

RICHARD H. RAHE
and
RANSOM J. ARTHUR

INTRODUCTION

A substantial amount of theoretical discussion in Psychosomatic Medicine has been devoted to the relationship between various life events and nearly simultaneous physical illnesses (Graham & Stevenson, 1963; Rahe et al., 1964; Weiss & English, 1957; Wolff, 1953). Despite voluminous work, certain basic issues remain unclarified. A constant recurring theme in such discussions is the question: "How many of the life-changes occurring around the time of an illness are really a result, rather than a cause, of the illness episode?" This paper utilizes questionnaire data from over three thousand subjects to examine life-change patterns surrounding episodes of unselected physical illnesses in an attempt to shed light on this unresolved problem.

Previous studies of life-changes and illness onset have investigated only life-changes antecedent to illness detection (Graham & Stevenson, 1963; Rahe, in press; Rahe & Christ, 1966; Rahe & Holmes, 1965; Rahe, McKean, & Arthur, 1967; Rahe et al., 1964; Weiss & English, 1957; Wolff, 1953). In this study, however, life-change patterns which occurred before, during, and after an illness episode were documented. Recent life-change patterns in individuals who reported recent illness were compared to life-change patterns from identical time periods of persons with similar social and cultural

Report Number 67-23, supported by the Bureau of Medicine and Surgery, Navy Department, under Research Unit MF022.01.03-9002.

backgrounds to the ill subjects but without concomitant health change.

The psychophysiologic significance of a wide variety of life-changes has been documented in previous reports (Rahe, in press; Rahe & Christ, 1966; Rahe, McKean, & Arthur, 1967; Rahe et al., 1964). A method for weighting the various life-changes, according to their significance for the average individual, was also presented. Therefore, it was assumed in this report that all life-changes reported by the subjects had some degree of psychophysiologic importance for the subjects in terms of the demands these changes placed upon the individual's life style which in turn influenced his overall resistance to disease through disturbances of his internal milieu.

For the sake of clarity and simplicity, a dichotomy was formulated in which all life-changes preceding clinical recognition of an illness were considered to have exerted a causal influence on the illness process and all those life-changes following documented illness onset were assumed to have resulted from the illness. A group of life-changes that occurred in very close temporal proximity to an illness was assumed to have exerted both a causative influence upon the illness process as well as reflecting behavioral changes resulting from the illness experience itself.

METHODS

The questionnaire utilized throughout the study was a military version of the Schedule of Recent Experience (SRE). The SRE instrument has been described in previous publications (Rahe, in press; Rahe et al., 1964). Basically, the instrument is a self-administered paper and pencil questionnaire that documents significant changes in the subject's life in the areas of his personal, family, community, social, religious, economic, occupational, residential, and health experience over the past few years. The military version of the SRE restricted its inquiry of these changes to the past 4 years, rather than as done in previous retrospective analyses which covered the past 10 years. Also, each of the four previous yearly periods inquired about was split into two 6-month intervals. Finally, the wording of a few questions was changed to communicate more meaningfully with the servicemen. For instance, instead of asking about whether the man was fired from work recently, the question was revised to ask about possible recent courts-martial.

As in previous reports, each life-change subscribed to by a subject was given a weight to indicate its relative amount of inherent change in one's life pattern and the ensuing amount of necessary adjustment in one's life style. These weights were developed on a sample of the American public and have been compared to weights given by persons of different cultures in foreign countries (Masuda & Holmes, 1967). The uniform agreement in the relative weights assigned to the various life-changes, even between persons of different cultures, gave support to the method of using these weights with a U.S. serviceman (Navy) population.

The various life events elicited by the military SRE, along with their assigned weights, were presented in detail in a recent publication (Rahe, McKean, & Arthur, 1967). In brief, the weights for each life-change are indicated through the use of a Life-Change Units (LCU) scale. This scale ranges from 11 LCU (minor violation of the civilian law) to 100 LCU (death of spouse). The total number of life-changes indicated by a subject over either a yearly or 6-month time interval was represented by ascribing to each life-change its LCU equivalent and then totalling all LCU for a given interval. The common denominator was therefore not the number of recent life-changes each subject registered over the past 4 years, but the intensity of life-change, for each subject, over 6 month and yearly intervals of this time span.

The criterion data on health change were determined by the subject's recall and indication of significant physical and mental illnesses over the past 4 years. All types of health changes were counted including infectious illnesses, exacerbations of chronic diseases, accidents, psychoses and so forth. Since most of the men in the study were recent recruits into the Naval service, there could be no systematic verification of the illnesses reported on their questionnaires.

Each subject could indicate the occurrence of a recalled health change or health changes during any or all of the previous 8 half-yearly intervals and the following criteria were used for analyzing the temporal relationship of life-change patterns to illness experience. For every 6-month interval where an illness experienced was indicated, that 6-month interval was termed an 'illness period'. LCU totals for all illness periods were pooled separately. The illnesses themselves did not contribute to the LCU totals. Six-month and yearly intervals preceding an illness period, which were themselves free from illness and were not preceded by an illness period, formed the pools for pre-illness intervals. Similarly, 6-month and yearly intervals following an illness period, which were not indicated as times of health change and did not precede another illness period, composed the pools for the post-illness intervals. (Because of the strict criteria for pre- and post-illness intervals, which prevented one type of interval from being contaminated by the other, there were fewer observations for these intervals than there were for the total number of illness periods.) Finally, before a 6-month or yearly LCU total was included in the pools for intervals of extended good health they had to be both preceded and followed by similar intervals of stated good health. All LCU totals, both yearly and 6-month, were ultimately dichotomized into a peri-illness category and an extended good health category.

Two thousand nine hundred U.S. Navy officers and enlisted men, virtually the entire ship's company of three cruisers, completed the military SRE questionnaire. Another 365 naval officers and enlisted men, virtually every beginning trainee in the Underwater Demolition Team training program at one training center, over an 18-month time span, also completed the instrument. These men were generally young (20–30), of lower and middle social class backgrounds, and had a high school education. A full description of the demographic characteristics of U.S. Navy enlisted recruits, who composed over 75 per cent of the sample, has been detailed in publications by Plag and Goffman (1966a; 1966b).

RESULTS

The LCU totals for the yearly (and 6-month) intervals were seen to steadily rise in magnitude over the 4 years inquired about by the questionnaire. [For the period] four years prior to the completion of the SRE the subjects recalled a mean LCU total of 100 for the entire year. [For] three years back they recorded a mean yearly LCU total of 140; 2 years back it was up to 185 LCU. [For] the two 6-month intervals prior to completion of the SRE the subjects recalled as much life-change, on the average, as they did during their third and second years back. The mean LCU total for 12–7 months prior to completion of the questionnaire was 145; the mean total for the most recent 6-month interval was 175 LCU.

Analyzing the dichotomization of the LCU intervals into a peri-illness category and an extended good health category it could be seen that intervals of long-standing good health had consistently lower LCU totals. The most striking difference between peri-illness intervals and intervals of extended good health was found between the 6-month illness periods and chronologically identical 6-month intervals of good health. Mean LCU totals for the illness periods were uniformly twice the magnitude of the corresponding mean LCU totals for comparable healthy intervals.

In order to graphically reflect the mean differences between the peri-illness intervals category and the extended good health intervals category a few simplifications were made in the presentation of the data (see Fig. 2.1). First, the intervals of extended good health were all expressed in terms of 6-month LCU totals. In other words, yearly healthy LCU totals were divided by two in order to establish the 6-month LCU interval as the common denominator. Second, a grand LCU mean was calculated for a 6-month interval of extended good health. This grand mean, 85 LCU, was used to give the best approximation of a 'baseline' 6-month LCU total that was reportedly concomitant with excellent health status. In Fig. 2.1 this baseline is represented by the horizontal broken line. Third, as was done with the intervals of extended good health, all peri-illness LCU intervals were expressed in terms of a 6-month LCU total. Lastly, grand LCU means were derived for all illness periods, for all 6-month intervals prior to and following an illness period, and for all 6-month intervals occurring seven through 12 months prior to and following an illness period. In Fig. 2.1 the grand mean LCU magnitudes of these five peri-illness intervals are indicated by solid-line bars. The illness period grand mean was the greatest in magnitude—174 LCU. Grand means for the 6-month LCU intervals immediately preceding and following an illness period were nearly identical in magnitude—125 LCU and 120 LCU, respectively. Seven through 12 months prior to an illness period the grand mean was 100 LCU. For the comparable 6-month interval following an illness period the grand mean was 130 LCU.

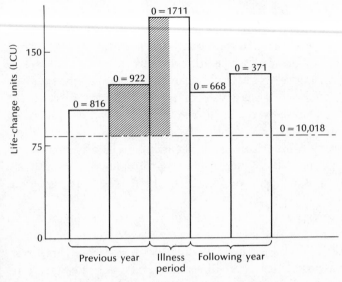

Fig. 2.1. Life-change units for peri-illness and extended good health intervals. See text for detailed explanation.

Fig. 2.1 also indicates the number of observations present in the data for each of the 5 peri-illness intervals and for the intervals of long-standing good health. There were 1,711 illness periods recorded. Six-month intervals immediately prior to and following an illness period were 922 and 668, respectively. The two peripheral 6-month peri-illness intervals were seen with the least frequency—816 for 12–7 months prior to an illness period and 371 for the comparable time span following an illness period. Intervals of long-standing good health were seen most frequently in the data, their number being 10,018.

Finally, the differences between the mean LCU values for the peri-illness intervals and those for comparable intervals of extended good health were analyzed by use of the *t*-test. For each of the 5 peri-illness intervals the differences were statistically significant at the 0.001 level of confidence.

DISCUSSION

Since the majority of persons in the study were recent recruits into Naval service it is not surprising that the most recent of the past 4 years contained the bulk of the recorded life-changes. In fact, entrance into the military entails changes in most of the areas of social adjustment and life style enquired about by the questionnaire. Also, in accordance with the theory that illness of all varieties increases in incidence during periods of significant increases in life-change, the bulk of the illness periods were also recorded during the most recent time intervals. The skewing of illness periods towards the most recent time intervals is reflected in the data by the fact that there were relatively few 6-month intervals occurring 7–12 months following an illness period. Also, there were one-third fewer 6-month intervals following an illness period than there were preceding an illness period.

An alternative explanation for the findings mentioned in the above paragraph would be that the subject's memory for recent events was much better than it was for events which occurred 3–4 years back. Because of this possibility, peri-illness intervals were always compared to long-standing good health intervals of identical chronological occurrence. In this way any systematic impairment of recall over time would be operating equally for both sets of data.

The major finding of the study was that life-change intensity, as measured by the LCU method, rose significantly above a healthy baseline value before, during and after illness occurrence. This LCU build-up and fall-off surrounding illness experience attained a peak of LCU build-up at the 6-month illness period. LCU build-up to a peak at the illness period would support previous reports in the literature on life stress build-up prior to the onset of a variety of physical illnesses (Fischer et al., 1962; Graham & Stevenson, 1963; Greene & Miller, 1958; Rahe, in press; Rahe & Christ, 1966; Rahe & Holmes, 1965; Rahe, McKean, & Arthur, 1967; Rahe et al., 1964; Weiss & English, 1957; Wolff, 1953). A notion adduced from previous studies, that life stress found prior to illness onset increases in a curvilinear fashion, with the majority of the life stresses found in close temporal proximity to the illness, was also supported (Fischer et al., 1962; Greene & Miller, 1958; Rahe & Christ, 1966; Rahe & Holmes, 1965; Rahe et al., 1964). In Fig. 2.1 it can be seen that LCU build-up prior to illness demonstrates just such a curvilinear increase. The existence of a nearly symmetrical LCU fall-off following illness experience, however, is a new and important finding. Using the temporal relationship of the life-changes to the illness to define their causal or resultant relationship to the illness, as stated in this paper's Introduction, it appears that life-changes resulting from illness experience are virtually equal in timing and intensity to those life-changes having a causal influence on the illness.

A seeming exception to the near-symmetrical LCU build-up and fall-off surrounding an illness period is the relatively high LCU grand mean for 7–12 months following an illness period. This finding is in part a function of the previously stated steady increase in LCU magnitude for each of the four previous years inquired about by the questionnaire. The horizontal broken line in Fig. 2.1 is slightly misleading because of this steady LCU increase. A true baseline of extended good health would have a positive slope to it.

From a preventive medicine point of view the cross-hatched area in Fig. 2.1 represents the most crucial data in the study. These significantly evaluated LCU levels may well become a useful indicator of increased vulnerability, in a subject, to a wide variety of illness processes. Pilot studies on a small, highly educated population have indicated that this may be the case (Rahe, in press). In large-scale studies of persons of average education the results could be quite different. At the present time most all the subjects in this retrospective study are also included in ongoing prospective studies of documented (health record) physical and mental illness during a 4- to 8-month follow-up period.

SUMMARY

Over 3,000 U.S. Navy personnel, primarily recent recruits into military service, completed a recent life-changes and health status questionnaire. Retrospective data were collected not only on life-change patterns occurring prior to illness, but also on life-changes recorded concomitant with and following illness experience. Subjects indicating recent illnesses provided life-change data which were compared to life-change patterns of a larger group of reportedly healthy subjects over chronologically identical time periods.

Life-change data seen prior to illness experience confirmed previous work done on life stress build-up prior to illness onset. A new and important finding was that life-change data seen following illness experience was a reversed and nearly symmetrical picture of its counter-part prior to illness. These data suggest that previous and seemingly opposing arguments on whether life-changes precede (causal relationship) or follow (resultant relationship) a wide variety of illnesses have equal validity.

3

Ethology and Stress Diseases

NIKOLAAS TINBERGEN

Many of us have been surprised at the unconventional decision of the Nobel Foundation to award this year's prize for Physiology or Medicine to three men who had until recently been regarded as "mere animal watchers." Since at least Konrad Lorenz and I could not really be described as physiologists, we must conclude that our *scientia amabilis* is now being acknowledged as an integral part of the eminently practical field of medicine. It is for this reason that I have decided to discuss today two concrete examples of how the old method [1] of "watching and wondering" about behavior (which incidentally we revived rather than invented) can indeed contribute to the relief of human suffering, in particular of suffering caused by stress. It seems to me fitting to do this in a city already renowned for important work on psychosocial stress and psychosomatic diseases (Levi, 1971).

My first example concerns some new facts and views on the nature of what is now widely called early childhood autism. This is a set of behavioral aberrations which Leo Kanner first described in 1943.[2] To us, that is, my wife Elisabeth and me, it looks as if this set of aberrations is actually on the increase in a number of Western or Westernized societies. From the description of autistic behavior, or Kanner's syndrome,[3] it is clear, even to those who have not themselves seen

[1] I call the method old because it must already have been highly developed by our ancestral hunter-gatherers, as it still is in non-Westernized hunting-gathering tribes such as the Bushmen, the Eskimo, and the Australian Aborigines. As a scientific method applied to man it could be said to have been revived first by Charles Darwin (1872).

[2] Recently, Kanner (1973) has published a selection of his papers.

[3] When I speak of Kanner's syndrome, I refer to the largely descriptive list of symptoms given by O'Gorman (1970). This is a slightly modified version of the description given by

these unfortunate children, how crippling this affliction is. In various degrees of severity, it involves, among other things, a total withdrawal from the environment; a failure to acquire, or a regression of, overt speech; a serious lagging behind in the acquisition of numerous other skills; obsessive preoccupation with a limited number of objects; the performance of seemingly senseless and stereotyped movements; and an electroencephalogram (EEG) pattern that indicates high overall arousal. A number of autists recover (some of them spontaneously), but many others end up in mental hospitals, where they are then often diagnosed and treated as schizophrenics.

In spite of a growing volume of research on the subject,[4] opinions of medical experts on how to recognize autism, on its causation, and therefore on the best treatment vary widely. Let me consider this briefly, point by point.

(1) There is disagreement already at the level of diagnosis and labeling. For instance, Rimland (1971) compared the diagnoses for 445 children, as given by the doctor who was consulted first, with a

Creak (1961). Many other definitions of autism in its various forms are mixtures of observed behavioral deviations and interpretations. For a discussion of the confusion surrounding the word "autism" see Tinbergen and Tinbergen (1972, pp. 45–46).

[4] For the purpose of finding one's way in this literature we can refer to Rutter (1965) and to the quarterly, started in 1971 (*Journal of Autism and Childhood Schizophrenia,* published by Winston, Washington, D.C.), which prints original articles as well as reviews. The most recent and most exhaustive review is by Ornitz (1973). Throughout the literature (not only on autism but on many other psychiatric issues as well) one finds one fundamental error in scientific reasoning. Time and again we receive the comment that we overlook the "hard" evidence of internal malfunctioning in autists as well as in other categories of the mentally ill. I assure my readers that we do not *overlook* such evidence (such as that on blood platelets, on lead contents, and on electronencephalogram patterns). The erroneous assumption underlying most of the arguments in which such facts are used for the purpose of throwing light on the causation of the behavioral deviation is almost invariably due to *the confusion between correlations and cause-effect relations.* With some exceptions (such as the deleterious effect of lead) the physiological or biochemical evidence is considered, without any ground whatsoever, to indicate causes, whereas the correlations found could just as well point to consequences or side effects. It is just as nonsensical to say that retarded bone growth, or abnormalities in the blood platelet picture (or for that matter speech defects, or high overall arousal) are causes of autism as it is to say that a high temperature is the cause of typhoid or pneumonia. Unless there is evidence, clinical and ultimately experimental, indicating what is cause and what is effect, the opinions based on hard evidence are in fact worthless. Our experimental evidence discussed on pages 21 and 22 [of original article] is hard, whereas evidence on correlations—however impressive the techniques might be by which they are found—are scientifically useless until an attempt is made to place it into cause-effect context. This is what I mean in my final paragraphs by "the glamor of apparatus"—the idolization of techniques, coupled with the failure to think about the meaning of evidence, is a serious disease of medical research.

"second opinion." If the art of diagnosis has any objective basis, there should be a positive correlation between first and second opinions. In fact, as Rimland points out, there is not a trace of such a correlation—the diagnoses are practically random (Table 3.1). What these doctors have been saying to the parents is little more than, "You are quite right; there is something wrong with your child."

And yet, if we use the term autism in the descriptive sense of "Kanner's syndrome," it does name a relatively well-defined cluster of aberrations.

(2) The disagreement about the causation of autism is no less striking. It expresses itself at two levels. First, there is the usual nature-nurture controversy. The majority of experts who have written on autism hold that it is due either to a genetic defect or to equally irreparable "organic" abnormalities, for instance, brain damage such as can be incurred during a difficult delivery. Some of the specialists are certainly emphatic in their assertion that autism is "not caused by the personalities of the parents, nor by their child-rearing practices" (Wing, 1970; p. 381; see also Tinbergen & Tinbergen, 1972, p. 51). If this were true, the outlook for a real cure for such children would of course be bleak, for the best one could hope for would be an amelioration of their suffering. But there are also a few experts who are inclined to ascribe at least some cases of autism to damaging environmental causes, either traumatizing events in early childhood or a sustained failure in the parent-infant interaction.[5] If this were even partially correct, the prospect for a real cure would, of course, be brighter.

The confusion about causation is also evident in the disagreement about the questions of what is primary in the overall syndrome, what is at the root of the trouble, and what are mere symptoms. Some authors hold that autism is primarily either a cognitive or (as is often mentioned in one breath) a speech defect (Rutter, Bartak, & Newman, 1971). Others consider the hyperarousal as primary (Hutt & Hutt, 1970a; Hutt et al., 1964). Those who subscribe to the environmental hypothesis think either in terms of too much overall input (Stroh & Buick, 1970), or in terms of failures in the processes of affiliation and of subsequent socialization.[6]

[5] One of the most prominent exponents of this view is Bettelheim (1967); see also Clancy and McBride (1969).

[6] See Footnote 5.

Table 3.1. Comparison of First and Second Opinions about 445 Children Showing Severe Behavior Disorders. [From Rimland (1971)]

First Opinion	Second Opinion								
	Autistic	Infantile Autism or Early Infantile Autism	Childhood Schizophrenia	Emotionally Disturbed or Mentally Ill	Brain or Neurological Damage	Retarded	Psychotic	Deaf or Partly Deaf	Total
Autistic	33	5	53	18	23	51	10	7	200
Infantile autism or early infantile autism	1	10	6	0	4	6	0	2	29
Childhood schizophrenia	17	3	1	2	8	1	0	0	32
Emotionally disturbed or mentally ill	12	2	4	2	9	13	3	0	45
Brain or neurological damage	14	3	2	5	4	15	0	1	44
Retarded	21	2	6	18	16	5	2	2	72
Psychotic	4	0	1	1	2	2	0	0	10
Deaf or partly deaf	4	1	0	2	0	5	1	0	13
Total	106	26	73	48	66	98	16	12	445

(3) In view of all this it is no wonder that therapies, which are often based on views concerning causation, also differ very widely. Nor is it easy to judge the success rates of any of these therapies, for the numbers of children treated by any individual therapist or institution are small; also, the descriptions of the treatments are inevitably incomplete and often vague. Unless one observes the therapist in action, it is not really possible to judge what he has actually been doing.

In short, as O'Gorman put it not long ago (1970, p. 124), ". . . our efforts in the past have been largely empirical, and largely ineffectual."

In view of all this uncertainty, any assistance from outside the field of psychiatry could be of value. And it is such assistance that my wife and I have recently tried to offer (Tinbergen & Tinbergen, 1972). Very soon our work led us to conclusions which went against the majority opinion, and we formulated proposals about therapies which, with few exceptions, had not so far been tried out. And I can already say that, where these treatments have been applied, they are leading to quite promising results, and we feel that we begin to see a glimmer of hope.

Before giving my arguments for this optimistic prognosis, let me describe how and why we became involved. Our interest in autistic children, aroused initially by what little we had seen of the work that was being done in the Park Hospital in Oxford, remained dormant for a long time. But when, in 1970, we read the statement by Drs. John and Corinne Hutt that ". . . apart from gaze aversion of the face, all other components of the social encounters of these autistic children are those shown by normal nonautistic children . . ." (1970b, p. 147), we suddenly sat up, because we knew from many years of child watching that normal children quite often show all the elements of Kanner's syndrome.

Thinking this over we remembered the commonsense but sound warning of Medawar, namely, that "it is not informative to study variations of behaviour unless we know beforehand the norm from which the variants depart" (1967, p. 109), and we realized that these words had not really been heeded by psychiatrists. In their literature we had found very little about normal children that could serve as a basis for comparison.

We also realized that, since so many autists do not speak (and are often quite wrongly considered not to understand speech either), a better insight into their illness would have to be based on the study of their nonverbal behavior. And it is just in this sphere that we could apply some of the methods that had already proved their value in studies of animal behavior.[7]

Therefore we began to compare our knowledge of the nonverbal behavior that normal children show only occasionally, with that of true autists, which we had not only found described in the literature but also began to observe more closely at first hand.

The types of behavior to which we soon turned our attention included such things as the child's keeping its distance from a strange person or situation, details of its facial expressions, its bodily stance, and its consistent avoidance of making eye contact—an extremely rich set of expressions that are all correlated with overt avoidance (Figs. 3.1 and 3.2). The work of professional child ethologists is beginning to show us how immensely rich and subtle the repertoire is of such nonverbal expressions (see Jones, 1972).

But, apart from observing these behaviors themselves, we also collected evidence about the circumstances in which normal children reverted to bouts of autistic behavior. What emerged from this dual approach was quite clear. Such passing attacks of autistic behavior appear in a normal child when it finds itself in a situation that creates a conflict between two incompatible motivations. On the one hand, the situation evokes fear (a tendency to withdraw, physically and mentally); on the other hand, it also elicits social, and often exploratory, behavior, but the fear prevents the child from venturing out into the world. And, not unexpectedly, it is naturally timid children (by nature or by nurture, or both) that show this conflict behavior more readily than more resilient, confident children do. But my point is that they all respond to the environment.

Once we had arrived at this interpretation, we tested it in some simple experiments. In fact, we realized that in our years of interaction with children we had already been experimenting a great deal. Such experiments had not been aiming at the elicitation of autistic

[7] For a recent review about the analysis of nonverbal signs of mixed motivation, or motivational conflicts, see, for example, Manning (1972, Chapter 5) and Hinde (1970, Chapter 17); both books give further references.

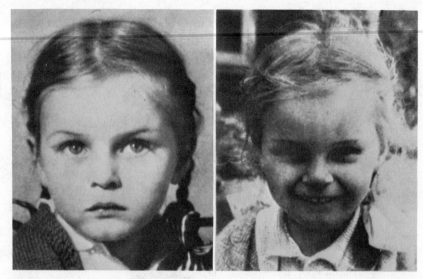

Fig. 3.1. Two photographs of a girl (aged 6 years) taken in the same spring; (left) taken by a school photographer; (right) taken by her elder sister. These illustrate some non-verbal expressions as used in motivational analysis. (According to E. A. & N. Tinbergen, 1972; Courtesy of Verlag Paul Parey, Berlin)

behavior, but rather at its opposite: its elimination. As we have written before, each of these experiments was in reality a subtly modulated series of experiments. For a description of what we actually did, I quote from our original publication. We wrote (Tinbergen & Tinbergen, 1972, pp. 29–30):

What we invariably do when visiting, or being visited by a family with young children is, after a very brief friendly glance, [to] ignore the child(ren) completely, at the same time eliciting, during our early conversations, friendly responses from the parent(s). One can see a great deal of the behaviour of the child out of the corner of one's eye, and can monitor a surprising amount of the behaviour that reveals the child's state. Usually such a child will start by simply looking intently at the stranger, studying him guardedly. One may already at this stage judge it safe to now and then look briefly at the child and assess more accurately the state it is in. If, on doing so, one sees the child avert its glance, eye contact must at once be broken off. Very soon the child will stop studying one. It will approach gingerly, and it will soon reveal its strong bonding tendency by touching one—for instance by putting its hand tentatively on one's knee. This is

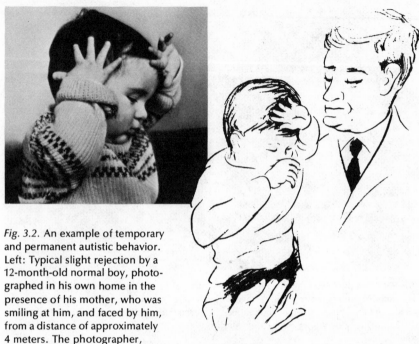

Fig. 3.2. An example of temporary and permanent autistic behavior. Left: Typical slight rejection by a 12-month-old normal boy, photographed in his own home in the presence of his mother, who was smiling at him, and faced by him, from a distance of approximately 4 meters. The photographer, who was his (rarely met) grandfather, was approximately 1½ meters away from the child. (According to E. A. & N. Tinbergen, 1972; Courtesy of Verlag Paul Parey, Berlin.) Right: Response of an autistic child to repeated attempts of adult to make eye-to-eye contact (drawn from 8-mm motion picture film). (From Hutt & Hutt, 1970b; Courtesy of Charles C. Thomas, Publisher, Springfield, Illinois.)

often a crucial moment: one must *not* respond by looking at the child (which may set it back considerably) but by cautiously touching the child's hand with one's own. Again, playing this "game" by if necessary stopping, or going one step back in the process, according to the child's response, one can soon give a mildly reassuring signal *by touch,* for instance by gently pressing its hand, or by touching it quickly, and withdrawing again. If, as is often the case, the child laughs at this, one can laugh oneself, but still without looking at the child. Soon it will become more daring, and the continuation of contact by touch and by indirect vocalisation will begin to cement a bond. One can then switch to the first, tentative eye contact. This again must be done with caution, and step by step; certainly with a smile, and for brief moments at first. We find that first covering one's face with one's hands, then turning towards the child (perhaps saying "where's Andrew?" or whatever the child's name) and then briefly showing one's eyes and covering them up at once, is very likely to elicit a smile, or even a laugh. For this, incidentally, a child often takes the initiative [see e.g. Stroh and Buick (1970)]. Very soon the child will then begin to solicit this; it will rapidly tolerate increasingly long periods of direct eye contact and join one. If this is played further, with continuous awareness of and adjustments to slight reverses to a more negative attitude, one will soon find the child literally clamouring for intense play contact. Throughout this process the vast variety of expressions of the child must be *understood* in order to monitor it correctly, and one must oneself *apply* an equally large repertoire in order to give, at any moment, the best signal. The "bag of tricks" one has to have at one's disposal must be used to the full, and the "trick" selected must whenever possible be adjusted to the child's individual tastes. Once established, the bond can be maintained by surprisingly slight signals; a child coming to show proudly a drawing it has made is often completely happy with just a "how nice dear" and will then return to its own play. Even simpler vocal contacts can work; analogous to the vocal contact calls of birds (which the famous Swedish writer Selma Lagerloef correctly described in "Nils Holgersson" as, "I am here, where are you?") many children develop an individual contact call, to which one has merely to answer in the same language.

The results of this procedure have been found to be surprisingly rapid, and also consistent *if one adjusts oneself to the monitoring results.* Different children may require different starting levels, and different tempos of stepping-up. One may even have to start by staying away from the child's favourite room. It is also of great significance how familiar to the child the physical environment is. Many children take more than one day; with such it is important to remember that one has to start at a lower level in the morning than where one left off the previous evening. We have the impression that the process is on the whole completed sooner if one continually holds back until one senses the child longing for a more intense contact.

With all these experiences with normal children in mind, we began to reconsider the evidence about permanently autistic children—again using our own observations as well as the reports we found in the literature. And two things became clear almost at once. Neither for genetic abnormalities nor for gross brain damage was there any convincing, direct evidence; all we found were inferences, or arguments that do not hold water.

The main argument for a genetic abnormality is the statement (and one hears it time and again) "these children have been odd from birth." And we also found that, for various reasons, neither the specialists nor the parents are very willing to consider environmental influences. But in view of what we know about the effects of nongenetic agents that act in utero, of which the recently indicated effect of rubella contracted by pregnant women is only one (Chess, 1971),[8] the "odd-from-birth" argument is of course irrelevant. And at least two cases are known of identical twins of whom only one developed Kanner's syndrome (Kamp, 1964; Vaillant, 1963).[9]

Equally unconvincing are the arguments in favor of gross brain damage, and this idea too is based mainly on inference.

On the other hand, the body of positive evidence that points to environmental causes is growing. For instance, many workers report that the incidence of autism is not random. Relatively many autists are firstborn children (see, for example, Wing, 1971, p. 8). There is also a pretty widespread conviction that the parents of autists are somehow different; for instance, many of them are very serious people, or people who are themselves under some sort of strain. And to a trained observer it is also very obvious that autists respond to conditions, which to them are frightening or intrusive, by an intensification of all their symptoms. Conversely, we have tried out our "taming procedure," as described for normal children, on some severely autistic children, and succeeded in drawing them out of their shells, in making them snuggle up to us, and even in making them join us in, for instance, touch games. I cannot possibly go into all the evidence, but there are several good indications: first, that many autists are potentially normal children, whose affiliation and subsequent socialization processes have gone wrong in one way or another; and second, this can often be traced back to something in the early environment—on occasion a frightening accident, but most often something in the behavior of the parents, in particular the mothers. Let

[8] The point I want to make with this brief reference is that, while one should call rubella an early environmental influence and therefore not congenital in the sense of genetic, it might well be correct to call it organic, even though rubella could well create a state of anxiety already during pregnancy in mothers who have heard about other damaging effects of the disease. And this in itself could well cause a complex psychosomatic state.

[9] While I do not of course intend to underrate the possibility of genetic predisposition, the hypothesis of a purely genetic deviation conflicts with this type of observation. At the same time we know that even when twins grow up in the same family, their experiences can never be identical.

me hasten to add that in saying this we are not blaming these unfortunate parents. Very often they seem to have been either simply inexperienced (hence perhaps the high incidence among firstborns); or overapprehensive; or overefficient and intrusive; or, perhaps most often, they are people who are themselves under stress. For this and many other reasons, the parents of autists deserve as much compassion, and may be as much in need of help, as the autists themselves.

Now, if we are only partially right in assuming that at least a large proportion of autists are victims of some kind of environmental stress, whose basic trouble is of an emotional nature, then one would expect that those therapies that aim at reducing anxiety, by allowing spontaneous socialization and exploration whenever it occurs, would be more successful than those that aim at the teaching of specific skills. Unfortunately, as I have already said, it is hardly possible to judge from published reports what treatment has actually been applied. For instance, one speech therapist may behave rather intrusively and turn a child into a mere "trained monkey," leaving all the other symptoms as they were, or even making them worse. Another speech therapist may have success simply by having proceeded in a very gentle, motherly way. One has to go by those instances where one has either been involved oneself or where one knows pretty precisely how the therapist has in fact proceeded. It is with this in mind that I will now mention briefly three examples of treatments that seem to hold great promise.

First, even before we published our first paper, the Australian therapist Helen Clancy had been treating autistic children and their families along lines that are very similar to, and in fact are more sophisticated than, those recommended by us in 1972.

The gist of Clancy's method is as follows (Clancy & McBride, 1969). (i) Since she considers the restoration of initially defective affiliation with the mother as the first goal of treatment of autism, she treats both mother and child, and the family as well. She does this by provoking in the mother an increase in maternal, protective behavior. (ii) She uses a form of operant conditioning for speeding up the child's response to this change in the mother. In other words, she tries to elicit a mutual emotional bond between mother and child, and refrains, at least at first, from the piecemeal teaching of particular skills.

With those mothers who were willing to cooperate, Clancy has achieved highly encouraging success, although of course a few families (4 out of approximately 50 treated over a period of 14 years) have failed to benefit.

Second, after the first public discussion of our work, my wife received invitations to visit some schools for autists and to observe what was being done. She found in one of them, a small day school which already had an impressive record of recoveries, that the treatment was likewise aimed at the restoration of emotional security, and teaching as such, including some gentle speech therapy, was never started until a child had reached a socially positive attitude. Much to our dismay, this school has since been incorporated into a school for maladjusted children—the experiment has been discontinued.

Third, a regional psychiatrist invited us a year ago to act as advisers in a fascinating experiment which she too had begun well before she had heard of our work. Three boys, who are now 9, 9½, and 11½ years of age, and who had all been professionally diagnosed as severely autistic, are now being gently integrated into a normal primary school. This involves a part-time home tutor for each boy, a sympathetic headmaster, and willingness of the parents to cooperate. The results are already little short of spectacular. In fact, a specialist on autistic children who visited the school recently said to us: "Had the records not shown that these three children were still severely autistic a couple of years ago, I would not now believe it." This experiment, which is also run along lines that are consistent with our ideas, is being carefully documented.

It is this type of evidence, together with that provided by a number of already published case histories, [10] that has by now convinced us that many autists can attain a full recovery, if only we act on the assumption that they have been traumatized rather than genetically or organically damaged. I cannot go into further details here, but I can sum up in a few sentences the gist of what the ethological approach to early childhood autism has produced so far.

[10] Although not all the authors of the following books label their subject as "autistic," I mention them because the descriptions of the initial behavior conform in whole or in part to Kanner's syndrome; and, as I have said, I consider such descriptions the only acceptable starting points: Axline (1971); Copeland and Hodges (1973); d'Ambrosio (1971); Hundley (1973); Park (1972); Thieme (1971); Wexler (1971). No two of these seven children received the same treatment, but on the whole one can say that those who were treated primarily at the emotional level rather than at the level of specific skills showed the most striking improvement.

(1) There are strong indications that many autists suffer primarily from an emotional disturbance, from a form of anxiety neurosis, which prevents or retards normal affiliation and subsequent socialization, and this in its turn hampers or suppresses the development of overt speech, of reading, of exploration, and of other learning processes, based on these three behaviors.

(2) More often than has so far been assumed these aberrations are not due to either genetic abnormalities or to gross brain damage, but to early environmental influences. The majority of autists, as well as their parents, seem to be genuine victims of environmental stress. And our work on normal children has convinced us not only that this type of stress disease is actually on the increase in Western and Westernized countries, but also that very many children must be regarded as semiautistic, and even more as being seriously at risk.

(3) Those therapies that aim at the reduction of anxiety and at a restarting of proper socialization seem to be far more effective than, for instance, speech therapy per se and enforced social instruction, which seem to be at best symptom treatments, and to have only limited success. Time and again treatment at the emotional level has produced an explosive emergence of speech and other skills.

If I now try to assess the implications of what I have said, I feel at the same time alarmed and hopeful. We are alarmed because we found this corner of psychiatry in a state of disarray, and because we discovered that many of the established experts—doctors, teachers, and therapists—are so little open to new ideas and even facts. Another cause for alarm is our conviction that the officially recognized autists are only a fraction of a much larger number of children who obviously suffer to some degree from this form of social stress.

We feel hopeful because attempts at curing such children at the emotional level, while still in the experimental stage, are already leading to positive results. And another encouraging sign is that, among the young psychiatrists, we have found many who are sympathetic to our views, or even share them, and have begun to act on them.

In the interest of these thousands of unfortunate children we appeal to all concerned to give the stress view of autism at least the benefit of the doubt, and to try out the forms of therapy that I have mentioned.

•   •   •   •

4

On the Concept of Psychological Stress

MORTIMER H. APPLEY
and
RICHARD TRUMBULL

PSYCHOLOGICAL STRESS

1. On the *stimulus* side, the term has been used to describe situations characterized as new, intense, rapidly changing, sudden or unexpected, including (but not requiring) approach to the upper thresholds of tolerability. At the same time, stimulus deficit, absence of expected stimulation, highly persistent stimulation, and fatigue-producing and boredom-producing settings, among others, have also been described as stressful, as have stimuli leading to cognitive misperception, stimuli susceptible to hallucination, and stimuli calling for conflicting responses. Any one of these procedures has at some time actually been used as an operational means for defining and producing stress.

2. On the *response* side, the presence of emotional activity has been used *post facto* to define the existence of stress. This usually refers to any bodily response in excess of "normal or usual"—states of anxiety, tension, and upset—or for that matter any behavior which deviates momentarily or over time from normative value for the individual in question or for an appropriate reference group. Indices used include such overt emotional responses as tremors, stuttering, exaggerated speech characteristics, and loss of sphincter control—or such perfor-

This chapter combines and extends the introductory remarks made by the two authors to the Opening Session of the Conference on Psychological Stress, May 10, 1965.

mance shifts as perseverative behaviors, increased reaction time, erratic performance rates, malcoordination, error increase, and fatigue.

3. The existence of a stress state *within* the organism has alternatively been inferred from one or more of a number of partially correlated indices, such as a change in blood eosinophils, an increase in 17-ketosteroids in the urine, an increase in ACTH-content or glucocorticoid concentration in the blood, or changes in any number of psychophysiological variables, such as heart rate, galvanic skin response (GSR), change in critical flicker fusion (CFF) threshold, inspiration:expiration $\left(\dfrac{I}{E}\right)$ ratio, and so on. (These are response measures, of course, but they can be usefully distinguished from responses which are of the order of overt performance changes or observable symptoms of emotionality, such as those noted above.)

THE PROBLEM OF DEFINITION

Investigators have usually sought both a condition which produces stress and a measure which indicates its presence as the most frequent combination of circumstances in which to study the phenomenon. Unfortunately, the choices have been selective—as often governed by the convenience or tradition of a given laboratory as by rational considerations. There are, then, clearly wide variations in specific uses, specific definitions, and specific purposes with which the term *stress* has been associated. However, one is reminded of Whitehorn's comments:

We may be able to get some use out of the term stress, even if it is left vague and not very clearly defined, provided we succeed in specifying fairly sharply some of the aspects of the biological reactions to stress.

If we were dealing with inanimate objects, the conceptual and terminological problem would be greatly simplified, because in physics action and reaction are equal, and stress can be expressed in dynes per square centimeter; but in biology this is not so. Living organisms are specially organized to accumulate and spend energy on their own discriminately, and not in exact equality to the forces acting upon them. We take this one step further and recognize the psychological factors which further influence this discriminating function and appreciate that our difficulties of description and evaluation have been geometrically expanded. (1953, p. 3)

Without a doubt, this geometrical expansion has served as a deterrent to exploring the psychological complex which produces the inequality of response to the forces acting.

Let us look next at the pattern of stress experiments. Typically, the experimenter manipulates the environment in a manner intended to produce a response, and then measures the extent and/or direction of the behavior change produced. (This is, of course, the pattern of all psychological experiments. Stress studies are usually distinguishable primarily in the selection of stimulating conditions).

Experimenters in these studies choose environmental manipulations which would, in their consideration, serve to produce not just change in the direction of ongoing behavior—which after all is what any response must be, and would not distinguish stress studies—but a disruption of behavior, or its disorganization. Accompanying such disorganization one expects to find certain physiological changes, and it is here that much of this research is concentrated. In fact, the most widely accepted types of operational definitions of the existence of stress are changes in physiological indices. Unfortunately, one investigator relies on the GSR, a second on blood volume changes, a third on pulse rate or heart rate, a fourth on muscle action potential, and so on. In animals, the presence of stress is often inferred from feces counts, trembling, "freezing" or washing behavior, and so on. The use of these measures rests on the simple assumption that certain environmental conditions induce not only overt behavioral effects but common autonomic and other internal effects as well.

We would not so much disagree with the logic of this argument as with the facts it has produced. In the studies with which we have acquaintance there are marked individual differences, as has already been noted. All subjects apparently do not respond to given environmental conditions as a given experimenter expected or intended. We may either conclude that the conditions were not stress-producing or, if we insist that they were, we must face the problem of explaining why some subjects were thereby *not* put into a stress state. We surely needn't labor this point, which could be made in connection with most psychological studies. It is of particular importance here, however, because of what we have described as the assumption of the commonality of intervening responses in stress situations. Further, the dependence on the stimulus to define a situation as stressful is obviously too limiting.

If we accept that a physiological index is a proper monitor of the presence of stress, which may be reasonable in some respects, we must nevertheless parallel our studies of these responses with investigations of those conditions which precipitate stress in the individuals under study. It is clear that if we cannot rely upon the stimulus we must look for some pattern of stimulus-organism interaction to understand why stress occurs in some exposed organisms and not in others.

With the exception of extreme and sudden life-threatening situations, it is reasonable to say that no stimulus is a stressor to all individuals exposed to it.[1] The earlier assumption of a common all-or-none psycho-physiological stress state is untenable in the face of evidence to the contrary. James Miller and his associates (1953), after surveying the available stress-sensitive tests more than a dozen years ago, concluded that "in a specific situation it becomes necessary to recognize the many different kinds of stress" (p. A-4). Lazarus, Deese, and Osler (1952), after reviewing the literature on the effects of stress on performance, concluded that these effects are not general, but "will depend upon what the individual expects or demands of himself" (p. 296). In a more recent paper, Lazarus [and Alfert (1964)] suggested what he called "cognitive appraisal" as a mediating condition for such determination,[2] and Appley (1962) has placed emphasis on the importance of "threat perception" as a mediator of stressfulness. A similar point was made earlier by Pascal (1951) in defining stress "in terms of a perceived environmental situation which threatens the gratification of needs . . ." (p. 177).

Basowitz et al. (1955), in an elaborate study of anxiety and stress in paratroopers, started with a situational definition but concluded that "in future research . . . we should not consider stress as *imposed* upon the organism, but as its *response* to internal or external processes which reach those threshold levels that strain its physiological and psychological integrative capacities close to or beyond their limits" (pp. 288–89).

---

[1] An interesting contrast can be made within the category of life-endangering situations. Attempted strangulation, for example, may be a psychological stressor of great import, whereas significant levels of irradiation (which may be near fatal but are not "detected" by the organism) may have no discernible effect on behavior at all.

[2] See Lazarus, this volume, for an elaboration of this point, and related concepts in Arnold's chapter and in discussion elsewhere in the volume [Appley and Trumbull, 1967b].

Cofer and Appley (1964) defined stress as "the state of an organism where he perceives that his well-being (or integrity) is endangered and that he must divert all his energies to its protection" (p. 453). In all of these instances we see an emphasis on individual determination of when stress will or will not occur.

It is further evident from the definitions cited that another area in which separation of psychological from physical aspects is required is that of "threat." In reports of studies involving physical "threat" we sometimes do not know and cannot determine if the "threat" is really "perceived" by the subject as such. Often the experimenter merely assumes that the situation *should have been* threatening or would have been threatening had he been the subject. The point to be made is that the first necessary step in such studies is to determine how the subject perceives the stimulus or situation presented. We know many ways to change deliberately his perception of the situation, but seem often to ignore other subtle forces which may be present and acting to change the value of an "objective" stressor. The extreme stimuli which some experimenters have used—such as electric shock or pistols fired close to the ear—indicate their awareness of this point. However, the very use of such strong stimuli probably obscures the influence of intervening perceptual factors, the understanding of which is so important. Obviously, it would be unreasonable to insist that the experimenter know what constitutes a stressor for his subject before beginning an investigation, when often that is to be its end point. However, the implications of this are found in Haggard's (1949) discussion of emotional stress:

An individual experiences emotional stress when his over-all adjustment is threatened, when his adaptive mechanisms are severely taxed and tend to collapse. Some of the factors which influence an individual's ability to tolerate and master stress include: the nature of his early identifications and his present character structure, and their relation to the demands and gratifications of the present stress-producing situation; the nature of his reactions to the situation; his ability to master strong and disturbing emotional tensions; the extent to which he knows about all aspects of the situation, so that he is not helplessly unaware of the nature and source of threat; his available skills and other means of dealing effectively with it; and the strength and pattern of his motivations to do so. (p. 458).

It would take months if not years to know a subject well enough to meet these demands. However, this does delineate those interests which are primarily psychological in nature, and we will briefly note a few studies which emphasize them. Lazarus, Deese, and Osler (1952) summarize their extensive review in the following terms:

Very little information has been obtained about the relationship between various measures of personality and reaction to stress. The problem has theoretical as well as practical importance. On the one hand, while great individual differences in response to stress have been recognized, few fruitful attempts have been made to discover their nature. On the other hand, it would be most useful to be able to predict which people will be adversely affected by a stressful situation. (p. 307)

Essentially, this boils down to a consideration of interactions between persons and types of stress. It would be interesting to know what kind of individual develops anxiety reactions to task-induced stress. We might guess that such people are highly motivated to perform well. The successful understanding of any individual's performance under stress depends upon some way of measuring the kinds and strength of his motivations and relating them to the characteristics of the situation in which he must perform. The fulfillment of this aim is, indeed, no simple affair. (p. 314)

If measurement of performance is the criterion, there would have to be decrement but one would never be certain as to why. The teasing out of truly psychological factors would appear to be the major contribution to come from psychologists.

Once again, literature reviews show us how pursuit of these many psychological factors without definitional clarity has produced little or nothing.

Some investigators have studied the effects of subject variables upon performance under short-term stress situations. Stopol (1954) tested twelve hypotheses involving Rorschach responses . . . and found no relationship between such responses and performance under stress. Lofchie (1955), however, found that subjects who scored high on a Rorschach index of perceptual maturity performed better on a psychomotor task under distraction stress than did subjects who scored low on the index. Katchmar (1953) selected anxious and nonanxious subjects by the Taylor Manifest Anxiety Scale. Under failure stress conditions, the anxious subjects did worse than the nonanxious subjects on a form-naming and substitution task, although the performance of both groups showed a decrement over control conditions. Hutt (1947) found that maladjusted children did more poorly than well-adjusted children on the Stanford-Binet Test under failure stress conditions. Further studies on the personality correlates of behavior under stress are cited by Lazarus et al. (1952). (Harris, Mackie, and Wilson, 1956, p. 34)

These definitions and comments generally suggest that stress is a response state and that its induction depends on the mediation of some appraising, perceiving, or interpreting mechanism. As was suggested earlier, certain universally adequate stimuli may be expected to lead to stress more rapidly than others—as, for example, cutting off the air supply.[3] This should lead to a stress state in *all* persons, with little variation in the rate of its development. However, any less severe stimulation—and particularly where the effectiveness of the stimulation is dependent on prior conditioning (as in the case of social stimuli)—will give rise to response patterns that vary greatly from person to person and may induce anxiety or stress much more rapidly in one person than another.

What must be taken into account is not only the objective reality of any given situation, as perceived by an independent observer, but the series of subtle, subjective equations comprising the individual's own assessments of possible success or failure in motive satisfaction. Simultaneous equations must be solved for the multiple motives, multiple response modes (as these are evaluated in terms of situational feasibility), and for motive-mode interactions. We must also recognize *time* as an important additional factor, altering both absolute and relative strengths of motives and the efficacy of different response modalities. We have not even mentioned the to-be-expected effects of stress, as these feed back into the subjective equations which modify the thresholds for threat perception from moment to moment.

STRESS AND INDIVIDUAL VULNERABILITY

We have emphasized the personal equation in assessing reactions to stress. It is consistently found that these reactions vary in intensity from person to person under exposure to the same environmental event. (This has been shown when the conditions studied were combat, oppressive leadership, internment, threat to life, threat to status, threat to livelihood, and others.) It has also been noted that,

[3] See Footnote 1.

with few extreme exceptions, the *kind* of situation which arouses a stress response in a particular individual must be related to significant events in that person's life. Many people have used the terms "ego-strength," "stress-tolerance," and "frustration-tolerance." It is perhaps doubtful that there is such a thing as a general stress-tolerance in people. There is more likely to be a greater or lesser insulation from the effects of certain kinds of stress-producers rather than others. The common idea of a threshold of tolerance for stress implies that stress-producing agents must reach a given strength in order to arouse this response. It seems more likely that there are differing thresholds, depending on the kinds of threats that are encountered and that individuals would be differentially vulnerable to different types of stressors. In other words, *not only must a situation be of a given intensity to lead to stress, it must also be of a given kind for a particular person.* To know what conditions of the environment are likely to be effective for the particular person, the motivational structure and prior history of that individual would have to be taken into account. Where the particular motives are known—where it is known what a person holds important and not important, what kinds of goals he will work for and why, what kinds of situations have for him been likely to increase anxiety or lead to aversive or defensive behavior—a reasonable prediction of stress proneness might be made. It is clear that what we would then have is a *vulnerability profile,* perhaps analogous to the industrial psychologist's job-profile, but based on strengths of motives and of motive-satisfying possibilities in situations rather than on strengths of skills and of skill requirements in particular jobs.[4]

If one tries to gain some overall perspective on what stress studies have so far revealed, and especially on their relation to studies of frustration, conflict, and anxiety, one is led to these kinds of general observations:

1. Stress is probably best conceived as a state of the total organism under extenuating circumstances rather than as an event in the environment.

2. A great variety of different environmental conditions is capable of producing a stress state.

---

[4] See Cofer and Appley (1964, pp. 449–65) for related discussion for this and subsequent section.

3. Different individuals respond to the same conditions in different ways. Some enter rapidly into a stress state, others show increased alertness and apparently improved performance, and still others appear to be "immune" to the stress-producing qualities of the environmental conditions.

4. The same individual may enter into a stress state in response to one presumably stressful condition and not to another.

5. Consistent *intra*-individual but varied *inter*-individual psychobiological response patterns occur in stress situations. The notion of a *common* stress reaction needs to be reassessed.

6. The behaviors resulting from operations, intended to induce stress may be the same or different, depending on the context of the situation of its induction.

7. The intensity and the extent of the stress state, and the associated behaviors, may not be readily predicted from a knowledge of the stimulus conditions alone, but require an analysis of underlying motivational patterns and of the context in which the stressor is applied.

8. Temporal factors may determine the significance of a given stressor and thus the intensity and extent of the stress state and the optimum measurement of effect.

.   .   .   .

5

Settings, Measures, and Themes: An
Integrative Review of Some
Research on Social-Psychological
Factors in Stress

JOSEPH E. McGRATH

SOME GENERAL THEMES AND VARIATIONS

There are at least five underlying themes which seem to emerge as
reasonable empirical generalizations from detailed scrutiny of the
findings in the sample of 200 stress studied reviewed [in McGrath,
1970b]. These five themes seem to cut across substantive problem
areas, although they have not been specifically tested in all areas. The
themes are interrelated with one another, as will be apparent in the
discussion to follow. . . . They are also highly convergent with the
central themes and issues drawn by Appley and Trumbull (1967b,
pp. 400–12), and by Lazarus (1966, pp. 24–29).

The cognitive appraisal theme. Stress is in the eye of the beholder,
and one of the most pervasive themes, both theoretically and empirically, can be stated as follows: *Emotional experiences, and to some extent physiological and performance measures, are in part a function of the
perceptions, expectations, or cognitive appraisal which the individual makes
of the (stressing) situation* (Fritz, 1957; Harris, Mayer, & Becker, 1955;
Lazarus et al., 1957; Lazarus, Deese, & Osler, 1951; Reid, 1948).

For example, this proposition is suggested in the drug studies;
physiological effects seem predictable from the biochemical nature of
the drug, but feeling states and behavior seem more predictable from
knowledge of the subjects' expectations (Goldberger, 1966; Schachter

& Singer, 1962). This same theme occurs in studies of reactions to threat of painful injections or puncture (Bem, Wallach, & Kogan, 1965; Brehm, Back, & Bogdonoff, 1964; Wrightsman, 1960). Furthermore, Lazarus and his colleagues, using vicarious physical threat, have succeeded in manipulating their subjects' cognitive processes or expectations, with associated changes in physiological (for instance, GSR) and psychological indices of arousal (Lazarus et al., 1957; Speisman et al., 1964). As a related comment, one of the major criticisms of sensory deprivation studies has been that whether or not Ss produce the deprivation syndrome—hallucinations and the like— seems to depend partly upon their knowledge of what one is supposed to experience under the circumstances (Jackson & Pollard, 1962). While this has been treated as an artifact, limiting external validity (Orne, for example, considers it an instance of experimental demand), it can equally well be construed as a finding of substantive significance which fits nicely with the empirical and theoretical proposition stated above.

This· general theme has several aspects.

1. Individual differences. One man's stress is another man's challenge. (Eckerman, 1964; Goldstein, 1959).
2. Adaptation. Yesterday's novelty is today's routine. (Lazarus et al., 1957; Miller, 1959).
3. Learning. Expectation is father to perception. (Sanua, 1960; Speisman et al., 1964; Ulrich, 1957).

The cognitive appraisal theme, and its variations, add up to a very general, and conceptually crucial, proposition about the nature of human stress. It presents that old bogeyman of the stress area—individual differences—in a new perspective, one which makes it much more a potentially researchable problem, rather than an inevitable and undesirable source of error variance. Furthermore, some of the other major themes to be discussed here can be construed as special cases of the cognitive appraisal theme.

The experience theme. "Practice makes better—usually." Another pervasive theme, related to the first, can be stated as follows: *Prior experience, with the task, the stressor and/or the situation, attenuates the effects of stress.* This theme occurs in several variations. For example, prior exposure to shock makes the threat of shock less threatening (Elliott, 1966). Furthermore, disruptive effects of shock and of auditory and visual distractions on task performance tend to "wear off" during extended series of trials, even when the stressor keeps occurring on the later trials (Ross, Rupel, & Grant, 1952). (A caution, however: there is some evidence for a generalization of stress from shock and distractors to later trials even when the stressor is not present on those later trials—Katkin, 1965; Miller & Shmavonian, 1965; Stopol, 1954.) Moreover, virtually every study of task performance under stress shows practice or exposure or experience to be effective in reducing performance deterioration (Berkun et al., 1962; Capretta & Berkun, 1962; Farber & Spence, 1956; Hill & Hansen, 1962; Miller, 1959; Pronko & Leith, 1956; Stopol, 1954; Ulrich, 1957). Generally, performance improves with practice on the task, either with a stressor present or for control conditions (although, of course, the former may be accompanied by unmeasured compensatory costs). Finally, a somewhat related point is that subjects will seek information about the occurrence of a potential stressor even when they cannot avoid it, presumably because advance knowledge somehow affects their expectations, and/or their coping responses (Luby et al., 1962). (Forewarned is, in some sense, forearmed.) Training, in the sense of deliberate practice in performance of the correct responses, appears to be an unmixed blessing with respect to alleviation of stress effects, and has been highly recommended as a remedy for potential stresses in space missions, civil defense, community disaster, and other real-life situations (Fritz & Marks, 1954; Malmo, Smith, & Kohlmeyer, 1956; Rohrer, 1959). Also, prior information (warning) reduces stress and its adverse consequences, provided it is not too little or too late (Elliott, 1966; Fritz & Marks, 1954).

However, the one instance in our sample of studies which attempted a deliberate indoctrination of attitudes and expectations (about life on an Arctic base) was unsuccessful (Eilbert, 1960). Furthermore, extended practice on a task (overlearning) is *detrimental* to later performance in a stressful situation, if conditions have changed so that the learned response is no longer the "correct" response (Castaneda & Palermo, 1955; Palermo, 1957).

This experience theme is closely related to the cognitive appraisal theme. Exposure or practice can be viewed as another form of change in S's expectations: prior exposure to a stressor lets S know better what is coming. The matter of experience is also part of a complex set of temporal factors, including practice and adaptation effects. . . .

The negative experience theme. "Failure breeds failure." A third major theme, which represents a variation of the first and a qualification of the second, can be stated as: *The experience of failure on a task is stressful in itself and has a number of effects which subsequently lead to decreased performance effectiveness.* Induced or actual failure, or evaluation situations involving potential failure, leads to a lowering of level of aspiration, and (therefore?) to a decrement in performance on psychomotor, problem solving, reasoning, learning, and other tasks (Ainsworth, 1958; Feather, 1965; Harleston, 1962; Hokanson & Burgess, 1962; Kalish et al., 1958; Osler, 1954; Parkes, 1963; Smock, 1955b) but enhances performance on sensorimotor and conditioning tasks (Beam, 1955; Vogel, Raymond, & Lazarus, 1959). It also leads to rigidity, to quick or impulsive closure, to decisions based on partial information, to increased conformity (Ainsworth, 1958; Cowen, 1952; Darley, 1966; Dittes, 1961; Parkes, 1963; Rosenberg, 1961; Smock, 1955a). There is evidence that task failure is accompanied by increases in the 17-ketosteroids (Berkeley, 1952).

Effects of failure can be modified by experience on the task, especially *successful* experience (Feather, 1965; Hill & Hansen, 1962). Thus, this principle can be seen as an extension to the second one: *Prior experience influences stress and its effects.* If that experience is unsuccessful (that is, negatively reinforcing, or of negative affect), prior experience will increase stress and degrade performance. If the prior experience is successful (positively reinforcing, of positive affect, or otherwise leading to learning, mastery, or adaptation), stress will be decreased and its negative effects on task performance will be attenuated.

Effects of failure can also be modified by manipulation of the S's expectations of success—for example, by telling him that subsequent tasks will be easy, or easy for him (Feather, 1966; Postman & Brown, 1952). It is interesting that one study (Eriksen, Lazarus, & Strange, 1952) found Ss able to predict their own subsequent performance levels, although the investigator's measures of personality could not. This suggests that what is being altered here is the S's level of aspiration, and that perhaps failure itself operates similarly, by altering level of aspiration downward. The latter, in turn, makes it clear that the failure theme is a special form of the cognitive-appraisal principle discussed above.

The inverted-U theme. "Stress comes from too much of a good thing—or not enough of it." Perhaps one of the most widespread ideas in the stress area is the notion (deriving from Selye's pioneer work) that stress represents a kind of abnormal stimulus load, and that stress responses reflect an increase in arousal. There is a related notion, deriving from the work on sensory and perceptual deprivation, that a condition of subnormal stimulus load is also stressful. . . . It is not so clear how the deprivation stress relates to either physiological or psychological arousal.

From these two notions, it is a fairly short step to the proposition that stress can be viewed as arising from increments or decrements of some stimulus parameters (intensity, complexity, information, uncertainty, and so forth) away from some optimal zone. A plot of degree of "felt stress" resulting from various magnitudes of a potentially stressing stimulus condition is, therefore, a U-shaped function; while a plot of performance effectiveness over that range of stimulus levels is an inverted U-shaped function.

This hypothesis is very complex, to say the least. First of all, there are problems arising from lack of calibration of degrees of stressor conditions, and lack of comparability of different stressors. . . . The inverted-U hypothesis becomes very complex when we add the individual-differences axiom (optimal level changes for a given individual, as a function of time, development, the state of the organism, and/or learning).

Nevertheless, there appears to be a good bit of evidence supporting (or at least not refuting) the proposition that *the intensity of environmental stimulation (broadly conceived) is curvilinearly related to degree of felt stress and to degree of effectiveness of subsequent performance* (Davis, 1956; Schmale, 1964; Torrance, 1954; see also Haythorn, Steiner, in McGrath, 1970b.) For example, degree of time pressure or pacing of a task, plotted against productivity or errors, shows the curvilinear (U-shaped) form (Pepinsky, Pepinsky, & Pavlik, 1960). Also, studies using various measures of situational, test, or trait anxiety [for example, Taylor's Manifest Anxiety Scale (MAS)], along with external stressors (such as shock), tend to support the curvilinear-function hypothesis.[1] In a number of such studies, high-anxiety subjects per-

---

[1] The meaning we have given this result, of course, depends on several qualifying assumptions. First, it is based on the assumption that "anxiety in the person"—trait anx-

formed *better* than low-anxiety Ss under low or no (external) stress conditions, but performed *poorer* than low-anxiety Ss under high (external) stress. This finding seems to hold for shock, distractors, task-difficulty, pacing, evaluation threat, and task failure as (external) stress conditions, and for performance problem solving, learning, and other types of tasks (Feather, 1966; Matarazzo & Matarazzo, 1956; Weiner, 1966).

The evidence is not all clear-cut, though. For example, there is evidence that *reaction time increases* with degree of task-based conflict on a variety of learning tasks (Atthowe, 1960, 1961; Berlyne, 1957; Kamano, 1963). On the other hand, there is also evidence that *response time decreases* as a function of evaluation threat and task failure, as well as so-called impulsive closure or decisions on the basis of limited information (Fenz, 1964; Katchmar, Ross, & Andrews, 1958). Steiner (in McGrath, 1970b) presents evidence to suggest that Ss who are most stressed (as indicated by GSR) by an interpersonal disagreement situation show *shorter* decision time than Ss relatively unstressed by the same situation; whereas control Ss, performing the same task but without presence of the stressor, showed *even shorter* decision times.

Studies using shock as a stressor have shown conflicting results regarding task performance. Shock impairs time and error scores, distraction does not, and *both* shock and distraction improve those scores (Murphy, R. E., 1959). Shock improves performance on reasoning tasks (Block, 1964) but impairs performance on a group escape task (Kelley et al., 1965). Finally, shock does not affect reaction times (Farber & Spence, 1956).

To some extent, dissenting evidence can be rejected by the argument that the conditions of a given study did not encompass a sufficient span of the stimulus continuum to yield the expected U-shaped curve. If degree of stimulus intensity correlates positively and linearly with performance, the high level was not high enough; if degree of stimulus intensity correlates negatively and linearly with performance, the low condition was *in,* rather than below the optimal zone of stimulation or arousal. Until we can calibrate either

---

iety—is the same kind of thing as stress arising from an external source. Second, it assumes that such stresses are additive, and this is a tenuous assumption (see discussion of calibration of stressors in Chapter 4 [of McGrath, 1970b]).

degrees of stress or degrees of stimulus intensity in some systematic way, such explanations will have an aura of circularity about them. . . .

The social-interaction theme. "We can't live with people, and we can't live without them." Social interaction is a two-edged sword in the context of stress research. There is at least scattered evidence that presence of, and communication with, other human beings acts to attenuate effects of some physical threats, as well as effects of restricted environments (Murray et al., in press; Schachter et al., 1965; Weller, 1963). The notion that presence of others increases the stress threshold has been suggested (Milburn, 1961). There is some evidence that the opportunity for social interaction—with its presumed positive reinforcement value—reduces the psychological and psychosomatic symptomatology of Ss under conditions of sensory-perceptual restriction (Gullahorn, 1956). Furthermore, the attenuation of stress effects is greater if the others are persons with whom S has a prior positive affect relationship (presumably, therefore, a source of more positive reward to him) than if the others are strangers (Davis et al., 1961; Kissel, 1965). This differential is further enhanced as a function of the strength of S's affiliation motivation (Dohrenwend & Dohrenwend, 1966a, 1966b; Kissel, 1965).

But presence of others is not an unmixed blessing, it would seem, especially in the context of long-term isolation in a constraining environment (see Haythorn in McGrath, 1970b). Social interaction and enforced intimacy may be a source of irritation to S. And the crowding of a behavior setting of fixed physical (and interpersonal) dimensions may lead to an increase of the stressing effects of a physical threat, as well as to stress effects deriving directly from restriction of environment. Indeed, presence of, and interdependence with, other people may in itself generate new stresses—ego threats and interpersonal threats—which could not be present if S were in the situation alone.

The degree to which such positive or negative effects will operate appears to depend on: the personality and motivational patterns of the Ss, singly and in relation to each other (for example, Davis et al., 1961; Dohrenwend & Dohrenwend, 1966b; Gifford & Murewski, 1964; Silverman & Blitz, 1956); the size and the formal and informal structure of the group (for example, Milburn, 1961; Smith, 1959;

Sutcliffe & Hoberman, 1956); features of the ecological setting (Gullahorn, 1956; Milburn, 1961); and, of course, the nature of the tasks and stressors involved in the situation (Feldman & Rice, 1965; Hamblin, 1958; Orr, 1964). (See also the work of Haythorn and Altman on small groups in isolated and confined settings in McGrath, 1970b.)

It would appear then that social interaction is a kind of stimulation which, like other kinds, has an optimal level. Too little or too much is stressful. Ss will work for social reinforcement (for example, emit operant responses) when deprived of it (Dohrenwend & Dohrenwend, 1966a, 1966b), just as they will seek sensory-perceptual stimulation, or information, when in a stimulus-deprived environment (Zuckerman & Haber, 1965); and they will develop means for reducing social interaction if they are satiated (Guetzkow & Gyr, 1954). The optimal zone, of course, depends on the behavior setting. It is also likely that the optimal zone varies over individuals and changes or adapts over time for the same individual.

SUMMARY

These five themes add up to something less than a systematic theory of stress, but they do represent a beginning in that direction. It must be kept in mind, of course, that these themes are induced as empirical generalizations from a limited sample of stress research by loose inference processes which overlook many specific points of evidence in order to remain general. They should be viewed as suggestive, not definitive.

Nevertheless, they do represent some general conceptual propositions which, together with the methodological problems noted previously, can be used as a basis for a summary formulation. That formulation, given below, can serve three functions: (1) as an overview of some empirical convergences, (2) as a warning of some of the methodological problems which need research, and (3) as a set of substantive issues for future research.

Social-psychological stress can arise from situational conditions which lead to a subjective or cognitive appraisal of threat. The threat can involve actual or anticipated harms to the physical self, the psychological self, and/or interpersonal relations. The threat may also derive from conditions of the physical and/or social environment which deprive the individual of opportunities to satisfy physical, psychological, and/or interpersonal needs.

The occurrence of stress and its effects can be measured at physiological, psychological, behavioral (task and interpersonal performances), and organizational levels. Within each of these levels, various operational types of measures can be applied: subjective reports, aided or unaided observation, trace measures, archival records. Alternative measures within level and type do not always agree; nor is there always convergence of measures across types and/or levels. Such lack of convergence of measures can be viewed as methodological weakness (alternate measures of the same property—stress—yield different results), or as substantive information (alternative measures represent alternate and more or less substitutable responses to stress).

The effects of stress conditions are mediated through subjective psychological processes (for example, cognitive appraisals of threat, secondary appraisals of coping resources) which are affected by many perspectives of the individual. Because of this, there are substantial interindividual differences in what stimulus situations lend to the perception of threat. Moreover, adaptation effects and learning effects make for intraindividual differences in perception of threat over time, under the "same" stimulus conditions. Finally, many individual physiological, psychological, and behavioral processes vary through time as a function of factors (such as motivation, diurnal cycles) which are more or less orthogonal to environmental stressing events; this introduces further inter- and intraindividual variability in the perception of threat and in responses to it. These considerations, also, are both methodological problems and crucial substantive issues for future stress research.

Stress, and responses to stress, also vary as a function of experience—both experience with the situation or conditions giving rise to stress, and practice in behaviors to cope with or avoid the consequences of stressor conditions. Past experience leading to successful mastery or to positive reinforcements tends to reduce the perception of threat (to raise the threat threshold); past experience leading to failure or to negative reinforcements (for example, negative evaluations by others) tends to lower the threat threshold; furthermore, failure and expectations of failure are in themselves threatening.

Situational or stimulus conditions seem to be related to perceived threat and to performance in a curvilinear manner. Extremely low levels or lack of variability of physical and/or social stimulation tend to induce threat and to impair functioning. Extremely high levels or high complexity or ambiguity of physical and/or social stimulation also tend to induce threat and to impair functioning. Moderate intensities tend to be nonthreatening and motivating, and to be conducive to optimum functioning. However, the implied optimal zone probably varies as a function of properties of the physical and social setting, personal attributes, adaptation, and learning. These considerations, too, pose critical methodological problems and offer crucial substantive issues for future investigation.

section II

~~~~~~

STRESS AND THE ENVIRONMENT

There is currently a great deal of interest in the ways environmental factors determine and influence man's behavior. Appropriately, the readings in Section II deal with the ways in which two broad classes of environmental stimuli, cultural and physical, operate in the production of stress reactions. The selections by Cannon (1942) and Zborowski (1969) examine the role of cultural environments in shaping threat appraisals while those by Dubos (1965), Hay and Oken (1972), and Glass and Singer (1972) examine the role of adverse or demanding physical environments in the etiology of stress.

Many people in Western culture have great difficulty in accepting the existence of "voodoo death," especially its often presumed supernatural basis. Nevertheless, reports of its occurrence have fascinated lay persons and scientists for some time, including the noted physiologist Walter Cannon (1942). In a now classic article Cannon presents documented cases of death by "voodoo" and then proceeds to offer an explanation based upon naturally occurring physiological processes under conditions of extreme stress. In essence, Cannon proposes that "voodoo death" may be due to prolonged overexcitation of the inner (medullary) portion of the adrenal glands caused by terror. This is an internal state very similar to surgical shock. The terror, Cannon hypothesizes, occurs because the individual believes he or she has transgressed a cultural norm (e.g., eating taboo food) and death must ensue as just punishment. This belief is reinforced by the individual's social group which takes steps first to isolate the victim and then to subject him or her to a mourning ritual. (For other explanations of "voodoo death" the reader should consult the work of Barber, 1961, and Frank's, 1961, fascinating comparative account of psychotherapy and religious healing.)

Zborowski has been interested in the cultural determinants of how we perceive and respond to pain for some twenty years and has recently published a book summarizing his research findings (1969; see also, 1952). While pain is a universal stressor and has obvious biological value as a signal of tissue damage, the amount and quality of pain we feel is determined not only by the extent of tissue damage but also our previous experiences, our understanding of the causes and consequences of the pain, and our cultural background (Melzack, 1973).

In the selection here, the individuals studied by Zborowski in a New York City Veterans Administration hospital included male patients from Jewish, Italian, and Irish ethnic groups as well as "Old Americans" (patients of Anglo-Saxon origin, usually of the Protestant creed with relatives residing in America for more than three generations). While Zborowski's findings are too complex to detail here, there were clear trends indicating similarities in reactions to pain between Jewish and Italian patients and between Irish and Old American patients. For example, Jewish and Italian patients tended to exaggerate their pain and openly sought support and sympathy from family members as well as physicians and nurses. In contrast, Irish and Old Americans adopted an accepting, matter-of-fact attitude towards pain and its expression. They rarely exhibited any public show of emotion and would withdraw when pain became intense—in their privacy, and here alone, one would hear moans or cries of anguish. Whether or not Zborowski's findings are relevant to individuals in the 1970s, to other ethnic groups, or, for that matter, females, remains to be seen. Nevertheless, it is apparent from his work that cultural factors influence our perceptions of pain and determine in large part how we cope with this significant source of stress.

In the selection by biologist Dubos (1965), the reader is introduced to the stresses resulting from overpopulation with the high population density and crowding it can produce. As may be seen from Dubos's analysis, much of our knowledge about the harmful effects of overcrowding is based on animal studies (e.g., Calhoun, 1962) and may or may not be relevant to humans. Dubos makes an important distinction (see also, Stokols, 1972), usually overlooked by others, between population density and crowding. Density is defined in terms of physical or spatial conditions which can be evaluated differently by diverse individuals or groups, while crowding is a psychological or experiential state in which the individual is troubled by the spatial restrictions. Understanding the effects of crowding on human behavior is extremely difficult, especially in comparison with animals, because the effects are so strongly determined by cultural, social, and psychological factors.

While many job situations may be characterized as "high pressured," perhaps none is more so than intensive care unit (ICU) nursing. In the next selection, Hay and Oken (1972) have portrayed graphically the special problems faced by the ICU nurse (e.g., formidable work load, heavy responsibility for life and death, patient pain and distress, and repeated observation of death) and how she copes with them. To protect herself from many stress-related emotions (e.g., grief, anxiety), the ICU nurse often uses defense mechanisms, particularly gross denial and detachment. The nature of the ICU work situation also promotes breakdowns in communication between the nurses and other hospital personnel and with relatives of the patients, adding further to the overall stress.

Because of its potentially damaging effects and relevance to city life, Glass and Singer (1972) have initiated a series of laboratory studies on the behavioral and psychophysiological consequences of noise. The selection included here reviews the literature in this area, and suggests that noise may indeed be a potent stressor depending on a number of cognitive and social factors such as being able to predict and/or control the onset and cessation of noise. For example, according to Glass and Singer, unpredictable noise is much more disruptive during and following certain complex tasks than predictable noise of equal intensity. Moreover, the adverse effects of unpredictable noise are appreciably reduced when the person can, or simply believes he or she can, exercise control over the noise. Of course, considerably more effort along naturalistic lines must be undertaken before we fully understand the role of noise in the production of stress or the generality of the above findings regarding predictability and control.

6

"Voodoo" Death

WALTER B. CANNON

In records of anthropologists and others who have lived with primitive people in widely scattered parts of the world is the testimony that when subjected to spells or sorcery or the use of "black magic" men may be brought to death. Among the natives of South America and Africa, Australia, New Zealand, and the islands of the Pacific, as well as among the negroes of nearby Haiti, "voodoo" death has been reported by apparently competent observers. The phenomenon is so extraordinary and so foreign to the experience of civilized people that it seems incredible; certainly if it is authentic it deserves careful consideration. I propose to recite instances of this mode of death, to inquire whether reports of the phenomenon are trustworthy, and to examine a possible explanation of it if it should prove to be real.

First, with regard to South America. Apparently Soares de Souza (1879, pp. 292–93) was first to observe instances of death among the Tupinambás Indians, death induced by fright when men were condemned and sentenced by a so-called "medicine man." Likewise Varnhagen (1875, pp. 42–43) remarks that generally among Brazilian Indian tribes, the members, lacking knowledge, accept without question whatever is told them. Thus the chief or medicine man gains the reputation of exercising supernatural power. And by intimidation or by terrifying augury or prediction he may cause death from fear.

There is like testimony from Africa. Leonard (1906) has written an account of the Lower Niger and its tribes in which he declares:

I have seen more than one hardened old Haussa soldier dying steadily and by inches because he believed himself to be bewitched; no nourishment or medicines that were given to him had the slightest effect either to check the mischief or to improve his condition in any way, and nothing was able to divert him from a fate which he considered inevitable. In the same way, and under very similar conditions, I have seen Kru-men and others die in spite of every effort that was made to save them, simply because they had made up their minds, not (as we thought at the time) to die, but that being in the clutch of malignant demons they were bound to die. (p. 257 ff)

Another instance of death wrought by superstitious fear in an African tribe is reported by Merolla in his voyage to the Congo in 1682 (cited by Pinkerton, 1814, p. 237 ff). A young negro on a journey lodged in a friend's house for the night. The friend had prepared for their breakfast a wild hen, a food strictly banned by a rule which must be inviolably observed by the immature. The young fellow demanded whether it was indeed a wild hen, and when the host answered "No," he ate of it heartily and proceeded on his way. A few years later, when the two met again, the old friend asked the younger man if he would eat a wild hen. He answered that he had been solemnly charged by a wizard not to eat that food. Thereupon the host began to laugh and asked him why he refused it now after having eaten it at his table before. On hearing this news the negro immediately began to tremble, so greatly was he possessed by fear, and in less than twenty-four hours was dead.

Also in New Zealand there are tales of death induced by ghostly power. In Brown's *New Zealand and Its Aborigines* (1845, p. 76) there is an account of a Maori woman who, having eaten some fruit, was told that it had been taken from a tabooed place; she exclaimed that the sanctity of the chief had been profaned and that his spirit would kill her. This incident occurred in the afternoon; the next day about 12 o'clock she was dead. According to Tregear (1890, p. 100) the *tapu* (taboo) among the Maoris of New Zealand is an awful weapon. "I have seen a strong young man die," he declares, "the same day he was tapued; the victims die under it as though their strength ran out as water." It appears that among these aborigines superstitions associated with their sacred chiefs are a true though purely imaginary barrier; transgression of that barrier entails the death of the transgressor whenever he becomes aware of what he has done. It is a fatal power of the imagination working through unmitigated terror.

Dr. S. M. Lambert of the Western Pacific Health Service of the Rockefeller Foundation wrote to me that on several occasions he had seen evidence of death from fear. In one case there was a startling recovery. At a Mission at Mona Mona in North Queensland were many native converts, but on the outskirts of the Mission was a group of nonconverts including one Nebo, a famous witch doctor. The chief helper of the missionary was Rob, a native who had been converted. When Dr. Lambert arrived at the Mission he learned that Rob was in distress and that the missionary wanted him examined. Dr. Lambert made the examination, and found no fever, no complaint of pain, no symptoms or signs of disease. He was impressed, however, by the obvious indications that Rob was seriously ill and extremely weak. From the missionary he learned that Rob had had a bone pointed at him by Nebo and was convinced that in consequence he must die. Thereupon Dr. Lambert and the missionary went for Nebo, threatened him sharply that his supply of food would be shut off if anything happened to Rob and that he and his people would be driven away from the Mission. At once Nebo agreed to go with them to see Rob. He leaned over Rob's bed and told the sick man that it was all a mistake, a mere joke—indeed, that he had not pointed a bone at him at all. The relief, Dr. Lambert testifies, was almost instantaneous; that evening Rob was back at work, quite happy again, and in full possession of his physical strength.

A question which naturally arises is whether those who have testified to the reality of "voodoo" death have exercised good critical judgment. Although the sorcerer or medicine-man or chief may tacitly possess or may assume the ability to kill by bone-pointing or by another form of black magic, may he not preserve his reputation for supernatural power by the use of poison? Especially when death has been reported to have occurred after the taking of food may not the fatal result be due to action of poisonous substances not commonly known except to priests and wizards? Obviously, the possible use of poisons must be excluded before "voodoo" death can be accepted as an actual consequence of sorcery or witchcraft. Also it is essential to rule out instances of bold claims of supernatural power when in fact death resulted from natural causes; this precaution is particularly important because of the common belief among aborigines that illness is due to malevolence. I have endeavored to learn definitely whether poisoning and spurious claims can quite certainly be excluded from instances of death, attributed to magic power, by addressing enquiries to medically trained observers.

Dr. Lambert, already mentioned as a representative of the Rockefeller Foundation, wrote to me concerning the experience of Dr. P. S. Clarke with Kanakas working on the sugar plantations of North Queensland. One day a Kanaka came to his hospital and told him he would die in a few days because a spell had been put upon him and nothing could be done to counteract it. The man had been known by Dr. Clarke for some time. He was given a very thorough examination, including an examination of the stool and the urine. All was found normal, but as he lay in bed he gradually grew weaker. Dr. Clarke called upon the foreman of the Kanakas to come to the hospital to give the man assurance, but on reaching the foot of the bed, the foreman leaned over, looked at the patient, and then turned to Dr. Clarke saying, "Yes, doctor, close up him he die" (i.e., he is nearly dead). The next day, at 11 o'clock in the morning, he ceased to live. A postmortem examination revealed nothing that could in any way account for the fatal outcome.

Another observer with medical training, Dr. W. E. Roth (1897), who served for three years as government surgeon among the primitive people of north-central Queensland, has also given pertinent testimony. "So rooted sometimes is this belief on the part of the patient," Roth wrote, "that some enemy has 'pointed' the bone at him, that he will actually lie down to die, and succeed in the attempt, even at the expense of refusing food and succour within his reach: I have myself witnessed three or four such cases" (p. 154).

Dr. J. B. Cleland, Professor of Pathology at the University of Adelaide, has written to me that he has no doubt that from time to time the natives of the Australian bush do die as a result of a bone being pointed at them, and that such death may not be associated with any of the ordinary lethal injuries. In an article which included a section on death from malignant psychic influences, Dr. Cleland (1928, p. 233) mentions a fine, robust tribesman in central Australia who was injured in the fleshy part of the thigh by a spear that had been enchanted. The man slowly pined away and died, without any surgical complication which could be detected. Dr. Cleland cites a number of physicians who have referred to the fatal effects of bone pointing and other terrifying acts. In his letter to me he wrote, "Poisoning is, I think, entirely ruled out in such cases among our Australian natives. There are very few poisonous plants available and I doubt whether it has ever entered the mind of the central Australian natives that such might be used on human beings."

Dr. Herbert Basedow (1925), in his book, *The Australian Aboriginal,* has presented a vivid picture of the first horrifying effect of bone pointing on the ignorant, superstitious, and credulous natives, and the later more calm acceptance of their mortal fate:

The man who discovers that he is being boned by an enemy is, indeed, a pitiable sight. He stands aghast, with his eyes staring at the treacherous pointer, and with his hands lifted as though to ward off the lethal medium, which he imagines is pouring into his body. His cheeks blanch and his eyes become glassy and the expression of his face becomes horribly distorted. . . . He attempts to shriek but usually the sound chokes in his throat, and all that one might see is froth at his mouth. His body begins to tremble and the muscles twist involuntarily. He sways backwards and falls to the ground, and after a short time appears to be in a swoon; but soon after he writhes as if in mortal agony, and, covering his face with his hands, begins to moan. After a while he becomes very composed and crawls to his wurley. From this time onwards he sickens and frets, refusing to eat and keeping aloof from the daily affairs of the tribe. Unless help is forthcoming in the shape of a countercharm administered by the hands of the Nangarri, or medicine-man, his death is only a matter of a comparatively short time. If the coming of the medicine-man is opportune he might be saved. (pp. 178–79)

The Nangarri, when persuaded to exercise his powers, goes through an elaborate ceremony and finally steps toward the awestricken relatives, holding in his fingers a small article—a stick, a bone, a pebble, or a talon—which, he avows, he has taken from the "boned" man and which was the cause of the affliction. And now, since it is removed, the victim has nothing to fear. The effect, Dr. Basedow declares, is astounding. The victim, until that moment far on the road to death, raises his head and gazes in wonderment at the object held by the medicine-man. He even lifts himself into a sitting position and calls for water to drink. The crisis is passed, and the recovery is speedy and complete. Without the Nangarri's intervention the boned fellow, according to Dr. Basedow, would certainly have fretted himself to death. The implicit faith which a native cherishes in the magical powers of his tribal magician is said to result in cures which exceed anything recorded by the faith-healing disciples of more cultured communities.

Perhaps the most complete account of the influence of the tribal taboo on the fate of a person subjected to its terrific potency has come from W. L. Warner, who worked among primitive aborigines in the Northern Territory of Australia. In order to provide a background for his testimony I quote from William James's *Principles of Psychology* (1905):

A man's social me is the recognition which he gets from his mates. We are not only gregarious animals, liking to be in sight of our fellows, but we have an innate propensity to get ourselves noticed, and noticed favorably, by our kind. No more fiendish punishment could be devised, were such a thing physically possible, than that one should be turned loose in society and remain absolutely unnoticed by all the members thereof. If no one turned round when we entered, answered when we spoke, or minded what we did, but if every person we met "cut us dead," and acted as if we were nonexisting things, a kind of rage and impotent despair would ere long well up in us, from which the cruelest bodily tortures would be a relief; for these would make us feel that, however bad might be our plight, we had not sunk to such a depth as to be unworthy of attention at all. (pp. 179–80)

Now to return to the observations of Warner regarding the aborigines of northern Australia, creatures too ignorant, he assured me, to know about poisons. There are two definite movements of the social group, he declares, in the process by which black magic becomes effective on the victim of sorcery. In the first movement the community contracts; all people who stand in kinship relation with him withdraw their sustaining support. This means everyone he knows—all his fellows—completely change their attitudes towards him and place him in a new category. He is now viewed as one who is more nearly in the realm of the sacred and taboo than in the world of the ordinary where the community finds itself. The organization of his social life has collapsed and, no longer a member of a group, he is alone and isolated. The doomed man is in a situation from which the only escape is by death. During the death illness which ensues, the group acts with all the outreachings and complexities of its organization and with countless stimuli to suggest death positively to the victim, who is in a highly suggestible state. In addition to the social pressure upon him the victim himself, as a rule, not only makes no effort to live and to stay a part of his group but actually, through the multiple suggestions which he receives, coöperates in the withdrawal from it. He becomes what the attitude of his fellow tribesmen wills him to be. Thus he assists in committing a kind of suicide.

Before death takes place, the second movement of the community occurs, which is a return to the victim in order to subject him to the fateful ritual of mourning. The purpose of the community now, as a social unit with its ceremonial leader, who is a person of very near kin to the victim, is at last to cut him off entirely from the ordinary world and ultimately to place him in his proper position in the sacred totemic world of the dead. The victim, on his part, reciprocates this feeling.

The effect of the double movement in the society, first away from the victim and then back, with all the compulsive force of one of its most powerful rituals, is obviously drastic. Warner (1941) writes:

An analogous situation in our society is hard to imagine. If all a man's near kin, his father, mother, brothers and sisters, wife, children, business associates, friends and all the other members of the society should suddenly withdraw themselves because of some dramatic circumstance, refusing to take any attitude but one of taboo and looking at the man as one already dead, and then after some little time perform over him a sacred ceremony which is believed with certainty to guide him out of the land of the living into that of the dead, the enormous suggestive power of this two-fold movement of the community, after it has had its attitudes crystallized, can be somewhat understood by ourselves. (p. 242)

The social environment as a support to morale is probably much more important and impressive among primitive people, because of their profound ignorance and insecurity in a haunted world, than among educated people living in civilized and well protected communities. Dr. S. D. Porteus [personal communication], physician and psychologist, has studied savage life extensively in the Pacific islands and in Africa; he writes:

Music and dance are primitive man's chief defenses against loneliness. By these he reminds himself that in his wilderness there are other minds seconding his own . . . in the dance he sees himself multiplied in his fellows, his action mirrored in theirs. There are in his life very few other occasions in which he can take part in concerted action and find partners. . . . The native aboriginal is above all fear-ridden. Devils haunt to seize the unwary; their malevolent magic shadows his waking moments, he believes that medicine men know how to make themselves invisible so that they may cut out his kidney fat, then sew him up and rub his tongue with a magic stone to induce forgetfulness, and thereafter he is a living corpse, devoted to death. . . . So desperate is this fear that if a man imagines that he has been subjected to the bone pointing magic of the enemy he will straight away lie down and die.

Testimony similar to the foregoing, from Brazil, Africa, New Zealand and Australia, was found in reports from the Hawaiian Islands, British Guiana, and Haiti. What attitude is justified in the presence of this accumulation of evidence? In a letter from Professor Lévi-Bruhl, the French ethnologist long interested in aboriginal tribes and their customs, he remarked that answers which he had received from inquiries could be summed up as follows. The ethnologists, basing their judgment on a large number of reports, quite independent of one another and gathered from groups in all parts of the world, admit that there are instances indicating that the belief that one has been subjected to sorcery, and in consequence is inevitably condemned to death, does actually result in death in the course of time. On the contrary, physiologists and physicians—men who have had no acquaintance with ethnological conditions—are inclined to consider the phenomenon as impossible and raise doubts regarding clear and definite testimony.

Before denying that "voodoo" death is within the realm of possibility, let us consider the general features of the specimen reports mentioned in foregoing paragraphs. First, there is the elemental fact that the phenomenon is characteristically noted among aborigines—among human beings so primitive, so superstitious, so ignorant that they are bewildered strangers in a hostile world. Instead of knowledge they have a fertile and unrestricted imagination which fills their environment with all manner of evil spirits capable of affecting their lives disastrously. As Dr. Porteus pointed out, only by engaging in communal activities are they able to develop sufficient *esprit de corps* to render themselves resistant to the mysterious and malicious influences which can vitiate their lives. Associated with these circumstances is the fixed assurance that because of certain conditions, such as being subject to bone pointing or other magic, or failing to observe sacred tribal regulations, death is sure to supervene. This is a belief so firmly held by all members of the tribe that the individual not only has that conviction himself but is obsessed by the knowledge that all his fellows likewise hold it. Thereby he becomes a pariah, wholly deprived of the confidence and social support of the tribe. In his isolation the malicious spirits which he believes are all about him and capable of irresistibly and calamitously maltreating him, exert supremely their evil power. Amid this mysterious murk of grim and ominous fatality what has been called "the gravest known extremity of fear," that of an immediate threat of death, fills the terrified victim with powerless misery.

In his terror he refuses both food and drink, a fact which many observers have noted and which, as we shall see later, is highly significant for a possible understanding of the slow onset of weakness. The victim "pines away"; his strength runs out like water, to paraphrase words already quoted from one graphic account; and in the course of a day or two he succumbs.

The question which now arises is whether an ominous and persistent state of fear can end the life of a man. Fear, as is well known, is one of the most deeply rooted and dominant of the emotions. Often, only with difficulty can it be eradicated. Associated with it are profound physiological disturbances, widespread throughout the organism. There is evidence that some of these disturbances, if they are lasting, can work harmfully. In order to elucidate that evidence I must first indicate that great fear and great rage have similar effects in the body. Each of these powerful emotions is associated with ingrained instincts—the instinct to attack, if rage is present, the instinct to run away or escape, if fear is present. Throughout the long history of human beings and lower animals these two emotions and their related instincts have served effectively in the struggle for existence. When they are roused they bring into action an elemental division of the nervous system, the so-called sympathetic or sympathico-adrenal division, which exercises a control over internal organs, and also over the blood vessels. As a rule the sympathetic division acts to maintain a relatively constant state in the flowing blood and lymph, i.e., the "internal environment" of our living parts. It acts thus in strenuous muscular effort; for example, liberating sugar from the liver, accelerating the heart, contracting certain blood vessels, discharging adrenaline and dilating the bronchioles. All these changes render the animal more efficient in physical struggle, for they supply essential conditions for continuous action of laboring muscles. Since they occur in association with the strong emotions, rage and fear, they can reasonably be interpreted as preparatory for the intense struggle which the instincts to attack or to escape may involve. If these powerful emotions prevail, and the bodily forces are fully mobilized for action, and if this state of extreme perturbation continues in uncontrolled possession of the organism for a considerable period, without the occurrence of action, dire results may ensue (see Cannon, 1929).

When, under brief ether anesthesia, the cerebral cortex of a cat is quickly destroyed so that the animal no longer has the benefit of the organs of intelligence, there is a remarkable display of the activities of lower, primary centers of behavior, those of emotional expression. This decorticate condition is similar to that produced in man when consciousness is abolished by the use of nitrous oxide; he is then decorticated by chemical means. Commonly the emotional expression of joy is released (nitrous oxide is usually known as "laughing gas"), but it may be that of sorrow (it might as well be called "weeping gas"). Similarly, ether anesthesia, if light, may release the expression of rage. In the sham rage of the decorticate cat there is a supreme exhibition of intense emotional activity. The hairs stand on end, sweat exudes from the toe pads, the heart rate may rise from about 150 beats per minute to twice that number, the blood pressure is greatly elevated, and the concentration of sugar in the blood soars to five times the normal. This excessive activity of the sympathico-adrenal system rarely lasts, however, more than three or four hours. By that time, without any loss of blood or any other event to explain the outcome, the decorticate remnant of the animal, in which this acme of emotional display has prevailed, ceases to exist.

What is the cause of the demise? It is clear that the rapidly fatal result is due to a persistent excessive activity of the sympathico-adrenal system. One of my associates, Philip Bard (1928), noted that when the signs of emotional excitement failed to appear, the decorticate preparation might continue to survive for long periods; indeed, its existence might have to be ended by the experimenter. Further evidence was obtained by another of my associates, Norman E. Freeman (1933), who produced sham rage in animals from which the sympathetic nerves had been removed. In these circumstances the behavior was similar in all respects to the behavior described above, excepting the manifestations dependent upon sympathetic innervation. The remarkable fact appeared that animals deprived of their sympathetic nerves and exhibiting sham rage, so far as was possible, continued to exist for many hours without any sign of breakdown. Here were experiments highly pertinent to the present inquiry.

What effect on the organism is produced by a lasting and intense action of the sympathico-adrenal system? In observations by Bard, he found that a prominent and significant change which became manifest in animals displaying sham rage was a gradual fall of blood pressure towards the end of the display, from the high levels of the early stages to the low level seen in fatal wound shock. In Freeman's research he produced evidence that this fall of pressure was due to a reduction of the volume of circulating blood. This is the condition which during World War I was found to be the reason for the low blood pressure observed in badly wounded men—the blood volume is reduced until it becomes insufficient for the maintenance of an adequate circulation (see Cannon, 1923). Thereupon deterioration occurs in the heart, and also in the nerve centers which hold the blood vessels in moderate contraction. A vicious circle is then established; the low blood pressure damages the very organs which are necessary for the maintenance of an adequate circulation, and as they are damaged they are less and less able to keep the blood circulating to an effective degree. In sham rage, as in wound shock, death can be explained as due to a failure of essential organs to receive a sufficient supply of blood or, specifically, a sufficient supply of oxygen, to maintain their functions.

The gradual reduction of blood volume in sham rage can be explained by the action of the sympathico-adrenal system in causing a persistent constriction of the small arterioles in certain parts of the body. If adrenaline, which constricts the blood vessels precisely as nerve impulses constrict them, is continuously injected at a rate which produces the vasoconstriction of strong emotional states, the blood volume is reduced to the degree seen in sham rage. Freeman, Freedman, and Miller (1941) performed that experiment. They employed in some instances no more adrenaline than is secreted in response to reflex stimulation of the adrenal gland, and they found not only marked reduction of the blood plasma but also a concentration of blood corpuscles as shown by the percentage increase of hemoglobin. It should be remembered, however, that in addition to this circulating vasoconstrictor agent there are in the normal functioning of the sympathico-adrenal system the constrictor effects on blood vessels of nerve impulses and the cöoperation of another circulating chemical substance besides adrenaline, viz., sympathin. These three agents, working together in times of great emotional stress, might well produce the results which Freeman and his collaborators observed when they injected adrenaline alone. In the presence of the usual blood pressure, organs of primary importance, e.g., the heart and the brain, are not subjected to constriction of their vessels, and therefore they are, continuously supplied with blood. But this advantage is secured at the deprivation of peripheral structures and especially the abdominal viscera. In these less essential parts, where constriction of the arterioles occurs, the capillaries are ill-supplied with oxygen. The very thin walls of capillaries are sensitive to oxygen want and when they do not receive an adequate supply they become more and more permeable to the fluid part of the blood. Thereupon the plasma escapes into the perivascular spaces. A similar condition occurs in the wound shock of human beings. The escape of the plasma from the blood vessels leaves the red corpuscles more concentrated. During World War I we found that the concentration of corpuscles in skin areas might be increased as much as fifty per cent (see Cannon, Fraser and Hooper, 1917).

A condition well known as likely to be harmful to the wounded was a prolonged lack of food or water. Freeman, Morison, and Sawyer (1933) found that loss of fluid from the body, resulting in a state of dehydration, excited the sympathico-adrenal system; thus again a vicious circle may be started, the low blood volume of the dehydrated condition being intensified by futher loss through capillaries which have been made increasingly permeable.

The foregoing paragraphs have revealed how a persistent and profound emotional state may induce a disastrous fall of blood pressure, ending in death. Lack of food and drink would collaborate with the damaging emotional effects, to induce the fatal outcome. These are the conditions which, as we have seen, are prevalent in persons who have been reported as dying as a consequence of sorcery. They go without food or water as they, in their isolation, wait in fear for their impending death. In these circumstances they might well die from a true state of shock, in the surgical sense—a shock induced by prolonged and tense emotion.

It is pertinent to mention here that Wallace, a surgeon of large experience in World War I, testified (1919, p. 7) to having seen cases of shock in which neither trauma nor any of the known accentuating factors of shock could account for the disastrous condition. Sometimes the wounds were so trivial that they could not be reasonably regarded as the cause of the shock state; sometimes the visible injuries were negligible. He cites two illustrative instances. One was a man who was buried by the explosion of a shell in a cellar; the other was blown up by a buried shell over which he had lighted a fire. In both the circumstances were favorable for terrifying experience. In both all the classic symptoms of shock were present. The condition lasted more than 48 hours, and treatment was of no avail. A *postmortem* examination did not reveal any gross injury. Another remarkable case which may be cited was studied by Freeman at the Massachusetts General Hospital. A woman of 43 years underwent a complete hysterectomy because of uterine bleeding. Although her emotional instability was recognized, she appeared to stand the operation well. Special precautions were taken, however, to avoid loss of blood, and in addition she was given fluid intravenously when the operation was completed. That night she was sweating, and refused to speak. The next morning her blood pressure had fallen to near the shock level, her heart rate was 150 beats per minute, her skin was cold and clammy and the measured blood flow through the vessels of her hand was very slight. There was no bleeding to account for her desperate condition, which was diagnosed as shock brought on by fear. When one understands the utter strangeness, to an inexperienced layman, of a hospital and its elaborate surgical ritual, and the distressing invasion of the body with knives and metal retractors, the wonder is that not more patients exhibit signs of deep anxiety. In this instance a calm and reassuring attitude on the part of the surgeon resulted in a change of attitude in the patient, with recovery of a normal state. That the attitude of the patient is of significant importance for a favorable outcome of an operation is firmly believed by the well-known American surgeon, Dr. J. M. T. Finney, for many years Professor of Surgery at the Johns Hopkins Medical School. He (1934) has publicly testified, on the basis of serious experiences, that if any person came to him for a major operation, and expressed fear of the result, he invariably refused to operate. Some other surgeon must assume the risk!

Further evidence of the possibility of a fatal outcome from profound emotional strain was reported by Mira (1939) in recounting his experiences as a psychiatrist in the Spanish War of 1936–39. In patients who suffered from what he called "malignant anxiety," he observed signs of anguish and perplexity, accompanied by a permanently rapid pulse (more than 120 beats per minute), and a very rapid respiration (about three times the normal resting rate). These conditions indicated a perturbed state deeply involving the sympathico-adrenal complex. As predisposing conditions Mira mentioned "a previous lability [changeability] of the sympathetic system" and "a severe mental shock experienced in conditions of physical exhaustion due to lack of food, fatigue, sleeplessness, etc." The lack of food appears to have attended lack of water, for the urine was concentrated and extremely acid. Towards the end the anguish still remained, but inactivity changed to restlessness. No focal symptoms were observed. In fatal cases death occurred in three or four days. *Postmortem* examination revealed brain hemorrhages in some cases, but, excepting an increased pressure, the cerebrospinal fluid showed a normal state. The combination of lack of food and water, anxiety, very rapid pulse and respiration, associated with a shocking experience having persistent effects, would fit well with fatal conditions reported from primitive tribes.

The suggestion which I offer, therefore, is that "voodoo death" may be real, and that it may be explained as due to shocking emotional stress—to obvious or repressed terror. A satisfactory hypothesis is one which allows observations to be made which may determine whether or not it is correct. Fortunately, tests of a relatively simple type can be used to learn whether the suggestion as to the nature of "voodoo death" is justifiable. The pulse towards the end would be rapid and "thready." The skin would be cool and moist. A count of the red blood corpuscles, or even simpler, a determination by means of a hematocrit of the ratio of corpuscles to plasma in a small sample of blood from skin vessels, would help to tell whether shock is present; for the "red count" would be high and the hematocrit also would reveal "hemoconcentration." The blood pressure would be low. The blood sugar would be increased, but the measure of it might be too difficult in the field. If in the future, however, any observer has opportunity to see an instance of "voodoo death," it is to be hoped that he will conduct the simpler tests before the victim's last gasp.

7

Differences and Similarities

MARK ZBOROWSKI

Data collected in [an earlier part of] our study were presented as patterns of behavioral and attitudinal responses to pain manifested and related verbally by patients of Old American, Jewish, Irish, and Italian origin. Our emphasis was on the regularities in responsive patterns for each ethnic group, and our aim was to document the original thesis . . . that responses to pain are learned and patterned as part of the individual's cultural heritage. The patient's information about his pain experience was seen as a description of a cultural experience, characteristic of each ethnic group; and, although no attempt was made to draw specific comparisons between the four groups, our approach was obviously crosscultural.

Now . . . we summarize the results of the study in the form of a comparative exploration of what we have learned about all four groups in terms of their differential responses to specific elements of the pain experience, such as the intensity of pain, its quality and duration, and its interpretation and significance in illness and medical treatment. These comparisons, based primarily on the qualitative material collected in the process of our study, are, wherever possible, tested by statistical computations of the incidence with which identifiable responses to pain occur within each ethnic group.[1] These responses are grouped in a list of fifty items derived from our un-

[1] All statistical computations were executed by Jack Cohen, Chief Research Psychologist at the Veterans Administration Hospital, Bronx, New York. Because of the complexity of the computations and their limited appeal to anyone but a small research minority, tables reflecting these computations have been omitted from the text. They are available on request from the author (Mount Zion Hospital and Medical Center, San Francisco, California 94115).

structured interviews, questionnaires, and direct observation of patients' behavior and their manner in describing their perceptions and feelings {not included here}.

First we shall examine how our four groups of patients compare in terms of such general background variables as age, education, occupation, socioeconomic status (SES), ethnicity (extent of cultural identification with the ethnic group), and, finally, the disease which is the cause of pain. Such an examination is helpful, as frequently questions are raised as to the effects which age, education, or disease of the patient might have upon his behavior in pain. The statistical analysis of the above variables for all patients suggests a number of differences in the composition of each of the ethnic groups.

All four groups were comparable in terms of age. However, there were significantly more Old Americans than Irish in the older age group (forty-six and over). The Jewish group included more higher-educated patients on the college level than any of the remaining three groups, which were comparable in terms of their education. The Jewish group included significantly more patients of middle-class background than the Irish, Old American, and Italian groups, which did not seem to differ with regard to their socioeconomic background.[2] Significantly more Old Americans and Irish were in occupations requiring physical effort than Jewish and Italian patients, who tended to be blue-collar workers or in small businesses. Among the three immigrant groups, the Irish expressed less ethnic self-identification than the Jewish and Italian patients, who were much more emphatic about their cultural background in such areas as customs, values, food habits, and interpersonal relationships. This response may have occurred because there were relatively more Irish of a third American-born generation than Jews and Italians, who were mostly of first and second generations. . . .

With regard to the pain-causing pathology, we differentiated among three major groups of patients—those suffering from herniated discs and backache; those whose pain was caused by migraine and other illness; and those whose pain was associated with a physical

[2] As the general patient population of a Veterans Administration hospital is of lower and lower-middle-class background, no attempt was made to assess rigorously the patients' SES. It was evaluated by the study group on the basis of the patients' education, occupation, and life style as revealed in the interviews.

disability such as paraplegia, quadriplegia, or amputation. The statistical analysis of ethnic groups in relation to the disease revealed that there were relatively more patients suffering from a physical disability among the Old Americans than in any other group.

Thus, if there is a correlation between the patients' background variables and their responses to pain, there were sufficient differences among the four groups to warrant a detailed examination of such correlations, which will be attempted in the process of our crosscultural comparisons.

Altogether we explored statistically five sets of comparisons: (1) Jewish and Italian patients versus Irish and Old American; (2) Irish versus Old American; (3) Italian versus Old American; (4) Jewish versus Old American; and (5) Italian versus Jewish. The reasons for such a selection of comparative sets derived from the analysis of the data [presented earlier in the study]. It seemed important to test the overall impression that most of the major differences in responding to pain were noticeable between the Irish and Old Americans on the one hand and the Italian and Jewish patients on the other. Another impression to be tested was that in spite of behavioral differences between the Old American and Jewish patients, in some areas their responses appeared to be similar. Finally, although the Jewish and Italian patients manifested many behavioral similarities, our observations suggested that their attitudes and orientations toward the experience were quite different; a similar reason underlay the sets of comparisons between the Irish and Old American patients.

The clinical impressions of medical practitioners that patients of Jewish and Italian origin tend to be more emotional while experiencing and expressing pain than the Anglo-Saxon—that is, the Old American—was confirmed by the observations derived from our study. Emotional description of pain experience occurred more frequently in the interviews with the Jewish and Italian patients than with the Old American and Irish. This emotionality was also expressed in the tendency of the Italian and Jewish patients to emphasize their perception of pain (to play up pain), whereas the Old Americans and Irish tended to deemphasize their perception (to play down pain). The former two groups also tended to describe the intensity of their pain as "very severe," whereas the latter two groups were more apt to differentiate between slight, severe, and very severe pain. The characteristic unemotional reporting on pain of the Old American which was commented upon earlier was confirmed by statistical computations, as also the vague and confused information offered by the Irish.

The literature on pain tends to differentiate between various qualities to the pain sensation, such as aching, pricking, or burning pain (see Hardy, Wolff & Goodell, 1952). Patients, on the other hand, tend to speak of sharp or dull pain, of a stabbing or aching sensation, or of a burning pain. Some of them try to convey their feelings by using illustrations from common experiences, such as sharp as if cut by a knife, burning like fire, or stabbing as with a needle. Our observations revealed that the Old Americans and the Irish were inclined more than the others to describe their pain as stabbing and sharp as well as to use comparative illustrations to describe their pain sensation. It is interesting to note that in identifying pain as burning, patients did not differ along ethnic lines.

Medical practitioners rely heavily on patients' descriptions of their pain in assessing its symptomatic significance. Such characteristics of pain as its intensity, location, and duration are important elements in the history of a disease and its etiology. It seems, however, that less precision can be expected from the Irish and the Italian patients than from the Old American and Jewish, who, despite their striking differences in behavior, tend to be more precise in describing their pain experiences. Among all the four groups, the Irish patients seem to be most confused in their description of perceptions and feelings about pain.

The perception of the time element in pain when defining its duration is probably affected by cultural time orientation. This impression seems to be supported by the fact that the Italian patients who were described earlier as present-oriented related more frequently than others that their pain was constant and present all the time, whereas patients from other ethnic groups described their pain as intermittent ("it comes and goes"), which clinically is probably more accurate.

The lack of inhibitions in exhibiting suffering manifested in the expressive behavior observed among the Italian and Jewish patients, and the nonexpressive behavior characteristic of the Irish and Old Americans was also documented statistically. Thus, while the Irish and American patients said that they prefer to hide their pain, the Jewish and Italian patients admitted freely that they show their pain and they do it by crying, by complaining about pain, by being more demanding, and by stating unequivocally that they cannot tolerate pain. Groaning and moaning in pain seemed to be common to all four groups; but our statistical computations suggest that they tended to be more frequent among the Italian and the Jewish patients, whereas withdrawal from other people when in pain was most characteristic of the Old American patients.

The expressive behavior of Jewish and Italian patients, which suggested their desire to communicate their suffering to others, was manifested also in various motor responses to pain such as body movements, gestures, twisting, and jumping. Such communication through body movements has also been observed by other investigators of the function of gestures and body movements in the communication patterns of the Italian and Jewish cultures (see Efron and Foley, 1937).

Our observations suggested that anxiety and worry, which are usually associated with pain, are most frequently expressed by Jewish patients. This observation was confirmed statistically. They stated more frequently than others that pain was the primary reason for seeking admission to the hospital, and they, more than others, were concerned with the symptomatic significance of pain. On the other hand, the Old Americans, who, as stated earlier in the book, were also preoccupied with pain, denied seeking hospitalization because of pain and were more prone to rationalize their pain by attributing it to external reasons rather than to illness or other causes.

The preoccupation with the immediate sensation of pain which we found as characteristic of the Italian patients was illustrated by their tendency to speak primarily of their pain only, rather than in association with other symptoms of illness, and to be less preoccupied with the future effects of their pain—in contrast to the future-oriented Jews.

The Jewish patients' concern about the symptomatic significance of pain was further indicated by their tendency to seek immediate consultation with a physician. One may wonder whether the Jewish patients' higher level of education and economic comfort might not have influenced their readiness to seek immediate medical help. The statistical tests indicate, however, that neither education nor socio-economic status seemed to influence significantly the patients' proneness to consult a physician as soon as they perceived pain.

The statistical tests suggest that both the Jewish and Italian patients tended to interpret their pain independently of the physician. The qualitative analysis of the interviews suggests that this tendency is more pronounced in the Jewish than in the Italian patients, even though this impression is not confirmed statistically. The preoccupation with the symptomatic meaning of pain so characteristic of the Jewish patients is also expressed in their insistence upon understanding the meaning of their pain, an insistence significantly more pronounced than even that of the rational and pragmatic Old Americans, who tended to leave it all to the physician and who in general seemed to have more confidence than the Jewish patients in the skill of the doctors.

The attitudes toward the doctor and his role in pain and illness seem to be strongly affected by the cultural background of the patient. Both the Old American and the Irish patients tended to express confidence in the doctor's skill—more so than the Jewish and Italian patients; the Jewish patients were significantly more likely to check up on doctors and shop around, thus suggesting a lesser degree of confidence in the physician.

The attitudes of the Irish and Old American patients toward pain, illness, and medical intervention, and their confidence in doctors and their skill were reflected in their total behavior in the hospital. They accepted their sick role as defined by the hospital and assumed what the hospital staff identified as a cooperative attitude. This attitude was reflected in their tendency to express satisfaction with the care they received as patients and their readiness to cooperate with the staff. Among all the patients the Irish seemed to stand out as most cooperative, which could be a manifestation of the resigned and defeated attitude that they seemed to adopt after a prolonged period of pain and illness. In contrast, the Jewish and Italian patients seemed to be more dissatisfied, more critical of the hospital care, and more demanding.

Looking back on the fifty items which were tested for statistical significance we find that the Irish and American patients differed from the Jewish and Italians on more than half of them, on the ones dealing with such aspects as pain description, attitude toward pain, and its meaning in illness, as well as with attitudes toward doctors, medical intervention, and hospital care.

The comparison between the Old American and the Irish patients supports much that was stated [in an earlier part of the study]. Thus, although both groups of patients tended to deemphasize their pain by playing it down, the Irish more so than the Old Americans tended to describe its intensity as "very severe." This tendency may result from a lack of precision in relating their pain experience in general and a need to dramatize their pain, which allows them to legitimize their defeat in fighting pain.

The tendency to delay consultation with a physician, which was expressed by the Irish as well as by the Old American patients, seems to be more frequently stated by the Old Americans than by the Irish. This tendency would be consistent with the apprehensions which this former group seems to experience with regard to the doctors' ability to determine a major threat to their health.

Throughout the study the Irish patients expressed worry and pessimism about the outcome of their illness and its effect upon their body and masculinity. This worry was substantiated by their frequently expressed concern about the symptomatic significance of the pain they suffered in the course of their illness; this concern exceeded that of the more rational patients of Old American stock. It is interesting that in this respect the Irish attitude was more like that of the Jewish patients, from whom they differed in such a striking manner in relation to other behavioral and attitudinal aspects of their pain experience.

The tendency of the Old American patients to attribute pain and illness to external causes was evident when compared to the Irish, who tended to be rather helpless in explaining their illness and were prone to seek the cause within themselves. This helplessness as well as a resigned attitude toward the impact of illness seemed to be reflected in their passive and uncomplaining role as patients, which differentiated them from the cooperative but frequently griping patients of Old American background.

Finally, the Old American patients differed from the Irish in their detached and precise manner of describing their pain experience. The latter had greater difficulties in talking and describing their suffering.

Much like the Old American and Irish patients, the patients of

Jewish and Italian origin frequently manifested similar behavior but differed in many attitudes toward pain. They were highly emotional and expressive in responding to their pain experience and tended to be less tolerant of pain than the other two groups, but here the similarities end. The Jewish patients expressed much more frequent concern about the significance of pain as a symptom of illness and therefore did not wait as long as the Italians to seek admission to the hospital or to consult a physician. In their desire to identify the pathological cause of pain, the Jewish patients cooperated with the physician in being more precise in describing their experience. The Italians tended to be more confused under the immediate impact of painful sensations and dramatized them more than the Jewish patients, who in comparison with them behaved almost like the "reporting" Old Americans.

In keeping with their cultural time orientation, the Italians unlike the Jews were mostly concerned with the immediacy of their sensation rather than with its future effects or its symptomatic significance. When in pain, they seemed to feel it all the time—as an ever-present, constant, intolerable sensation—and even more frequently than the Jewish patients claimed that they could not tolerate pain.

The Jewish patients, on the other hand, in their anxiety about the cause and future implications of pain, rather than about the sensation itself, were concerned with finding the most skillful physician to make the correct diagnosis and prescribe the best treatment. In many of these attitudinal responses to pain, the Jewish patients manifested many similarities with the Old Americans, with whom they shared many health values as well as their orientation toward the future, even though they behaved differently under the actual impact of pain.

The Jewish patients tended to describe their pain mostly as very severe, they openly manifested their pain, they tended to express their pain by groaning and moaning more so than the Old Americans and by tears and more frequent demands for help. In comparison with the Jewish patient, the Old American appeared to be unemotional and to be trying to play down his suffering. When in pain he tended to withdraw from other people in order not to show his pain, which he seemed to be able to tolerate better than the Jew.

From the point of view of the medical and paramedical staff in the hospital, the Old American patient lives up to the image of a desirable patient. He is not as demanding as the Jewish patient, and he has confidence in doctors and their skill, which is important in his role as an active member of the health team.

Many of the observations described and interpreted throughout the book were supported by statistical computation wherever it was possible to translate qualitative data into figures. The following summary of results will facilitate an overview of the responses which were analyzed and tested statistically:

Table 7.1. *Comparative Listing of Statistically Significant Differences in Response to Pain*

(OA = Old American, IR = Irish, IT = Italian, J = Jewish)

PAIN DESCRIPTION

Intensity of pain

	OA	IR	J	IT
Reported by degrees (slight, severe, very severe)	OA	IR		
	(OA more than IR)			
Reported usually as very severe			J	IT

Quality of pain

	OA	IR	J	IT
Stabbing, sharp	OA	IR		
Aching, dull			J	IT
Burning	No difference			
Comparative description of pain	OA	IR		

Duration of pain

	OA	IR	J	IT
Constant pain				IT
Intermittent pain	OA	IR	J	

Description of sensation

	OA	IR	J	IT
Tendency to be precise in description of sensation	OA		J	
Tendency to be vague and confused		IR		IT
Emotional description			J	IT
Unemotional description	OA	IR		
Playing up pain			J	IT
Reporting on pain	OA		(J)	
Playing down pain		IR		
Detailed spontaneous description	OA			
Detailed answers to probing questions	OA			

BEHAVIOR IN PAIN

Expressive versus unexpressive behavior

	OA	IR	J	IT
Showing pain			J	IT
Hiding pain	OA	IR		
Moaning and groaning			J	IT
Crying			J	IT

Table 7.1. *Comparative Listing of Statistically Significant Differences in Response to Pain* (Continued)

(OA = Old American, IR = Irish, IT = Italian, J = Jewish)

BEHAVIOR IN PAIN

	OA	IR	J	IT
Motor responses and reactions	OA		J	
Tendency to withdraw when in pain	OA	IR		
No tendency to withdraw when in pain			J	IT
Demanding behavior when in pain			J	IT
Complaining behavior when in pain			J	IT
Uncomplaining behavior when in pain	OA	IR		

Tolerance of pain

	OA	IR	J	IT
'I can take pain'	OA	IR		
'I cannot take pain'			J	IT

Attitudinal response to being in pain

	OA	IR	J	IT
Worry			J	IT
Bothered by immediate effects of pain				IT
Bothered by future effects of pain			J	
Bothered by symptomatic significance of pain			J	IT
Concern with understanding pain			J	IT

Reasons for being in pain

Symptomatic interpretation of pain	No significant difference			
External causes	OA			

PAIN AND MEDICAL INTERVENTION

	OA	IR	J	IT
Pain and symptoms as reason for hospitalization			J	IT

Attitude toward doctor as related to pain

	OA	IR	J	IT
Immediate consultation			J	IT
Delayed consultation	OA	IR		
(OA more than IR)				
Seeing doctor because of pain	OA	IR		
Seeing doctor because of pain and symptoms			J	IT

Attitude toward doctors

	OA	IR	J	IT
Confidence in skill of doctor	OA	IR		
Checking on doctors			J	

Attitude toward surgery

	OA	IR	J	IT
Confidence in surgery	OA	IR		

Attitude toward hospital care

	OA	IR	J	IT
Demanding attitude			J	IT
Undemanding attitude	OA	IR		
Satisfaction with hospital care	OA	IR		
Dissatisfaction with hospital care			J	IT
Cooperative attitude	OA	IR		
Critical attitude			J	IT

In commenting on patients' responses to pain, most of the clinical practitioners tended to attribute differences in behavior and attitude to four major independent background variables: illness being the cause of pain, the patients' age, his education, and his socioeconomic status. In analyzing the results of our study we attempted to test these impressions with regard to the items that were our guidelines for testing the differences and similarities among the four groups. The logical procedure would have been to test the possible influence of these independent variables for each ethnic group independently. However, the rather small number of informants within each group disallowed this procedure, and we had to test the interrelation between the independent variables and the patients' responses for all four groups.

There seems to be little doubt that the nature of a patient's illness seemed to affect to a great extent his behavior and attitudes with regard to his pain experience. In thirteen out of fifty items (26 percent) on our list, the pathology influenced the patients' responses on a high level of statistical significance ($p < .05$ and less). Thus, it influenced their reasons for hospitalization. It made them more prone to show their pain by moaning and groaning, by crying, and by motor manifestation. Depending on the nature of their illness, they were more or less worried and more or less concerned about the immediate as well as symptomatic significance of their pain and the future effects of their illness. The pathology also affected the manner of presentation of their sensation (precise or confused) and their being more or less emotional and dramatic.

No other independent variable appeared to be as important in affecting the patients' responses as the nature of their illness. The age variable was important only in three areas: (1) whether the patients would show or hide their pain, the oldest patients being more prone to show pain than hide it; (2) how soon the patients would consult a doctor after experiencing pain, the middle age group tending to delay the least; and (3) the patients' feelings about their doctors, the oldest age group valuing the doctor's personality over his skills. The educational variable seemed to play a role only in two areas: it influenced the anxiety of the patient, the less-educated individuals seeming to worry more; also, the more educated seemed to have more confidence in surgery than the less educated. Finally, the socioeconomic status of the patient seemed to affect his response only in one area: the less privileged group tended to say that they visited the physician only because of pain.

As can be seen from this summary, the disease variable was clearly a major influence on patients' responses in those areas of their experience where differences were attributed to ethnic background. Hence, to assess the relative importance of the disease variable in comparison with the significance of ethnic background, we compared the responses of Irish and Old American patients with the responses of Italian and Jewish patients in those critical areas by keeping the disease variable constant. We selected all patients suffering from herniated discs and backache and compared their responses in relation to their ethnic background.

In response to six items, these two groups of patients suffering from pain associated with a similar pathology showed significant differences. The Italian and the Jewish patients tended to show their pain more than the Irish and Old American. Moaning and groaning, tears, and motor manifestations of pain were more frequently observed among the Jewish and Italian patients, who also tended to be more emotional and dramatic about their pain than the other two groups. Thus, we can conclude that, along with the major role which pathology might play in influencing a patient's response to his pain experience, the cultural background of the individual appears to be a most important, if not the determining, factor in shaping his behavior in pain and illness.

These same conclusions were reached independently by a number of social and medical scientists who investigated the role of ethnicity in affecting the patients' responses to pain and illness. During the years since we published the first results of our study (Zborowski, 1952), social scientists interested in health and human behavior (Croog, 1961; Mechanic, 1963; Suchman, 1964 and 1965) also found significant differences between ethnic as well as religious (Jewish, Catholic, and Protestant) groups in their responses to questions pertaining to health and illness.

An investigation of special relevance to our study was conducted by Sternbach and Tursky (1965), two scientists who explored the psychophysiological aspects of pain.

Following Zborowski's (1952) findings, [they] interviewed and tested Yankee, Irish, Jewish, and Italian housewives, and corroborated the differences in pain attitudes. They found in addition that the Irish attitude involved deliberate suppression of suffering and concern for the implications of pain. Italian subjects had significantly lower pain tolerance to electric shocks and the Yankees demonstrated a more rapid and complete adaptation of diphasic palmar skin potentials to repeated strong shock. In a latter report, Tursky and Sternbach (1967) presented additional physiological differences among the groups in noting mean heart rate, palmar skin resistance, and skin potential levels. *The differences among the groups in physiological activity seemed to parallel the culturally acquired attitudinal sets toward pain.* (Italics mine)

It is interesting to note that these findings were arrived at in a laboratory setting where subjects were responding to "experimental pain" without the complicating, anxiety-provoking elements experienced under the impact of the pathological (clinical) pain (Beecher, 1952).

Pain and illness are stress situations to which individuals respond as people, as humans equipped with intricate biophysical, biochemical, physiological, and psychological mechanisms which enable them to adapt to stress, whatever its origin (Dubos, 1965). However, stress is also a cultural experience in perception as well as in interpretation, and as such is responded to by behavior and attitudes learned within the culture in which the individual is brought up. To ask whether the man's biopsychophysical endowment or his cultural background is more important in allowing him to survive under stress is pointless and futile. The most we can hope to achieve is to assess the functions of different components in the biocultural process of man's struggle for survival.

8

∿∿∿∿∿∿∿∿∿∿∿∿∿∿∿∿∿∿∿∿∿∿∿∿∿∿∿∿∿∿∿∿∿

The Living World

RENE DUBOS

THE SOCIAL ENVIRONMENT

Physiological Responses to Population Density

The word crowd has unpleasant connotations. It evokes disease, pestilence, and group-generated attitudes often irrational and either too submissive or too aggressive. Congested cities call to mind unhealthy complexions and harassed behavior; city crowds are accused of accepting despotic power and of blindly engaging in acts of violence. In contrast, rural areas and small towns are thought to foster health and freedom. The legendary Arcadia and the Utopias of all times are imagined as comfortably populated by human beings enjoying vast horizons. The nature and history of man are far too complex, of course, to justify such generalizations, but there is some truth nevertheless in the belief that crowding generates problems of disease and behavior. However, these problems are poorly understood and their formulation is rendered even more difficult by a number of oversimplified and erroneous concepts inherited from the late nineteenth century.

During the Industrial Revolution, the crowding in tenements, factories, and offices was associated with tremendous increases in morbidity and mortality rates. Along with malnutrition, the various "fevers" were the most obvious causes of ill health. Epidemic outbreaks and chronic forms of microbial disease constituted the largest medical problems of the late nineteenth century because they were extremely prevalent, not only among the economically destitute but also among the more favored classes. The new science of microbiology that developed during that period provided a theory that appeared sufficient at first sight to explain the explosive spread of infection. The germ theory made it obvious that crowding facilitates the transfer of microbes from one person to another, and this led to the reasonable conclusion that the newly industrialized communities had been caught in a web of infection, resulting from the increase in human contacts.

The expression "crowd diseases" thus became, and has remained ever since, identified with a state of affairs conducive to the rapid spread of infective agents, particularly under unsanitary conditions. Epidemiologists have built their science on the hypothesis that the pattern of microbial diseases in a given community of animals or men is determined by the channels available for the spread of microbes. In reality, however, the rise and fall of animal populations, both in confined environments and in the field, present aspects that cannot be entirely accounted for by these classical concepts of epidemiology. The reason, as we shall now see, is that crowding has several independent effects. On the one hand, it facilitates the spread of infective agents; on the other hand, it also modifies the manner in which men and animals respond to the presence of these agents and thereby increases indirectly the prevalence and severity of microbial disease. In fact, crowding affects the response of the individual and social body, not only to infection, but also to most of life's stresses.

In many species, the numbers of animals increase continuously from year to year until a maximum population density is reached; then suddenly an enormous mortality descends. This phenomenon, known as "population crash," has long been assumed to be caused by epidemics corresponding to those which have been so destructive in the course of human history, for example plague or yellow fever. Indeed, several different kinds of pathogens have been found to attack animal populations at the time of the crash. Pasteurellae and salmonellae are among the bacterial organisms that used to be most commonly incriminated; two decades ago a particular strain of *Mycobacterium muris* (the vole bacillus), isolated from field mice in England, was thought for a while to be responsible for population crashes in these rodents. Now that viruses have taken the limelight from bacteria, they in turn have been made responsible for occurrences of widespread mortality in several animal species.

It has become apparent, however, that the relation between population crashes and microbial diseases is far less clear than was once thought. On the one hand, several different types of pathogens can be associated with crashes in a given animal species. On the other hand, there are certain crashes for which no pathogen has been found to account for the pathological picture. These puzzling observations have led to the theory that the microbial diseases associated with population crashes are but secondary phenomena, and that the primary cause is a metabolic disturbance. . . .

Food shortages, or at least nutritional deficiencies, were long considered as a probable cause of drastic population decline. It is well known, in fact, that when wild animals multiply without check under natural conditions they exhaust their food supply, lose weight, and bear fewer young; this occurs for example when their predators are eliminated. However, a poor nutritional state can hardly account alone for population crashes. Its effect is rather to limit reproduction, either by failure of conception or by abortion; the overall result is an automatic adjustment of population size to the food supply instead of a massive crash. In fact, drastic population declines commonly occur even when the food supply is abundant.

The trend during recent years has been to explain population crashes by a "shock disease" related in some obscure way to overactivity of the adrenopituitary system. A notorious example of this type of crowd disease is the mass migration of the Norwegian lemmings from the mountaintops of Scandinavia. According to an ancient Norwegian belief, the lemmings periodically experience an irresistible "collective urge" either to commit suicide or to search for their ancestral home on the lost Atlantic Continent, and consequently they march unswervingly into the sea. In reality, such migrations take place whenever the lemmings become overcrowded, a situation that occurs every third or fourth year, as each mating pair produces 13 to 16 young annually. The migration of Norwegian lemmings was so massive in 1960–61 that a steamer entering the Trondheim Fjord took one hour to pass through a two-mile-long pack of swimming and sinking rodents!

Although the nature of the initial stimulus that prompts the lemmings to migrate is not understood, crowding is almost certainly one of its aspects. As the rodents become more and more crowded they fall victim to a kind of mass psychosis. This results in a wild scrambling about that, contrary to legend, is not necessarily a march toward the sea but merely random movement. The animals die, not by drowning, but from metabolic derangements associated with stress; lesions are commonly found in the brain and the adrenals.

Profound changes have also been observed to occur at more or less regular intervals in the population of snowshoe hares. According to a classical description, these animals observed in Minnesota during periods of crash

characteristically died in convulsive seizures with sudden onset, running movements, hind leg extension, retraction of the head and neck, and sudden leaps with clonic seizures upon alighting. Other animals were typically lethargic or comatose. . . . This syndrome was characterized primarily by decrease in liver glycogen and a hypoglycemia preceding death. Petechial or ecchymotic brain hemorrhages, and congestion and hemorrhage of the adrenals, thyroid, and kidneys were frequent findings [Deevey, 1960].

Interestingly enough, many of the signs and symptoms observed in wild animals dying during population crashes have been reproduced in the laboratory by subjecting experimental animals to crowding and other forms of stress. Voles placed for a few hours a day during a month in cages containing another pair of aggressive voles eventually died, but not of wounds. The main finding at necropsy was a marked increase in the weight of their adrenals and spleen and a decrease in the weight of the thymus. Similar findings have been made on captive and wild rats.

Crowding can act as a form of stress in most species of experimental animals. In chickens, mice, rats, and voles, it causes an enlargement of the adrenals chiefly through cellular hyperplasia in the cortical areas; in addition it interferes with both growth and reproductive function.

Crowding affects many other biological characteristics of animal population; for example, the reproducibility of the response to various abnormal states, such as barbiturate anaesthesia, is affected by population density. The toxicity of central nervous system stimulants such as amphetamine is remarkably enhanced when the animals are placed in a crowded environment; central depressants protect to some degree against this aggregation effect. The experimental hypertension produced in rats bearing regenerating adrenals is increased by crowding, and coronary arteriosclerosis develops more rapidly and more intensely in chickens that are grouped than in animals kept isolated.

Field studies of voles in England have revealed the puzzling fact that their population continues to fall the year after the crash. It would appear, therefore, that the reduced viability responsible for the crash is transmitted from one generation to another. This finding is compatible with other observations which indicate that crowding of the mother affects the physical development and behavior of the offspring.

The response to almost any kind of stimulus can be modified by crowding, as is illustrated by the production of experimental granuloma. Cotton pellets impregnated with turpentine were introduced subcutaneously into groups of mice that were then either caged individually or in groups. The granulomas that developed in the grouped mice weighed 19 per cent less than in the other animals, a result probably due to the fact that the greater adrenocortical activity in the grouped mice had exerted a suppressive effect on the inflammatory reaction.

It is probable that the effect of crowding on tissue response accounts for the decrease in resistance to infection. In order to put this hypothesis to the test, mice were infected with a standardized dose of *Trichinella* and then were either isolated in individual jars or caged in groups immediately after infection. When these mice were sacrificed 15 days later, it was found that all the grouped animals had large numbers of worms (15 to 51) in their intestines, whereas only 3 out of 12 of the isolated animals showed any sign of infection. Although exposure to infection had been identical, crowding had therefore increased the ability of trichinella to invade the intestinal wall, probably by decreasing the inflammatory response to the parasite. Analogous observations have been made with regard to infantile diarrhea of mice. The incidence of clinical signs of this disease remains small or is nil when the population density in the animal room is low, but it increases as the colony approaches peak production. The infection is endemic in most colonies, but the disease does not become overt until the animals are crowded.

The grouping of several organisms of one given species has certainly many physiological consequences more subtle than those mentioned above. One such curious effect has been observed in male ducks kept constantly either in the dark or exposed to artificial light for periods of over two years. In both cases, these abnormal conditions of light exposure resulted in marked disturbances of the sexual cycles, which were no longer in phase with the seasonal rhythms. However, the animals within each group exhibited a remarkable synchronism of testicular evolution, thus revealing a "group effect" on sexual activity that was independent of light, of season, and of the presence of animals of the opposite sex.

Territoriality, Dominance, and Adaptation to Crowding

As we have just seen, the epidemiology of "crowd" diseases involves factors other than those affecting the spread of infectious agents. Association with other living things modifies the total response of the organism to the various environmental forces and thereby affects susceptibility to a multiplicity of noxious influences, including infection.

A quantitative statement of population density is not sufficient, however, to forecast the effects of crowding on human beings or animals. Even more important than numbers of specimens of a given species per unit area is the manner in which each particular person or animal responds to the other members of the group under a given set of conditions. The response to population density is determined in large part by the history of the group and of its individual members; furthermore, it may be favorable or unfavorable, depending upon the circumstances.

Many types of rodents, such as laboratory rats and mice, prefer to be somewhat crowded. In fact, individually housed rats and mice usually behave in a more "emotional" or "frightened" manner than their group-housed counterparts; they are also less able to adapt to a variety of experimental procedures such as food restriction, food selection, or cold stress. Isolated mice are less able than grouped mice to overcome the disturbances in intestinal ecology caused by antimicrobial drugs and other physiological disturbances (unpublished observations). . . . The practice of mutual cleaning accelerates wound healing in many animal species, and isolation has unfavorable effects on the behavior and personality structure of animals and man.

In most animal species, probably in all, each group develops a complex social organization based on territoriality and on a social hierarchy comprising subordinate and dominant members, the so-called pecking order. The place of each animal in the hierarchy is probably determined in part by anatomical and physiological endowments and in part by the history of the group. In any case, the behavioral differences that result from the pecking order eventually bring about anatomical and physiological differences far more profound than those initially present. For example, the dominant animals usually have larger adrenals than the subordinates and they grow more rapidly because they have more ready access to food. It appears also that in rhesus monkeys the young males issued from females with a high social rank have a better chance than other males to become dominant in the colony.

Under a given set of conditions, the relative rank of each individual animal is fairly predictable. Social competition is often restricted to the male sex, the reproductive fortunes of the female being determined by the status of the male which selects her. Females associated with subordinate males in experimental populations may entirely fail to reproduce. However, the pecking order is valid only for well-defined environmental conditions. For example, each canary bird is dominant in the region near its nest; and similarly chickens in their home yard win more combats than strangers to that yard. The successes of animals on their own territorial grounds bring to mind the better performance of baseball teams on their home fields.

Successful competition within the group naturally confers advantages. The despot has first choice with regard to food and mates, and its position may even increase its resistance to certain forms of stress such as infection. In a particular experiment involving tenches, one fish in the group was found to dominate the whole territory and to be the first one to feed. This dominance had such profound physiological consequences that when all the tenches were infected with trypanosomes, the infection disappeared first from the dominant fish. When this fish was removed from the tank, fighting started among those remaining; the fish that became dominant in the new grouping in its turn had first access to the food, and soon got rid of its trypanosome infection.

The phenomenon of dominance has a social meaning which transcends the advantages that it gives to the dominant individuals. Acceptance of the hierarchical order reduces fighting and other forms of social tensions and thus provides a stability that is beneficial to the group as a whole. In an undisturbed organized flock of chickens, for example, the individual animals peck each other less frequently and less violently, eat more, maintain weight better, and lay more eggs than do chickens in flocks undergoing social reorganization through removal of some animals or addition of new ones. Furthermore, the subordinate animals do not suffer as much as could be expected from their low rank in the pecking order. There is no direct competition for food or for mates in the well-organized group; the subordinates readily yield their place to the dominants at the feeding box; they exhibit no sexual interest, often behaving as if they were "socially castrated." Thus, the establishment of an accepted hierarchy in a stable group of animals almost eliminates the stresses of social tension and results in a kind of social homeostasis.

Needless to say, there are limits to the protective efficacy social organization can provide against the dangers created by high population density. Excessive crowding has deleterious effects even in the most gregarious rodents. When laboratory rats are allowed to multiply without restriction in a confined space, an excess of food being available at all times, they develop abnormal behavior with regard to mating, nest building, and care of the young as soon as the population becomes too dense. However, such conditions of life are extremely artificial. Under the usual conditions of rodent life in the wild, animals migrate or are killed when the population becomes too large for the amount of food available.

Although man is a gregarious animal, sudden increases in population density can be as dangerous for him as they are for animals. The biological disturbances created during the Industrial Revolution by lack of sanitation and by crowding in tenements and factories were aggravated by the fact that most members of the new labor class had immigrated from rural areas and were totally unadapted to urban life. In contrast, the world is now becoming more and more urbanized. Constant and intimate contact with hordes of human beings has come to constitute the "normal" way of life, and men have eagerly adjusted to it. This change has certainly brought about all kinds of phenotypic adaptations that are making it easier for urban man to respond successfully to situations that in the past constituted biological and emotional threats.

There may be here an analogy with the fact that domesticated animals do not respond to various types of threatening situations in the laboratory as do wild animals of the same or related species. In any case, the effects of crowding on modern urban man are certainly very different from those experienced by the farmer and his family when they were first and suddenly exposed a century ago to the city environment of industrialized societies.

The readiness with which man adapts to potentially dangerous situations makes it unwise to apply directly to human life the results of experiments designed to test the acute effects of crowding on animals. Under normal circumstances, the dangerous consequences of crowding are mollified by a multiplicity of biological and social adaptations. In fact, crowding per se, i.e. population density, is probably far less important in the long run even in animals than is the intensity of the social conflicts, or the relative peace achieved after social adjustments have been made. As already mentioned, animal populations in which status differences are clearly established are likely to reach a greater size than those in which differences in rank are less well defined.

Little is known concerning the density of population or the intensity of stimulation that is optimum in the long run for the body and the mind of man. Crowding is a relative term. The biological significance of population density must be evaluated in the light of the past experience of the group concerned, because this experience conditions the manner in which each of its members responds to the others as well as to environmental stimuli and trauma.

Laying claim to a territory and maintaining a certain distance from one's fellow are probably as real biological needs in man as they are in animals, but their expressions are culturally conditioned. The proper distance between persons in a group varies from culture to culture. People reared in cultures where the proper distance is short appear "pushy" to those coming from social groups where propriety demands greater physical separation. In contrast, the latter will appear to the former as behaving in a cold, aloof, withdrawn, and standoffish manner. Although social anthropologists have not yet adequately explained the origin of these differences, they have provided evidence that ignorance of them in human relations or in the design of dwellings and hospitals can have serious social and pathological consequences.

The problems posed by crowding in human populations are thus more complex than those which exist in animal populations because they are so profoundly conditioned by social and cultural determinants. Indeed, there is probably no aspect of human life for which it is easier to agree with Ortega y Gasset that "man has no nature. What he has is a history." Most experimental biologists are inclined to scorn discussions of mob psychology and related problems because they feel that the time is not yet ripe for scientific studies on the mechanisms of collective behavior. Yet the phrase "mob psychology" serves at least to emphasize that the response of human beings to any situation is profoundly influenced by the structure of the social environment.

The numerous outbreaks of dancing manias that occurred in Europe from the fourteenth to sixteenth century constitute a picturesque illustration of abnormal collective behavior; such an event was witnessed by P. Breughel the Elder and became the subject of one of his most famous paintings, "The Saint Vitus Dancers," now in Vienna. Even today, revivalists, tremblers, and shakers often outdo the feats of the medieval performers during the dancing manias. And millions of people can still be collectively bewitched by the antics of a Hitler or other self-proclaimed prophet, to whom they yield body and soul. What happens in the mind of man is always reflected in the diseases of his body. The epidemiology of crowd diseases cannot be completely understood without knowledge of mob psychology.

BIBLIOGRAPHY

Allee (1951); Barnett (1960, 1963, 1964); Barrow (1955); Benoit, Assenmacher, and Brard (1955, 1956); Bernardis and Skelton (1963); Bronson and Eleftheriou (1965a, 1965b); Calhoun (1949, 1962); Carpenter (1958); Chitty (1958), Christian and Davis (1956); Christian, Flyger and Davis (1960); Christian and Williamson (1958); Curry-Lindahl (1963); Davis and Read (1958); Deevey (1960); Ellis and Free (1964); Elton (1958); Etkin (1964); Flickinger and Ratcliffe (1961); Greenwood (1935); Hall (1959, 1964); Hediger (1950); Hinde (1960); Keeley (1962); Koford (1963); Lasagna (1962); Mackintosh (1962); Mason (1959); McDonald, Stern, and Hahn (1963); McKissick, Flickinger, and Ratcliffe (1961); Siegal (1959); Thiessen (1963); Tinbergen (1953); Washburn and Devore (1961); Welty (1957); Zeuner (1963).

9

The Psychological Stresses of Intensive Care Unit Nursing

DONALD HAY
and
DONALD OKEN

Much has been written about the stressful psychological experience of being a patient in an Intensive Care (ICU) or other special care unit (Abram, 1965; Bishop & Reichert, 1969; DeMeyer, 1967; Hackett, Cassem, & Wishnie, 1969; Margolis, 1967). Less well recognized, however, are the problems posed for those who work in an ICU that provides the complex nursing care required by critically ill, often dying, patients. Notable exceptions include the contributions of Vreeland and Ellis (1969) and of Gardam (1969).

The quality of a patient's care, and, hence, outcome, depends greatly upon the people providing that care, and the effectiveness of the latter is a function of their psychological state no less than of their technical expertise. This has special meaning for the ICU patient, whose very life hangs upon the care provided by the nursing staff. Yet, in this special environment, the psychological burdens imposed upon the nurse are extraordinary. Her situation resembles, in many ways, that of the soldier serving with an elite combat group.

Our understanding derives from the experience of one of us (DH) working directly as a member of the nursing staff of a 10-bed university hospital ICU over a period of approximately one year, plus mul-

A condensed version of this paper was delivered at the workshop "Psychiatric Contributions to Management of Intensive Care Units" at the Annual Meeting of the American Psychosomatic Society, Denver, Colorado, April 2, 1971.

tiple interviews and informal contacts with ICU nurses.[1] From these observations, we have developed some insights into the nature of the nurses' experience and the methods they develop to handle it. These, we believe, provide useful clues for lessening the stressful nature of the experience, and hence benefit the nurses and (through them) their patients.

THE ICU ENVIRONMENT

A stranger entering an ICU is at once bombarded with a massive array of sensory stimuli (DeMeyer, 1967), some emotionally neutral but many highly charged. Initially, the greatest impact comes from the intricate machinery, with its flashing lights, buzzing and beeping monitors, gurgling suction pumps, and whooshing respirators. Simultaneously, one sees many people rushing around busily performing lifesaving tasks. The atmosphere is not unlike that of the tension-charged strategic war bunker. With time, habituation occurs, but the ever-continuing stimuli decrease the overload threshold and contribute to stress at times of crisis.

As the newness and strangeness of the unit wears off, one increasingly becomes aware of a host of perceptions with specific stressful emotional significance. Desperately ill, sick, and injured human beings are hooked up to that machinery. And, in addition to mechanical stimuli, one can discern moaning, crying, screaming and the last gasps of life. Sights of blood, vomitus and excreta, exposed genitalia, mutilated wasting bodies, and unconscious and helpless people assault the sensibilities. Unceasingly, the ICU nurse must face these affect-laden stimuli with all the distress and conflict that they engender. As part of her daily routine, the nurse must reassure and comfort the man who is dying of cancer; she must change the dressings of a decomposing, gangrenous limb; she must calm the awakening disturbed "overdose" patient; she must bathe the genitalia of the helpless and comatose; she must wipe away the bloody stool of

---

[1] While our detailed observations were made on a single ICU, superficial contact with several other such units, which have many features in common, leads us to believe that our conclusions have significant generalizability. However, there may be some significant differences from other types of specialized units such as coronary care units, neurosurgical ICUs, transplant and dialysis units, etc.

the gastrointestinal bleeder; she must comfort the anguished young wife who knows her husband is dying. It is hard to imagine any other situation that involves such intimacy with the frightening, repulsive, and forbidden. Stimuli are present to mobilize literally every conflictual area at every psychological developmental level.

But there is more: there is something uncanny about the picture the patients present. Many are neither alive nor dead. Most have "tubes in every orifice." Their sounds and actions (or inaction) are almost nonhuman. Bodily areas and organs, ordinarily unseen, are openly exposed or deformed by bandages. All of this directly challenges the definition of being human, one's most fundamental sense of ego integrity, for nurse as well as patient. Though consciously the nurse quickly learns to accept this surrealism, she is unremittingly exposed to these multiple threats to the stability of her body boundaries, her sense of self, and her feelings of humanity and reality.

To all this is added a repetitive contact with death. And, if exposure to death is merely frequent, that to dying is constant. The ICU nurse thus quickly becomes adept at identifying the signs and symptoms that foretell a downhill trend for her patient. This becomes an awesome addition to the burden of the nurse who has been caring for the patient and must *continue* to do so, knowing his outcome.

THE WORK LOAD AND ITS DEMANDS

If the sense of drama and frightfulness is what most forcefully strikes the outsider, what the experienced nurse points to, paradoxically, is the incessant repetitive routine. For each patient, vital signs must be monitored, commonly at 15-minute intervals, sometimes more often. Central venous pressures must be measured, tracheas suctioned, urimeters emptied and measured, intravenous infusions changed, EKG monitor patterns interpreted, respirators checked, hypothermia blankets adjusted, etc., etc. And every step must be charted. The nurse begins to feel like a hamster on a treadmill: she finishes the required tasks on one patient just in time to start them on another; and when these are completed she is already behind in doing the same tasks all over again on the first, constantly aware of her race with the clock. A paradox soon becomes apparent. Nowhere more than in the ICU is a *good* nurse expected to make observations about her patient's condition, to interpret subtle changes and use judgment to take appropriate action. But often, the ICU nurse is so unremittingly involved in collecting and charting information that she has little time to interpret it adequately.

The work load is formidable—even in periods of relative calm. Many tasks, which elsewhere would be performed by nurse's aides, require special care in the ICU and become the lot of the ICU nurse. Changing a bed in an ICU may require moving a desperately ill, comatose patient while watching EKG leads, respirator hoses, urinary and intravenous catheters, etc. Moreover, the nurse must maintain detailed records.

Night shifts, weekends, and holidays all mean less work on other floors. Only urgent or fundamental procedures are performed. But, in an ICU, emergency is routine: there is no surcease—no holidays. In fact, the regular recovery room in our hospital shuts down on weekends and holidays so that patients must be sent to the ICU after emergency surgery. It is not rare, on a weekend, to see several stretchers with these patients interposed between the fully occupied beds of the ICU, leaving the nurses with barely time enough to suction patients and keep them alive.

The quantity and variety of complex technical equipment poses tremendous demands on the knowledge and expertise of the nurse (Gardam, 1969; Vreeland & Ellis, 1969). Because of this and the nature of her tasks, temporarily floating in nurses from elsewhere when staff is short provides little in the way of help; indeed, this may even prove a hindrance. Yet, ICU nurses are fully able to fill in elsewhere when staff shortages occur; and they are not infrequently asked to do so, leaving the ICU understaffed.

The emergency situation provides added work. Although an ICU's routine is another floor's emergency, obviously there are frequent situations of acute crisis, such as cardiac arrest. These require the nurse's full attention and prevent her from continuing her regular tasks on her other patients. A few remaining nurses must watch and calm all other patients, complete as many of their regular observations and treatments as possible, and prevent other emergencies. Meanwhile, the nurses assisting at the emergency are called upon not only to do things rapidly but to make immediate and accurate decisions that oftentimes include determining the priority of several emergencies (Vreeland & Ellis, 1969).

Habituation is both inevitable and necessary if the nurse is not to work in an exhausted state of chronic crisis. Yet, she must maintain an underlying alertness to discern and respond to cues which have special meaning. This is like the mother who hears the faint cry of her baby over the commotion of a party.

Nor is the work without its physical dangers, and the nurses know this. It is impossible to take fully adequate isolation precautions against infections because of time pressures and the bodily intimacy required to provide the needed level of care. Portable x-rays are sometimes taken with inadequately shielded nurses holding immobile patients in proper positioning. Heavy comatose patients must be lifted. Sharp needles, scalpels, etc., must be handled rapidly. Electric equipment must be moved, adjusted, and attached. Physical assaults on nurses by a delirious patient, though infrequent, can and do occur.

There are occasions also when distraught relatives misinterpret a situation, feel that their loved one is getting inadequate care and become verbally—and sometimes physically—abusive. The roots of these more dramatic misunderstandings lie in more general problems about visitors. On other floors, visiting hours occur daily at specified times, but in the ICU, there can be no such routinized schedule. Close relatives are allowed to see the patient at any time of the day or night. Though restricted to a brief (commonly 5-minute) period, their presence soon becomes a burden. In his constant inquiries about the patient's condition and prognosis, the relative is asking for more than information. He is seeking reassurance and support (Salter, 1970; Vreeland & Ellis, 1969). The nurse may wish to respond at this deeper level, but usually she cannot, because she has tasks that require more immediate attention. The relative, feeling rebuffed, begins to critically scrutinize the nurse's every action. With so much to be upset about, he is prone to jump to unwarranted conclusions. While many visitors see the nurses as "angels of mercy," others develop a projection of their worst fears. Seeing a nurse spend more time with another patient, he may feel his loved one is not getting adequate attention. Or, he may see blood, vomitus, or excreta soiling the patient's bed and misinterpret this as an indication of poor care, not appreciating the nurse's preoccupation with lifesaving activities. Moreover the nurse has little escape from hovering relatives: she has "no place to hide."

DOCTORS AND ADMINISTRATORS

Visitors are not the only ones who cause problems. Some of the very people who might be expected to provide substantial support add to the stresses on the nurse. The potentially fatal outcome in the gravely ill ICU patients tends to stimulate feelings of frustration, self-doubt and guilt in their physicians. The ways he deals with these may have major consequences for the nurse. He may, for example, use projection and behave in a surly, querulous manner. He may bolster his self-esteem by becoming imperious and demand that the nurses "wait on" him.[2] He may also rely on avoidance as a way of distancing himself from his feelings about his seeming failure as a lifesaver. Though the nurse must remain on the unit for almost her entire shift, the physician can make good use of his prerogatives to move about freely. Especially at the time of a patient's death, the physician seems to have a way of not being present; the full burden of breaking the news and supporting the family through the acute grief reaction is left to the nurse to handle as best she can. Conversely, compensatory overzealousness may occur, and unnecessary heroic gestures be made to save someone beyond recovery. The physician may order special treatments and an unrealistic frequency of monitoring. The not uncommon incongruity of orders is especially revealing about this. A patient on "q15 minute" vital signs will have nothing done—and correctly so—when these deteriorate. Or, the physician will recognize the inappropriateness of frequent monitoring, yet insist on fruitless *emergency* attempts at resuscitation (e.g., a pacemaker) when death supervenes. This not only increases the nurse's work load but adds to her frustration by diverting her energies from patients who could be saved.

·   ·   ·   ·

[2] Another factor in this overdemanding behavior may be his sense of inadequacy and self-doubt if he is unfamiliar with the unit and its highly organized functions (Kornfeld, 1969b). This may culminate in his issuing dictatorial orders and commands that are not commensurate with the realities of the situation.

THE PSYCHOLOGICAL EXPERIENCE

We will now shift from a situational frame of reference to a psychological one and take a closer look at the concerns and feelings of ICU nurses. We will also examine the adaptive devices, individual and group, which they use to cope with their situation.

The work load, so great in its sheer quantity, is unusual also in its variety and the intricacy of its tasks as well as in the rapidity with which these must be performed. Great flexibility is required (which may partly explain why ICU nurses are predominantly in their early twenties).

Mistakes are, of course, inevitable. But, when every procedure is potentially lifesaving, any error may be life-endangering. Hence the ICU nurse lives chronically under a cloud of latent anxiety. The new nurse, particularly, begins to view the never-ending, life-dependent tasks as a specter of potential mistakes and their imagined dreadful sequelae. Some, of course, cannot shake this and soon arrange a transfer. The experienced nurse achieves a more realistic perspective, but a degree of residual uncertainty always remains, given the complexity of machines and procedures. Especially at times of stress, she too may become anxious. When this anxiety exceeds minimal levels, it reduces efficiency and decision-making capacity, inviting additional mistakes—the classic vicious circle.

When the inevitable error does occur, the nurse is in a dilemma. To make it public is likely to enhance her guilt and invite criticism. Moreover, it leads to the need to fill out an incident report, a further drain on her time and a potential blot on her record. Yet to fail to do so may compound the error by blocking corrective treatment. The experienced nurse develops a subtle adaptive compromise, reporting serious mistakes but fudging-over inconsequential ones. In either case, she must live with her guilt.

The ICU nurse has much in which she can take great pride. Yet her self-esteem takes an awful beating in many ways. Her awareness of her mistakes, both real and exaggerated, is one such factor. Another is her repeated "failure." The ultimate goal of the health professions is to save lives; yet, frequently, her patients die. Nor do the dying patients or mourning relatives provide much source of gratification, as do patients on other floors who go home well. (Even the

ICU major successes are usually still seriously ill and are merely transferred.) On the bulletin boards of other units there are warm, sentimental cards and notes of appreciation. In the ICU, the cards are of a different and macabre quality. They say: "Thank you. You did all you could."

Further, the deaths provide a situation of repetitive object-loss, the intensity of which parallels the degree to which the nurse has cathected her patient. The intimacy afforded by the amount and frequency of direct personal contact, involving some of the most private aspects of life, promotes this attachment. This is further enhanced when the patient is conscious and verbal, since he is then so obviously human. Young patients are easily identified with friends and spouses—or with the self, stimulating anxiety about one's own vulnerability. In this country, with its cultural premium on youth, the death of a young patient tends to be regarded as inherently more tragic. Older patients may become transference objects of parental or grandparental figures.

All these warm personal attachments obviously provide great comfort for patients and family and make the job worthwhile. But they expose the nurse to a sense of loss when the patient dies. The balance is a delicate one. With comatose patients, it is easy to limit emotional involvement and subsequent grief. But here, paradoxically, one often sees the nurse project vital qualities into her patient.[3]

The threat of object-loss is pervasive. The nurse simply must protect herself—from grief, anxiety, guilt, rage, exhausted overcommitment, overstimulation, and all the rest. She has no physical escape. But she can avoid, or at least attenuate, the meaning and emotional impact of her work (Rome, 1969). For example, she may relate more to the machines than to the patient. And it comes as a surprise to an outsider to observe routinely some of the nurses in the ICU joking and laughing. Even whistling and singing may be observed, phenomena which are inexplicable and unforgivable to distraught relatives. Some of this ebullience arises as a natural product of the friendly behavior of young people working closely together. But a

---

[3] Sometimes this mechanism backfires in an interesting way. The nurse begins to project specific attributes onto the comatose patient. When he recovers and asserts his real personality, especially if this has unpleasant characteristics, she feels a sense of disappointment and betrayal.

major aspect is gross denial as a defense against their stressful situation. Schizoid withdrawal or a no-nonsense businesslike manner (isolation) also are used, but cheerful denial is more common. The defensive and, at times, brittle nature of this response is especially evident at times of crisis. At a lull in procedures after a cardiac arrest, for example, giggling and outrageous joking of near hysterical proportion suddenly may supervene. Sometimes the blowup is in the form of anger. But, there are great constraints placed upon the expression of anger by the situation and the group.

THE GROUP

The new ICU nurse experiences the trials of her early days on the job as a *rite de passage.* Some do not make it through. Those who do, learn that they have become members of a special, tightly knit group.[4] Naturally, they work together on a common job, sharing common experiences. But, there is far more to it than this. Most have volunteered. They have one of the most difficult jobs in the hospital. Nowhere else does a nurse so often literally save lives by her own direct actions. It stands to reason that nurses who operate special machines and perform special procedures for special patients must be special too! Rightfully, they take pride in their abilities and accomplishments. The very stressfulness of the job is a further source of pride, albeit with masochistic overtones. Like Commandos or Green Berets, they have the toughest, dirtiest, most dangerous assignment; and they "accomplish the impossible."

Further cementing group ties are the conditions of work. They carry on their duties in a common area, using common equipment (Vreeland & Ellis, 1969). In emergency situations particularly, they share the responsibility for each other's patients. Even in non-emergency situations there is a general factor of enforced interdependency. Routinely, for example, one nurse must ask another to cover her patients when she goes for a meal. Here an unspoken but potent group norm becomes manifest. Refusal is impossible. Cooperation is absolutely essential for unit function. When a nurse returns from an absence, she may well find that only the most minimal monitoring

[4] We have seen similar, though usually less intense, group formation among psychiatric nursing personnel, for some of the same reasons.

has been carried out on her patient. No matter how justified its basis, she is likely to be irritated. Yet, group pressures for cooperation and the very fact that there is no time for anger on the job make it imperative to suppress or repress the hostility. These same forces inhibit the expressions of anger that arise inevitably during the course of everyday work when people are in regular close contact. In the total context, this ambivalent hostility serves to bind the group ties with still more intensity.

At the end of a shift of constant work and emotional turmoil, it is nearly impossible for the nurse to "turn it off" and return to normal pursuits. She needs to unwind. To do so requires the understanding ear of someone who knows what she has been through. Who then is a more logical choice for an off-duty companion than another ICU nurse? Thus, one finds much group social activity: parties, showers, and just informal, off-duty get-togethers. While these might provide an opportunity to express interpersonal hostility, they more often result in "bull sessions" of shared experiences and problems. Similar discussions take place at lunch or coffee breaks, to which they go preferentially with coworkers. These shared feelings feed back to enhance group ties further.

External forces further define the group. The ICU is typically located in an area away from other nursing units. Frequently ICU nurses wear scrub gowns or other protective devices to decrease contamination and soiling; thus they have a distinctive uniform. Very significant is the attitude of other nurses throughout the hospital. Many tend to regard ICU nurses with considerable ambivalence in which envy and projection play a part, and react to being treated as outsiders by retaliatory disregard, isolating the group further.

Group cohesiveness is a logical solution to the multiple practical problems on the job and provides essential emotional support. Being a part of a special group is a major advantage in bolstering the nurse's pride and strength. However, there are not so desirable consequences. The force of the group and the extent of its activities can become all-encompassing, taking over the roles of family and friends. Thus, it can interfere with personal autonomy and outside social relationships. The pressures of the job and group activities may limit healthy introspection. (This may have temporary adaptive value for the girl beset with life problems, or tangled in inner conflict, allowing her to retrench while thus losing herself. But obviously, this can be seriously maladaptive if pursued as a long-term escape.) Absence from the group due to a concurrent social activity may be seen unconsciously as disloyal by both the nurse and the group, though inevitably the familial and social aspect of the group will wear thin for the girl who has achieved maturity and seeks a life of her own. Yet the nurse who fails to use the group may find herself taking out the tensions of work on her family. She may let off steam to a boyfriend, roommate, or husband. But soon, she learns that this can strain the relationship since the person on the receiving end cannot know what it is like to work in the ICU.

Group loyalty reinforces work pressure in stimulating guilt about any absence. The nurse with a minor illness (or one suffering from "combat exhaustion") cannot, in good conscience, stay away as she should. This would increase the work load for her peers. If she does stay home, she cannot "rest easy." Nor, as described above, can she say no to a request to cover another girl's patients, even if she is already working at peak load. This would violate the group norms and threaten the shared fantasy of omnipotence linked to the concept of being special and to the defensive denial of anxiety about mistakes.

This same mechanism can work also to the collective detriment of the group. Like the individual nurse, the group self-destructively cannot say no to situations where its total work load is unrealistic. Paradoxically, the individual almost never can get the group to support protests about realistic problems or unfair exploitation so that changes can be made. Intragroup competitiveness and rivalry may play a part in this. The nurse who will not tailor constructive criticism to the group norm finds she must leave. Since many such nurses will be thoughtful, aggressive people with good ideas, leadership potential is drained away. The whole situation lends itself to perpetuating the status quo and to no recourse but permanent flight (i.e., resignation) when the pressures on an individual build to the point of intolerability.

SOME POSSIBLE SOLUTIONS

From the foregoing, it seems obvious that a constructive approach will capitalize on the many positive aspects of the group process, while attenuating its pathological features. One excellent way to accomplish this is through regular group meetings devoted to exploring the work experience, especially its stressful aspects (Kornfeld, 1969b). These discussions can provide: (a) an avenue for ventilating suppressed intragroup hostilities as well as shared gripes; (b) a recognition that fears, doubts, guilt, and uncertainty are shared, acceptable feelings; (c) the abreaction and working through of feelings aroused at times of stress but which cannot be expressed due to work demands; (d) the sharing of innovative *ad hoc* techniques which individuals have found helpful in dealing with problems arising on the job; (e) recognition of realistic superior abilities and their delineation from masochistic fantasies of omnipotence; (f) a realization that minor mistakes are ubiquitous and inevitable, leading to the detoxification of guilt and shame; and (g) the development of constructive solutions for problems and effective suggestions for communication to administration.

·   ·   ·   ·

While this group process can enhance the appropriate sense of pride and "special-ness," more can be done to bolster self-esteem. Here, we have something to learn from studies of morale in combat troups (Grinker & Spiegel, 1945). A distinctive uniform or an identifying patch may be helpful. A small pay differential, like that paid for special shifts, "hazardous duty pay," is an indication of special regard as well as a material reward. Periodic, brief, extra vacations (R and R—Rest and Recreation Leave) will do the same. Such periods might involve work on other nursing units rather than a true vacation, thereby providing education and communication for both staffs. One might consider also whether there should be a finite tour of duty on the ICU, with an enforced interval before a second tour. At the least, transfer to another unit should be made accessible and free from stigma; our experience suggests that often ICU nurses work past the point of "combat exhaustion" and then resign, sometimes with a sense of failure.

Another alternative might be to create a Unit Coordinator position through which the ICU nurses would periodically rotate. Freed from the regular nursing role and its duties, she could fulfill a number of important functions. In an emergency, she could help the head nurse organize the situation or provide an often crucial extra pair of hands.

She could help orient new personnel. When consulting physicians arrive on the unit, she could familiarize them with its facilities and routine, thereby reducing their need for direct nursing assistance. She could serve as a major communication link with visitors, providing them with crucial emotional support, and keeping them "out of the hair" of others.

Competitive selection of nurses with superior skills appropriate for the job also will add to pride. In addition to technical expertise, applicants should be screened for psychological aptitude, perhaps by the liaison psychiatrist. In any event, an initial period of training and orientation (Boklage, 1970) is essential, and should focus on job characteristics specific to the ICU. The group leader(s) should play a major role in this, so that the psychological aspects of the job experience are fully considered.

A sufficiently large nursing staff is necessary to allow coverage for vacations, weekends, and holidays without the use of outside "floating" assignees. The special characteristics of the unit should also be reflected in the assignment of other personnel. Insofar as the acuteness of its patients and the difficulty of their care are concerned, the ICU is highly specialized. In another sense, however, it is general: it provides care for almost every type of disease process. To provide the full range of treatment required, and to do so on a 24-hour, everyday basis, means that the ICU must be "a hospital within a hospital." Thus representatives of all relevant hospital services always must be at hand. Given a unit of sufficient size, a permanent pharmacist, inhalation therapist, x-ray technician, etc., may become a necessity as part of the regular ICU staff. At the very least, the person "on call" in each of these fields should be given the ICU as his regular assignment to ensure familiarity with the unit.

A *full-time* physician is an especial necessity, constantly and immediately available to examine patients, and as a source of information, advice, and support (Kornfeld, 1969a). Whether a member of the attending or house staff, he must be delegated sufficient authority to be able to write new "orders" whenever indicated by the constantly changing condition of the patients, without necessarily consulting senior physicians of the specialty services to which the patients may be administratively assigned.

·   ·   ·   ·

CONCLUSIONS

Perhaps it will seem as if we have been overly dramatic in our descriptions of the ICU as being so stressful. Most such units function very well. Other parts of the hospital (e.g., emergency and operating rooms) share many of the same stresses; and each deserves examination to understand its particular features. Moreover, nurses who work in the ICU do so by choice, suggesting that, for them, other assignments might be less gratifying or even more stressful. Yet, we believe that the seeming dramatization is, on careful scrutiny, an accurate portrayal and that the intensity and variety of the sources of stress in the ICU is somewhat unique. In any event, stress is there. Doubtless it is useful to an extent, enabling the nurses to maintain their critical alertness and ability to respond effectively to the needs of their patients. Yet there are many signs that its intensity goes well beyond this adaptive level. And since there are approaches to deal with this, it behooves us to utilize these for the benefit of both staff and patients.

10

Environmental Stress and the Adaptive
Process

DAVID C. GLASS
and
JEROME E. SINGER

NOISE AS A STRESSOR

We suggested [in an earlier part of this study] that the effort entailed
in adapting to aversive events may be achieved at some expense to
the individual's behavioral functioning. Alternatively, deleterious aftereffects may be the direct result of a cumulative experience of
stress, despite the fact that the individual has adapted to repeated occurrences of the aversive event. In either case, we might expect task
degradations and other impairments of behavior following termination of the stressor. Any number of stimuli could have been used to
test for these effects, including such familiar procedures as electric
shock, the cold-pressor test, sudden noise, attacks on the self-esteem
of subjects, and routinized performance of frustrating tasks. Unfortunately, there is no set of rules about why this variety of stimulus conditions produces the reactions typically identified as stress. Indeed,
there is evidence suggesting that different stressors produce different
consequences (Appley & Trumbull, 1967a; Parsons, 1966), in which
case it would be unwise to treat various stressor stimuli as equivalent.

We were faced, therefore, with the necessity of selecting a single
aversive event that would enable us to test our basic hypothesis about
behavioral aftereffects of stress and adaptation. As we noted in the
previous chapter, high-intensity broad-band noise was selected as the
principal source of stress. We chose noise for three reasons: (1) it is

easier to manipulate in the laboratory than many other stressors; (2) people more frequently encounter it than they do stressors such as electric shock and hypoxic atmospheres; (3) it is alleged to be an increasingly important hazard to public health in modern cities. The latter point had a particular attraction for us, since there is a growing concern in psychology (e.g., Miller, 1969), with which we agree, to engage in research having relevance to pressing social problems. The public policy implications of the effects of noise satisfy requirements of relevance.

There are many ways in which noise can be defined, some technical, others popular. It can be considered as "random fluctuations . . . which distort all observations" (Freeman, 1958); as a broadband energy without periodicity (Burns, 1968); or as any unwanted sound (Berrien, 1946; Rodda, 1967). The latter definition implies that noise is any sound that is physiologically arousing and harmful, subjectively annoying, or disruptive of performance (Anastasi, 1964). We follow this definition throughout the monograph.

But do we have any evidence that noise is in fact a stressor and that measurable consequences result from its repeated application? There have been dozens of newspaper accounts and magazine stories (e.g., Bailey, 1969; Blum, 1967; Mecklin, 1969) that suggest an affirmative answer. The mere fact that many cities have created task forces on noise control (e.g., Anderson, 1970) affirms that noise is one of "the most impertinent of all interruptions." However, psychoacousticians are not all convinced that noise has deleterious consequences for man.[1] Comprehensive reviews of systematic research on noise (Broadbent, 1957; Kryter, 1950, 1970) conclude that there is no compelling evidence of adverse effects of noise, *per se,* on mental and psychomotor performance, providing the tasks do not involve auditory communication. A typical explanation of the null effect is that man adapts to the noise and any initial task deficits soon disappear.

---

[1] They are not, of course, referring to hearing loss due to repeated exposure to high-intensity noise. There is a sizable literature on temporary and permanent threshold shifts (e.g., Glorig, 1958; Kryter, 1970) which shows that loud noise can damage the peripheral mechanisms of hearing, and the development of damage-risk criteria for exposure to sound has been increasingly occupying the energies of large numbers of psychoacousticians (e.g., Kryter et al., 1966). More recently, we have seen studies of auditory fatigue and permanent hearing defects from rock-and-roll music. At least one controlled experiment (Dey, 1970) has demonstrated such effects.

Positive effects of noise have even been noted, as where it masks distracting sounds (Rodda, 1967), stimulates the individual to remain alert on an otherwise boring task (McGrath & Hatcher, 1961), or arouses a sleep-deprived subject to perform better than under quiet conditions (Wilkinson, 1969). A recent summary of conclusions drawn from research on noise and human task performance is contained in the following excerpt from Kryter.

. . . [O]ther than as a damaging agent to the ear and as a masker of auditory information noise will not harm the organism or interfere with mental or motor performance. Man should be able, according to this concept, to adapt physiologically to his noise environment, with only transitory interference effects of physiological and mental and motor behavior activities during this period of adaptation (1970, p. 587).

Another body of systematic research, however, suggests that high-intensity noise does have negative effects on performance. A major contributor of this evidence is D. E. Broadbent (e.g., 1958). His experimental paradigm usually involves a vigilance task in which the subject is required to maintain long-term monitoring of various dials, any one of which may unexpectedly show a deflection. Signal detection on such tasks is adversely affected by high-intensity noise (Broadbent, 1954; Jerison & Wing, 1957). Other studies have shown that task degradations are most likely to occur on those complex tasks that exceed the individual's total information-processing capacity. Thus Boggs and Simon (1968) demonstrated that 92-dB noise produced significantly greater increments in auditory monitoring errors when the monitoring task was paired with a complex reaction-time task than with a simple reaction-time task. Several studies have demonstrated that the nature of the noise is critical to the demonstration of task impairments; that is, intermittent noise has a greater tendency to impair performance than does steady noise. Smith (1951) has shown that subjects exposed to 100-dB intermittent sound bursts 10 to 50 seconds in length tried more items on name and number checking tests, and scored more correctly and incorrectly than the control group. Corso (1952) and Woodhead (1959) have replicated these effects, and Sanders (1961) has shown that randomly varying noise intensities also produce greater impairment on mental tasks than does steady noise. Although not explicitly so done in these intermittent-noise studies, it is reasonable to describe the noise bursts as aperiodic or unpredictable, in which case we may conclude that unpredictable sound has a more aversive impact on performance than predictable sound. We will return to this point later in the section.

There is still another psychological factor that appears to affect the noise—performance relationship. Azrin (1958) reports that high-intensity sound can become an aversive stimulus and reduce performance quality if it becomes associated with incorrect behavior. He has also shown that noise can facilitate task performance if it is perceived as rewarding, or contains information relevant to the task. Kryter has suggested that experimental results showing noise-induced task degradations (e.g., vigilance task data) may be attributable to such "stimulus and response contingency interpretations of the meaning of the noise by the subjects" (1970, p. 556). For example, the task becomes disliked and is performed poorly because it is seen as contingent on the noise (stimulus contingency), or subjects view noise as punishment and are motivated to perform better if they believe their responses will reduce the noise. What Kryter seems to be saying here is that the context in which noise occurs is a principal determinant of its effects on task performance. As we noted earlier, one way of coping with urban stress is to pay less and less attention to each stimulus, lessening the impact of each (Milgram, 1970). But this strategy can only work if one is willing to forego the information contained in the stimulus. Little is gained if, after asking a passerby in the city for directions to your destination, you ignore his answer. When noise is actually, or is perceived to be, part of a necessary task, it is less easily ignored and consequently shows greater task-related effects.

Stressful effects of noise can be assessed not only by performance deficits, but also by subjective reports of annoyance. That noise is considered a nuisance by most people would hardly seem to require documentation, yet there is considerable literature on the problem indicating that persons exposed to noise object to it (Broadbent, 1957; McKennell & Hunt, 1966). Among the factors affecting degree of annoyance are such properties of the sound as intensity, frequency, aperiodicity, and unexpectedness (Kryter, 1970). Even more important, perhaps, in determining degree of annoyance are various psychological and sociological factors. Thus, for example, the extent to which people take actions to control environmental noise reduces the annoyance caused by the noise. A survey by Irle and Rohrmann (1968) of several hundred men and women living near the Hamburg airport showed that those who did not attempt to escape from aircraft noise reported being more sensitive to and annoyed by noise than those who said they had taken a variety of direct actions, such as insulating their walls, attending protest meetings, and so forth. Aside from the factor of control, other studies have shown that individual differences play an important role in noise tolerance. Thus, anxiety neurotics suffer more under noise than do nonneurotic subjects (Jansen, 1969), and even sociocultural backgrounds have been found to contribute to differences in complaints about noise (Jonsson et al., 1969). Studies by Kryter (1968) indicate that the specific noise levels found unacceptable also depend on the activity in which the individual is engaged; that is, variations in work and living requirements result in different sound-level tolerabilities. In addition, Broadbent (1957) has noted that the source of noise may affect degree of annoyance. Special meanings associated with given sources require different tolerable limits for different noises; for example, the sound of a neighbor slamming a door is more annoying than the sound of a truck delivering a parcel to the neighbor. At times, even the same noise may receive different interpretations. Our secretary's typewriter is less annoying than that of a colleague's secretary.

If noise causes annoyance, it is entirely possible that mental disorders are correlated with prolonged exposure to noise. Clinical experience suggests that there is such a relationship. For example, Tomkins (in Blum, 1967) asserts that "since a high level of noise arouses in us either distress or anger . . . we're paying a very high price for the noise that surrounds us . . . we are all much more ready to cry or become angry than we need to be." This tendency to "fly off the handle" at the least provocation has received much anecdotal documentation (e.g., New York Post, April 16, 1968; New York Times, March 2, 1970). Consider the former newspaper account. Four boys were playing in a Bronx residential neighborhood. They were shouting and running in and out of an apartment building. Suddenly, there was a pistol shot from a second-floor window and one of the boys fell dead on the pavement. The killer eventually confessed to police that he was a nightworker, and that he lost control of himself because the noise was interfering with his sleep (Mecklin, 1969). An extreme example, perhaps, but it does lend support to the allegation of disturbed emotional consequences stemming from noise exposure.

Systematic evidence for this relationship is, however, far from conclusive. Rodda (1967) cites data from a survey of aircraft carrier crews which showed no evidence of a higher incidence of mental disorders among this group as compared with military personnel who were not exposed to intense noise. On the other hand, Jansen (1961) found that steelworkers in the noisiest work environments had a higher frequency of social conflict at home and in the plant. Weybrew (1967) also notes that under conditions of prolonged noise exposure, most people show symptoms of irritability and aggression. However, all of these and related studies are subject to criticism on one or more methodological grounds. It is therefore premature to conclude that there is or is not a relationship between noise exposure and emotional disturbance.

A third way of assessing the stressful impact of noise is through measurements of physiological functioning. The former Surgeon General of the United States, William H. Stewart, has stated that noise produces physiological changes such as "cardiovascular, glandular, and respiratory effects reflective of a generalized stress reaction" (1969, p. 9), and Rosen has given the following summary of nonauditory reactions to loud noise: "The [peripheral] blood vessels constrict, the skin pales, the pupils dilate, the eyes close, one winces, holds the breath, and the voluntary and involuntary muscles tense. Gastric secretion diminishes and the diastolic pressure increases. Adrenaline is suddenly injected into the blood stream . . ." (Rosen, 1970, p. 57). To this list might be added GSR increments, and certain chemical changes in the blood and urine from glandular stimulation. There is experimental evidence to support these statements (cf. reviews by Broadbent, 1957; Kryter, 1950, 1970; Plutchik, 1959), and the work of Davis (e.g., Davis, Buchwald, & Frankmann, 1959) and Jansen (e.g., 1969) has been particularly important in demonstrating autonomic responses to high-intensity sound. Davis notes that these responses cannot necessarily be called "fear" or "startle," for some of them are associated with emotion-arousing stimulation whereas others are related to emotion-suppressing activities of the autonomic nervous system. There is usually a change in heart rate from startle that is not found in the arousal caused by noise. It has been alleged, and there is some support for the allegation (e.g., Teichner, Arees, & Reilley, 1963) that autonomic arousal, not S—R or cognitive linkages, is responsible for the noise-associated task impairments described above. This notion is consistent with the assumption that noise produces stress arousal and concomitant behavioral consequences.

More important, perhaps, than physiological response to noise is the pervasive phenomenon of adaptation to sound. All laboratory tests show that autonomic adaptation or habituation invariably occurs with repeated presentations of noise (Kryter, 1970). This does not mean, however, that people experience the noise as acceptable. Data on annoyance reactions cited above are a case in point, for people continue to complain about intense sound even though they show physiological adaptation. There is also some evidence that autonomic reactions do not always wane with repeated noise presentations. Jansen (1969) reports that subjects continued to show constriction of the peripheral blood vessels when exposed to noise for the successive times they returned to the laboratory. Other studies have found similar effects. Rosen cites research indicating that "while after 5 minutes of noise, constriction of the blood vessels begins to disappear, the reaction may persist for as much as 25 minutes before disappearing completely" (Rosen, 1970, p. 57). Still other data show that if the noise occurs in a particular cognitive context, physiological adaptation may not occur. For example, Davis and Berry (1964) found that subjects who could avoid a loud tone by pushing a switch at the correct time exhibited greater gastrointestinal motility during the tone (i.e., when they failed to press the switch) than did subjects who had no means of avoiding the same tone. The noise became a more aversive stimulus because it signified incorrect behavior (see the Azrin study cited earlier in this section).

There is also evidence of harmful physiological effects because of longterm exposure to noise. Data from industrial settings suggest greater circulatory, heart, and equilibrium problems in workers from more intense noise environments than from less intense environments (e.g., Jansen, 1961). However, Kryter (1970) correctly points out that other important factors in these industrial situations (e.g., poor ventilation, anxiety over job security, danger from accidents) may be responsible for the presumably noise-induced health problems. In short, there is really little evidence to connect noise with identifiable physical disease (Burns, 1968; Kryter, 1970), but the possibility cannot be completely dismissed at this time. Even if intense noise does not produce measurable effects on health, it does induce stress under certain conditions, with a resultant increase in autonomic reactions, irritability, and social conflicts at work and at home (Cohen, 1969).

To sum up, there are three ways in which noise-produced stress may be exhibited: by disruption of ongoing tasks or behaviors; by subjective displeasure or annoyance as indexed by complaints; and by reaction of autonomic, cardiovascular, and neuromuscular systems. We may relate these three types of measures by stating that aside from reactions of annoyance, high-intensity noise does not have adverse effects on performance probably because of the adaptation of disruptive physiological and behavior responses. There are, however, data that seem to disagree with this conclusion. First, there is evidence that autonomic reactivity does not always habituate with repeated noise presentations, and that even when it does, initial physiological responses to noise have been shown to correlate with initial impairments of task performance. Second, task degradations that do not disappear with habituation are noted when: (a) the performance entails long-term vigilance; (b) the task is otherwise complex; (c) the noise itself is intermittent; and (d) the noise occurs in a context in which the individual associates it with certain stimulus and response contingencies.

There is one general consistency in these exceptions to the conclusion that noise, *per se,* does not have adverse effects on behavior. All four cases appear to reflect the operation, not of noise alone, but of noise mediated by cognitive processes. The first two are presumably situations in which the organism becomes overloaded; that is, task inputs are so numerous as to inhibit adequate information processing, and the noise becomes still another input for the organism to monitor (Weitz, 1970). The noise continually overloads the subject and in such a situation produces performance deficits that do not wane with repeated exposure. The deleterious effects of intermittent noise probably reflect the fact that such noise is often aperiodic, and unpredictable stressors have a more aversive impact on behavior than predictable stressors (e.g., Berlyne, 1960; Broadbent, 1957). Indeed, it has been suggested that where sound is aperiodic or unexpected, the absence of precise knowledge about when to anticipate the stimulus services to increase its unpleasant effects (Broadbent, 1957). We may suppose, therefore, that unpredictable noise has consequences equal to those of a higher-intensity predictable noise, and to the extent that intensity relates to performance, the individual should have greater difficulty in performing under unpredictable than predictable noise stimulation. The fourth case, stimulus and response contingencies, also reflects the impact of cognitive processes, for such contingencies really refer to the information or signal value of the sound. If the subject associates noise with punishment, task performance is impaired. If he associates it with reward, or if the noise contains task-relevant information, performance is facilitated, or at least remains unimpaired.

That the effects of noise should depend on cognitive factors is nicely consistent with our earlier discussion of the role of cognition in stress arousal and reduction. It would appear that high-intensity noise becomes a stressor contingent on the cognitive and social context in which stimulation occurs. But it is also true that physiological and behavioral adaptation to noise eventually occurs even in these special contexts. To return to our original question, are these adaptations achieved at some cost to the individual such that deleterious behavioral aftereffects are observed? And do such consequences vary with the meanings attributed to the noise as it originally occurred? Unfortunately, there is a virtual absence of systematic research demonstrating postnoise effects, and there is certainly no evidence linking performance impairments after noise exposure with the adaptive process itself. This monograph is designed to fill these gaps in our knowledge.

section III

~~~~~~

THE NATURE OF COPING

Section III marks a transition from an emphasis on the nature of stress to the ways in which people handle stress, i.e., coping behaviors. The readings in this section deal primarily with issues relevant to coping processes and styles, with the former articles being largely, though not exclusively, theoretical and the latter primarily descriptive. The selections by Lazarus (1974a), Menninger (1954), and Spiro (1965) provide different though not incompatible perspectives on coping processes and their contributions to, and relationships with, the self-regulation of emotion, the degree of threat, and religious ideology. Shapiro (1965) and Friedman and Rosenman (1974), on the other hand, deal with various coping styles or dispositions and how they affect our daily lives and our health.

In his paper on emotions, Lazarus (1974a) emphasizes the key role of cognitive processes in coping activity and the importance of coping in determining the quality and intensity of emotional reactions. There is impressive anecdotal and research evidence suggesting that we are constantly "self-regulating" our emotional reactions, e.g., escaping or postponing unpleasant situations, actively changing threatening conditions, deceiving ourselves about the implications of certain facts, or simply learning to detach ourselves from unpleasant situations (like medical students witnessing an autopsy—see Lief & Fox, 1963). Lazarus's emphasis is on the individual (i.e., the *self*) actively appraising the situation and what he or she can do, rather than on the environmental contingencies presumably manipulating the individual's behavior (e.g., Skinner, 1953). These alternative outlooks constitute one of the major ideological splits in modern psychology, and reflect very different ways of defining the problem of emotion and in designing research observations.

Menninger (1954) offers a classification of coping processes based upon the influential concept that the ego, or executive function of the psyche, is a homeostatic regulator. In an effort to maintain psychic equilibrium, the ego employs coping techniques appropriate to the degree of threat that is perceived. Minor stresses are typically handled by fairly "healthy" or "normal" devices while more severe or prolonged stresses require the ego to expend more energy and employ rather "primitive" strategies in an effort to avoid psychological disintegration. Menninger views coping devices as being hierarchically arranged (along a continuum) into five differentiable though often overlapping groups, each representing increasingly greater degrees of failure in ego functioning. For example, stress-relieving efforts of the "first and second order" are temporary emergency devices including efforts at self-control, increased alertness or vigilance, and fantasy, while efforts of the "fifth order" may reach the point of violent loss of control and death.

Menninger's article, though interesting and thought-provoking, is not without its problems and biases. Notice, for example, how Menninger devotes essentially his entire article to "failures" of coping, thus almost completely ignoring "successful" coping devices—and, in fact, though he mentions so-called "normal" or "healthy" devices, these are never described. Also, the issue of measuring or scaling the degree of threat and/or degree of primitivity is largely side-stepped. In order to avoid circularity, we must be able to assess independently threat and its effects, and Menninger does not explicitly indicate techniques for achieving this. Despite these shortcomings, Menninger's work is a pioneering effort to classify coping devices and provides an interesting parallel (on the psychological level) with the work on bodily homeostasis by noted research physiologists (e.g., Cannon, 1929; Selye, 1956). (For a more thorough account of Menninger's views on coping and stress, see his influential 1963 book.)

In Section II, we saw how cultures may influence our appraisals of stress (e.g., Cannon, 1942). Spiro (1965), focusing on coping, presents a similar argument but from a slightly different perspective, namely, that religion often serves as a highly efficient coping device by being a culturally constituted and approved defense mechanism. To illustrate this, Spiro examines the personalities of Burmese Buddhist monks by studying data obtained from interviews and Rorschach test protocols and concludes that the monks display a clear picture of psychopathology—i.e., they are highly defensive, show regressed expression of oral and anal drives, are latent homosexuals, etc. However, in addition to their private coping resources, the monks are also able to use one provided by their culture, namely, the traditions of the monastic order. Religious tradition, argues Spiro, resolves the inner conflicts of the Burmese male by allowing expression and gratification of their drives in a disguised and socially acceptable manner, thus precluding mental disorders, like schizophrenia, and/or social punishment. Although stress may be resolved by idiosyncratic strategies (leading often to neurosis and psychosis), "culturally constituted defenses" protect both the individual and society from the disruptive consequences of powerful needs and private defensive maneuvers.

While Spiro's views on religion as a defense against inner conflicts are fascinating and in line with general psychoanalytic thought (cf. Ellenberger, 1970), other interpretations of his observations are certainly possible. For example, one could argue that the monks show "pathological" Rorschach responses because of the type of life they lead, rather than because of personality traits presumably existing even before they entered the monastic order. Specifically, in an all-male vocation which forbids work and encourages "an exclusively otherworldly existence," a withdrawal from reality, and meditation, it is not surprising to find Rorschach responses indicating "erotic self-cathexis," latent homosexuality, avoidance of "emotionally ladened" situations, etc. The fact that these characteristics are also found in the Burmese layman, though to a lesser degree, may also suggest they are positive attributes in that society and, therefore, are striven for consciously rather than resulting from unconscious defense mechanisms.

The neurotic has often been described as an individual who persistently experiences feelings of threat and anxiety and must rely increasingly on neurotic patterns for relieving these stresses (e.g., Coleman, 1976). In our next selection, Shapiro (1965), adopting a psychoanalytic orientation, maintains that neurotic "styles," that is, consistent ways of perceiving, thinking, feeling, and behaving characteristic of the various neurotic conditions, are basically major forms of coping with stress which have become well entrenched in every area of psychological functioning. The selection included here gives a descriptive clinical account of the rigidity in thinking and sense of being "driven" which characterize one particular neurotic style, the obsessive-compulsive. Notice how this style narrowly focuses the person's attention to avoid new facts and different points of view—a coping strategy, one might argue, used to overcome anxiety generated by doubt and uncertainty (Buss, 1966). While rigidity and overconcern for detail may limit aspects of the obsessive-compulsive individual's cognitive and emotional experience, they can also be an asset in situations requiring great concentration and attention to technical detail (Zax & Cowen, 1972). It should be noted as a caution, however, that while Shapiro's observations are undoubtedly useful, they are also inconclusive. As Page (1975) states, many kinds of personalities are represented in any given form of neurosis, and furthermore, any given personality type associated with a specific neurotic disorder also occurs in other neuroses as well.

One of the more recent links between styles of living, coping, and somatic illness has been suggested by Friedman and Rosenman (1974), who argue that a primary cause of heart disease is a distinctive pattern of behavior they call Type A. This behavior pattern involves constant pressured interactions with the environment and a compelling sense of time urgency, aggressiveness, competitiveness, and generalized hostility. In a sense, this pattern is a mode of coping with societal values of achievement and the work ethic in which these values have been internalized by the Type A person.

Exactly how this pressured style of living can lead to an increased risk of heart disease is as yet unclear, although Friedman and Rosenman implicate increased levels of adrenaline (epinephrine) and noradrenaline (norepinephrine), as well as other hormones in the Type A person. The idea that one's style of coping with the demands and stresses of living contributes to somatic illness is a highly important one even though it is not yet clear how large a share in the causation of heart disease such behavioral factors play compared with direct physiological ones (like high cholesterol levels).

11

Cognitive and Coping Processes in Emotion

RICHARD S. LAZARUS

I believe that emotion cannot be understood or even adequately researched without asking about the cognitive factors underlying the emotional reaction. It has always seemed to me that when Freud (1936) spoke of anxiety in his monograph *Inhibitions, Symptoms, and Anxiety* as arising from the perception of danger, he was pointing the way toward a cognitive approach to emotion. The unanswered implicit question he posed there concerns the rules by which danger is recognized or cognized by the person or the ego-system.

My presentation here has two main themes: First, that cognitive processes determine the quality and intensity of an emotional reaction; and second, that such processes also underlie coping activities which, in turn, continually shape the emotional reaction by altering the ongoing relationship between the person and the environment in various ways. Let me begin with the first theme.

From my point of view (Lazarus, Averill, & Opton, 1970), emotions reflect the continuing nature of the person's or animal's adaptive commerce with his environment and the way this commerce is evaluated. The commerce can be judged by him as either damaging, threatening, challenging, or conducive to positive well-being. Each of us maintains special motives, belief systems, and competencies to cope with problems, and each also arranges and interprets his commerce with the environment in particular ways. *Cognitive appraisal* is the cornerstone of my analysis of emotions; and this appraisal, from which the various emotions flow, is determined by the interplay of personality and the environmental stimulus configuration.

From this perspective, emotion is defined in the following way: It is a complex disturbance which includes three main components—namely, subjective affect (which includes the cognitive appraisal), physiological changes related to species-specific forms of mobilization for action, and actions having both instrumental and expressive features. The somatic disturbance arises from an impulse to action which, in part, defines the particular emotion and reflects the mobilization for the action. The quality or intensity of the emotion and its action impulse depend on a cognitive appraisal of the present or anticipated significance of the adaptive commerce for the person's or animal's well-being. In lower animals, such as those studied by Tinbergen, the evaluative or appraisal feature of the emotion-eliciting perception is built into the nervous system. In higher mammals, such as man, symbolic thought processes and learning play a predominant role.

In stressing the importance of cognitive appraisal in the mediation of emotional states, it is useful to point to a debate between Hans Selye, with his "general adaptation syndrome" (GAS) on the one hand, and John Mason and I on the other. Selye argues that the GAS is a universal biological defense reaction aroused by any physically noxious agent. Mason (1971) points out, however, that coping processes are constantly shaping the endocrine response to stressor conditions. To express this mediation of the physiological response by coping and other psychological processes, Mason used the compound term "psychoendocrinology," thus attributing to psychological processes an important portion of the variance in endocrine reactions under noxious conditions. Mason and I have gone even further in this direction: We both have suggested (Lazarus, 1966; Mason, 1971) that the essential mediator of the GAS may be *psychological.* Therefore, we are saying that the pituitary-adrenal cortical response to disturbed commerce with the environment may require that the animal or person somehow recognize his plight. Any animal that has sustained an injury is apt to sense that he is in trouble; and if he does not, there will be no GAS. Moreover, in research on the GAS, psychological mediation has almost never been ruled out. Thus, one could argue with some justification that this cognitive appraisal of harm via cerebrally controlled processes is necessary to initiate the body's defensive adrenal cortical response.

An animal that is unconscious can sustain bodily harm without the psychoendocrine mechanisms of the "general adaptation syndrome" becoming active. Data from Symington et al. (1955), for example, suggest that unconsciousness and anesthesia eliminate the adrenal effects of physiological stress. In their study, patients who were dying from injury or disease showed a normal adrenal cortical condition as assessed during autopsy as long as they have remained unconscious during the period of the fatal condition. In contrast, patients who were conscious during the periods of the fatal disease process did show adrenal cortical changes. A study by Gray et al. (1956) has also demonstrated that general anesthesia, by itself, does not produce a significant adrenal reaction. These studies raise the question of whether it is the *psychological significance of injury* rather than its physiologically noxious effects that produce the adrenal cortical changes associated with stress.

We have a great need for a transactional language that describes individual differences in the way a person relates to the environment. I have constructed a simple hypothetical example to bring the point home. Consider two different persons who perceive that they are facing a demand, or the juxtaposition of several demands, which seem to them to be at the borderline or beyond their capacity to master— too much is expected of them. As a result of their individual histories and particular personalities, Person A feels that failure of mastery reflects his own inadequacy, while Person B, by contrast, feels the same pressure but interprets the situation as one in which people are constantly trying to use or abuse him. Both experience similar degrees of anticipatory stress and are mobilized to cope with the problem. Prior to the confrontation with the dangerous situation, both experience anxiety, an anticipatory emotion produced by appraised threat. In Person A, the anxiety is mixed with depression, while in Person B, the anxiety is mixed with external blaming and anger. Following the confrontation in which both perform badly, Person A will experience mainly loss and depression, while Person B mainly anger and resentment. Thus, a similar set of overwhelming demands has been construed or appraised quite differently by these two individuals. If, on the other hand, these persons do well in the confrontation, one may experience more elation than the other, depending on whether the explanation of the success is luck or their own perseverance and skill. In any case, such subtle differences in appraisal of a stressful commerce with the environment underlie variations among individuals in the severity (and possibly the pattern) of bodily reactions, the intensity and chronicity of the accompanying emotion, the quality of the affects experienced, and the types of solutions for which they opt, including seeking and accepting clinical help.

You will recognize that in this analysis of cognitive appraisal and emotion I come close to the efforts of attribution theorists . . . to spell out the cognitions underlying variations in achievement striving and the person's response to success and failure. Such concepts, in my view, can defeat circularity by leading to the identification of variables within the person and in the situation producing particular kinds of cognitive mediations and one or another type of action.

There is, incidentally, a tendency, especially in psychological research on emotion in the laboratory, to focus only on the immediate stimulus situation that provokes an emotion, while forgetting what is or has been going on in the general life of the person, as if the latter did not exist and played no role. An emotion then becomes an immediate "figure" in the person's life, so to speak, with the "ground" simply ignored. The person is momentarily occupied by certain transactions with the environment (his or her figure), but there remains a background of other problems, concerns, moods, and emotions that might well be considered in our attempts to understand emotions in nature. Perhaps the person has been struggling with multiple problems about which he may feel despair or depression much of the time, and suppressing such feelings as much as possible. He goes to work (or into our laboratories) and fulfills the day to day demands of his responsibilities against this depressive background. Although we know almost nothing about the possible interpenetrations of the figure and the ground of emotion, there may be important dynamic relationships. For example, the ongoing activities of the job (the figure) may suddenly make salient the wider problems being faced outside of the work situation in such a way as to elicit anger or depression then and there. Or, perhaps the job activities are sought out as ways of mastering, or at least momentarily preventing through attention deployment, a general sense of despair. In short, whatever the person is momentarily experiencing, be it emotional or not, happens against a background of other psychological conflicts and states, even if these are tentatively pushed into the background. This background of latent emotionality is constantly lurking in the shadows and is undoubtedly a major influence on the immediate figure states, just as is the immediate stimulus.

Now what about the second theme concerning coping or self-regulation? Emotion is not a constant thing. Rather, it ebbs and flows and changes over time as the nature of the adaptive commerce and the information about it changes. Anger suddenly melts and changes to guilt, depression, relief, or love; anxiety changes to relief or euphoria; guilt changes to anger; and so on. Most strong emotional states are complex and have more than one quality; emotions typically involve complex combinations of affect, each deriving from multiple cognitive appraisal elements to be found in any complex human transaction with the environment. These shifts in intensity and quality over time reflect perceived and evaluated or appraised alterations in the person's relationship with the environment, based in part on feedback from the situation and from his own reactions. In the stress emotions, the changes reflect, in part, the person's constant efforts to master the interchange by overcoming the damage, by postponing or preventing the danger, or by tolerating it. Thus, as a result of constant feedback and continuing efforts to cope with the situation or to regulate the emotional response, the person is also constantly reappraising his relationship with the environment, with consequent alterations in the intensity and quality of the emotional reaction. Thus, expectations about his power to deal with the environment and master danger are a factor in determining whether the person will feel threatened or challenged by what happens.

This latter theme is especially important for an understanding of emotional states because it places emphasis not only on cognitive processes, but also on *coping processes* as central features. We are sometimes accidentally confronted by a situation having major relevance for our welfare, but we also do a great deal of active regulating of our emotional reactions. People select the environments to which they must respond; they shape their commerce with it, plan, choose, avoid, tolerate, postpone, escape, demolish, manipulate their attention, and also deceive themselves about what is happening, as much as possible casting the relationship in ways that fit their needs and premises about themselves in the world. In regulating their emotional life, they are also thereby regulating the bodily reactions which are an integral part of any emotional state.

There are countless observations of the important role played by such coping activities in emotion. In a previous discussion of these (Lazarus, 1973), I cited everyday life anecdotal examples, such as the management of grief, the escalation or discouragement of a love relationship, and being a good loser. I also cited formal research examples, such as field studies of combat stress, the psychoendocrine research of the Bethesda group on parents of children dying of leukemia (Wolff et al., 1964; Wolff, Hofer, & Mason, 1964), the observations of Lief and Fox (1963) on reactions to viewing a medical autopsy, and research from my own laboratory (Koriat, et al. 1972) dealing with the self-control of emotional states. There is insufficient time here to do full justice to the problem, but it will be useful to illustrate two interesting examples of the role of intrapsychic as opposed to direct-action coping processes.

Lief and Fox (1963) have conducted extensive interviews with medical students witnessing a medical autopsy for the first time—an experience that can be quite distressing. Students, who are probably self-selected to a high degree, usually achieve detachment from the experience, though there are some failures to do so, too. Certain institutional features of the procedure itself provide help to the student in the process of achieving detachment. For example, during the autopsy the room is immaculate and brightly lit and the task is approached with seriousness and a professional air which helps achieve a clinical and impersonal attitude toward death. Certain parts of the body are kept covered, particularly the face and genitalia. The hands, which are so strongly connected with human, personal qualities, are usually not dissected. Once the vital organs are removed, the body is taken from the room, bringing the autopsy down to mere tissues which are more easily depersonalized. The deft touch, skill, and professional attitudes of the prosector make the procedures neater and more bloodless than might otherwise be the case, and this increases intellectual interest and makes it possible to approach the whole thing scientifically rather than emotionally. Students avoid talking about the autopsy; and when they do, the discussion is impersonal and stylized. Finally, humor, which is typical as a defense in laboratory dissection, is absent in the autopsy room, perhaps because joking would appear too insensitive in the case of recent death. In short, the student struggles to achieve a proper balance between feeling things and looking at them objectively, an effort in which detachment or distancing is facilitated by a variety of institutional procedures. Some professional individuals in medicine and nursing appear to overdo the coping strategy of detachment and are seen by their patients as cold and indifferent.

The second example is, I believe, the only experimental psychophysiological study explicitly designed to investigate whether and how people can alter their emotional states volitionally. Arguing that most research in the area of emotional control has been oriented to the *reduction* of stress reactions, while healthy management of one's emotional life requires also the *release* of emotional reactions, as in love, empathy, joy, distress over the suffering of others, etc., my colleagues and I (Koriat et al., 1972) instructed laboratory subjects to do both. In two experimental sessions they were exposed to four presentations of a film showing wood-shop accidents in which one man lacerates the tips of his fingers, another cuts off his middle finger, and a third dies after a plank of wood is thrust through his midsection by a circular saw. During the first two presentations there were no special instructions. However, half the subjects were instructed prior to the third presentation to *detach* themselves from the emotional impact of the accidents, and before the fourth presentation they were asked to *involve* themselves more fully and emotionally in them. The other half were given reverse order instructions, that is, on the third film presentation they had to involve themselves, while on the fourth, to detach themselves. They were not told how to do this, since one of the objectives of the experiment was to evaluate the cognitive devices they might use.

Among the findings of the research, two are of particular interest here. First, it was found that subjects could indeed exercise some degree of control over their emotional reactions to the accidents, as evidenced by their reported emotional state and changes in heart rate. Second, certain strategies were reported being used most commonly in involvement, and others in detachment. The most frequently reported *involvement* device was trying to imagine that the accidents were happening to the subject himself. Other less frequent strategies included trying to relate the scene to a similar experience he had or to which he was a witness, and trying to think about and exaggerate the consequences. The most popularly reported *detachment* strategy was reminding oneself that the events were dramatized for the film rather than being real, followed by the strategy of concentrating on the technical aspects of the production. In this study, we see clearly the operation of self-generated rather than situationally-induced modes of emotional control.

I have thus far avoided making explicit some of the theoretical issues or controversies inherent in this way of viewing emotion and its self-regulation by means of intrapsychic (cognitive) mechanisms, and some of these should now be examined.

WHAT IS BEING REGULATED?

In speaking of the self-regulation of emotion, I have actually meant control not only over the overt behavior that can be associated with an emotion (e.g., the expressive gestures and postures and instrumental action), but of the entire organized state that is subsumed under the emotion construct.

There would be little argument that we are capable of inhibiting emotional behaviors such as avoidance, aggression, etc., or the behavioral expression of emotions such as grief, love, depression, and joy. I am saying, of course, more than this, namely, that intrapsychic forms of coping such as detachment, denial, etc., are also capable of modifying, eliminating, or changing the emotion itself, including its subjective affect and the bodily states which are a normal feature of it. When successful, these mechanisms not only modify the outward signs of emotion, but they dampen or eliminate the entire emotional syndrome. Thus, in the Bethesda studies of parents with children dying of leukemia (Wolff et al., 1964; Wolff, Hofer, & Mason, 1964), by denying the fatal significance of their child's illness the Bethesda parents were no longer as threatened, and they exhibited lower levels of adrenal cortical stress hormones, than those parents who acknowledged the tragic implications; and by successfully distancing themselves from the personal emotional features of the autopsy, the medical students observed by Lief and Fox not only behaved unemotionally, but in all likelihood, if the appropriate measurements had been made, reacted with little or no affect and without the bodily disturbances that are an integral part of any stress emotion.

Moreover, much coping activity is anticipatory; that is, the person anticipates a future harmful confrontation such as failing an examination, performing in public, or confronting a flood, tornado, or a personal criticism, and such anticipation leads him to prepare against the future possibility of harm. To the extent that he prepares effectively, overcoming or avoiding the danger before it materializes, or being better able to function adequately in the anticipated confrontation, he thereby changes the nature of the ultimate transaction, along with the emotions that might have been experienced in the absence of such anticipatory coping. Overcoming the danger before it materializes can lead to exhilaration rather than fear, grief, depression, or whatever, depending upon the nature of the harm or loss that might have been experienced and the appraisal of the reasons for success.

You will note that this analysis reverses the usual wisdom that coping always follows emotion (or is caused by it) and suggests that coping can precede emotion and influence its form or intensity. In fact, my general position requires the assertion that coping never follows emotion in anything but a temporal sense, a stance in direct opposition to the longstanding and traditional view that emotions (such as anxiety) serve as drives or motives for adaptive behavior. The exception to this is when the person is trying to regulate the bodily state directly, but more about this in a moment.

Unfortunately, the psychology of coping is largely descriptive in nature, rather than systematic and predictive. People use a wide variety of coping processes, depending on their personal characteristics, the nature of the environmental demands and contingencies, and how these are appraised. They engage in a variety of preparatory activities. For example, they may worry without taking adequate steps to increase their effectiveness in confrontation; they reduce intense arousal by periodic disengagements from stressful transactions; they take tranquilizers to lower excessive levels of arousal; they use antispasmodics to quiet their bowels; they practice positive mental attitudes; they try to tell themselves that the problem will work itself out or that there is really no problem; they seek support from loved ones or those they trust; they try this or that stress-prevention fad or fashion, such as transcendental meditation, psychotherapy, relaxation, hypnosis, yoga, etc.; they direct their attention away from the source of threat and toward benign or escapist literature or movies; they cope with loss ultimately by giving up what was previously a central portion of their psychological domain. However, we still know extremely little about the conditions, both within the person and in the stimulus configuration, that lead to one or another coping process. We also know little about the relative effectiveness of such diverse coping processes in regulating emotional states or about the comparative costs in energy and other maladaptive consequences of each form of coping.

WHAT IS THE MODE OF SELF-REGULATION?

Here I should make a distinction of importance between two kinds of emotion-regulatory processes—a distinction others too have made (cf. Mechanic, 1962). One type, which might properly be called "coping," concerns efforts by the person to deal with the problem generating the stress emotion in the first place. Whether the person takes direct action, say by attacking or escaping the harmful agency, or engages in intrapsychic forms of coping (which we typically refer to as defense mechanisms), the focus of the coping effort is on the plight in which the person finds himself. The other type, which might be called "direct control" of emotion, is focused on ways of reducing the visceral or motor reactions that are part of the stress emotion generated by troubled commerce with the environment.

For example, if a student who is facing an important and very threatening examination spends the anticipatory interval reading relevant books and articles, rehearsing his understanding of the subject matter with other students or teachers, trying to guess or find out the questions that will be asked, and so on, he is engaged in coping with the problem whether he does this effectively or ineffectively. He is attempting to alter his basic relationship with the environment or, put differently, to change the nature of his troubled commerce with it. To the extent that such activity leads to a more benign appraisal of the potential outcome of the examination—for example, by giving him a sense of preparedness and mastery—the emotional reaction attendant on the threatening character of the situation for him is to some extent short-circuited. His anxiety is reduced, along with its bodily concomitants, and he is better able to sleep, think, draw upon his knowledge in the examination, etc. From the standpoint of the emotional state, it does not matter whether or not he has been kidding himself about his mastery, although, of course, it will ultimately matter during or after the exam, say if he fails.

On the other hand, if the same student takes tranquilizers or drinks to control his disturbed bodily state, takes sleeping pills, engages in muscle relaxation, diverts his attention for a time, or tries other techniques designed to quiet his heightened arousal, he is seeking directly to control the emotional response itself rather than to cope with the environmental transaction which generated the arousal in the first place. He is dealing with the somatic reaction rather than its cause. In all likelihood the rules by which these two divergent kinds of processes operate are quite different.

I do not intend any derogation of this latter, response-oriented or peripheral approach. We all use a variety of emotion-regulating devices, including those involving direct-control activities, and this often helps greatly. Sometimes they are the only ones available to the person, perhaps because the tendency to appraise certain situations as threatening is very deep-rooted, or the source of threat is unknown and therefore fairly refractory to change. Moreover, as in the handling of test anxiety, sometimes effective coping in the problem-oriented sense is severely impaired by the emotion itself, as when the person finds he cannot think clearly about his problem and prepare adequately in the face of the interfering effects. Under such conditions, reducing the anxiety or the correlates of anxiety by *any* means available may serve to facilitate adaptive coping.

Moreover, in chronic or repeated situations of threat, even merely lowering debilitating arousal may swing the balance of the approach-avoidance conflict in favor of approach and commitment and away from avoidance and disengagement, and this may make possible the attainment of goals of great importance. For example, I am usually very uneasy about commercial flying, although I have flown extensively for much of my professional Life. Were I not able to subdue my apprehensions and calm my overactive viscera on landings and takeoffs by alcohol or meprobamate, I might eschew making trips to professional meetings, with the attendant loss of important professional commitments and ultimate damage to my life goals. You will recognize, incidentally, that emotional control which aims at direct management of somatic turmoil rather than at the resolution of its psychodynamic origins is the arena in which biofeedback research and its use in therapy falls. We need to have more knowledge of the myriad forms of self-regulation that are available and serviceable to given kinds of people and in given types of situations in managing their emotional lives.

WHY SELF-REGULATION?

In speaking of the control of emotion by means of intrapsychic processes, I have deliberately used the expression "self-regulation" to convey the theme that it is the person, appraising the personal and social requirements of an emotional situation, who manages his emotional reactions willfully, as it were, rather than merely passively and automatically responding to internal and environmental pressures.

The concept of self-regulation (often called self-control and sometimes impulse-control) has a long history, especially in clinical and personality psychology. It is also a common-sense or lay concept. To some, self-regulation might suggest a flirtation with the philosophical idea of free will or a quarrel with determinism. Yet the concept does not require that such acts of will or self-control be said to occur outside of natural laws, or that we cannot discover the determinants of self-control, some of which lie within the person.

When behaviorally oriented psychologists have spoken of self-control, they have done so in what I consider to be a strange and contradictory way. Skinner (1953), for example, speaks of it as manipulating one's own behavior just as one might do in the case of another person or, as the environment does, through its pattern of reward and punishment contingencies. To decrease an undesirable behavior in oneself, for instance, the person makes the undesirable response less probable by altering the variables of reward and punishment on which it depends. Thus, if a person wishes not to overeat, he can place a time-lock device on the door of the refrigerator to eliminate snacks between meals. To prevent shopping sprees, he can leave his credit card or money at home. Thus, in this view, which has become exceedingly popular in behavior modification circles, the key agency of control seems to be the environmental contingencies rather than the person.

Although such environmental contingencies are very important, what is often missed is that an *executive agency within the person* determines which of many competing trends and impulses are to be encouraged or discouraged. Oftentimes it is not the environment that is manipulated, but what the person attends to in that environment, or how he interprets that environment. This is precisely what is meant by intrapsychic or cognitive control mechanisms. To speak of manipulating environment contingencies seems contradictory to me because it makes the environment the locus of self-control rather than the person, and this emphasis distorts the meaning inherent in the term *self*-control. It is the person who makes a commitment or decision on the basis of cognitive activity, whether he is conscious of it or not.

While speaking of self-regulatory or coping processes, let me offer what I think is an important qualification. We should not expect given self-regulating strategies to be effective in every context. Rather, depending on the environmental demands and options open to the person, some strategies should be serviceable and others not. Frances Cohen and I (1973) found that patients who approached surgery with avoidant strategies, that is, those who did not want to know about their illness and the nature of the surgery, showed a smooth and more rapid post-surgical recovery than did patients adopting a vigilant strategy. We speculated that vigilance might actually be a handicap for the surgical patient because there was nothing constructive he could really do in the postoperative recuperation period except simply to ignore or deny the sources of threat and pain. Trying postoperatively to pay attention vigilantly to every possible cue of danger or sign of discomfort resulted in a longer and more complicated recovery, and this appears to be maladaptive in this situation.

However, a very different strategy seems called for in the stressful context studied by Reuven Gal (1973), namely, seasickness among Israeli navy personnel. Holding constant the degree of seasickness, which incidentally can be assessed quite objectively, it was found that sailors who, through personality testing, displayed the trait or disposition to cope in an active, purposive, and vigilant fashion despite being sick, functioned much better at their normal jobs. Forgetting for a moment several possible sources of confounding, such as the measures of coping and the type of population, the juxtaposition of these two studies points up the potential interaction that might exist between the type of coping and the nature of the environmental demands. This suggests the importance of investigating the nature of the environmental demands that interact with coping dispositions and activities.

In closing, let me say that I am inclined to believe that the best strategy for such research on the cognitive mediators of emotion and coping is idiographic and naturalistic rather than nomethetic or normative and experimental. I no longer believe we can learn much by experimentally isolating coping processes, say, or personality variables, or situational demands, from the total context of the individual person in his usual environment. We need to study given classes of normally functioning persons longitudinally, that is, day to day or week to week, as they range from one situational context to another, to analyze and put together effectively the multiple forces to which their emotional reactions respond. I am not rejecting laboratory experiments for many problems, but I am merely questioning their adequacy for the study of emotional processes which are difficult to generate in sufficient intensity with adults in the laboratory setting within the confines of our present-day ethical standards.

Naturalistic research would lack some of the measurement precision and control possible in the laboratory, which is best suited for isolating variables, but it would increase our ability to uncover what has been most lacking in our understanding to date, namely, how the various individual response systems of emotion, and the mediating processes of appraisal and self-regulation, are organized or integrated within the person who is struggling to manage his relations with the environment.

12

Regulatory Devices of the Ego Under Major Stress

KARL MENNINGER

The general point of view taken is that all clinical phenomena may be advantageously viewed as belonging within a continuum between the state of adjustment which we call health and an ultimate state of disintegration or extreme "illness." This would tend to dispense with the controversial and essentially useless traditional designations of nervousness, neurasthenia, neurosis, psychasthenia, psychosis, etc., and would bring into some systematic organization our dynamic concepts of "defence measures," reactions, etc., for use in clinical psychiatry.

One can view the functions of the ego in dealing with external and internal stimuli as those of a homeostatic regulator. The drives of the organism must be so directed and modified, in view of the superego system and the reality system, as to permit the maintenance of a level of tension which is tolerable, productive, maximally satisfying, and consistent with growth. Events persistently occur which tend to disturb the adjustments and reconciliations achieved, and these stresses require the ego to improvise adaptive expedients for maintaining the integrity of the organism. Minor stresses are usually handled by relatively minor, "normal," "healthy" devices. Greater

I acknowledge with gratitude the assistance of my associate, Dr. Martin Mayman (K.M.). The complete version of this presentation was published under the title "Psychological Aspects of the Organism under Stress," Part I; "The Homeostatic Regulatory Function of the Ego," Part II; "Regulatory Devices of the Ego under Stress" in the *Journal of the American Psychoanalytic Association* 2 (1954), No. 1, 67–106; No. 2, 280–310. I have ventured to submit here, at the request of the editor, a condensation of the clinical application of these theories presented before the 18th Int. Congress in London on 28 July 1953.

stresses or prolonged stress excite the ego to increasingly energetic and expensive activity in the interests of homeostatic maintenance.

One of the first evidences of failure of the "normal" devices of the ego for handling emergencies is the development or persistence of *stress awareness.* The subject is conscious of discomfort in connection with efforts at concentration or self-control. Aware of this, he consciously exerts an extra measure of "will power" in the mastery or concealment of these phenomena. Perhaps we should think of this *hypersuppression* as the most nearly normal of any of the secondary defences.

Less uncomfortable because unconscious is the greatly increased use of *repression.* Externally this appears as restriction and increased inhibition.

Another well-known representative of this order of emergency-coping devices is the increase of alertness, irritability, distractability, "tenseness," flushing, sweating, and "nervousness" so typical of the initial phases of acute mental illness. (To call this "anxiety" is to confuse the meaning of the term.) It is often most uncomfortable in its effect upon the sleep habits of the individual. This *hyperalertness* represents a protective vigilance. Almost inseparable from hyper-alertness are *hyperemotionalism* and *hyperkinesis.* The exaggerated use of crying and/or of laughing is one form; but increased "sensitiveness," touchiness, and irascibility to the point of rage attacks are also of this order. Other excesses of emotion are also familiar, particularly fear-someness and depression. The latter may represent "mourning" for a real or anticipated loss of love, or it may be a consequence of some special and excessive *introjection.*

Depression tends to retard the hyperkinetic phenomena which otherwise appear characteristically in association with hyperalertness and hyperemotionalism. The hyperkinesis may be somewhat directed, as in the normal *"acting to alter."* But it is now much more likely to appear as insufficient, impulsive, or compulsive (see below) pointless muscular activity. Beginning with restlessness, jumpiness, and other phenomena often considered quasinormal, it reaches extremes of various kinds of overactivity and distorted activity. The hostile impulses seem sometimes to be deflected to substitute persons or inanimate objects, sometimes to no particular object (or end) at all.

Instead of acting it out with one's muscles, however, the individual may make persistent attempts to think it out, to worry it through, with distorted emphases in mild *"obsessional" thinking* or "worrying." Excessive talking is a combination of hyperkinesis and hyperintellection.

Excessive fantasy formation is a common first order device, which belongs properly in the broader category of the overuse of compensatory measures. When it replaces necessary reality thinking or effective acting, it is pathological. Hypercompensation is also accomplished, however, in numerous other ways, particularly by elaborate *reaction formations* (reversing the effect of the aggressive wish) and *ad hoc identifications* (e.g., with the enemy).

Somatic reactions characteristic of "anxiety" probably serve the same purpose as the psychological devices described, namely, that of relieving tension. The patient rarely experiences them as other than uncomfortable, and would be loath to accept the proposition that they relieve him. Indeed, they may constitute his chief complaint. They vary greatly in form, intensity, frequency of recurrence, or degree of constancy in different individuals. Tremor, flushing, palpitation, "weak" feelings, giddiness, anorexia, tachycardia, nausea, enuresis, diarrhea, and other evidences of sympathetic nervous system liability and excitation are the more frequent. To this should be added various *quantitative and qualitative disturbances in the sexual function.*

To recapitulate, regulatory devices of a first order or degree of pathological nature may be employed by the ego in situations which overtax the ordinary or normal devices. These consist essentially in exaggerations of normal functions, but they now appear uncomfortably and unpleasantly. They are apt to be described as evidences of "nervousness." The more familiar ones are:

Hypersuppression
Hyperrepression
Hyperalertness
Hyperemotionalism
Hyperkinesis
Hyperintellection, including mild obsessional thinking
Hypercompensation
Minor somatic dysfunctions

        •   •   •   •

There seems to be a limit to the utilization of First Order devices, beyond which *qualitative* rather than merely *quantitative* alterations are necessary. These are in the nature of strategic retreats,[1] with compensating features. The ego system, burdened beyond the Plimsoll mark, capitulates to the necessity of an altered (lowered) level of homeostatic balance, and effects it by a *Second Order* of regulating devices *characterized by partial detachment from the world of reality*— from loved objects, feared objects, and hated objects. Real objects of cathexis are abandoned in favor of substitutions which may have a flavor or façade of "reality," but which yield a gratification only dereistically. This partial withdrawal from reality is not affected for the sake of getting out of harm's way—for that would be a realistic withdrawal. This is the withdrawal for the sake of the ego—i.e., to diminish the tension resulting from excessive internal pressures.

Simple withdrawal by dissociation is accomplished by or reflected in a variety of internal modifications of consciousness and of the mnemonic such as ("hysterical") fainting, amnestic periods, and amnestic states. Presumably the withdrawal here goes far, for the whole world is temporarily forgotten—but it all returns rather promptly. What unconscious *fantasies* occupied the internal screen we can rarely discover. These are "acted out" in the more complicated phenomena of "dual personalities," and fugues.

Less dramatic, less extreme, but far more frequent are those *formes frustes* in which there is to be seen only social shyness or avoidance or gaucherie, while subjectively there is a sense of strangeness, of unreality, or even of depersonalization. (Oberndorf, Federn, etc.) Since these are subjective phenomena, they may be long concealed.[2]

However widespread such withdrawal and dissociation may be, it is clinically important (at present) chiefly when it is uncomfortable. For this discomfort itself indicates that a tolerable equilibrium has not been established; the device (withdrawal) has bettered things,

---

[1] The term "regression" is sometimes applied, rather confusingly, I think.

[2] One is tempted to speculate, at this point, regarding the extent of this "symptom" in the world's population. We psychiatrists usually think of it from the standpoint of those who suffer from their isolation; both we and they are accustomed to think them more or less "sick." How much less sick are they, perhaps, than the many "healthy minded" millions who scotomatize the misery of most of mankind, and by means of denial, avoidance, studied ignorance, preoccupation, snobbery, and distractions of all kinds manage to avoid even the awareness of worldwide tragedy, and hence of reality in a larger sense!

but has added another burden from the diminished object attachment (positive and negative). The ego, like Nature, abhors a vacuum! Thus the world of reality is subjectively recreated, modified to fit the needs of the beleaguered ego. New objects in the outside world are substituted for those with which the ego felt unable to cope because of the uncontrollable impulses excited by them. This device of *displacement,* which Freud so brilliantly rediscovered clinically, is as old as the race, as old as dolls and idols and scapegoats. To what extent it pervades all our thinking can only be conjectured. For, indeed, what are prejudices, extreme aversions, and fanatical attitudes *pro* or *con* but the substitution of something symbolic for the truly feared or hated or loved object?

We know more about this device, thanks to Freud, as it appears in obsessional and phobic states than we know about it in crusaders and class-haters. We know that even phobias may be converted into or replaced by a reversal, i.e., a pathological (ungenuine) boldness and intrepidity with particular respect to the thing feared. Anna Freud has elaborated this *"counterphobic"* phenomenon.

Corresponding to its displacement of *fear* to a substituted symbolic object, the ego logically ascribes to that object threatening intentions. The selection of this object is partly determined by previous— often forgotten—experience, although propinquity and chance play roles in the choice also. We speak of this device as *projection.* It must be considered a more desperate measure, particularly when it is accompanied by its often associated phenomena—hallucinations, ideas of reference, and delusions. It is then a signal of gross ego failure.

Closely allied to projection and, indeed, making much use of it, is an unhappily familiar syndrome of rapidly shifting displacements, with alternating reality acceptance and reality denial. The characteristic motivation here seems to be provocativeness; it would seem as if the ego accepted or effected potentially unstable object attachments for the very sake of being able to disappoint them and inciting retaliation as a combined form of love and punishment. Individuals who are forced into a program of this semirational, semirealistic, semicriminal, semipsychotic behavior have been called by many names—most commonly, perhaps, "psychopathic personalities." I have previously described them as characterized by this saltatory phenomenon, this device of transiliency, but probably the basic mechanism involved is the compulsion toward provocativeness. Of course, in its simplest form this device is frequently used by others than the individuals just described who are so completely characterized by it.

The substitution of symbolic objects for the displacement of otherwise uncontrolled impulses differs from the substitution of *modified modalities* of "dealing" with objects. The high value of symbols in psychic life is such that it is possible to use speech, rituals, and other things in place of the unconsciously formulated intent of destruction. Cursing someone may be a sufficiently satisfying equivalent of ridding one's self of him by *magic*. There are, as we know, many other ways than cursing in which "murder" may be attenuated. This attenuation may be almost to the vanishing point, so far as practical effect on the subject is concerned, but there is always an effect on the *subject*. One effect is to release aggressive energy and hence diminish ego tension. But another effect is to arouse the superego to require placatory undoing, restitutive, penitential, and similar activities. What we call "compulsions" are acts or strong inclinations toward such acts which symbolically destroy the danger and simultaneously appease the conscience. The balance achieved in this combination will by no means satisfy an objective observer, but because of the impaired reality sense, it partially satisfies the doer. Symbolically doing-and-undoing constitute the essence of a large number of modality substitutions all of which represent a partial detachment from reality and an attempted arrangement for releasing an "irresistible impulse" of a dangerous kind in a disguised "magic" form.

Prominent among these substitution techniques as seen in clinical material are the various perversions of mode or object in the gratification of sexual desire. The sexual urge may be considered primarily a derivative of the life instinct—a partial instinct, some would call it. But it is always "contaminated" or fused with some derivatives of the aggressive instinct. According to the proportions of admixture, a sexual act may be predominantly loving or predominantly hostile (but never wholly either). For some individuals the expression of the sexual impulse in a predominantly loving form, according to biologically "normal" modes and toward the appropriate objects, is blocked in respect to one of these three criteria. This frustration still further increases the proportion of aggressive component (which, in turn, may still further intensify the blocking). A bargain is finally struck, so to speak, by means of displacement, substitution, and—as with all these devices—some reality denial. The conditioning of some egos is such that in spite of the superego pressure and in spite of reality pressure (danger, inconvenience, etc.) the perverse act can be tolerated, i.e., permitted, whereas the normal act cannot be. Expression of the "sexual" needs in this distorted, substituted way relieves ego pressure by permitting destructive urges to emerge in disguise.[3]

Finally, among the Second Order devices of stress relief, there are the phenomena in which the ego effects a semirealistic withdrawal through the offering of sacrifices, or as some (Rado) prefer to phrase it, by a choice of the lesser evil. In the psychological system the sacrifice may be made either to conscience demands or to reality demands. Most reality sacrifices represent normal choice behavior and are usually conscious ("A half loaf is better than no bread"; "a bird in the hand is worth two in the bush," etc.). Sacrifices offered the conscience are more self-destructive and are usually only dimly recognized for what they are. The principle of sacrifice is based on a rather complicated equation, in which a part is made to stand for the whole, and is yielded or offered in order to preserve the integrity of the remainder of the whole. I have illustrated in *Man Against Himself* in how many different ways the superego can be placated by a sacrifice which involves such magical choice of a lesser evil. The solution by sacrifice is accomplished, in clinical experience, by self-immolation and penalization, as in the case of asceticism and martyrdom; by mutilation of one's own body or by exploitation of the opportunity for obtaining surgical operations or sustaining semipurposive accidents which accomplish mutilation; by self-intoxication or narcotization; by entertainment of the fantasy of a somatic affection, as in hypochrondriasis; by exploitation and misinterpretation of sensations of somatic affection as in neurasthenia; by unconscious simulation of somatic affection as in conversion syndromes; by the physiological production of somatic affections as in psychosomatic disorders; by the psychological exploitation of an intercurrent somatic affection.

---

[3] Some colleagues will feel that sexual perversion is *prima facie* evidence of severe ego failures and hence should be assigned to a still higher order of tension-relieving devices. I think this is true only if violence and overt destructiveness characterize the modality. There are self-destructive and externally aggressive elements in all the Second Order devices, but they are concealed. If the aggression becomes obvious (and, of course, misdirected) we have sufficient evidence to ego rupture to assign such devices to the next order.

Regulatory Devices of a Second Order of Pathology

1. *Withdrawal by dissociation (intrapsychic)*
   Syncope
   Narcolepsy
   Amnesia
   Fugues
   Dual personality
   Sense of unreality (estrangement)
   Depersonalization
2. *Withdrawal by displacement of aggression to substituted objects*
   Aversion
   Prejudice
   Phobias
   Counter-phobic attitudes
   Obsessions
   Projection
   Provocative transiliency
3. *Substitution of (magic) symbols and modalities for more frankly hostile discharge*
   Compulsions
   Rituals
   "Kleptomania," "pyromania," etc.
   Undoing and restitutive gestures
   Perverse sexual modalities and objects, without violence
4. *Substitution of the self or a part of the self as an object of displaced aggression*
   Self-imposed restriction and abasement (asceticism)
   Body mutilation (self-inflicted, "accidental," surgical)
   Self-intoxication or narcotization
   Somatic involvement (fantasy, sensation, or function)
   a. Unconscious simulation
   b. Exploitation of somatic affection
   c. Physiological production of somatic disorder

REGULATORY DEVICES OF THE THIRD ORDER

All the stress-relieving devices of the first and second orders are temporary and emergency devices. The ego never "expects" to retain them permanently (although it often does!). If a woman sees a shocking automobile accident and faints, she doesn't think of her fainting as a symptom of illness; she doesn't expect to continue fainting. If a man has a fatiguing and discouraging day and takes a few drinks too many, he doesn't think of this narcotization as a symptom. It is only when the fainting becomes frequent or the alcoholic relief imperative, so that other satisfactions are sacrificed, that the "device" becomes a symptom. We may sometimes refer to these as "habits," but it is not merely the accustoming of one's self to an expedient, but rather the *hypertrophy and solidification of a definitely emergency measure which makes for pathology.*

Nevertheless, the actual intrapsychic state of affairs is never static. The stresses either recede, or they continue, and are added to by the necessary compromises. And the trend of pressure is in the direction of ego rupture, which could correspond to the neurophysiologist's "exhaustion state." An already stretched, compromised, injured, wearied, over-taxed ego may simply have to yield. It does the best it can as long as it can, but the pressures may be too great for it; it may give way. This does not mean that the ego is destroyed or annihilated; intact portions or functions persist, of course. But in certain "weak" spots it yields. The result is catastrophe—not for the ego, but for the total organism.

THIRD ORDER DEVICES

The uncontrollable emergence of dangerous instinctual impulses is always something of a catastrophe. As we shall see shortly, it is not *the* catastrophe, the ultimate and *most* dangerous explosion, but it is always serious, because of consequences to be expected from the environment (retaliation, punishment, etc.) and from the superego. In this ego rupture the dangerous impulses are apparently outwardly directed, but the "recoil," the concomitant self-damage, is always detectable also.

Clinically and empirically we know these catastrophes in *two forms*—as continuous phenomena over a considerable period of time, and as relatively brief, episodic, discontinuous phenomena from which there is prompt recovery with a continued tendency for them to recur. It would seem that these episodic explosions serve to relieve enough tension to prevent the development of the continuous forms.

Sudden homicidal violence or less extreme assaults and uncontrollable attacks of rage are the most familiar exhibitions of such primitive impulse explosions. These are occasionally self-directive, either as suicide or self-mutilation. Unhappily the pages of history, particularly those of criminologic and psychiatric history, are full of dramatic illustrations of the catastrophe in the form of "impulsive" homicide. In many such instances there is so much "isolation" that the patient has no explanation at all for his crimes. In other cases there are rationalizations for the deed, and for the selection of the individual attacked, but as Wertham has shown, these reasons, convincing as they may sound in mystery stories, and even in some criminal trials, usually have little to do with the real motivation of the murder.

Assaultive forms of violence may contain an admixture of sexuality, used chiefly as a cloak. But sexual assaults of all kinds, including rape and the aggressive types of sexual perversion, represent modified forms of ego rupture.

．　　　　　．　　　　　．　　　　　．

To summarize, stress-relieving devices of a Third Order of pathology are represented by episodic, explosive outbursts of aggressive energy, more or less disorganized, including:

1. Assaultive violence—homicidal or suicidal
2. Convulsions
3. Panic attacks
4. Catastrophic demoralization
5. Schizoid attacks (e.g., ten-day schizophrenia)

REGULATORY DEVICES OF THE FOURTH ORDER
(PERSISTENT DEREISTIC DISCHARGE)

Rupture of the ego permitting an episodic explosion may be sufficient to relieve the tension, and the ego quickly "heals" with or without a "weak spot." Its boundaries are restored (Federn) and a catastrophe has been averted. Freud pointed out how suicide may be a substitute for murder, and Reichard and Tillman have recently proposed and illustrated the idea of murder and suicide as "defences" against psychosis.

Thus, the victory may be a Pyrrhic one. The cost of salvation may be fatal. The damage done may be irreparable. Or, the rupture may be too great for the ego to reconstitute its homeostatic patterns in a quick restoration. The ego may be exhausted or semipermanently damaged. In that case, a further retreat and detachment from reality must occur. This actually represents the net effect of the aggressive intent: destruction is accomplished symbolically in the form of a repudiation of reality and of reality testing to a penultimate degree. Not only is the process of reality testing abandoned, but the established loyalty to reality is (largely) renounced. With this, of course, goes a disruption of interpersonal linkages and the separation from love objects which presages psychological starvation of the ego (Ernest Jones's aphanisis).

It is this state of affairs to which most psychiatrists refer with the word "psychosis," a word which I earnestly hope we can abandon. (Adolf Meyer, George Stevenson, Karl Bowman and other psychiatrists have expressed the same wish.) It is illustrated in the delirious states, many schizophrenic pictures, some stupors, and various conditions associated with organic brain damage. I am not concerned now with names of specific "causes," but rather with the psychological picture and the psychological process that is represented.

I believe this stage of the process represents a near catastrophic rearranging of homeostatic balance in which the dangerous impulses, aroused by threat, pain, fear, guilt, and frustrations are controllable only (or chiefly) by absorption into fantasy, including narcissistic preoccupations, denial, and destruction in fantasy of some or all of the real world. Disorganization of a high degree is conspicuous. An internal equilibrium and relative peace are indeed reestablished, but at a fearful cost in effectiveness. Edward Kempf described this as his fifth and most extreme stage of personality decompensation—"a further flight from adjustment, really an almost complete failure to compensate, so that the individual is dominated by the uncontrollable elements of the unconscious. Then there appear, as if they were a part of real life, such very unreal things as delusions, hallucinations, etc. These, in short, are symptoms popularly known as 'insanity.' "

This is truly disorganization, and the sacrifice of much of the self to the situation. It is self-destructive. But from the other standpoint, which we have been emphasizing, it is also self-preservative, a device to *avert* a more complete self-destruction. It is not a complete self-destruction. It is not a complete surrender, but a retreat—almost a rout, perhaps. But the organism is saved, even though its productive level has fallen to almost zero. We know that such patients feel, on the one hand, desolate, estranged, and hopeless because of the disruption of their linkages with reality love objects; and, at the same time, seek to bolster their egos with omnipotent fantasies of destroying the whole world. The picture is apt to be complicated by numerous fragments of second and third order devices which are carried over. Indeed, it is these which give color and form to the various clinical pictures in which this near-total disorganization of psychic function appears. The following are some of the commonly observed varieties:

(1) *Erratic, disorganized excitement*—with corresponding verbal and motor productions—at times destructive, at times self-injuring, at times only bizarre and ineffectual. These pictures have been called delirious, manic, maniacal, catatonic, epileptic, and other names.

(2) *Conditions of extreme hyperthymia*—chiefly melancholy, with or without stupor, agitation, delusion formation, retardation, or restless activity. The characteristic feature is the overwhelming of the wish to live, the mood of resignation and obligation to suicide.

(3) *Silly, incoherent, manneristic, autistic speech and behavior,* without excitement or clear meaning or direction. Such pictures are often called hebephrenic.

(4) *Extreme and continuous apathetic inertia* and extreme inactivity, sometimes rigidity, often with mutism, hallucinations, and other rarely revealed fantasy indulgences and occasional outbursts. Such conditions are called hebephrenic, catatonic, "deteriorated," "regressed," and other undefinable and unjustifiable names.

(5) *Delusion preoccupation* with one or several themes, usually persecutory, and usually supported with defensiveness, suspiciousness, gradiosity, condescension, irascibility, etc. with or without hallucinations. A good façade of "normality" may partially or occasionally obscure the underlying picture. Such states have classically gone under many names containing the adjective "paranoid."

(6) *Disoriented, confused, uncertain, amnesic,* bewildered disorientation typical of senile regression and organic brain injury.

(7) *Gross intellectual defect,* typical of congenital or acquired hypophrenia.

    •   •   •   •

At this cost, then, the final catastrophe of dissolution has been averted. A kind of equilibrium has been reestablished at a very low level. Here it may remain until death. *But,* empirically we know that complete restoration may still occur! Thus the survival function of this catastrophic retreat is demonstrated, and the ego's regulatory powers seem to be justified even in its so-called failure.

THE ULTIMATE AND IRREVERSIBLE
CATASTROPHE: THE FIFTH ORDER

But despite the successive inauguration of progressively more "radical" measures, the ego may really fail completely. Things may go from good to bad, to worse, to worst. And what is the worst that can happen? From the biological standpoint, one would say death; from the psychobiological standpoint, and in line with the concept here presented, one would have to say complete disorganization, which is perhaps not quite the same. We might borrow the term entropy from physics.

Since the basic function of the ego is integration, i.e., holding the personality together, its complete failure is to be seen in disintegration, which occurs when the destructive drives overwhelm it. Complete failure of ego control releases enormous violent energies of destruction in all directions. Clinically one sees occasionally such dreadful cases of continuous, wild, furious, violent mania ending, nearly always I believe, in complete exhaustion and death.[4]

[4] Actual self-propelled physical self-destruction in the clinical form of suicide should probably be treated as an indication of *not-quite-total disintegration.* It is certainly terminal and irreversible, and it is certainly a kind of failure of ego control which turns out to be fatal. But it does involve some conscious direction, and hence falls a little short of complete reality renunciation. When Freud outlined his concept of the self-destructive instinct he made it clear that its manifestations are never nakedly visible. This is true even in suicide, as I have tried to point out in *Man Against Himself.* It is possible that those forms of suicide among primitives which are said to be accomplished by sheer determination to die represent an exception to Freud's statement, but suicide in the ordinary form represents a direction of violence toward the self which is always tinctured with elements of the integrative efforts of the ego. In other words, no suicide is ever completely wholehearted. There is certainly a considerable difference between the wish to die, the wish to *kill* (one's self), and the wish *to be killed* (by one's self or by someone else) as I have pointed out elsewhere (*vide infra*). And none of these are undisguised representations of the "death instinct," by definition. Suicide as an occasional fantasy, suicide as an obsessional preoccupation, and suicide as a gesture must be distinguished from successful or unsuccessful but *bona fide* suicidal attempts. (See Raines.) The great excess of suicidal attempts as compared with "successful" suicides (even

INTERPRETATIVE ADDENDA AND CONCLUSION

On this dismal note of complete disintegration, we must terminate this analysis of the progressive steps or stages in the temporary arrest of the trend toward disintegration by the various regulatory expedients available to the ego. Please bear in mind that this was, by design, a schematic rather than a clinical presentation. As has been pointed out repeatedly as we went along, the ego always does more than attempt to manage the immediate emergency. In spite of resistances implicit in the semistabilized emergency adjustment, the ego perennially endeavors to return to its original normal adjustment level. These restorative efforts of the ego have been little touched upon here for the reason that we have been trying to describe the disease process rather than the recovery process, which in no way diminishes the importance of a further consideration of the latter including . . . "treatment." That recovery actually may take place wholly or in part, after arrival at any of the stages described, has been repeatedly mentioned, but perhaps needs repeating. That recovery may fail to take place is unfortunately also an empirical fact.

•   •   •   •   •

Nor would I leave the impression that the demarcation of these five hierarchical orders of stress-relieving devices is something sharp, clear, and invariable. As in all scientific description, they appear more so in a verbal description of this kind than in real life. In the course of a progressive maladjustment in which second order devices, for example, are gradually or even suddenly superseded by third and fourth order devices, there is apt to be a trailing or continuing use of some of the devices belonging to earlier orders (i.e., the first and second). It should not be forgotten that we psychiatrists see the patient only after months or years of a fluctuating struggle to attain a tolerable adjustment. By recapitulating the history, we can determine which of the present devices are revivals and which are new, and

---

after one excludes "thwarted" suicides) suggests, as Stengel has recently pointed out, that many so-called "successful suicides" are actually bungled attempted-suicides. The gesture function, the appeal effect, and the ordeal character of the attempt are of great importance. Stengel agrees with us, however, that even the suicidal attempt is "a catastrophic reaction to an intolerable social and emotional situation."

what former "emergency reactions" had been partially accepted by the patient as inevitable character traits rather than symptoms. These may now have become hypertrophied to the point of rejection as "ego-alien," or they may have been supplanted by a new series. Thus a sequential order may be demonstrable, but often it is not.

I have tried to avoid the use of such terms as defences, defence measures, and defence mechanisms, because of the narrowness of their implications. They call to mind partial maneuvers which parry circumscribed threats. I have tried to employ terms which accent the more holistic implications of the ego's defence efforts, that is, its use of a wide range of expedients in the interest of preserving the best possible level of integration in the face of disintegrative pressures. At first, those expedients may be chosen which result in an increased state of tension within the system (First Order Devices). Ultimately, however, the organism may be forced to adopt devices which will relieve the painful state of tension. The devices it chooses must be the best available for maintaining organismic integrity with a minimum of loss.

Disease may be seen, then, not simply as *lack* of "ego strength," an absence of normality, but as a positive expression of the survival efforts of the organism, inept and costly as they may be. In this paper I have sketched out only in broad strokes and rough outline the implications of such a concept of disease. In the development of this idea, the term homeostasis was used to signify the efforts of the organism to realize its potentialities and maintain its integrity despite descriptive onslaughts from within and without. Treatment may be viewed in these terms as assistance in the effort to reestablish the optimal level of integration which had to be sacrificed for a more tenable level of homeostatic maintenance.

·   ·   ·   ·

13

Religious Systems as Culturally Constituted Defense Mechanisms

MELFORD E. SPIRO

BURMESE MONASTICISM

In Burma, one of the centers of Theravada Buddhism, the monastic vocation is the most venerated of all patterns of life. Almost every village contains at least one monastery with at least one resident monk. The monk, in theory at least, lives an exclusively other-worldly existence. His monastery is outside the village gates, and his interaction with the layman is confined to occasional ritual situations. The monk is prohibited from engaging in any form of physical labor, including any economic activity. All of his wants are attended to by the laymen, who provide his daily meals, his robes, and other necessities. Except for teaching young children, the monk's official responsibilities to the laymen are restricted to chanting of "prayers" at funerals and to public recitation of the Buddhist precepts on the "Sabbath" and other sacred days. His primary responsibility is to himself and to his attempt to attain nirvana. The latter goal is achieved through the study of Scripture and through various techniques of Buddhist meditation. These activities are believed to be instrumental to the attainment of Release from the round of rebirths because they lead to ultimate comprehension of the true characteristics of existence, viz., impermanence, suffering, and the absence of an ego. This comprehension, in turn, is believed to lead to the sever-

Materials in this section are based on field work carried out during 1961–62; I am grateful to the National Science Foundation for a research fellowship which made the research possible.

ance of all desire for, and cathexis of, the world. With the destruction of desire or "clinging" (*tanha*), the basis for rebirth is destroyed. Nirvana, whatever else it may be, is the cessation of rebirth. The true monk, then, is completely absorbed in his own "salvation." Although living in a state of absolute dependence on the laymen, he has withdrawn both physically and psychologically from the physical and social world, and even—in states of trance (*dhyānas*)—from his own self. This extreme withdrawal from reality is similar to that withdrawal behavior which, in our society, would be taken as symptomatic of severe pathology, most certainly schizoid, if not schizophrenic. Is the Burmese monk to be similarly characterized? Such a judgment, in my opinion, would be grossly in error. Phenotypically, the behavior of the monk and that of the schizoid or schizophrenic patient may be very similar. Genotypically and functionally, however, they are importantly dissimilar. All of the criteria suggested [in a previous part of this study] for assessing pathology are applicable to the schizophrenic; none is applicable to the monk.

In the case of the schizophrenic the actor resolves his inner conflict by constructing private fantasy and action systems; in the case of the monk, however, the actor uses culturally constituted fantasy and action systems (Buddhism) to resolve his inner conflicts. This difference not only provides the primary basis for a differential diagnosis of monk and schizophrenic, but it also provides, parenthetically, an important insight into the nature of religion. Culturally constituted religious behavior not only is not a symptom of pathology but, on the contrary, it serves to preclude the outbreak of pathology. The schizophrenic and the Burmese monk, alike, are characterized inially by pathogenic conflict, and schizophrenia and monasticism may each be interpreted as a means for resolving conflict. But this is where the similarity ends. Although schizophrenia and monasticism are both symptomatic of pathogenic conflict, the former represents a pathological, whereas the latter represents a nonpathological, resolution of the conflict. Let us examine these claims.

An analysis of monastic personality, based on the Rorschach records of a sample of Burmese Buddhist monks, and without reference to their (monastic) behavioral environment, would surely lead to a diagnosis of severe pathology. Dr. James Steele (1963), who has analyzed these records, finds the following "pathological" features, among others: (1) a very high degree of "defensiveness"; (2) "pathologically regressed" expression of aggressive and oral drives; (3) cautious avoidance of "emotionally laden" situations as a means of obviating the necessity of handling affect, for which there are no adequate resources; (4) a "hypochondriacal self-preoccupation" and "erotic self-cathexis," instead of a cathexis of others; (5) latent homosexuality; (6) above-average fear of female- or mother-figures.

One of the significant characteristics of the Rorschach protocols of these monks, according to Steele, is their similarity to the records of Burmese laymen. It is not that the monastic records do not differ from those of the laymen; but the difference is one of degree, not of kind. Monks differ from laymen, not because they have different problems, but because they have more of the same problems. The monk, in other words, is a Burman *in extremis.* Burmese laymen (like Burmese monks) are constricted, ruminative, defensive, anxious about females, distrustful of others, and, perhaps, latently homosexual. The monks differ from the laymen only in that, for all these characteristics, they are *more so.* Monks are *more* constricted, *more* ruminative, *more* . . . , etc. For other characteristics, however, monks are *less so.* Compared to laymen, monks are ". . . less phallic, less self-confident, less striving, and less impulsive." In summary, Burmese monks not only appear to have "more of the basic problems" which characterize Burmans in general, but they also seem to be characterized by a "more constricted adjustment." It is the latter feature, still quoting Steele, which makes them "less accessible to social interaction with the protection that this provides."

This picture of the Burmese monks is surely a picture of pathology. Are we to conclude then—holding in abeyance a specific psychiatric diagnosis, and assuming that the Rorschach test is a reliable instrument—that these monks are abnormal? If personality existed in a social and cultural vacuum, the answer would be an unqualified "yes." Acute psychological conflicts and attendant intrapersonal tensions are marked. That these conflicts have produced defensive distortions of various kinds—perceptual, cognitive, affective—is clearly indicated. That social impairment is a most likely consequence of these conflicts, tensions, and distortions can hardly be doubted. In brief, if personality existed *in vacuo* one would probably conclude that Burmese monks resolve their conflicts in a manner which issues in severe pathology (perhaps paranoid schizophrenia).

But the proviso, "if personality existed *in vacuo*," is crucial. Although Steele's analysis of their Rorschach records is remarkably similar to my clinical impressions of these monks, impressions derived from intensive participant-observation in a score of monasteries, and from personal interviews with more than twenty-five monks—thus providing a dramatic test of the reliability of the instrument and of Steele's skill in its use—I did not ever feel that these monks, with but one exception, were pathological or, specifically, schizophrenic. Nor is this a paradox. The psychological analysis (based on Rorschachs and clinical impressions) provides a set of statements concerning the emotional problems of the subjects; it also provides, to a somewhat lesser extent, a picture of their idiosyncratic defenses, i.e., of those defenses which the subjects have constructed for themselves, in an attempt to resolve their problems. That these defenses are hardly adequate to the task is obvious from the Rorschach analysis. Left exclusively to their own inner resources many of these subjects would have become, I believe, genuine psychotics.

But personality does not exist *in vacuo,* and Burmese males, characterized by the problems described, are not confronted with the necessity of solving these problems by means of their own resources. In addition to their private resources, they are able to utilize a powerful cultural resource for their solution, i.e., they can solve their problems by recruitment to the monastic order. By utilizing the role-set prescribed for this institution as a culturally constituted defense, Burmese monks can resolve their conflicts with a minimum of distortion. Since, moreover, the performance of the roles comprising this role-set satisfies their prohibited and/or shameful needs and reduces their painful fears and anxieties, these potentially disruptive psychological variables, rather than provoking socially disruptive behavior, provide the motivational basis for the persistence of the most highly valued institution—monasticism—in Burmese society. As a culturally constituted defense, the monastic institution resolves the inner conflicts of Burmese males, by allowing them to gratify their drives and reduce their anxieties in a disguised—and therefore socially acceptable—manner, one which precludes psychotic distortion, on the one hand, and criminal "acting-out," on the other. Hence, the monk is protected from mental illness and/or social punishment; society is protected from the disruptive consequences of antisocial behavior; and the key institution of Burmese culture—Buddhist monasticism—is provided with a most powerful motivational basis. Space permits only a brief examination of these assertions.

The monastic rules which interdict *all* labor, and those Buddhist norms which guarantee that the laity provide monks with *all* their wants, combine to satisfy the monk's "regressed oral drives." The monastic life, moreover, makes no demands, either social or psychological, which might render the monk's weak "phallic-orientation," his low degree of "striving and impulsivity," and his lack of "self-confidence" nonviable modes of adjustment. Quite the contrary, the physical isolation of the monastery, and the monastic norms proscribing social participation, preclude the stimulation of "disruptive affect." At the same time, the monk's "self-preoccupation" and "erotic self-cathexis" is wonderfully expressed and institutionalized in the prescribed techniques of Buddhist meditation. Latent "homosexual" needs can be satisfied in the exclusively male setting in which the monks live. Finally, the strong interdiction on interaction with females provides little opportunity for encounters with them and for the consequent fear attendant upon such encounters. Buddhist monasticism, then, is a highly efficient means for coping with the psychological problems of many Burmese men. The differences between a monastic and a psychotic resolution of these problems are instructive.

1. In general the genesis of the psychotic's conflict is idiosyncratic, while the genesis of the monk's problem is rooted in modal features of his society. That is, the source of the monk's conflict—which we cannot discuss here—is to be found in culturally constituted experiences which the monk shares with many other members of his social group. The monk differs from other Burmans in one of three ways: his potentially pathogenic experiences are more intense than those of other males; other Burmans utilize alternative, non-Buddhist institutions for the resolution of equally intense problems; still others (a minority) develop idiosyncratic methods of conflict-resolution (in extreme cases, these take the form of mental illness or criminal behavior).

2. The psychotic resolves his problems by means of idiosyncratic,

private defenses; the monk resolves his problems in an institutionalized manner, by utilizing elements of his religious heritage as a culturally constituted defense. The difference between these two types of defense accounts for the following differences between the psychotic patient, on the one hand, and the normal monk, on the other.

3. The behavior of the psychotic is incompatible with any normal social role within his society, and inconsistent with important cultural norms of the larger society. The psychotic is *psychologically incapable* of performing social roles or of complying with those cultural norms which he violates. The behavior of the monk, on the other hand, is entirely appropriate to—indeed, it is the enactment of—a most important and honorific social role. The monk may be psychologically incapable of performing nonmonastic roles, but he is ideally suited for performing the monastic role.

4. As a corollary of the above, the behavior of the psychotic is bizarre in the eyes of, and disapproved of by, his fellows. The behavior of the monk is not only approved by the other members of his society, but it is most highly valued.

5. Following from the last point, the behavior of the psychotic alienates him psychologically from his fellows. The behavior of the monk, on the contrary, though isolating him physically from his group, serves to integrate him psychologically into the group; for in his behavior he expresses the most cherished values of Burmese culture.

6. The world view constructed by the psychotic represents a dramatic distortion of reality, as the latter is structured by the world view of his culture; and the cognitions and perceptions that are derived from his idiosyncratic world view are highly distorted, relative to the behavioral environment in which expected social interaction of his society takes place. The world view of the monk, on the other hand, rather than being constructed from his private fantasies, is taught to him as an integral part of the cultural heritage of his society. The private world view of the monk corresponds to the public world view of his society; his world view, in brief, is a culturally constituted world view. The Buddhist world view, of course, may be false, a distortion of reality, relative to the world view of modern science; but it is true, relative to the knowledge available to Burmese

society. True or false, however, the monk's cognitions and perceptions are consistent with, rather than distortions of, reality, as the latter is structured by the world view and behavioral environment of his society. The perceptions and cognitions, the fantasies and emotions experienced by the monk in the course of Buddhist meditation and concentration may never be experienced by other Burmans— because the latter do not meditate or concentrate—but they are experiences consistent with the conception of reality which all Burmans hold, and they are vouchsafed to any Burman who is prepared to enter into these spiritual disciplines.

7. The psychotic sustains social relationships neither with the normal members of his society, nor with other psychotics. Psychotics, in short, do not participate in the society of which they are members, nor do they comprise a social group distinct from the larger society but nevertheless viable for its constituent members. Burmese monks, on the other hand, although socially isolated from Burmese society, are yet psychologically part of it. Moreover, although the monk may find difficulty in participating in the larger society, and in forming social relationships within it, he does enter into social relationships with other members of the monastic order. Monks are members of increasingly larger concentric groups, beginning with other members of the local monastery and extending to the entire order of monks. In short, while psychotics comprise a typological class, the monks constitute a social group, even if it be but a subgroup of the larger society.

8. Finally, and as a corollary of the last point, the behavior of the psychotic is anomic; it violates many of the rules of his society. The monk, on the other hand, not only exemplifies the rules of Burmese society, but he must, in addition, comply with the 227 rules of the monastic order (as outlined in the *Vinaya*). Should he violate these rules, he is expelled from the order as a charlatan, regardless of whatever wondrous visions he is alleged to have had, or miraculous powers he is supposed to possess.

In summary, then, a psychiatrically diagnosed psychotic is not only incapable of participating in his own society, he is incapable of participating in any society. An American psychotic would function no better in a Buddhist monastery than in an American city. A Buddhist monk, to be sure, while not capable of functioning in every cultural environment, functions very well indeed within *his* cultural environment. This is hardly surprising, since the latter environment is so structured that it satisfies his needs and resolves his conflicts. That he cannot function in a radically different environment does not render him "sick," nor his adjustment precarious. Typically, differential sets of human needs are differentially satisfied in different types of cultural milieux. It is doubtful if the typical Burmese peasant could adjust to an American urban environment, or a typical American to a Buddhist monastery. For neither is the new environment capable of satisfying the needs and resolving the conflicts which were produced by the old.

•   •   •   •

14

Obsessive-Compulsive Style

Wilhelm Reich (1933, p. 199) described compulsive characters as "living machines." It is an apt description and one that is, in fact, confirmed in the subjective experience of some of these people (see Shapiro, 1965, p. 40). It is, also, a good example of a general formal description. This machinelike quality is not to be derived from the content of any instinctual impulse nor from any mental content.

Many formal characteristics of obsessive-compulsive functioning are, in fact, quite familiar, probably more than for any of the other neurotic conditions. For example, we are familiar with a distinctive way of thinking marked by "rigidity," a certain mode of tense activity, and the like. Obsessive-compulsive people also show, in their intellectuality, what is probably the most familiar example of a formal characteristic with both conspicuous defensive and adaptive aspects. However, the fact that such traits are well known by no means necessarily indicates that their formal characteristics are well understood or have been seriously studied. For example, I know of no study of obsessive-compulsive intellectual rigidity, although it is certainly one of the most easily observed psychiatric phenomena. And this is true despite the fact that the obsessive-compulsive neurosis has been the subject of the most intensive study from a dynamic standpoint, that is, from the standpoint of the instinctual and counterinstinctual forces involved in it.

I have selected three aspects of the obsessive-compulsive style of functioning for examination: (1) rigidity, (2) the mode of activity and the distortion of experience of autonomy, and (3) the loss of reality. The first and third aspects are primarily those of cognition and thinking. The second refers to the sort of activity we often describe as "driven" and to aspects of the obsessive-compulsive's most characteristic form of subjective experience; this section comes closest, perhaps, to describing the obsessive-compulsive's way of living in general.

RIGIDITY

The term "rigidity" is frequently used to describe various characteristics of obsessive-compulsive people. It may refer, for example, to a stiff body posture, a stilted social manner, or a general tendency to persist in a course of action that has become irrelevant or even absurd. But, above all, "rigidity" describes a style of thinking.

What exactly is meant by rigidity of thinking? Consider as a commonplace example the sort of thinking one encounters in a discussion with a compulsive, rigid person, the kind of person we also call "dogmatic" or "opinionated." Even casual conversation with such a person is often very frustrating, and it is so for a particular reason. It is not simply that one meets with unexpected opposition. On the contrary, such discussion is typically frustrating just because one experiences neither real disagreement nor agreement. Instead, there is no meeting of minds at all, and the impression is simply of not being heard, of not receiving any but perfunctory attention. The following excerpt from a conversation will illustrate the point. Two friends, K and L, are discussing the buying of a house in which K is interested.

K: So you think I shouldn't buy it?
L: Never buy a house with a bad roof. It will cost you its price again in repairs before you're finished.
K: But the builder I hired to look it over did say it was in good condition otherwise.
L: The roof is only the beginning. First it's the roof and then comes the plumbing and then the heating and then the plaster.
K: Still, those things seem to be all right.
L: And, after the plaster, it will be the wiring.
K: But the wiring is. . . .
L: [interrupts with calm assurance] It will cost double the price before you're finished.

In this illustration, L does not exactly disagree with K. He does not actually object to or oppose K's arguments, and he cannot be called "negativistic." He simply does not pay attention. This is an inattention, furthermore, that has a special quality; it is quite different, for instance, from the wandering attention of a tired person. This inattention seems somehow to have an active and, as it were, a principled quality. It is in just such inattention to new facts or a different point of view that rigidity (or its more specific form, dogmatism) in the obsessive-compulsive person seems to manifest itself. It is this inattention that makes us experience these people as being so utterly uninfluenceable. Without defining it further for the time being, let me say, therefore, that some kind of special restriction of attention seems to be one crucial feature of obsessive-compulsive intellectual rigidity, although not necessarily the only one.

It may clarify this feature, as well as others, of the compulsive's rigidity to consider the fact that intellectual rigidity is not peculiar to obsessive-compulsive people. Specifically, quite dramatic forms of such rigidity are often observed in cases of organic brain damage. This comparison may seem a strange one, but it is valid enough. The phenomena described by the term "rigidity" in these two types of pathology do in fact have essential features in common. I would like to digress briefly to examine certain features of thought rigidity in organic cases, where it is certainly more vivid and, on the whole, better understood than in obsessive-compulsives.

Goldstein and Scheerer (1941) and others have shown that the rigidity of the organically brain-damaged person is an aspect of the concrete, "stimulus-bound" quality of their cognition and general mode of approach. The organically brain-damaged person's attention appears to be gripped or passively held by a more or less immediately manifest or concrete aspect of a situation or task (or by an aspect that has been otherwise imposed on his attention), and he cannot detach himself from it. His attention, held by one aspect of a situation or task, can be distracted, that is, it can be pulled away, but he is not able to shift it himself. He has, in other words, lost the capacity for volitional direction of attention.

For example, a patient who has just succeeded in reciting the days of the week is now asked to recite the alphabet. He cannot shift to this task, and only after repeated promptings, or better stated, after the examiner has commenced to call out the alphabet, can the patient follow in his recitation. . . . . Another patient can call out the number series from one on, but if the examiner asks him to begin with a number other than one, the patient is at a loss, he must start with one. (Goldstein & Scheerer, 1941, p. 5.)

The normal person, in contrast, has the capacity *not* to be gripped, the capacity to detach himself from the concrete or immediately manifest features of a situation or task and to shift his attention smoothly and rapidly, now to this aspect, now to that aspect. He has the capacity for volitional direction of attention.

What I am describing here is, of course, what we call "flexibility." I am suggesting that cognitive flexibility may be described as a mobility of attention of this sort, a volitional mobility of attention. Now, we concluded before that obsessive-compulsive intellectual rigidity, also, was characterized by some special limitation of attention. Can we say that, notwithstanding the obvious disparity between the obsessive-compulsive's and the brain-damaged person's rigidity, they have this feature in common: that both are characterized by some general loss or impairment of volitional mobility of attention?

Although the obsessive-compulsive's attention certainly cannot be described as stimulus-bound or flagrantly unable to shift volitionally, as in the brain-damaged person, it is in fact far from being free and mobile. Let me describe this mode of attention and its limitations more closely.

The most conspicuous characteristic of the obsessive-compulsive's attention is its intense, sharp focus. These people are not vague in their attention. They concentrate, and particularly do they concentrate on detail. This is evident, for example, in the Rorschach test in their accumulation, frequently, of large numbers of small "detail-responses" and their precise delineation of them (small profiles of faces all along the edges of the inkblots, and the like), and the same affinity is easily observed in everyday life. Thus, these people are very often to be found among technicians; they are interested in, and at home with, technical details. The same sharpness of attention is, of course, also an aspect of many obsessive-compulsive symptoms. They will notice a bit of dust or worry over some insignificant inaccuracy that, everything else aside, simply would not gain the attention of another person. But the obsessive-compulsive's attention, although sharp, is in certain respects markedly limited in both mobility and range. These people not only concentrate; they seem always to be concentrating. And some aspects of the world are simply not to be apprehended by a sharply focused and concentrated attention. Specifically, this is a mode of attention that seems unequipped for the casual or immediate impression, that more passive and impressionistic sort of cognitive experience that can include in its notice or allow one to be "struck" by even that which is peripheral or incidental to its original, intended focus of attention or that may not even possess a clear intention or sharp focus in the first place. These people seem unable to allow their attention simply to wander or passively permit it to be captured. Thus, they rarely seem to get hunches, and they are rarely struck or surprised by anything. It is not that they do not look or listen, but they are looking or listening too hard for something else.

For example, these people may listen to a recording with the keenest interest in, and attention to, the quality of the equipment, the technical features of the record, and the like, but meanwhile hardly hear, let alone are captured by, the music.

In general, the obsessive-compulsive person will have some sharply defined interest and will stick to it; he will go after and get the facts—and will get them straight—but he will often miss those aspects of a situation that give it its flavor or its impact. Thus, these people often seem quite insensitive to the "tone" of social situations. In fact—such is the human capacity to make a virtue of a necessity— they often refer with pride to their singlemindedness or imperturbability.

The sharp but narrowed focus of the obsessive-compulsive's mode of attention, then, misses certain aspects of the world even while it engages others quite successfully. Not every mode of cognition that is capable of intense concentration and sharply focused attention suffers these limitations. Some people are able to regard the casual impression with a casual attention, to entertain the hunch, to notice the element on the periphery of attention briefly, in other words, and then pass on (or not) with greater or lesser gain. This is a free mobility of attention, a flexible cognitive mode. But the obsessive-compulsive person is not so equipped. For him the hunch or the passing impression is only a potential distraction, and a discomforting one at that, from his single-minded concentration. And he seems to avoid that distraction exactly by the intensity of his sharp, narrow focus of attention. Let me explain this further.

We are not born with the ability to concentrate intensely, to look or listen technically, sharply, and intently for something, or to keep our mind's eye focused keenly on a single point for a long period of time and, as we say, follow a train of thought. The cognition of childhood is highly impressionistic and distractible; the child's attention is, at it were, open and ready to be captured. Those active and normally volitional cognitive capacities, such as the capacity for intense and sustained concentration, in which the obsessive-compulsive excels are capacities that mature slowly in childhood (Schachtel, 1959; see particularly Chapter 11, pp. 251-78) and quite possibly continue developing even into adolescence. Probably these capacities for volitional direction of attention develop, at least in their initial phases, along with the development of other capacities for volitional direction, including muscular direction, and of intentionality in general. At any rate, in the normal case these cognitive capacities *are* achieved; direction and maintenance of attention *at will* in such forms as sustained concentration becomes possible. Normally, in fact, these capacities for intense and sharply focused attention become sufficiently well established to permit them to be activated and relaxed at will and so smoothly as to be hardly noticeable. The normal person, in other words, can concentrate *and* entertain a hunch, and he can allow his attention to shift not only in direction, but also in intensity and can do all this smoothly. In some cases, however—and the obsessive-compulsive is one, although not the only one—this directedness of attention seems to be maintained, and is apparently maintainable, only under continuous tension, with great intensity and extreme narrowness of focus—in other words, in a continuous, rigid, and in some respects hypertrophied form.

We are, then, entitled to say that this cognitive mode does involve an impairment of the normal volitional mobility of attention. The normal capacity for smooth and volitional shifts between a sharply directed and a more relaxed, impressionistic cognition is absent here. Elements on the periphery of attention, the new or the surprising, that which can only be apprehended impressionistically—all these are only potentially distracting and disruptive to the obsessive-compulsive, and they are avoided exactly by the intensity and the fixed narrowness of his preoccupation with his own idea or aim. It is like shooting an arrow on a windy day; the greater the tension of the bow and force of the arrow, the less susceptible the arrow will be to incidental winds. This is what we mean by the obsessive-compulsive's intellectual rigidity and what we experience as a quality of "active inattention" to any external influence or any new idea on the part of the compulsive dogmatic person. It will, also, be understandable from this view of obsessive-compulsive cognition that the same qualities that make these people seem so rigid in one context endow them, in another, with excellent technical facility and an impressive capacity for concentration on a technical problem.

THE MODE OF ACTIVITY AND THE GENERAL DISTORTION OF THE EXPERIENCE OF AUTONOMY

In each neurotic style, one can describe, in addition to a characteristic cognitive mode, interrelated modes of activity, of affect experience, and the like. But there is no doubt that, among the neurotic styles, there are not only differences in form of functioning within such areas as these, but also differences in the significance the various areas may have in the overall psychological organization. In the hysterical style, for instance, affective experience virtually dominates the individual's existence. In the obsessive-compulsive style, on the other hand, affective experience as a whole shrinks, as will soon become plain; it is in the nature of this style that life pivots around work activity and certain sorts of subjective experience associated with it.

The most conspicuous fact about the activity of the obsessive-compulsive is its sheer quantity and, along with this, its intensity and concentration. These people may be enormously productive in socially recognized ways, or they may not; however that may be, they are, typically, intensely and more or less continuously active at some kind of work. In particular, they are perhaps most typically represented in intensive routine or technical work. In fact, many compulsive symptoms consist of grotesque intensifications of just such activities.

For example, there is the compulsive patient who spends all day intensively cleaning and recleaning the house or the obsessional patient who spends vast amounts of time carefully collecting and transcribing to index cards data on all the schools and colleges he can locate with the dim justification of some day attending "the best."

This basic fact of the more or less continuous absorption of these people in intensive activity of this sort is a significant one, and it is worth noting already that it is a mode of functioning that is well suited to their rigid, technical cognition; but there is another quality about this activity that is equally distinctive. I am speaking now about the special subjective quality of it. The activity—one could just as well say the life—of these people is characterized by a more or less continuous experience of tense deliberateness, a sense of effort, and of trying.

Everything seems deliberate for them. Nothing is effortless. This tense deliberateness or sense of trying cannot be regarded simply as a greater measure of the experience of effort felt by anyone engaged in an activity that in some way taxes his capacities. For the compulsive person, the quality of effort is present in every activity, whether it taxes his capacities or not. Or, to put it more accurately, every activity seems to be carried out in such a way as to tax his capacities. In the area of work, of course, such a quality of effort is generally more expected and, therefore, less noticeable, and there is no doubt that work is the obsessive-compulsive's preferred area of existence. But the effortfulness and tense deliberateness extends also into activities that are, for the normal person, playful or fun. The compulsive person tries just as effortfully to "enjoy" himself at play as he does to accomplish or produce at work.

One such person carefully scheduled his Sundays with certain activities in order to produce "maximum enjoyment." He determinedly set about enjoying himself and became quite upset if anything interfered with his schedule, not merely because he missed the activity, but because his holiday had been spent inefficiently. Another compulsive patient always tried hard, in his social life, to be "spontaneous."

How can we understand the continuous effortfulness, trying, and tense deliberateness of this way of living? How can we distinguish it, aside from its continuousness, from the normal person's effort to do something that taxes him? The normal person's effort, one might say, is hard, whereas the obsessive-compulsive's effort is labored. Let me clarify the distinction further in another way. When the normal person says that he will try to do something, he means that he intends to do his best to do it, but the obsessive-compulsive person does not mean exactly that. When the obsessive-compulsive person says that he will try, he means, not necessarily that he intends to *do* it or do his best to do it, but that he intends to tax himself with the task, admonish himself to do it, and perhaps worry about it. Sometimes, in fact, when he says he will *try,* he has no intention of *doing* it at all.

Thus, a patient announced that she was going to try to stop smoking, and with this announcement she did, indeed, look as if she were making some kind of mental effort. But at the same time she proceeded to take a cigarette out and light it. Clearly her statement did not reflect an intention to stop; it reflected, instead, an intention to achieve a special state of effort or, perhaps, an intention to worry about stopping.

Deliberateness, trying, effort of will are obviously a part of normal psychological life as well as that of the obsessive-compulsive. But the object of the normal person's will is, on the whole, something external to himself; he decides to stop smoking. The object of the obsessive-compulsive's will, on the other hand, seems in part at least to be himself; he decides to "try" to stop smoking.

Sometimes the obsessive-compulsive's activity is also described as "driven." No doubt, this description refers partly to the sheer quantity and intensity of his activity, suggesting, I suppose, that no one could possibly work as hard of his own free will. But the term is apt in another sense as well. The compulsive's activity actually has the appearance of being pressed or motivated by something beyond the interest of the acting person. He does not seem that enthusiastic. His genuine interest in the activity, in other words, does not seem to account for the intensity with which he pursues it. Instead he acts, and indeed he feels, as though he were being pressed by some necessity or requirement which he is at pains to satisfy. In actual fact, he *is* pressed by such a necessity or requirement. But it is not an external requirement. It is a requirement and a pressure that he applies to himself.

Thus, these people will frequently give themselves deadlines for various activities, which logically may be quite arbitrary. One patient decided that he must have a better job by his next birthday or else he would have to regard himself as a failure. Of course, he then felt extremely pressed as the day approached, as anyone would given his assumption. With the passing of his birthday, the deadline was shifted to the first of the year, and so on.

If, in other words, we choose to characterize the obsessive-compulsive's activity as driven, then we must also characterize him as the driver. He not only suffers under the pressure of the deadline; he also sets it. And he not only sets it, but also continually reminds himself of its existence and its nearness. He will never complain about this aspect of his behavior, incidentally, nor see it as "neurotic." Although, from an objective standpoint, this attitude is quite critical to the neurotic process, from his standpoint it is only good sense. He will often complain, however, and, in a sense, quite justifiably, about the experience of the pressure itself.

Thus, to speak of the drivenness of obsessive-compulsive activity, on the one hand, or the tense deliberateness and effortfulness of it, on the other, is only to describe variations of the same mode. It is a mode of activity in which the individual exerts a more or less continuous pressure on himself, while at the same time living and working under the strain of that pressure. The obsessive-compulsive person functions like his own overseer issuing commands, directives, reminders, warnings, and admonitions concerning not only what is to be done and what is not to be done, but also what is to be wanted, felt, and even thought. This is the meaning of the single most characteristic thought-content of obsessive-compulsive people: "I should." Depending on its tone, it may be a directive, a reminder, a warning, or an admonition; but in one tone or another, the obsessive-compulsive tells himself, "I should . . . ," almost continuously. I would like to suggest now that this mode of activity and experience reflects a remarkable distortion of the normal function and experience of will or volition, a general distortion comparable to the more specific one that we discussed in connection with the problem of intellectual rigidity.

In the relatively helpless infant, behaving reflexively, pressed from the inside by drives, compelled from the outside by drive objects, one hardly can speak of volition or intentionality, except, possibly, in the most rudimentary sense. In the course of development, however, human beings acquire the capacity for many kinds of volitional activity and function or, in general, the capacity to do things intentionally, deliberately, or at will. This capacity, insofar as it describes an individual's capacity to direct himself, that is, to direct various aspects of his behavior, his actions, his attention to a certain extent, and so on, may also be called a capacity for "autonomous" functioning. I cannot say, and it is not necessary here to attempt it, what kinds of maturational process and equipment are involved in that general development, although we know certain landmarks of it (such as the development of volitional bowel control). Its initial phases must involve not only the development of muscular equipment, but, for example, various cognitive capacities, such as the capacity for anticipation, elementary planning, and so on, which will be essential if the new muscular capacities are to achieve their normal significance and be exercised with their normal competency. In any case, in the course of this development—which probably extends throughout childhood and even adolescence and is not to be wholly identified with any brief developmental phase—much that was originally involuntary becomes supplemented or superseded by volitional behavior. The means of satisfying hunger, eliminative functions, and even ideational and thought processes come to be, at least to some extent, within the domain of intentional direction. This development of the capacity for deliberate and purposeful activity gradually must bring with it many new kinds of psychological experience and new kinds and dimensions of self-awareness. Among these is a new sense of self-direction, autonomy, or choice that we usually describe as the experience of "will," and we are used to seeing in children who are somewhat flush with this new experience that special interest and satisfaction in the exercise of their autonomy that we call "willfulness."

Not every aspect of psychological function and behavior becomes deliberate or comes under willful direction. While the satisfaction of instinctual drives becomes a subject, up to a certain point, of intention and will, the drives themselves never come under the domination of intentionality. It is not in the nature of drives or affects to be called up and banished at will (a fact that compulsive people, when they tell themselves that they "should" feel this way or "should not" feel that way refuse to recognize). In general, while the capacity for willful or volitional choice and action implies an immense enlargement of possibilities of satisfactions and interests, the nature of one's interests, preferences, or feelings is not itself subject to choice or determinable at will. For the normal person, the fact that one sector of life, so to speak, is within the domain of intentionality and volition and another sector is not presents no special problem. If the capacity for volition and the sense of autonomy and will are well established they can also be relaxed to make room for whim, playfulness, spontaneity of affective expression, and the like. A person whose direction of himself is secure can, in other words, afford abandonment of direction of himself in various forms and degrees with neither the expectation nor the fact of disastrous consequences. Altogether, in the normal case, intentionality becomes sufficiently well established to function smoothly, without self-consciousness and, for the most part, without any special tension, and the willfulness of childhood seems to develop into an adult's sense of competency and freedom to do with himself what he chooses.

In certain cases, however, the development of will and volition is achieved only in a markedly distorted and rigid form. The obsessive-compulsive represents one such case, and . . . the paranoid represents another. The obsessive-compulsive person lives in a continuous state of volitional tension. We have encountered one aspect of this state in the form of his intellectual rigidity, but it pervades every aspect of his life. In his psychology, self-direction is distorted from its normal meaning of volitional choice and deliberate, purposeful action to a self-conscious directing of his every action, to the exercise, as if by an overseer, of a continuous willful pressure and direction on himself and even, strange as it may appear, an effort to direct his own wants and emotions at will. These people are "willful" with a vengeance. Every action, every direction is weighty, heavy with deliberateness, like an act of state. They not only tolerate no interference with their own willful direction by others, that is, in the sense of being stubborn, but also, embarked on their deliberate course, they tolerate no interference even from themselves. Willful directedness has been distorted from its normal subjective significance as an extension and, so to speak, representative of one's wants to a position of precedence over wants, aimed even at directing them. Impulse, in this order of things, is not the initiator or the first stage of willful directedness and effort, but its enemy. Thus, for these people, impulse or wish is only a temptation which can corrupt their determination, interrupt their work, interfere with what they feel they "should" want to be doing, or otherwise endanger their rigid directedness. They are, therefore, cut off from the sources that normally give willful effort its direction, a fact that has, as will become plain, many consequences.

There are a great many manifestations of this general mode of functioning in the obsessive-compulsive's life, some of them, incidentally, so much a part of our culture, particularly our work culture, that they are taken for granted and hardly excite attention. One important and interesting example of this style of experience and activity is what we call "will power." Will power, so characteristic of the obsessive-compulsive and so adaptable to routine work activity, is comprised exactly of the experience of issuing willful commands and directives to oneself.

This style of activity and experience, it will be clear, also implies a special kind of self-awareness, an awareness of the overseer sitting behind and issuing commands, directives, and reminders, that the obsessive-compulsive person is never without. It is the self-awareness of a person who is working under pressure with a stopwatch in hand. Since, for the obsessive-compulsive, virtually all of life is transformed into such activity, the experience for him is continuous. We see this, for example, in the role-playing that is characteristic of these people. It is important for the obsessive-compulsive person always to be aware that he is a "this" or a "that." This awareness of and interest in establishing his role is an essential step in the transformation of whole areas of living into his characteristic mode. Once his role is established in his mind, it becomes a general directive for behavior, one that is often capable of including even the details of facial expressions, ways of speaking, and the like. Compulsive people are usually especially aware, in this way, of their professional role—the compulsive doctor plays the doctor—or their marital or parental role. They are often aware even of the role of themselves and act it; that is, they have an awareness, in certain respects, of what they are like, and they direct their behavior accordingly. It is this awareness of "role" and acting always under its directive that frequently gives the behavior of these people a stilted quality or a stuffy, pompous one. Fenichel gives a good example of this process, though without indicating its generality.

A patient felt well only as long as he knew what "role" he was supposed to "play." When at work he thought, "I am a worker," and this gave him the necessary security; when at home, "Now I am the husband who comes home from work to his beloved family." (Fenichel, 1945, p. 530.)

It should be added, however, that in this example it is not simply the *awareness* that is essential to this patient, but rather that the awareness is essential to the *directive* and the whole characteristic mode of activity and experience. Thus, when the patient thinks, "Now I am a worker," he means, also, "Now I should behave according to how workers behave."

Another, modern, example of the same process is the obsessional patient in psychotherapy who is interested in finding out from his dreams, fantasies, and so forth, what he "really" thinks, wants, and feels like. Once he finds out, he needs only to direct himself to act that way.

Where, and how, does the obsessive-compulsive person derive these directives, commands, and pressures, the "shoulds" which he issues to himself and under which he then lives? Objectively, there is no doubt that they come from him: *He* reminds himself of his "role," contrives and invokes his deadlines, issues his own commands. But notwithstanding that the authorship and the responsibility for these commands and directives may, objectively, be solely his, he does not feel that they are his. He does not feel that he issues these directives wholly on his own authority and by his own free choice. On the contrary, the obsessive-compulsive always feels that he is reminding himself of some compelling objective necessity, some imperative or higher authority than his personal choice or wish, which he is obliged to serve.

Thus, these people feel that propriety requires them to dress neatly, duty obliges them to visit Aunt Tilly, the boss's expectations make it necessary to finish the job early, health requires a certain amount of calisthenics every day, mental health necessitates a certain number of hobbies and a quantity of "relaxation," culture a certain amount of reading and music, and so on. It does not occur to the compulsive person that to many other people none of these duties and "necessities" carry any weight at all, and if it does occur, no matter—to him they do carry weight.

When the obsessive-compulsive person acts as his own overseer, he also feels that he acts in response to the requirements of some objective necessity, particularly some moral necessity. He feels in the capacity of agent or representative to himself of that objective necessity or imperative. These external pressures or imperatives, which the obsessive-compulsive person endows with such compelling authority, take many forms. These people are keenly aware of various kinds of external expectation, of the threat of possible criticism, of the weight and direction of authoritative opinion, of rules, regulations, and conventions, and, perhaps above all, of a great assemblage of moral or quasimoral principles. They do not feel literally forced to comply with these, and they do not precisely submit to them. They recognize their authority and press themselves, for example, feel duty-bound, to comply with them.

The necessity to maintain a rigid and continuous state of directed and purposive activity and a continuous pressure on himself requires an experience of this sort, that is, an experience of some compelling necessity or moral imperative superior to his own wishes or choices. This regime of rigid, willful pressure—the regime of effort, in other words—has no intrinsic direction. The obsessive-compulsive stands ready for duty, ready to exercise will power, ready to work or at least to "try," but he must have, in order to function in this way, some authoritative directive to transmit to himself. These people feel and function like driven, hardworking, automatons pressing themselves to fulfill unending duties, "responsibilities," and tasks that are, in their view, not chosen, but simply there.

One compulsive patient likened his whole life to a train that was running efficiently, fast, pulling a substantial load, but on a track laid out for it.

In other words, they do not feel like free men. In fact, they feel exceedingly uncomfortable in circumstances that do offer them a whiff of freedom. This is a common difficulty that obsessive-compulsive people experience on vacations or holidays. On just those occasions when the regular duties, responsibilities, and burdens of work, about which they have complained, are lifted, they show unmistakable signs of discomfort until they have located some new pressure or compelling duty.

One patient frequently expressed the complaint about weekends, "But I don't know what I want to do." He tried to solve the problem by a psychological search of himself, including even his dreams, in order to find out what he "wanted" to do, working on the theory that it was a rule of mental health to do what one wanted to do.

The pressures and directives with which the obsessive-compulsive person lives are beyond doubt extremely burdensome to him, but they are also authoritative guides. They provide a framework within which he can function comparatively comfortably, but outside of which he is extremely discomforted. At work, these people are often most comfortable feeling that they have their own little niche or bailiwick in which they devote themselves to carrying out their established duties ordained by higher authorities. Their choices become narrowed to technical ones—the best way to meet the deadline or satisfy the expectation. Their satisfactions are not the satisfactions of decision and freedom, but the satisfactions of duty for the time being done, authority temporarily pleased, and, frequently, the satisfactions of exercising a highly developed technical virtuosity and ingenuity.

　　　•　　　　　•　　　　　•　　　　　•

Obviously much of life, aside from work, shrinks and is severely restricted in this style of functioning. Certain areas of psychological life simply are not compatible with a continuous, rigid state of deliberate activity or tension. Certain kinds of subjective experience, affect experience particularly, require by their nature an abandonment or at least a relaxation of the attitude of deliberateness, and, where such relaxation is impossible, as in the obsessive-compulsive style, those areas of psychological life tend to shrink. Hence, the dry, mechanical quality or the dull heaviness that frequently characterizes these people. One sometimes witnesses the unhappy spectacle of such a person deliberately attempting to achieve a state of mind or a mood, such as a mood of gaiety, for which a relaxation of such deliberateness is the first prerequisite.

Sometimes this restriction of affect is mistakenly attributed to the obsessive-compulsive's "overcontrol," which suggests that these people can deliberately or by effort of will restrict or otherwise control their own experience of affect or impulse. This, of course, they cannot do, much as they might like to; they can only control to some extent the outward expression of affect. But, although they cannot curb or restrict affect experience *by* deliberate effort, the *existence* of that state of tense deliberateness—and the discomfort, should that deliberateness begin to relax, that moves them to resume it—*automatically* restricts not only affect experience, but also whim, playfulness, and spontaneous action in general.

The discomfort that these people feel in the face of any temptation to relax their attitude of deliberateness, their effortful activity, or their purposefulness takes many specific forms, is expressed in many attitudes, and often involves elaborate rationalizations.

For example, one patient maintained that he must avoid watching any television since he might enjoy it, want to watch more, become addicted to it and want to do nothing else, and then, what would become of the book he was writing?

In general, obsessive-compulsive people feel that any relaxation of deliberateness or purposeful activity is improper, unsafe, or worse. If they are not working, they usually feel that they should at least be thinking (that is, worrying) about some problem, and the prospect of not worrying about a problem that exists, even if it is one that they can do nothing about, seems quite foolhardy to them. They do not feel comfortable with any activity that lacks an aim or a purpose beyond its own pleasure, and usually they do not recognize the possibility of finding life satisfying without a continuous sense of purpose and effort, a continuous sense of advancing the career, making money, writing papers, or the like.

Sometimes obsessive-compulsive people experience an unusual impulse or temptation together with a specific kind of anxiety and discomfort that is worth mentioning here. I am referring to the fear of "going crazy" or, as it is sometimes described, the feeling of "loss of control" that is, at one time or another, quite commonly expressed by these people. It is sometimes assumed that this experience necessarily reflects an actual danger of psychosis, a weakness of defense and an actual pressure of primitive impulse of great intensity. Although sometimes this is no doubt the case, it is by no means invariably so. This fear seems to arise in obsessive-compulsive people when, for whatever reason, their usual rigid deliberateness is significantly interrupted, for example when they are tempted to some unusually abandoned, but by no means necessarily aggressive or primitive, behavior.

Thus, a fear of "losing control" is often experienced, and expressed in therapy hours, by rigid people when they start to laugh very hard or become unusually excited and lose their usual sober composure.

In other words, the experience by these people of an imminent "loss of control" often seems to represent no more than their sensation of a loss or relaxation of volitional tension, a relaxation of "will," and while this is an experience which from their standpoint may seem like "going crazy," it is by no means equivalent to a loss or breakdown of defensive or other such impulse-control structures as would be involved in an actual psychotic episode.

There is another kind of psychological experience that seems to be at least as discomforting to the obsessive-compulsive person as a temporary abandonment to impulse or whim. I am speaking of the process of decision-making. Among the activities of ordinary life, there is probably none for which this style is less suited. No amount of hard work, driven activity, or will power will help in the slightest degree to make a decision. Sometimes the difficulty and discomfort that these people experience when a decision is in prospect is explained as a reflection of their ambivalence. But what distinguishes obsessional people in the face of a decision is not their mixed feelings, but rather the fact that those feelings are always so marvelously and perfectly balanced. In fact, it is easy to observe that just at the moment when an obsessional person seems to be approaching a decision, just when the balance is at last tipping decisively in one direction, he will discover some new item that reestablishes that perfect balance. The obsessive-compulsive person, in other words, shrinks from the act of decision. It is not surprising that he should. To a person driven by a sense of pressure and guided by moral directives, to a rigid soldier devoted only to duty and cut off from his own wants, the act of decision, which, by its nature, pivots around wants and normally brings with it a sense of freedom and free choice, can only be extremely discomforting. Yet no one can avoid decision, and it is interesting to see the mental operations that appear in obsessive-compulsive people at such times and, as it were, carry them through these occasions.

When he is confronted by the necessity for a decision, even one which may be trivial from a normal standpoint, the obsessive-compulsive person will typically attempt to reach a solution by invoking some rule, principle, or external requirement which might, with some degree of plausibility, provide a "right" answer. He will, in other words, seek some means by which the process of decision-making can be fit into his regular mode of functioning. If he can find some principle or external requirement which plausibly applies to the situation at hand, the necessity for a decision disappears as such; that is, it becomes transformed into the purely technical problem of applying the correct principle. Thus, if he can remember that it is always sensible to go to the cheapest movie, or "logical" to go to the closest, or good to go to the most educational, the problem resolves to a technical one, simply finding which *is* the most educational, the closest, or such. In an effort to find such requirements and principles, he will invoke morality, "logic," social custom and propriety, the rules of "normal" behavior (especially if he is a psychiatric patient), and so on. In short he will try to figure out what he "should" do. Sometimes, with one or more principles in mind, he may add up pros and cons—the advantages to the children on the one side, but the expense on the other, and so on—hoping that the result of this more complicated technical procedure will be decisive. Sometimes it is, or rather, may appear to be, and many such "decisions" are a part of the obsessive-compulsive's daily life. Thus, he decides to wear one suit rather than another because it is more "appropriate." But many decisions, particularly those outside his already accustomed routine, are not easily susceptible to being dealt with in this way. No plausible principle appears, or a number appear, but none of them sufficiently authoritative. And this is almost as likely to happen in matters where the objective consequences are trivial as where they are not.

When the obsessive-compulsive person is unable to reach a decision by formula or rule, he may begin to stew. He will *struggle* to find the *right* solution. He will tax himself, work at it night and day, drive himself to "think" about it. But the obsessive-compulsive person's stewing has very little in common with the normal person's thinking over of the relevant facts. In the course of his stewing, the obsessive person will continue long after he has worn out the relevant facts, and exhausted any possibility of new understanding from them. He will have combined them in all their possible combinations, and done so many times. He has, in other words, tried once again to deal with the problem of decision according to his style. He tries to deal with it as if it were the most taxing technical problem—the search for the "right" answer. But most of the time this search is bound to fail. There is no "right" answer in his sense, in the sense that there is a right answer to a technical problem. The decision, as much as he shrinks from the fact, comes to a choice, a preference.

It is often noticeable that, despite all the hesitation and weighing of pros and cons that precedes the obsessive-compulsive's decision, the actual decision or the actual change will be made exceedingly abruptly. Despite the total length of time consumed, the decision itself will be quite attenuated as compared with the normal person's; it will be very much like a leap. He will finally say or feel something like, "What the hell!" or, "I've got to do something!" and pick the next suit that the salesman happens to offer or quickly sign the contract. Once the choice is made, then, these people will often regard it as a new directive, admitting no new evidence and preferring to feel that the situation no longer allows of modification. Once the obsessive-compulsive can experience this, he can again devote himself with relief to the narrower and more accustomed task of executing the directive. Will power and the general mode of driven activity once again find application. But the interplay between decision and the new data that continuously become available in the course of action, which is central to the activity of a more flexible person, hardly exists for the obsessive-compulsive.

THE LOSS OF REALITY

Sometimes obsessive-compulsive people worry (that is, do their taxing mental work) about things that are not merely unlikely but truly absurd. Their worries—hypochondriacal ideas, for example—can be so outlandish that they seem to border on the delusional. Even if one makes allowances for all the motives the obsessional person may have for worry, when he talks as if he believes he has contracted some serious disease through the most remote chain of contacts is this not at least an incipient delusion? Or, for that matter, when such a person has just finished meticulously cleaning a table and acts now as though he believes that the table has instantly again become dirty and requires cleaning, should this be considered delusion? To answer these questions, the fact that he behaves merely "as though" he believes must be considered carefully, for it turns out that the obsessional person does not really believe these things at all. He does not really believe that the table is dirty or that he has been dangerously contaminated in the sense in which we ordinarily use the word "believe." In fact, close examination shows that he never even states that he believes these things to be true. He never says, "I have cancer," or "I have been contaminated." He says, rather, that he might have been contaminated or that he could have cancer, and this is an important difference.

It may be noted, furthermore, that the obsessive-compulsive's interest at such times is different from what we might consider normal concern. Typically, his greatest interest is in what are essentially "technical details." He tells us with great concern, for example, that such and such a person might have touched such and such a person who, in turn, probably had contact with a doorknob that he has used—details that by their nature are incapable of decisively settling the important matter with which he is ostensibly concerned. These technical details seem to replace matters of substantial truth in his interest. The same issue comes up in connection with obsessional doubt in general. We see that obsessional people have doubts about obvious matters, in circumstances where lack of information, which may give rise to normal doubt, cannot possibly be held accountable. If one assumes that the sense of truth and the meaning of doubt are for the obsessive-compulsive what they are from the normal point of view, one would frequently be forced to the conclusion that the obsessional person is deluded. However, this assumption does not seem to be warranted.

· · · ·

15

The Key Cause — Type A Behavior Pattern

MEYER FRIEDMAN
and
RAY H. ROSENMAN

WHAT IS TYPE A BEHAVIOR PATTERN?

Type A Behavior Pattern is an action-emotion complex that can be observed in any person who is *aggressively* involved in a *chronic, incessant* struggle to achieve more and more in less and less time, and is required to do so, against the opposing efforts of other things or other persons. It is not psychosis or a complex of worries or fears or phobias or obsessions, but a socially acceptable—indeed often praised—form of conflict. Persons possessing this pattern also are quite prone to exhibit a free-floating but extraordinarily well-rationalized hostility. As might be expected, there are degrees in the intensity of this behavior pattern. Moreover, because the pattern represents the reaction that takes place when particular personality traits of an afflicted individual are challenged or aroused by a specific environmental agent, the results of this reaction (that is, the behavior pattern itself) may not be felt or exhibited by him if he happens to be in or confronted by an environment that presents no challenge. For example, a usually hard-driving, competitive, aggressive editor of an urban newspaper, if hospitalized with a trivial illness, may not exhibit a single sign of Type A Behavior Pattern. In short, for Type A Behavior Pattern to explode into being, the *environmental challenge must always serve as the fuse for this explosion*.

The person with Type B Behavior Pattern is the exact opposite of the Type A subject. He, unlike the Type A person, is rarely harried by desires to obtain a wildly increasing number of things or participate in an endlessly growing series of events in an ever decreasing amount of time. His intelligence may be as good as or even better than that of the Type A subject. *Similarly, his ambition may be as great or even greater than that of his Type A counterpart.* He may also have a considerable amount of "drive," but its character is such that it seems to steady him, give confidence and security to him, rather than to goad, irritate, and infuriate, as with the Type A man.

In our experience, based on extensive practices in typing and then observing many hundreds of individuals, the general run of urban Americans tend to fall into one or the other of these two groups. The Type As, we have found, predominate; they usually represent somewhat over half of all those in the open samples we tested. There are somewhat fewer true Type B individuals, perhaps 40 percent of the whole. People in whom Type A and Type B characteristics are mixed account for about 10 percent. If our testing procedures can be further refined—and we are, of course, constantly trying to do this—we believe that the number in this middle group can be reduced. In other words, most Americans are in fact either Type A or Type B, though in varying degrees.

Again we should like to reiterate that, with exceedingly rare exception, the socioeconomic position of a man or woman does not determine whether he or she is a Type A or Type B subject. The presidents of many banks and corporations (perhaps even the majority) may be Type B individuals. Conversely, many janitors, shoe salesmen, truck drivers, architects, even florists may be Type A subjects. We have not found any clear correlation between occupational position held and the incidence of Type A Behavior Pattern. Why is this so? Because (1) a sense of job or position responsiblity is not synonymous with the Type A sense of time urgency; (2) excessive drive or competitive enthusiasm may only too frequently be expended upon economic trivia rather than affairs of importance; and (3) promotion and elevation, particularly in corporate and professional organizations, usually go to those who are wise rather than to those who are merely hasty, to those who are tactful rather than to those who are hostile, and to those who are creative rather than to those who are merely agile in competitive strife. (And if you who are reading this happen to be a wife of a Type A executive, attorney, physician, or florist, this last should not be forgotten, even if your husband insists that it isn't true.)

Before we begin to draw a detailed portrait of the Type A man, we should like to forestall one rather important source of misunderstanding. We are not psychologists. What follows is an honest description of symptoms and signs as *we have observed them*. We are convinced that they form, in themselves, a significant behavior pattern, and we *know*, by virtue of our own professional expertise, that this group of traits is closely linked to the pathology of coronary artery and heart disease. It is possible that our *psychological* analysis may be criticized as superficial, perhaps rightly so. But this by no means invalidates its *medical* significance. The Type A man is prone to heart disease; these characteristic behavioral habits identify the Type A man.

SENSE OF TIME URGENCY, OR THE MODERN DISEASE, "HURRY SICKNESS"

Overwhelmingly, the most significant trait of the Type A man is his habitual sense of time urgency or "hurry sickness." Why does the Type A man so often feel that he doesn't have enough time to do all the things that he either believes should be done or that he wishes to do, whereas the Type B man feels that he has quite enough time to do all that he believes ought to be done? The answer is quite a simple one. The Type A man incessantly strives to accomplish too much or to participate in too many events in the amount of time he allots for these purposes. Even if by some miracle time could be stretched adequately just once for his activities, the Type A man still would not be satisfied. He would then seek to stretch time a second or third or fourth time.

The fundamental sickness of the Type A subject consists of his peculiar failure to perceive, or perhaps worse, to accept the simple fact that a man's time can be exhausted by his activities. As a consequence, he never ceases trying to "stuff" more and more events in his constantly shrinking reserves of time. It is the Type A man's ceaseless striving, his everlasting *struggle* with time, that we believe so very frequently leads to his early demise from coronary heart disease.

In an attempt to save time the Type A man often creates deadlines for himself. He subconsciously believes that if he fixes a date for the execution of a particular task that is actually too soon, somehow or other he will succeed in triumphing over his inveterate enemy, time. Since he very often has created not one but as many as a dozen such deadlines, he is subjecting himself to a more or less continuous time pressure. This voluntary tyranny frequently forms the very essence of Type A Behavior Pattern. To fill a life with deadlines to the exclusion of life's lovelinesses is a peculiarly dreadful form of self-punishment.

If this ever-increasing harassment by a sense of time urgency is not checked, eventually the Type A subject begins to indulge in a phenomenon that can and only too often does subvert his creative and judgmental attributes. This phenomenon is stereotyped thinking and action. More and more, again to save time, the Type A subject tends to think and do things in exactly the same way. Consciously or not, the Type A man apparently feels that if he can bring the previously "coded" thought and action processes again to bear on a new task, he can accomplish it *faster*. He more and more substitutes "faster" for "better" or "different" in his way of thinking and doing. In other words, he indulges in stereotyped responses. He substitutes repetitive urgency for creative energy.

But his challenges may demand nonstereotyped responses. It is particularly this tendency that so often makes the Type A person vulnerable to what he in the past had contemptuously regarded as the snail-like, noncompetitive pace of the Type B subject. The *intelligent* Type B man is capable, at least at times, of freeing himself from the steel meshes of stereotypal thought and behavior. He *does* find the time to ponder leisurely, to weigh alternatives, to experiment, to indulge in the sort of dialectical reverie from which two, three, or even four seemingly totally disparate events, facts, or processes can be joined to produce strikingly new and brilliant offshoots.

Far more often than not, then, the Type A man, because he tries so desperately to accomplish more and more in less and less time, finally impairs his creative power and only too often the acuity of his judgment. Thus bereft, he desperately seeks to substitute speed of execution. If sometimes he still seems to display brilliance, it usually is due to those original and creative concepts which he may have formulated in his younger years—before he became *totally* enslaved to his Type A Behavior Pattern. But this earlier collected cache of concepts can serve him well only as long as the milieu and its demands remain relatively unchanged.

One of the real tragedies of Type A Behavior Pattern is its tendency to erode the adaptability of its sufferer to the totally new challenges of contemporary society. It has been distressing for us to observe the severely afflicted Type A subject when he is confronted with one of these utterly new challenges. Desperate, he tries to run faster in his old ways to overcome a problem whose solution cannot be achieved by stereotyped and hasty thinking, but only by creative, time-free contemplation and deliberation. The ranks of corporate middle management contain more than just a few thousand such condemned hangers-on. Type A Behavior Pattern may be felling their hearts. It is almost certainly making tatters of their spiritual fabric.

THE QUEST FOR NUMBERS

Man's fascination with the quantitative accumulation of material objects is a trait, like speech or awareness of future time, which is not shared by any other species. Admittedly, squirrels accumulate nuts and bees honey, but they do so for strictly utilitarian reasons—to forestall winter's famine. They do not do so simply for the "human" joy of adding to that of which they already have enough.

This almost innate delight in acquisition probably begins quite early in our childhood. All of us have witnessed, for example, the delight a small boy takes in his first electric train set, even though it only consists of a locomotive and several freight cars. Later, as he experiences more birthdays and Christmases and receives more toy locomotives, freight cars, and tracks, he begins to *count* (rather than enjoy) the number of units he has. A similar process takes place when he begins to collect marbles, postage stamps, or anything else.

Most of us mature sufficiently to realize that it is better to love, marry, and mate with one rather than with a constantly increasing number of attractive girls. We tend to lay aside our childhood collections of trains, marbles, dolls, stamps, bottle tops, and so on as we buckle down to single, rather than to multiple, vocations. As parents, few of us strive to beget as many children as we can. We content ourselves with rearing several children well. Even in our vocations, at least half of us, while reasonably anxious to accumulate some of the goods of this world, still manage to preoccupy ourselves with matters that have nothing whatsoever to do with numbers. However, the severely afflicted Type A subject rarely matures in this regard.

Because of his obsession with numbers and because so many of the world's activities are expressed in currency units (that is, dollars, pounds, francs, and marks), the Type A subject more often than not appears to be absorbed in money. Before we thoroughly understood our own Type A patients and friends, we were inclined to believe that they were inordinately fond of making money for its own sake. This, however, is not true. The Type A businessman is not intrigued with money as such, nor is he miserly, nor is he necessarily eager to buy a better and bigger house or automobile than his friends (even if he frequently ends up doing just exactly that). Money for him merely represents the tokens or chips of the "numbers game" to which he has dedicated himself. "Last year my company grossed a profit before taxes of five million dollars," the Type A businessman proudly states. "Last year I performed one hundred fifty appendectomies," the Type A surgeon just as proudly announces. "Last year my laboratory published eighteen articles," the Type A scientist even more proudly announces. You will note that each is proud of his kind of "numbers."

The Type A individual simply uses money as a numeral of his prowess or achievements and then more often than not liberally disposes of a large fraction of it. You might compare a Type A man at work with an enthusiastic adolescent playing Monopoly. Both pay avid attention to their opportunities for acquiring the paper tokens necessary to win, but when the game is finished the Monopoly player counts them and then without a pang puts them away in the box. Likewise, the Type A man, after having striven for and obtained a certain *number* of dollars, doesn't care any more—and frequently even less—than the Type B about what use is made of the money. It is the *number* of dollars, not the dollars themselves, that appease—but unfortunately only partially—the insecurity of the Type A man.

THE INSECURITY OF STATUS

Perhaps no man, at first glance, seems less insecure than the typical Type A man. He bristles with confidence and appears to exude lavish amounts of self-assurance and self-conviction. How can we indict a man as being insecure who is always so eager to ask

"What is your problem and how can I help *you?*"—a man who is so loath to say, "I have a problem and I need your help"? We do so because we have found, after many years of studying the Type A man, that he either lost or never had any intrinsic "yardstick" by which he could gauge his own fundamental worth to his own satisfaction.

Somewhere in his development process he began to measure the value of his total personality or character by the *number* of his *achievements*. Moreover, these achievements invariably must be those he believes capture the respect and admiration of his peers and superiors. He does not, however, care whether these achievements gain him the love or affection of his fellow man, although he does not particularly care to be disliked.

Having chosen this yardstick, he has committed himself irretrievably to a life course that can never bring him true equanimity. The *number*, not the quality, of his achievements must constantly increase to satiate an appetite that, unchecked by other restraints, ceaselessly increases. Second, he believes that the number of his achievements are always being judged by his peers and subordinates, and since the latter are constantly changing as he ascends in the socioeconomic scale, he feels that the number of his achievements must continue to rise.

A young Type A bank clerk, for example, will strive first to accomplish a number of tasks that will be admired by his fellow bank clerks and the assistant cashier, his immediate superior. At this stage in his development, their respect and admiration are necessary to him. Later in his development, when he becomes a senior vice-president of the bank, he then strives to obtain the respect and admiration of his fellow vice-presidents and the president and chairman of the bank's board of directors. How enormously unhappy he would be if he failed to obtain their esteem and had only the awed admiration of the bank clerks. In a pinch, this Type A senior vice-president would gladly trade off the esteem of even the thirty or more other vice-presidents for the sole approbation of the president; it is probably not an exaggeration to say that the respect of a single superior is more sustaining to the personality of a Type A man than that of a score of his peers. It may be in only this particular matter that even the Type A subject prefers *quality* to sheer *numbers*.

Perhaps we are all of this mold in that we all desire the approbation of our peers and superiors. But not all of us are so constantly and all-consumingly possessed with frenzy to gain this esteem. Then, too, many of us, unlike the Type A person, do want affection and do find considerable emotional satisfaction from the continuing admiration of those we may have left behind in our economic ascent. We must add also that the Type A man is not a snob, if only because the social amenities appear a complete waste of time to him unless they further what he considers to be his cause. Certainly, if a Type A lieutenant were invited to a party at which his commanding colonel's wife were present, he would be more inclined to attend her than the other ladies in the room, regardless of their possible charm. (We describe these traits, you must remember, not because we wish to condemn the Type A man; we only wish to portray him to you.)

From what we have written so far, it should be obvious that the Type A man isn't very concerned about simply sustaining himself. He feels that he always can obtain food, shelter, and clothing (and the modern welfare state, of course, buttresses his confidence in this regard). Nor is his insecurity exclusively focused solely upon his status at any given instant. Rather, it appears to be directly attuned to the *pace* at which his status *improves*. This brings us, then, to the key reason for the insecurity of the Type A man: he has staked his innermost security upon the *pace* of his status enhancement. This pace in turn depends upon a *maximal* number of achievements accomplished in a *minimal* amount of time, achievements recognized as significant by constantly changing groups of his peers and superiors.

His only possible surcease from this almost continuous self-harassment occurs at those fleeting moments when he believes that the number of his achievements are increasing at a satisfactory rate. These moments have to be rare. In his frenzy to accumulate achievements, he necessarily tends at the same time to subvert their quality. Noting unconsciously this fall-off in quality, he desperately attempts on a conscious level to make up for the deficit, by heaping up a still greater number of achievements.

The never-ending conflict in which the Type A subject is involved is a solitary one. It is, moreover, one frequently unrecognized by his associates or even his wife and children. So very few of us can muster sympathy, particularly in these antiestablishment days, for a successful banker, an attorney, or a physician whose sole difficulty, it seems to us, is only that he may appear to be somewhat short of time and sometimes rather irritable.

How can the president of a city's largest bank, whose spirit is being torn to shreds by his enormously compulsive drive to prove to the board of directors that he is making a better president than the one he succeeded or the president of a rival bank, expect sympathy or solace, even from his wife? Or how can the professor of medicine in a mediocre state medical school, who is publishing reams of medical trash in order to attract the attention of his peers at Harvard, expect understanding of his plight from the rather insouciant, but far better adjusted, members of his department?

Even if a Type A subject's friends were to recognize his potentially deadly struggle and try to help him, he would probably reject their sympathy as of no value whatsoever. Again, only an increasing number of achievements and their recognition by his peers and superiors could serve as a temporary respite for his struggle. And one more thing. Even if a Type A man's peers and superiors were to laud his achievements, such praise would still not appease him unless he himself was certain that the number of such achievements truly warranted such encomium. The Type A man may have his faults, but hypocrisy and downright dishonesty are not among them. If a Type A man is found to be dishonest, you would be well advised to attribute this to ordinary human weakness, not to his behavior pattern.

AGGRESSION AND HOSTILITY

No man who is eager to achieve is totally lacking in aggressive spirit. Certainly we have met few if any Type A subjects who are deficient in this trait. On the contrary, most Type A subjects possess so much aggressive drive that it frequently evolves into a free-floating hostility. But excess aggression and certainly hostility are not always easily detected in Type A men, if only because they so often keep such feelings and impulses under deep cover. Indeed, very few of these men are even aware of their excess aggression, and almost none are aware of their hostility. Indeed, it is maybe only after fairly intimate acquaintance with a Type A man that his hostility becomes manifest.

Perhaps the prime index of the presence of aggression or hostility in almost all Type A men is the tendency always to compete with or to challenge other people, whether the activity consists of a sporting contest, a game of cards, or a simple discussion. If the aggression has evolved into frank hostility, more often than not one feels, even when talking casually to such men, that there is a note of rancor in their speech. They tend to bristle at points in a conversation where the ordinary person might either laugh self-deprecatingly or pass over the possibly contentious theme.

There are some persons whom we consider Type A, not because they are engaged in a struggle to achieve a maximal number of goals in a minimal amount of time (the usual complex making up this pattern), but because they are so hostile that they are almost continuously engaged in a struggle against other persons. Of course nature does not distinguish between a man struggling against time and one struggling against another man, but it does make the organs of this struggling man discharge the same kinds of chemicals regardless of the exact causes of the struggle. No Type A man is more difficult to treat than one whose pattern stems directly and wholly from his free-floating hostility. . . .

section IV
COPING WITH TRANSIENT LIFE CRISES

The readings in Section IV center on severely stressful life situations demanding difficult adjustments and sometimes, but not necessarily, involving death. Although coping under extreme conditions of stress is often dramatic and sometimes paradoxical to the casual observer, one must remember that cultural, situational, and personality factors are always operating in complex ways to influence the way an individual or group handles very threatening circumstances.

In an exploratory study looking at the relationships between personality factors in earlier life and the subsequent adjustment of burn patients during hospitalization, Andreasen, Noyes, and Hartford (1972) illustrated one of the major generalizations in this field. They found that poor adjustment (e.g., severe depression and violent behavior) occurred frequently among patients who had difficulty coping with life prior to their accidents. Again and again research has shown that success or failure in coping is, to some extent at least, a stable property of persons. Previously highly successful premorbid copers are also likely to show good adjustment during a later crisis, and unsuccessful copers poor adjustment, as in this example with burned patients. Persons with a history of premorbid difficulties may well need more professional help in coping with severely stressful life events than those already possessing adequate coping skills. Future research along these lines must determine in detail the particular premorbid coping skills that are most important for successful adjustment to various life stresses.

Katz et al. (1970b) interviewed women awaiting breast tumor biopsies in the hospital and also assessed their concomitant hydrocortisone production rates and levels of subjective distress. Even when facing a severe cancer-related threat like loss of life or removal of a breast, ego defenses served "effectively" to buffer these women against the stress of their ordeals—i.e., psychological and physiological indicators of stress were all rather unremarkable. In fact, Katz et al. found that six defensive patterns were employed, all of which, with the exception of projection and displacement, were highly effective in reducing the level of stress reactions. Of great importance also was the fact that some women who successfully used denial with rationalization actually jeopardized their chances for survival by waiting the longest to consult their physicians, suggesting, as we have said (see Introduction), that defenses may be effective from one vantage point (in this case, the physiological realm) but damaging when viewed from a different perspective (i.e., physical survival). Of great interest, too, was the fact that cultural background influenced defensive styles, e.g., black patients were more likely to rely on stoicism-fatalism or faith and prayer while whites primarily used displacement or projection.

Mechanic (1962) has argued that there are basically two components of adaptation, namely, dealing directly with the situation ("coping"), and dealing with one's feelings about the situation ("defense"). The amount of stress one experiences is therefore dependent upon the effectiveness and available means for coping and defense. In a naturalistic investigation of graduate students studying for a major examination, Mechanic carefully observed and interviewed students and their families for three months prior to and one month following the exam. The brief selection included here emphasizes "defensive" modes (such as joking and humor) used by students anticipating their examinations. Mechanic found that older and very anxious students found little about their plights to joke about and that, among all students, joking tended to occur most frequently at certain points in time (e.g., just prior to the examination week). Moreover, as the exams became imminent, the nature of the jokes changed from that of tension-release (i.e., poking fun at the study material) to "avoidance-banter" (i.e., humor which permitted avoidance of the anxiety-provoking material); as time was running out, the switch to the latter type of joking was "adaptive" in that it protected students from being confronted with new and potentially stressful ideas. Mechanic's study is one of the more thorough and wide-ranging naturalistic studies of stress and coping, and the reader may want to examine his book in its entirety.

Hazardous occupations provide excellent opportunities for studying coping processes, especially in times of disaster. Lucas (1969) reports a series of interviews obtained from coal miners following their rescue from a coal mine disaster, examining in detail the social and psychological forces operating while the men were trapped underground. One of their most pressing problems was a dwindling water supply and they quickly had to find an adequate solution. The men eventually decided they would have to drink their urine in order to survive but, before this could be initiated, severe inhibitions against the act had to be overcome. The social forces eventually legitimizing this normally repugnant act were complex, and Lucas's reconstruction and analysis of these forces provide penetrating insights into the cultural and social dynamics shaping coping behavior under life-threatening circumstances.

Janis (in Janis et al., 1969) reports on his pioneering work with surgical patients and discusses the importance of the "work of worrying" in coping with stress. For example, Janis notes that patients with a moderate amount of anticipatory fear were unlikely to show postoperative emotional disturbances while those displaying low levels of anticipatory fear were very likely to experience them. In attempting to explain this, Janis suggests that patients with moderate anticipatory fear felt somewhat vulnerable and hence sought realistic information and developed effective defenses to prepare themselves for the surgical risks and pain. In short, these patients worked through each potential source of stress by engaging in the "work of worrying." Low anticipatory fear patients, on the other hand, by employing denial defenses did not feel threatened and hence remained uninformed about their operations and the problems of post-surgery recovery. According to Janis, because these latter patients did not mentally rehearse the dangers of their situations (i.e., they did not do the "work of worrying"), they developed feelings of helplessness and resentment when "unexpected" postoperative pain and other sources of distress set in; consequently, they were unable to cope effectively with this stressful situation. There is some evidence (e.g., Cohen & Lazarus, 1973) that Janis's findings and "work of worrying" hypothesis may be restricted to certain kinds of hospital contexts, but the issues this research raises are of enormous significance to practitioners and theorists interested in factors influencing successful and unsuccessful coping.

Bernard, Ottenberg, and Redl (1965) provide a detailed and enlightening analysis of a seemingly prevalent coping device, dehumanization. The authors suggest that dehumanization is a result, in part, of modern social organization and, in turn, threatens our very existence—namely, the increased use of dehumanization greatly increases the risk of nuclear war. Examples of the dehumanization process abound (e.g., consider the behaviors of the workers on the assembly line, the prostitute, the prejudiced individual, and the soldier) and empirical studies have demonstrated how easy it is for people to adopt a dehumanized view, particularly of others (e.g., Carlson & Wood, 1972; Mansson, 1972; Milgram, 1965).

Several points in this selection are particularly important to mention here. First of all, Bernard, Ottenberg, and Redl maintain that dehumanization (like other defenses—see Introduction) has "adaptive" as well as "maladaptive" consequences. That is, there are times when dehumanization protects the individual from overwhelming stress and allows him or her to effectively fulfill an important role (e.g., the surgeon or military leader). Nevertheless, it is also possible for this dehumanization process to have damaging consequences such as promoting feelings of personal helplessness and increased emotional distance from other human beings. Secondly, the authors note that it is possible for an individual to adopt a dehumanized stance toward some people while retaining a capacity for emotional ties with certain others. This "selective" process is illustrated nicely by the lack of any help (including a simple phone call to the police) given to Kitty Genovese as she was brutally attacked three times near her house in a middle-class New York neighborhood. When the thirty-eight neighbors who had witnessed the attacks were interviewed it became clear that they were basically "decent, moral people" with families who had a deep fear of involvement, any kind of involvement. Thus, we see how people can compartmentalize their feelings of apathy (and dehumanization) from those of commitment and caring.

Bernard, Ottenberg, and Redl provide a solemn reminder of the dangers inherent in our highly "civilized" life style and point to the importance of learning how to "rehumanize" society. If nothing else, their article provides strong justification for increased efforts along empirical lines for understanding more fully the processes of dehumanization and for increased social consciousness and action to combat the damaging effects of this particularly important defense mechanism.

16

Factors Influencing Adjustment of Burn Patients During Hospitalization

N. J. C. ANDREASEN, RUSSELL NOYES, JR.,
and
C. E. HARTFORD

During recent years psychiatry has advanced with increased frequency and depth into an artificial and self-created frontier with general medicine, and studies of such colorful and topical areas as emotional reactions to renal dialysis or open heart surgery have abounded. Yet the number of patients who submit to these procedures is small, and often the medical miracle which seems to hold such promise for so many must be restricted to a very few because of technical or economic shortcomings. Meanwhile the emotional problems experienced by people suffering burn injuries, who number in the hundreds of thousands, have been largely ignored.

This exploratory study of factors which influence the adjustment of burn patients during hospitalization is part of a planned series of investigations of the burn-injured patient, his psychologic reaction to his injury, and the factors affecting his recovery (Andreasen, Norris, & Hartford, 1971; Andreasen et al., 1972). The adjustment problems which the burn patient faces during hospitalization were well described by Hamburg in 1953 (Hamburg et al., 1953; Hamburg, Hamburg, & deGoza, 1953). These include sudden enforced dependency, threats to identity or autonomy, handling of anger and hostility and prolonged pain and monotony. Visotsky et al. (1961) have also described the adjustment mechanisms by which patients adapt to burn injuries and to chronic illnesses in general. Our purpose in the present investigation has been to explore the environmental, personality, and physical factors which affect the burn patient's capacity to adjust during hospitalization. In particular, we have sought to identify those factors which are associated with a complicated course or adjustment difficulties.

We included in the present study all patients between the ages of 18 and 60 with a greater than 7% burn who were admitted over a period of 9 months to the burn unit at the University of Iowa Hospitals, a 12-bed unit staffed with nurses and physicians specializing in the care of burns. Our sample consisted of 20 men and 12 women ranging in age from 20 to 59 years (mean, 36) and in total body surface burn from 8 to 60% (mean, 29%). Duration of hospitalization ranged from several weeks to 3 months, with an average of about a month. Three patients in the study died, all of them about 1 month after initial injury. Three patients who died 1 or 2 days after admission were not included. Two patients with mental retardation who were unable to communicate verbally were also excluded.

Data consisted of a psychiatric history following a standardized format obtained from the patient by one of the investigators within several days after admission, a standardized social history from a close relative by a psychiatric social worker and daily progress notes made after regular rounds. In the initial psychiatric and social histories, special emphasis was placed on exploring premorbid personality and identifying major life changes or stresses prior to injury. Ten patients took a Minnesota Multiphasic Personality Inventory (MMPI), but this test could not be completed on others because of the severity of their illness or because they did not satisfy its intellectual criteria. The significant premorbid factors to be evaluated were defined for the purposes of this investigation as follows:

Disturbed Family Situation—poor marital relationship, emotional problems in first-degree relatives.
Recent Family Crises—serious illnesses or deaths among first-degree relatives during the previous year, significant financial problems.
Changes in Living Pattern—a move to a new location, new job, new person living in the home during the previous 2 months.
Below Normal Intelligence—inability to obtain an eighth grade education or completion of higher grades through a special education program.

(All patients in this group were judged to have an IQ below 90 on the basis of a mental status exam.)

Premorbid Psychopathology—prior psychiatric hospitalizations or treatment, description by the patient or his relatives of adjustment problems prior to injury sufficiently severe and/or chronic that a psychiatric diagnosis was made after the initial interview, alcoholism. (Diagnoses were made according to the nomenclature outlined in the American Psychiatric Association's *Diagnostic and Statistical Manual*, second edition.)

Prior Accidents—at least one prior accident (not including childhood accidents) for which the patient himself was responsible and which was serious enough to require inpatient care. (This was assumed to give some index of accident proneness.)

Self-Destructive Tendencies—prior suicide attempts, failure to follow a prescribed medical program when such neglect was life-threatening.

Physical Disabilities—prior medical diagnosis of such illnesses as seizure disorder, Huntington's chorea, ulcerative colitis, blindness.

The roles of *age* and *area involved by burn* were also explored. Age 30 was used as a cut-off point to divide patients into an *older* and a *younger* group. Patients were also divided into a group with greater-than-30% area involved by burn and a group with a less-than-30% involvement.

Like the above factors, what constitutes *good* or *poor* adjustment during hospitalization must be somewhat arbitrarily defined, for success or failure in adjusting is actually a continuum. Further, *good adjustment* is a concept analogous to *normality* in its slipperiness, imprecision, and defiance of quantitative measurement. As used herein, good adjustment is defined by exclusion and refers to those patients who adapted to their situation without developing significant emotional problems or a complicated course. Patients who were felt to represent adjustment failure were so classified if they developed one or more of the following complications: severe depression, severe regression, violent or nearly unmanageable behavior, delirium, or death. Those who did not develop such complications were, by exclusion, considered to have adjusted adequately to their situation.

Data were analyzed by using the x^2 test with Yates's correction.

RESULTS

Sixteen patients, or 50% of the sample, adjusted satisfactorily to the stresses they faced. Likewise, 50% did poorly, developing the

Table 16.1. *Factors Associated with Adjustment Outcome*

Factors	Total	Among Good Adjusters (N = 16)	Among Poor Adjusters (N = 16)	χ^2	P
Premorbid psychopathology	12	1	11	10.8	0.001
Physical disability	10	1	9	7.13	0.01
Burn > 30%	11	2	9	4.99	0.05
Disturbed family situation	7	1	6	ns	ns
Recent family crises	3	0	3	ns	ns
Changes in living pattern	7	5	2	ns	ns
Below normal intelligence	7	2	5	ns	ns
Prior accidents	7	2	5	ns	ns
Self-destructive tendencies	4	0	4	ns	ns
Age > 30	18	12	6	ns	ns
Totals *	68	14	54		

* Age not included in these totals

complications listed above. Specific data concerning adjustment and contributing factors are summarized in Tables 16.1 and 16.2.

Good Adjustment

Presenting striking tribute to the durability and adaptability of the human organism, a substantial number of our patients were able to handle the stresses presented by experiencing and recovering from a severe burn without developing serious emotional problems. Indeed, as the following brief case histories indicate, the 50% who adjusted adequately often overcame stresses which one might predict a priori would lead to significant difficulties.

R. P. was a 30-year-old married male lineman who sustained severe electrical burns when he accidentally came in contact with a hot line while at work. His injuries required complete amputation of his left arm and leg 2 days after admission. He was a tall, good-looking man who had been happily married for 11 years and who enjoyed such sports as swimming, boating and water-skiing. He had been a lineman for 13 years. During the course of hospitalization, he remained consistently cheerful and optimistic, making realistic plans for obtaining prosthetic limbs and eventually obtaining a desk job with his company. Denial was a prominent adjustment mechanism: he avoided discussing his disability and when asked about it he made replies such as, "I'll just have to get used to it . . . it'll work out

Table 16.2. *Factors Associated with Adjustment Problems*

Factor	Total	In Severe Depression (N=6)	In Severe Regression (N=7)	In Management Problems (N=5)	In Delirium (N=10)	In Death (N=3)
Premorbid psychopathology	12	3	7 *	5 †	7 ‡	3
Physical disabilities	10	2	5 ‡	3	5	2
Burn > 30%	11	3	5 §	4 §	7 †	3 §
Age > 30	18	2 §	3	2	7	2
Disturbed family situation	7	4 ‖	3	3 §	4	1
Recent family crises	3	1	1	0	2	1
Changes in living pattern	7	1	1	1	2	0
Below normal intelligence	7	1	4 ‡	3 §	4	1
Prior accidents	7	3	2	1	3	1
Self-destructive tendencies	4	2	2	3 †	3	2 ‡

* χ^2 significant at > .001 level
† χ^2 significant at > .01 level
‡ χ^2 significant at > .05 level
§ χ^2 significant at > .10 level
‖ χ^2 significant at > .02 level

. . . I've known others with artificial limbs and they have done OK." Discussing how he would manage the steps in his two-story home prior to obtaining a leg prosthesis, which could not be fitted for several months, he smiled wryly and drawled, "I dunno . . . I guess I'll just have to slither up and down." His wife remained with him almost continually and also remained cheerful and optimistic. He wept only once, when he voiced concern about how his young daughters might react to his injury and at no time showed any symptoms of depression or even grief about his loss. An MMPI showed a 6-9-3 profile with the 6 and K scales greater than 70, indicating that he was quite a sensitive person, prone to keep his feelings and thoughts well-hidden, with a high level of energy and a superficial air of optimism. He was seen about 1 month after discharge and at this time he and his wife indicated that he was doing quite well.

L. K. was a 24-year-old married housewife who sustained 20% burns of her face and hands when an unnoticed gas leak in her new subdivision home caused an explosion. Her husband was also severely burned and died 2 days after admission, while her 2 children had only minor injuries. Her marriage had been a close and happy one. Confronting the stresses of her husband's sudden death, possible facial deformity and separation from her 2 young children, she reacted initially with disbelief and then grief. She wept openly, discussed her loss and wondered what it would be like to raise her children without a husband and a father. She tended to rationalize that her husband's death was for the best, however, since he would not have to experience the intense suffering and deformity that his burns would have caused, and to express the religious faith that his death was God's will. As she worked through these problems, she too began to make plans about resuming her former work in nursing, perhaps on a burn unit. After about one month it became quite apparent that she would have some facial deformity and contractures of her hands. She was also able to work this through, placing considerable hope in future plastic procedures and gratefully accepting reassurance from the staff that she was doing quite well. An MMPI showed 5-8 profile with all scores below the 70 range, indicating some feelings of fear and isolation in a basically normal personality.

Both these patients adjusted well, although the mechanisms they used were quite different. The quality which they shared, and which tended to characterize the *good adjusters* as a group, was the capacity to achieve a satisfying and stable social and vocational adaptation prior to injury. As illustrated in Table 16.1, the patients who did well were charactarized by a significant absence of premorbid psychopathology and physical disability. They also tended to include the less severely burned.

Poor Adjustment

As a group the 16 patients who tended to respond poorly to the stress of injury and hospitalization had past histories suggesting rather consistent poor adjustment and/or a general tendency toward misfortune. They had a statistically significant prevalence of premorbid psychopathology, including chronic organic brain syndrome, 2; schizophrenia, 1; depression, 1; personality disorders, 5; and alcoholism, 3. Personality disorders were particularly prevalent and varied in type, including paranoid, 1; inadequate, 3; and passive-aggressive, 1. A statistically significant number also had physical disabilities: Huntington's chorea, 1; epilepsy, 4; blindness, 1; porphyria, 1; hypertension, 1; and ulcerative colitis, 1.

Their failure to adjust was manifested in a variety of ways. These included severe depression, marked regression, delirium, or becoming a significant management problem. Of the 3 patients who died, all fell into the *poor adjustment* category on the basis of developing one or more of these problems.

The following case history is representative of patients in this category: J. B. was a 51-year-old housewife who incurred 30% burns of her face (superficial), chest, and upper extremities when her clothes caught on fire as she was cooking a roast in her home. Prior to injury the focus of her life revolved around her home and family. Her family described her as a warm and open person. She had been legally blind from birth with associated nystagmus. She refused to wear glasses and denied visual defects. Her husband reported a gradual onset of symptoms of an organic brain syndrome recently, including agitation, poor recent memory, and mild confusion; they had urged her to seek medical help but she refused, again denying any problem. From the time of admission until a few weeks prior to discharge she had a marked intention tremor, and on mental status exam she consistently demonstrated poor calculations, perseveration, poor fund of general information, emotional lability, and little insight. When her severely burned left arm was placed in a splint, she indicated that her arm had been removed but would be put back eventually; she showed no other delusions. She frequently complained about the duration of her hospitalization (53 days) and felt that her doctors were keeping her unduly long. She was homesick for her husband and children, who were able to visit only occasionally on weekends. She became quite depressed, lapsing into periods of withdrawal and refusing to speak when anyone walked into the room. She was never a management problem, however. About 2 weeks prior to discharge, she became more talkative and alert and showed some interest in other patients on the unit, especially the children.

Severe Depression

Six patients developed this problem. Most patients who suffer a burn injury develop symptoms of depression at some time during their hospital course, but these symptoms usually last only a few days and are not incapacitating. The 6 who were judged to be severely depressed had symptoms lasting longer than 1 week, consisting of marked blueness, crying spells, loss of hope, feelings of worthlessness, decreased appetite, and insomnia. The factor most closely associated with the development of this problem (Table 16.2) is a disturbed family situation, although there is a trend toward association in the group of patients over 30. Four of the 6 patients came from disturbed family situations. These included (a) a marriage on the verge of break-up, (b) a problem offspring manifesting antisocial behavior leading to imprisonment, (c) a mother frequently hospitalized for symptoms suggestive of schizophrenia, and (d) a wife who was sexually promiscuous. Whether such disturbed family situations contributed indirectly to the patients' injuries or to their developing depressive symptoms after injury, or both, cannot be determined. None of these patients gave histories of being depressed prior to injury. Patients who became depressed tended to ruminate over their family problems and to express guilt feelings about their supposed responsibility for such problems during the course of their depression.

Severe Regression

Seven patients developed severe regression. Again, most patients became regressed to some degree for brief periods, but their symptoms differed in both intensity and duration from those who were judged to be severely regressed. The latter manifested behavior which was markedly infantile, demanding, dependent, and hypochondriacal. They showed a low frustration tolerance and poorly controlled anger when frustrated. Such behavior persisted for longer than one week. As indicated in Table 16.2, the tendency to develop this problem was associated with premorbid psychopathology, physical disability, and below normal intelligence. All 7 patients who became severely regressed had premorbid psychopathology, and 5 of these 7 had personality disorders. In these cases immature behavior was part of their life style prior to injury, and the tendency to react to life stresses in an ineffective and exaggerated way perhaps became more pronounced under the severe stress of being burned. Five had physical disabilities and 4 had below normal intelligence, both factors possibly tending to contribute to the ease with which they developed a demanding and dependent mode of behavior. Having a burn greater than 30% was also associated with regression, though not closely.

Management Problems

Five patients were severe management problems. These patients tended to disturb the entire unit and to sorely try its staff with their uncooperative, disruptive, and frustrating behavior. They refused to eat, tore off grafts, became violent and abusive and, against medical advice, threatened to leave. All 5 of these patients had premorbid psychopathology. Three were alcoholics (2 of whom also had personality disorders), one a schizophrenic and one a severe passive-aggressive personality. Thus all were predisposed toward impulsive behavior on the basis of their previous life style. Three of the 5 also fell into the rather small group of patients who had premorbid self-destructive tendencies, again probably reflecting a tendency to behave impulsively. Burns greater than 30%, below normal intelligence, and disturbed family situations were also somewhat less closely associated.

Delirium

Ten patients, or 31% of the sample, became delirious. Following the concept of delirium as defined by Lipowski (1967) and Romano and Engel (1944a; 1944b; Engel & Romano, 1959), we took cognitive impairment to be the primary symptom of delirium and diagnosed it in those patients who showed decreased memory, disorientation, or other such indications of decreased cognitive function. In about half of these patients the delirium was of an agitated type, characterized by anxiety, disturbing hallucinations, and thrashing or picking movements. In the other half the delirium appeared to be primarily of a retarded type, and patients were somnolent, obtunded, and difficult to arouse. The tendency to develop delirium was most closely associated with greater severity of burn and premorbid psychopathology. Seven of the 10 delirious patients had a burn greater than 30% and some type of psychopathology prior to injury. This suggests that both organic and emotional factors may be contributory to the development of delirium and that its etiology is probably multifactorial.

Death

Three patients in the study died, all of them after approximately one month of hospitalization. Strictly speaking, of course, death cannot be considered a failure to adjust, but all the patients who died had already demonstrated an adaptive failure by developing one of the four complications described above, and for all of them death was the terminal event in a series of adaptive failures. All were delirious prior to death, and prior to the delirium 2 had shown self-destructive tendencies, and for both of these death fulfilled a genuine death wish. The third did not have self-destructive tendencies as defined in this study, but she was depressed prior to injury and frequently expressed a death wish; her injury and death can probably be viewed as a *subintentional suicide*. The relationship of severity of burn to death is not clear. All 3 patients who died had a greater than 40% burn (X = 42%), but 6 other patients who had burns greater than 40% survived, suggesting that other factors may be as important as area involved by burn. The mean age of the deceased patients was 46, while that of survivors who had a burn greater than 40% was 32, indicating that age plays a significant role as well.

DISCUSSION

Hamburg and associates have explored and defined the adaptive problems experienced by burn patients during hospitalization and the adjustment mechanisms they used to cope with them (Hamburg et al., 1953; Hamburg, Hamburg, & deGoza, 1953), and by and large our observations confirm those of Hamburg's group. In this study we sought to supplement his inquiries of *What?* and *How?* by asking *Why?* We raised the question of what premorbid factors influence success or failure in achieving adaptation.

Our patients divided themselves neatly into two groups, 50% achieving a successful adaptation and 50% failing to do so. When these two groups were analyzed for predisposing factors, the most prominent appeared to be physical and emotional disorders in existence prior to their injury. Twelve patients out of the total sample of 32 were found to have premorbid psychopathology, and 11 of these 12 became adjustment failures during hospitalization. Statistically, this association is significant at the 0.001 level. Not only had the adjustment failures done poorly emotionally prior to injury, but they had also done poorly physically, with a prior history of physical disability being the second most significant predisposing factor.

That the previously successful would continue to be successful and that failures would continue to fail is, in a sense, exactly what one would anticipate, but this investigation was in fact begun with a different hypothesis, and the investigators were surprised at many of the adjustment successes which were achieved. We began with the suspicion that the life style helpful in coping with the vicissitudes of modern civilization, involving qualities such as independence, aggressiveness, and high energy levels, poorly prepares the individual who has been seriously injured for coping with the forced dependency, passivity, and monotony of prolonged *patienthood*. Yet we repeatedly observed individuals who defied our predictions and, after a brief period of depression or anxiety, rapidly learned to cope with the new stresses of hospitalization by using their old and familiar defenses and adaptive mechanisms. The previously active individual learned to put his prior life style to good use and recovered his prior identity by managing his work and family from his bed, educating himself on the care of burns, cooperating with physical therapy to hasten recovery, etc.

Some might also hypothesize that those whose quality of life has been poor prior to injury might be bothered less than the previously successful, since the change in their fortunes is less dramatic. But, in fact, the individual who has not been able in the past to work positively and persistently toward some goal soon comes to feel angry, helpless, and defeated when he must cope with the multiple stresses faced by the burn patient. He too soon learns to handle his new situation in terms of his old modes of adaptation, for it indeed is simply a more pronounced form of the old familiar situation of repeated pain and frustration; therefore, his familiar mechanisms such as regression, depression or poorly controlled hostility are also intensified. Our findings suggest that we need to dispose of the sentimental notion sometimes expressed that the emotionally disturbed, mentally dull, or chronically ill suffer less or are better able to cope with additional illness because it is familiar. They in fact suffer more and are less able to cope.

•   •   •   •

17

~~~~~~

Stress, Distress, and Ego Defenses: Psychoendocrine Response to Impending Breast Tumor Biopsy

JACK L. KATZ, HERBERT WEINER, T. F. GALLAGHER,
and
LEON HELLMAN

STUDY BACKGROUND AND ISSUES

The woman who discovers a lump in her breast is immediately confronted with a series of alternatives which will not be even preliminarily sorted out until after biopsy can take place and perhaps not definitively for many years. She is faced with perplexing questions and circumstances which cannot be quickly answered and which implicitly contain a major threat to her very existence.

Thus: is it a real lump she feels or perhaps just some thickening which will eventually disappear? In conjunction with this, should she immediately tell her physician about it or elect to wait a while to see if it will recede? If she does tell him, will he immediately launch into a variety of complicated tests and perhaps even hospitalize her or will he simply reassure her after a brief physical examination?

And once in the hospital, the patient with a breast tumor must face separation from her home and family, a bewildering array of unfamiliar personnel and medical procedures, and the knowledge that she will have to undergo anesthesia and surgery of at least some type (i.e., at the minimum, for biopsy).

This work was supported in part by NIMH Interdisciplinary Research Fellowship MH 6418-11 (Dr. Katz) and grants from the National Cancer Institute (CA-07304), the General Clinical Research Centers Branch of NIH (FR-53), and the American Cancer Society.

But it is the ambiguous and life-threatening aspects of the pre-biopsy situation which are most striking. Inherent in this situation are the following considerations: Will she awake from surgery to find her breast still present or no longer there? If mastectomy has been necessary, how will she look and feel about herself as a woman and how will others respond to the cosmetic insult she has sustained? Will she be learning that the tumor was diagnosed as "cancer"? If it is cancerous, will this mean an early and painful demise for her?

Confronted with these questions, the patient can reasonably be considered to be facing a major threat to her very being. The situation consequently provides an excellent opportunity for examining the human response to a naturally occurring major "stress."

Toward this end, this study reports our observations and experiences with such a group of women awaiting breast tumor biopsy in the hospital. This was an outgrowth of an investigation of psychoendocrine considerations in cancer, which was prompted by reports of the importance of the endogenous hormonal environment for the course of certain malignancies. Results of that aspect of the study have recently been published (Katz et al., 1970a).

In this paper, then, we are turning our attention to the following issues: (1) In this potentially life (or at least body) threatening situation, do any subjects really "defend" or "cope" with high effectiveness? (2) Are there differences in the affective states of these women, who are all confronted with the same set of unfortunate circumstances but who may perceive or interpret these differently? (3) Is there a constant or strong relationship between the kind of defense employed and its effectiveness? (4) Does extent of "success" of the defense (as defined by psychological and physiological parameters) coincide with extent of "appropriateness" of the defense (i.e., in terms of its reality-syntonic and adaptive qualities)?

METHODS

Thirty women, all with presumably operable breast tumors (should biopsy prove positive) but otherwise in generally good health, were admitted to the Clinical Research Center of Montefiore Hospital and Medical Center. The patients were told they would spend about one week there for complete medical evaluation; transfer to the surgical service for biopsy would then take place.

As a biochemical index of "distress," we relied upon adrenocortical activity. A substantial number of studies now exist in the psychoendocrine literature (Mason, 1968) which document the activation of the hypothalamic-pituitary-adrenal axis concomitant with psychological states characterized by failing ego defenses.

Thus, after at least a three-day period to permit adjustment to the hospital environment, each patient received an intravenous tracer of hydrocortisone tagged with carbon 14: total urine output was then collected for the next 72 hours. This permitted determination of the patient's average daily production rate of hydrocortisone during this period by radioisotope dilution technique; more complete details of the theory and method of this determination have been reported elsewhere (Katz et al., 1970a). All medication, other than chloral hydrate for insomnia, was discontinued upon admission to the Clinical Center.

Within several hours after administration of the hydrocortisone tracer, an extensive psychiatric interview was conducted with each of the 30 patients by the same investigator (J.K.). Whenever feasible (19 of the 30 interviews), the session was tape-recorded. These taped records were then independently assessed by three other investigators in addition to the interviewer.

The model for psychological assessment of the adequacy of ego defenses was that provided by the work of Wolff, and co-workers (Wolff et al., 1964; Wolff, Hofer, & Mason, 1964). The first of their three criteria was "affective distress," which was inferred from the presence of unpleasant affects, such as grief, anxiety, despair, or other discernible painful mental states. The second was "disruption of function," which was reflected in the subject's description of such psychophysiologic upheavals as anorexia, insomnia, constipation, etc., or such ego difficulties as decreased power of concentration, memory lapses, decreased frustration tolerance, etc. The third was "impairment of defensive reserve," which referred to a depletion of ego defensive capacity to the extent that any stress superimposed upon the immediate one simply could not be dealt with effectively; this might be reported by the subject or made manifest by the interviewer, providing the additional threat of "stressful confrontations" during the interview.

Thus, in the course of a single but lengthy interview, the interviewer in our study attempted to elicit from the patient a description of her affective state and functional intactness prior to and then subsequent to the discovery of the lump in her breast, and particularly since she had entered the hospital for tests and probable biopsy. More objective data, such as crying, tremulousness of voice, language errors or slips of the tongue, difficulty in attending to the content of the interview, etc., occurring during the interview, were used as further signs of affective display or functional disruption (in this regard, the interviewer had an obvious advantage over the other raters in that he could directly observe blushing or blanching, tearing, hand-wringing, etc.—this information was not conveyed to the other raters to prevent transmission of assessment bias). The area of "defensive reserve" was approached both by asking the patient how adequately she felt she had been dealing with any concurrent life problems since detecting the breast mass and by noting how effectively she maintained her emotional equilibrium within the interview under the threat posed by direct confrontations concerning her being separated from her family and her home, having anesthesia and surgery, and, finally, the possibility of losing a breast and having cancer.

In other words, "defensive adequacy" was being operationally defined in terms of the success the patient was having (as manifested by the three criteria defined by Wolff et al., 1964, and Wolff, Hofer, & Mason, 1964) in coping with a specific threat—namely, a breast tumor with all its ramifications.

In addition to covering these specific areas, however, the interviewer encouraged the patient to talk about whatever was on her mind: more specific information about her social, medical, family, marital, educational, and occupational history was also sought. This provided additional information about the patient's affective state, personality style and characterological defenses, and the overall quality of her ego functions.

For each of the three criteria of defensive adequacy, a seven-point rating scale was constructed. These scales were meant to reflect in a gross way, by assigning a numerical value, each rater's estimate of the degree (from absent, 0, to fulminating, $+6$) of unpleasant affect the patient reported or seemed to be experiencing, the degree of her functional disruption, and the degree of impairment of her defensive "reserve." A further modification of the original Wolff criteria was

also introduced by noting and rating pleasant affects, as well as unpleasant ones, since these have been reported (Sachar, Fishman, &
Mason, 1965; Wadeson et al., 1963) to be reflected in relatively
lower corticosteroid levels: thus, with regard to the criterion of affective state, we employed a bipolar rating scale which included both
unpleasant (0 to $+6$) and pleasant affect (0 to -6).

Scores on the three scales were then summed. The focus here,
then, was on how *effectively* the patient coped with the stresses confronting her, as judged by her affect, function, and defensive reserve.
We anticipated that the higher each subject's overall score was the
higher would be her production rate of hydrocortisone. Furthermore,
we anticipated that, if the "stress-strain" model was indeed valid for
humans, the psychological scores and hydrocortisone production rates
would be markedly skewed toward the high side of the possible distribution range.

In addition to scoring the three criteria, the raters were asked to
also specify the main components of each, i.e., the specific affects described by the subjects or inferred from the interview, the functions
which were disrupted, and the interview topics which elicited signs
of compromised defensive reserve. Each rater was also asked to infer,
whenever feasible, the patient's basic personality style and pattern of
psychological defenses, and to note which defenses, whether newly
employed or habitually used, were being most prominently relied
upon (with or without success) during the current stresses. The issue
here, then, was how (as contrasted with how *effectively*) did the subjects
defend against their threatening circumstances.

RESULTS

Identifying Data. (See Table 17.1) Of the 30 women in the study,
22 were white, 6 black, and 2 Puerto Rican. They came from predominantly lower-middle socio-economic backgrounds, 19 of the
women being referred by the hospital's clinic and only 11 by private
physicians. The range of ages was from 33 to 79 years, with 14 being
premenopausal and the remainder menopausal. Eleven were Jewish,
10 were Catholic, 7 were Protestant, 1 was Greek Orthodox, and 1
Puerto Rican woman described herself as "nonsectarian." On biopsy,
22 of the tumors were diagnosed as malignant.

Table 17.1. *Clinical, Psychiatric, and Endocrine Data*

Patient (Grouped by Principal Defense(s) Employed in Hospital)	Age	Racial Stock	Religion *	Tumor Diagnosis	Psychiatric Score for Extent of Failure of Defenses	Hydrocortisone Production Rate (mg/gm Creatinine)
Projection						
16	71	W	P	M	+10	19.0
20	48	W	C	M	+12	23.0
Displacement						
8	72	W	J	M	+13	24.5
18	66	W	J	M	+8	16.5
Denial With Rationalization						
3	62	W	J	M	−2	11.5
4	42	W	J	B	+2	23.0
6	64	W	C	M	−1	16.0
7	46	PR	NS	M	−3	18.0
9	52	W	C	M	+2	13.5
10	48	W	C	B	+3	17.5
11	38	PR	C	M	+2	15.5
12	41	B	P	M	+10	13.0
13	48	W	GO	B	0	13.0
15	40	W	C	M	+2	12.0
23	58	W	C	M	+2	16.5
Prayer and Faith						
14	60	W	C	M	−2	14.0
17	45	B	P	B	0	8.0
24	63	W	C	M	+7	24.0
27	33	B	P	M	0	12.0
Stoicism-Fatalism						
1	47	B	P	M	−3	15.5
19	54	B	P	B	−1	11.0
Mixed						
2	79	W	J	B	+7	29.5
5	69	W	J	B	+7	16.0
21	50	W	J	M	+4	16.0
22	44	W	J	B	+9	12.5
25	57	W	J	M	+10	15.5
26	36	W	J	M	+7	21.0
28	56	W	C	M	+3	13.0
29	45	N	P	M	+5	12.0
30	37	W	J	M	+11	24.0

* P = Protestant; C = Catholic; J = Jewish; NS = nonsectarian; GO = Greek Orthodox.

Endocrine Data. Hydrocortisone production rates for our subjects had a range of 8.0 to 29.5 milligrams per gram of creatinine (mean = 16.5). (These figures represent the means between values for hydrocortisone production rate as determined from both principal metabolites, tetrahydrocortisone and tetrahydrocortisol; for a more complete discussion of the assumptions and issues involved in this measurement, the interested reader is referred to other papers by us—Fukushima et al., 1968, 1969; Katz et al., 1970a.) When compared with results obtained in other studies with females by our Steroid Institute, these values for production rate fell within a low normal to high normal range; the mean value is similarly unremarkable. Thus, not only is the range and mean value for hydrocortisone production rate grossly unremarkable for our group of women in their presumably very remarkable set of circumstances, but the distribution of their values (Fig. 17.1) also shows a rather typical clustering about the normal mean. Indeed, only 7 of the 30 patients had rates of 20 or more milligrams per gram of creatinine, and 10 patients, despite their "stressful" circumstances, actually had values of 13 or less, which is in the low normal range.

Psychiatric Ratings for Defensive Adequacy. Using the three criteria previously defined, the interviewer obtained scores with the 30 patients which ranged from − 3 to + 13 (the possible limits having obviously been from − 6 to + 18). A plot of the distribution of these ratings (Fig. 17.2) reveals, again despite the circumstances, that the majority of women did not manifest signs of significant defensive breakdown—namely, a *major* elaboration of unpleasant affect, disruption of function, and/or impairment of defensive reserve.

Correlation Between Psychological and Endocrine Variables. A rank ordering of the interviewer's scores for extent of defensive failing in each patient and of the values of their hydrocortisone production rates gave a correlation (r_s) of 0.48 between the two variables, significant at less than the 0.02 level. Figure 17.3 is a plot of ratings vs. the production rates.

Breaking down the criteria by category, we found that affect had the most significant covariance with hydrocortisone production rates ($r_s = 0.55$, $P < 0.01$), function was intermediate ($r_s = 0.40$, $P < 0.05$), and defensive reserve had the least ($r_s = 0.31$, $P < 0.10$).

Thus, it is clear that (1) our subjects showed a broad but not star-

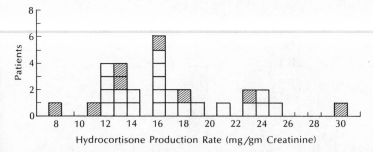

Fig. 17.1. Distribution of values for hydrocortisone production rate (white squares indicate malignant tumors; cross hatched squares indicate benign tumors).

tling range of values for both the endocrine and psychological parameters of defensive adequacy, (2) the majority of corticosteroid values clustered unremarkably around the normal mean, and (3) there was a significant (although not perfect) rank order correlation between the two variables.

Inter-rater Reliability. The inter-rater reliability between the four raters for their scoring of the 19 taped interviews was excellent, the Kendall coefficient of concordance (W) for their total scores being 0.85 ($P < 0.001$). Breaking this down by categories, agreement was found to be highest for ratings of function, intermediate for affect, and lowest for defensive reserve.

Patterns of Defense. Six basic defensive maneuvers or styles characterized our group of 30 women awaiting breast tumor biopsy. These were displacement, projection, denial with rationalization, stoicism-fatalism, prayer and faith, and a mixture of multiple defenses without any single one being solely or predominantly relied upon.

The following examples are representative of each of the defense patterns.

Displacement. This was observed in 2 elderly Jewish women. Typically, patient No. 18, 66 years old, responded to the very initial query in the interview ("What brought you into the hospital"?) with concern focused virtually exclusively on her sick husband:

I don't know whether you noticed my husband [visiting] in the room, but if you had, you would have noticed that he's a very sick man. He has cancer of the stomach . . . I have had a lump on my breast for the past

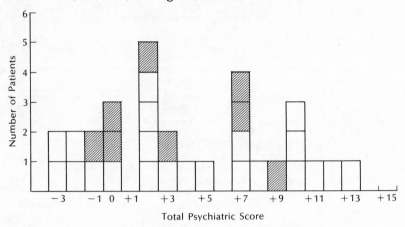

Fig. 17.2. Distribution of total psychiatric scores for extent of failure of the defenses, obtained by summing ratings for patients' affective state (−6 to +6), functional disruption (0 to +6), and defensive reserve impairment (0 to +6) (white squares indicate malignant tumors; crosshatched squares indicate benign tumors).

two months. I had noticed it but it didn't bother me . . . and besides, I just couldn't leave him alone. Everything went through my mind: What if I had to go into the hospital? What if I had to leave him alone?

Whenever confronted in the interview with the implications of the tumor in her breast, the patient would similarly respond by minimizing her concerns about herself and emphasizing rather her fears about her husband's health.

Projection. This was conspicuous in 2 white women, one a 7 1-year-old Protestant and the other a 48-year-old Catholic. The former patient (No. 16), for example, was convinced that the interviewer and staff were withholding information from her that she had disseminated cancer and that they were simply using her as a guinea pig:

I don't like the expression on your face. . . . I think there's something you want to tell me but are withholding. . . . I think you know [something] and don't want to come out with it. . . . Why are you asking me all these questions? . . . You want to make me nervous. . . . You're trying to find out something. . . . You're trying to tell me there is something wrong with me—worse than what I think it is. . . . I think you know.

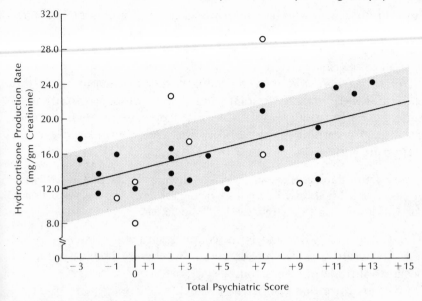

Fig. 17.3. Total psychiatric scores for extent of failure of the defenses vs. values
for hydrocortisone production rate, with regression curve (±1 SE) determination
(circles indicate benign tumors; r = 0.48[P < 0.02]).

Interestingly, both of these patients were the only two in the study
who refused to sign consent for mastectomy; they permitted only
needle biopsy to be done and, in both cases, this revealed cancer.

Denial With Rationalization. This was clearly the most commonly
employed defense pattern in our group of subjects. It was primarily
employed by 11 of the women, including older and younger subjects, black, white, and Puerto Rican, Protestant, Catholic, and Jewish. Representative is patient No. 3, a 62-year-old Jewish woman.
She had not reported the lump in her breast for many months because she thought she had gotten it from "falling in the bathtub."
(She finally went to a physician at her daughter's insistence.) In the
hospital, she reported "never feeling better" in her life and being certain that the tumor was "nothing" because she had always been such
a "strong" person, had been "healthy all my life," and had such a
good family medical history.

Stoicism-Fatalism. This style was observed in 2 of the black patients, both Protestant, and is illustrated by patient No. 1, a 47-

year-old housewife who had a "grin and bear it" philosophy. She repeatedly emphasized her belief that "What will be, will be . . . all one can do is hope for the best and go about one's business . . . getting all upset isn't going to change what's fated to be."

Prayer and Faith. Four of our subjects relied primarily upon this pattern; 2 were black Protestants and 2 were white Irish Catholics. Patient No. 14, a 60-year-old Catholic widow, responded to a confrontation concerning the possibility the tumor would prove to be malignant with:

> I try not to think about that: I just keep hoping for the best and trusting in God. . . . I hope and I pray it's nothing serious. . . I'm not a fanatic but I try to live up to my religion half way decent.

This turning to prayer and faith (coupled with suppression) typified how she dealt with the breast tumor whenever thoughts about it began to intrude into consciousness.

(We recognize that the defenses which we have termed "stoicism-fatalism" and "prayer and faith" have not been traditionally listed among the principal ego defenses. Nevertheless, a careful review of our material left us with little doubt these are indeed real and distinct defensive maneuvers; while they both do contain elements of denial, rationalization, ritualization, isolation, regression, and repression, they are not identical with any one or even the sum of these and would thus seem to warrant categories of their own.)

Mixed. For a number of the patients, no single type of defensive maneuver appeared to be dominant. Rather, several different defenses were all being employed, the patient one moment using one defense, a few minutes later another, then another, and then perhaps returning to the initial one. For example, patient No. 2, an elderly Jewish woman, was noted from the one interview to have clearly employed repression (she reported having "forgotten" that a breast lump had been discovered during a hospitalization for eye surgery, "remembering" again only when a letter came from the breast clinic confirming an appointment), displacement (her main medical concern was the health of the brother who lived with her and had recently fractured his hip), rationalization (she stated that, since her general health had been pretty good and since she was feeling well, "Perhaps the tumor is benign"), prayer and faith (when thoughts about the tumor began to emerge into consciousness, she would pray to God that it prove "not serious"), projection (she would emphasize the concern of her friends, rather than her own, over her hospitalization), and stoicism (she would accept "things as they come").

· · · ·

Pattern of Defense vs. Effectiveness of Defense. One of the questions we posed at the outset of this report was whether certain defenses are more effective than others, "effectiveness" being defined by psychological (affect, function, and defensive "reserve") and physiological (hydrocortisone production rate) parameters.

It will be noted that Table 17.1 groups our subjects by predominant defense. In the 19 cases where all 4 raters assessed the interviews, at least 3 had to concur about the defense being of prime importance to the patient for her to be assigned to that category; if there was less agreement than this, the patient was placed in the "mixed" group (certain patients were, of course, initially diagnosed by the raters as showing principally "mixed" defense styles as well). In the remaining 11 cases, the judgement was solely that of the interviewer.

As judged by both the hydrocortisone production rates and the psychiatric rating scores, the following trends are discernible (with several of the categories, the number is obviously too small to permit specific statistical analysis).

On the whole, those patients who employed stoicism-fatalism, prayer and faith, and denial with rationalization appeared to experience considerably less psychological and concomitant physiological disruption than those who depended primarily upon projection or displacement (mixed patterns showed a very broad range).

Nevertheless, given any single pattern of defense, with the possible exceptions of projection and stoicism-fatalism, one could not automatically assume low or high defensive adequacy.

A further complicating consideration, however, may be whether a defense is being employed only after other defenses have already proved inadequate and thus been "discarded" by the patient's ego. This was obviously an exceedingly difficult issue for the raters to assess, but in at least one case (patient No. 24), where several of the raters expressed the feeling that for her prayer was being used only as a last resort, her hydrocortisone production rate and psychiatric score were both relatively elevated (the only patient in this category with such values).

•   •   •   •

Pattern of Defense vs. "Reality," Background, and Diagnosis. If one accepts the ego defenses as indeed having as their prime function the prevention or control of unpleasant affective states, it is obvious from our data that the defenses of many of our subjects were operating with great success.

Nevertheless, an additional finding confirms a frequently observed phenomenon in clinical psychiatry, namely that an effective defense is not necessarily a healthy, reality-oriented one. Most dramatically illustrative of this is the defense of denial with rationalization. While a number of our patients were observed to utilize this with impressive efficiency, it was also precisely these women who tended to delay the longest in seeking medical help and so most impaired their chances for surgical cure if their lesions were malignant.

With regard to background, several trends suggestive of cultural influences on defensive style are clearly discernible, even within the admitted confines of our subject number of only 30. First, black patients (4 of the 6) were more likely to rely on stoicism-fatalism or faith and prayer than on other defenses; conversely, white patients were less likely to use these defenses (only 2 of 22; interestingly, both of these women were Irish Catholics). Only white subjects primarily employed displacement or projection, the former being used by 2 Jewish women and the latter by 1 Catholic and 1 Protestant. Denial with rationalization apparently is ubiquitous. It was utilized by persons of all religions (including the 1 Greek Orthodox woman in the study) and races (including the 2 Puerto Rican women).

•   •   •   •

COMMENT

Our findings vividly document the importance of weighing individual psychological and physiological variability in assessing the response to "stress." Clearly, even in the face of potentially disastrous circumstances, one cannot assume that what "stresses" also "dis resses" in proportional fashion. The perception and interpretation f, and particularly the defenses against, threat remain sufficiently aried between humans to give a panorama of responses.

The ego's defenses are obviously able to "buffer" the individual rom threat with great efficiency and, therefore, psychological-physiological arousal should never be automatically assumed in any est situation. In our group of subjects, who were soon to learn whether they would lose a breast consequent to a cancerous tumor, many showed psychological states and hydrocortisone production ates which could not be deemed remarkable.

Clinically, of course, this cannot be considered surprising. It is merely a formal confirmation of a fact generally evident to surgeons nd internists, namely that they are able to guide most of their patients through "stressful" hospitalizations and surgery without having to put them on tranquilizers or call for psychiatric consultation.

There also appear to be various defenses that can work effectively a warding off distress. Whether one prays or rationalizes may matter ss than the "expertise" one develops with the defense over the ears. The ineffectiveness of projection is perhaps the exception and a reating physician should probably be alert to the possibility of rious psychological complications to management when this defense is noted in his patient.

Moreover, despite the sameness of the circumstances confronting ur patients, they displayed a variety of affects, which highlights the sue of the interpretation of a stress. Clearly, some of our patients ere responding to the element of potential loss (breast, life) in their tuation, while others focused on the uncertainties and ambiguities volved, and still others saw it as a test of their strength, determina-on, will, or faith. Thus, even if a "stress" is indeed "distressing" to many subjects, an investigator cannot assume it is distressing in the ime way, i.e., having the same meaning and eliciting the same affect or all the subjects.

· · · ·

Perhaps, however, the most intriguing finding in our study was ne wide disparity between the ego's twin goals of maintaining psy-nological equilibrium (via the defenses) and adapting to the realities f the situation. Thus, two women who used projection became con-inced they were being used as "guinea pigs"; they refused to sign consents for mastectomy, and needle biopsies proved positive for malignancy in both cases. Meanwhile, many other women who employed denial with rationalization had been so well defended that they delayed seeking medical evaluation; they thus significantly impaired their chances for successful medical treatment.

Not only, then, does the "stress-distress" model appear to be an overused concept, but it should not be assumed that the "distress" part need always be detrimental for humans. Incapacitating psychic anxiety may not ultimately prove any more disastrous for a person than the pleasant, "no need to do anything" calm observed with denial-rationalization. The implication here is obvious. A moderate amount of "distress" probably is actually needed for the most effective and realistic handling of a threat.

Finally, the determinants of defense style and effectiveness are obviously an exceedingly complicated issue, but our study does point to the importance of cultural influences. While denial-rationalization may be ubiquitous, certain other defenses may well be relatively characteristic of certain groups; this means that cultural background is simply one more variable that influences the subject's response to a situation which is perhaps being viewed as "stressful" by an investigator who may himself be from an entirely different cultural background.

SUMMARY

It is frequently assumed that "strain" or "distress" in a subject is essentially proportional to the severity of "stress" imposed upon that subject. This model may, however, be a relatively crude one for human beings, even when the threat is a potentially life-taking one.

Thirty women, while awaiting breast tumor biopsy in the hospital, were intensively interviewed to determine the adequacy of their ego defenses in this serious and highly ambiguous circumstance. The criteria for this psychological assessment were affective state, functional intactness, and defensive "reserve." Concurrent with the psychiatric evaluation, radioisotopic determination of hydrocortisone production rate was carried out to provide a concomitant physiological parameter of adequacy of defenses.

The principal finding was that, whereas the "stress-strain" theory would predict major psychological and associated psychoendocrine upheavals in these subjects, the majority of patients did not manifest significant defensive breakdown, as judged by these criteria.

Six basic defense patterns were observed in these women: displacement, projection, denial with rationalization, hope and prayer, stoicism-fatalism, and a mixture of defenses. The first two types tended to be associated with greater defensive failure than the others, but despite the high effectiveness of denial with rationalization, many of the women who successfully employed the latter impaired their chances for survivial by waiting the longest to consult their physician as a direct consequence of the defense. Defense pattern also showed some correlation with cultural background.

A variety of affects was also present in these women, suggesting that, although they were all awaiting biopsy, the event was perceived or interpreted differently by various subjects.

Our findings indicate that all that "stresses" does not necessarily evoke comparable distress; rather, the latter is contingent upon how the former is perceived, interpreted, and defended against.

18

Some Modes of Adaptation: Defense

As we see it, a person's behavior represents a more or less consistent pattern of response—what we call his *personality*. He attempts to maintain cognitive integration by controlling the information that enters the cognitive system and by making it congruent with his views and needs (Festinger, 1957).

Organizing his behavior around attitudes of the self and the relations of the self to the external world, he deals not only with objective situations, but also with perceived subjective threats. The information that enters the cognitive system may be relevant or irrelevant, important or unimportant to the task at hand or to the attitudes the person holds about himself in relation to the task. In instances where relevant information does enter the system, the individual either may integrate it into his cognitive orientation or attempt to reject it. In doing this he seeks various kinds of support from others in the communication structure of which he is a part and from cues which he finds in his environment.

The system of defenses described by the classical psychoanalytic theorists attempts to indicate *what* occurs, but tells us little that is clear as to *how* this occurs. Thus, whereas the descriptions of behavior—repression, denial, projection, intellectualization, and so on—sensitize us to these happenings, the conditions under which these distortions occur and how they develop remain unclear.

A step in the direction of solving this problem has been provided by some interesting studies by David Hamburg and his associates (Hamburg, Hamburg, & deGoza, 1953). Studying the adaptive processes of badly burned soldiers, they observed that many of the adaptive processes were social—that these processes involved communication as well as cognition, and that cognitive defenses were associated with environmental cues. These insightful papers suggested that perhaps we might learn a good deal more if we would attempt to understand the social and social-psychological contexts within which defense occurs.

THE NEED FOR DEFENSE

The students under study most definitely saw stress as a major factor in the challenge of passing the examinations. Many of them believed that if they could defend adequately and maintain their anxiety at some comfortable level, they would be adequate in their performance. Both students and faculty were asked to indicate the importance of the ability to remain relaxed and the ability to work under pressure for students taking preliminary examinations. The difference in perception of stress as a factor was quite considerable when viewed through the eyes of students and faculty in Table 18.1.

Table 18.1. *Perceived Importance of Defending Against Stress by Students and Faculty*

Items	Percent of Students Responding Very or Fairly Important (N-22)	Percent of Faculty Responding Very or Fairly Important (N-21)
Ability to remain relaxed	68	29
Ability to work under pressure	100	76

Since students do find that preparation is a major factor in reducing anxiety, tasks that keep them from working on examination preparation were likely to raise their anxiety level. We expected, therefore, that students would think it more important than faculty to put aside everything for their studies in order to pass the examinations. And, as analysis of Table 18.2 shows, they did just this.

Table 18.2. *Rated Importance of the Ability to Put Aside Everything for Studies by Students and Faculty*

	Percent Responding Very or Fairly Important
Students (N-22)	91
Faculty (N-21)	38

COMFORTING COGNITIONS AND FAVORABLE SOCIAL COMPARISON

The most consistently observed defense device used by the students under study was that of seeking comforting information from the environment that was consistent with the attitudes and hopes the student held about the examinations. Often these comforting cognitions were made on the basis of comparing oneself favorably with others, or by finding cues in the environment that made the person more confident about his situation. A number of these comforting cognitions have already been pointed to in preceding chapters. For example: "most students who had failed preliminary examinations in the past had had difficult personalities"; "the faculty expects less from this year's group as compared with earlier ones because most of the people in the present group have been here for only two years."

This is not to say that what is necessarily comforting for one student is comforting for all. But in general the persons who most often verbalized these attitudes were those for whom they were most comforting as measured by other criteria. For example, as we have pointed out, the attitude concerning the faculty expecting less of second-year students was developed and communicated by second-year students. It is true that one or two of the older students also accepted this idea, but these students had little to lose by its acceptance. In addition, the fact that a belief may be accurate does not invalidate it as a defense; on the contrary, accurate beliefs are valuable as defenses because they do have environmental support. Thus, while the inaccurate defenses may be more striking to the observer, they are probably more likely to lead to later problems of adaptation. The student who can draw satisfaction from the fact that he is competent and that others think him competent is in a better position than the student who holds this as an illusion.

A number of comforting thoughts, verbalized in early interviews with the students, were included in the questionnaire administered to students. They were asked to indicate how often they had felt, thought, said, or done each of a number of things (see Table 18.3).

The assurance that occurred most frequently resulted from favorable social comparison—a student compared himself with other students who had taken examinations in prior years and passed, and told himself that he was as knowledgeable or more so than the student

Table 18.3. *Students' Reported Use of Comforting Cognitions*

	Percent of Students	
Comforting Cognitions	Who Report Using This Cognition Very or Fairly Often	Who Report Using These Cognitions With any Frequency
I'm as bright and knowledgeable as other students who have passed these examinations	64	91
I've handled test situations in the past—there's no good reason why not now	59	86
I am doing all I can to prepare—the rest is not up to me	50	86
I wouldn't have gotten this far unless I knew something	50	86
I'm well liked in this department	45	77
I've already demonstrated my competence on past work, they will pass me	26	77
You can't fail these examinations unless you really mess up	23	73
They wouldn't fail me—they've already decided I'm going to pass	18	30
This is a test of stress; I can deal with that	14	59
If I'm not cut out for the field, it's best that I know it now	14	55

with whom he was comparing himself. Others *drew on past experience,* and, by reassuring themselves of their competence in the past, they felt more competent in the present: "I wouldn't have gotten this far unless I knew something," "I've handled situations in the past," and other such similar statements. Still others saw themselves as well liked, and almost all of the students believed to some extent that if you were liked, your chances of having a good outcome on the examinations were better. Others sought to externalize responsibility: "If I am doing all I can, what's the use of worrying?" Let us take some examples from the interviews to illustrate how the student verbalized these comforting comparisons and cognitions.

I think I'll pass because I think that if decisions have been made previously, that I'm one who will pass rather than fail. . . . So I'll really have to botch up writtens to get them to alter their opinion of me. . . . I evaluate the people on the faculty as being reasonable people . . . who should make reasonable demands for performance on writtens which I should be able to meet.

[I was saying] that we are pretty scared of the questions that were asked on the old examinations and yet we haven't seen the answers that people have given to these questions to see what they were like; to see the quality of the answers—the answers which were acceptable in terms of passage. Perhaps, if we were able to see some of the answers that have been acceptable, we would feel a little better. I don't feel that we are significantly more defective than other people who have passed these . . . or that we worked any less. From this standpoint, it would seem that our chances of passing are just as good as those who passed.

I was afraid that reading so few books wouldn't be enough. Then I found out that other people were reading these and felt secure with them. Now I feel better.

It seems that people pass [the examinations] pretty easily.

I have a much better memory than most people.

[I tell] myself how clever I am. . . . I usually have done better. I think it contributes to my normal state of well-being.

Considering the people who passed previously, I think my chances are at least even.

Hundreds of such statements came up in the interviews with students. The examples took many forms, and enumerating them would be unnecessary for our argument. What is important to recognize is that these beliefs arose in the interaction process; they were exchanged back and forth among students, and many were held commonly and were consensually validated.

This is not to suggest that all social comparisons are favorable. As we indicated earlier, social comparison often aroused anxiety. It is through social comparison processes that the individual attempts to ascertain both his strengths and his weaknesses, and to evaluate what soft spots need plugging. The student who fails to take part in this type of social comparison can lose considerable information about the examinations and possible modes of preparation, although as a result he may be able to keep his anxiety at a lower level. This was especially true of two, low-anxiety, isolated students who were not comparing themselves to others, and who had little idea how much others were studying. Both of these students studied considerably less than the rest of the group, and both performed at a level below the expectations of faculty. One of these two students had communicated and compared himself so little with others, that he had no idea that other students were aiming to pass at the Ph.D. level. All along, he prepared casually, feeling that he would be satisfied attaining an M.A. pass. After the examinations the student became considerably agitated about his performance, knowing that had he set his expectations higher he might have performed better and closer to the expectations others had of him. The reactions of these two low-anxiety persons were somewhat similar to the reactions that Grinker and Spiegel (1945, p. 128) observed among some soldiers: "One sometimes sees men who err in the opposite direction and fail to interpret danger when they should. As a consequence, they are protected against developing subjective anxiety. . . . The defect in discrimination gives them the appearance of being unrealistic and slaphappy, illustrating the maxim that fools walk where angels fear to tread."

It is thus the process of social comparison that allows the student to pace himself. For example, one student decided a few weeks prior to examinations to postpone them until the following fall. Notice how social comparison was a prime influence in this decision.

I think, to a great degree, interacting with people like you who keep asking me what I am doing and other people who are doing things, sort of hearing that certain people are reading this, that, and the other, has kind of gotten me to the point of feeling that I'm not preparing for them like other people are. I really don't have a chance to. Maybe it would be best that I didn't take them at all rather than take them and not do so well. . . . I talked to a couple of people, [student X] and [student Y], in Central Building, and I've heard some from my office partner who knows [students A, B, and C] who are taking them and he related some of the things that they are doing. I feel, myself, that I would like to do some of these things . . . I don't have the time this semester. . . . So these sorts of things have gotten me to think that I'm not preparing too well. And I think that it would be best that I don't take them at all.

JOKING AND HUMOR

Joking as a useful form of defense has been given considerable attention by philosophers, psychologists, and humorists, but only in recent years have its social functions been noted to any significant degree. In recent studies by Coser (1959), Fox (1959), and Hamburg and associates (Hamburg, Hamburg, & deGoza, 1953) on the hospital ward, some of the social functions of joking under stress have been pointed out.

Four weeks prior to examinations students were asked to indicate how much they joked about examinations. Every student indicated that he had joked to some extent.

Table 18.4. *The Extent of Student Joking About Examinations*

Extent of Joking	Percent of Students (N-22)
Joked a great deal	23
Joked some	54
Joked not very much	23
Joked none	—

The older students who were more anxious and more upset about examinations seemed to find it more difficult to find humor in the examination situation.

Table 18.5. *Student Status and Joking*

	Percent of Students Who Joked		
	A Great Deal	Some	Not Very Much
Older students (N-8)	—	62	38
Second-year students (N-14)	36	50	14

Since joking is an interpersonal event and may serve as an avoidance device in interaction, we would expect that joking about examinations would be more likely to arise among the second-year students, who are more centrally located in the communication structure, than among those more isolated. Table 18.6 confirms this.

It appears that joking occurred primarily among those who were high-moderate and moderate-anxiety types. Students who were very anxious, with some exceptions, did not see the examinations as humorous as did some of the moderate-anxiety students. This was true especially of the older students who felt that they had suffered considerably in going through the process; yet it did appear that humor was an important mode of anxiety reduction. Also it seemed that joking occurred most frequently at certain points in time. For example, it seemed to increase in intensity just prior to the week of examinations, and the form that it took also seemed to change. Well before examinations, joking consisted mainly of poking fun at the material—a form of tension release. As examinations approached, however, tension-release humor still was present, but avoidance banter seemed to increase in significant quantity. A possible explanation for the change in the kind of joking forms was that as the examinations approached, time pressures increased and students became aware that time for future coping effort was limited. Therefore, a useful defense would allow for avoidance of serious discussion about examinations and avoidance of the kinds of anxiety stimuli that were

Table 18.6. *Joking Among Second-Year Students and Centrality in the Communication Structure **

	Percent of Students Who Joked		
Degree of Centrality	A Great Deal	Some	Not Very Much
Three or more communication links (N-6)	67	33	—
Less than three communication links (N-8)	12	63	25

* This relationship did not hold among older students. Having three or more communication links was atypical of older students.

discussed in an earlier chapter. For example, a few days prior to examinations, it would be of little use for a student to discover that five important textbooks had been read by others while he had spent his time on less significant details. Joking as an avoidance technique allowed for keeping further information that might have been disruptive out of one's frame of reference.

Before going on to describe and give some examples of the kinds of humor that developed, the reader should be warned that he might not find student humor terribly humorous. Humor is highly situational, and often specific to those sharing a common frame of reference. Regardless of how the jokes appear to the reader, they were in fact funny from the student's perspective.

Joking as a form of tension release. Joking is a useful device to reduce tensions resulting from uncertainty. One of the more common problems for students in dealing with examinations is the uncertainty they feel as to which questions or areas will appear on examinations and the sampling used in choosing these questions. Students feel that it is conceivable that one can know an area well yet encounter an examination where he cannot answer the questions. Put in another way, students believe that an element of chance is operating, that the student may be lucky or unlucky in the questions he encounters. In the student story that follows, the uncertainty in the examination process was made to appear ludicrous.

I heard a cute story the other day about the manner in which certain people go around assigning questions for the examinations. . . . He grabs down a great big book and goes thumbing through it and happens to pick up one little area, one little section in the bottom of the page in the middle of the volume. And he says: "Hmmmm, this strikes my fancy. I've never seen this before. I think I'll put this on the examinations and see what they could tell me about this."

One of the situations found most amusing by the students concerned a discussion about a possible question on examinations. As the reader will remember, most of the students felt that if you do not know the answer to a question, you still should attempt to write something. The situation described below deals with a discussion of this strategy.

When I walked into the Monday class, everyone was joking around . . . [student *D*] was telling us his point of view of what he would do if he didn't know a question. . . . He would give another answer to it. . . . The other fellows said, "Okay, we'll test you out. What is the [Spencer] hypothesis?" or some obscure thing I never heard of. And so [student *D*] sort of laughed and said, "Well, I never heard of that but I'm sure getting familiar with the [Zipp] effect."
[Later student *D*] came in and said, "Okay, I found out what [Spencer] is." And [student *A*], who doesn't take our other course, said, "WHAT???" And everybody said, "You better be sure you know that, that's very important." And someone said it was such and such and such. And somebody else turned around and said, "What is its present status?" and everybody laughed.

Here again, the question, "What is its present status?" was experienced by the group as a humorous remark. This is probably due to the fact that many of the questions on doctoral examinations ask students to discuss the development and present status of various concepts. In a sense the group was having a good laugh over the examinations and, to some extent, over the stereotyped forms the questions sometimes take.

Another source of humor was the obscure items that students often pick up in their reading for examinations, that they then go around and jokingly ask other students about. In a sense this represents a take-off on the anxiety-arousing effect students have on one another, and also is sometimes used as a device to hide one's own anxiety about examinations. Below are some examples:

Generally we joke about things that don't mean too much . . . and obscure things. [Student *F*] said something like, did I know that the average visual acuity of an eight-year-old elephant was the same as a female horse? He came across a little bit about Meyer, the photosensitive crab. So this seemed like a particular bit of nonsensical information which he passed all over the department. "You got to know about Meyer." It has kind of been the joke of the week.

One of the students who participated a great deal in joking described what he perceived to be the function of joking about examinations.

All of this doesn't mean anything. It's not going to be useful in preparing for the writtens . . . but I think it's a tension-reducing mechanism. It keeps you from getting too serious about them, in a sense, letting the thing get the better of you, which I'm sure has happened to some people in the past, and I'm sure it has had an adverse effect.

Students also made seemingly silly comments to one another, or thought of funny comments they might make. Apparently this made the whole process seem a little more unreal, a little less serious.

I was thinking about walking in on the first examination and yelling, "Hey, I thought this was going to be multiple choice."

"Sick" Humor. This type of humor is represented by jokes about failing. Usually these jokes involve saying, "I'm going to fail, ha, ha, ha," or "We'll fail and then we can go out and kill ourselves." By attaching an absurdity to the situation, the student seemed to make the real situation and the threat it presented more remote and more impossible.

Another kind of "sick" humor pertained to what the student should do should he fail. Once again the same function was apparent. By making the possibilities absurd, failure seemed more remote.

[Student *C*] said, "Next year at this time, I'll be getting ready to get out of this place, and I'll be looking for a job." And I said, "Yeah, next year at this time I might be selling shoes." Someone else said, "Yeah, if it weren't for these writtens."

We got into a discussion, you know, how I always wanted to sell shoes. . . . A lot of talk is this sort of humorous thing about it.

Whether the jokes were concerned with selling shoes or picking cotton, their intent was the same: to debunk the seriousness of the possible outcomes. This could take various forms; for example, one student usually referred to the examinations as the "spring quizzes."

Joking as an Avoidance Device. Joking is one of the most effective methods for avoiding a serious discussion. Certainly anyone who has ever tried to have a serious discussion with a person who insists on being jovial will realize how effective humor may be as an avoidance device. It allows an individual to fend others off in a friendly but effective fashion, and it makes them keep their distance. It also can be used as a form of attack on others, and should they object, one always can have the recourse to "I was only joking." It is this ambiguous function of joking that allows one to attempt attack and avoidance without making himself too vulnerable to being charged with his offense. One student explained how joking might be utilized in this fashion:

When [student *X*] comes in, he wants to talk seriously about the examinations. But I don't want to talk seriously about them because I feel that I'm not going to pass and that isn't very funny. Another thing is that I don't want to tell him that I don't think I'm going to pass. . . . [Student *X*], he's pretty serious and I tease him. He comes in and asks, "What are you studying for statistics?" And I spend the next five minutes reeling off all this nonsense (laughs), and he's getting more and more anxious. He just bothers most people more because he is serious. He's pretty anxious really. . . . Everybody is just real childish and real silly. It's easier to be funny than to be serious.

The joking playfulness one can observe here combined teasing, hostility, and anxiety avoidance. One student, for example, related how he became very anxious after he had found a question he could not answer on an old examination. After asking another student if he knew the answer, he reported that the other student also became anxious, and, feeling that he had done his duty, he went to bed. Another student, from the viewpoint of the recipient of the communication, related a somewhat similar situation:

When I try to study in the office, somebody will come up to me and say, "What are you studying? What are you studying?" When I tell them, they say, "Oh, you don't want to study that. What do you want to study that for?" And they'll go on. It makes me angry. They're doing it because they feel threatened sort of. . . . . Everyone wants to be sure that nobody knows anything more than they do. . . . . So instead you tease.

One student who generated considerable anxiety, and who a number of students were avoiding, was sometimes heavily sanctioned by names. This was done to discourage his serious attitude toward examinations, which made the other students anxious.

Students also did a considerable bit of clowning.

[Student B] was on a jag a couple of weeks ago. Every time someone walked into the room, he asked them, "Why are you so hostile to me?". . . . It's just easier to keep laughing. It doesn't bother you as much to joke about it.

This kind of joking, especially among one of the cliques, continued until writtens began, and then to some extent seemingly subsided. At any rate, there was an apparent decrease in the hostile jabbing that had taken place just before the examinations. Once examinations started, however, students became more genuinely friendly to one another and supported one another more than they had at any prior period. It would appear that once the examinations had begun, and some of the tension was reduced, the competitive jockeying was no longer necessary. The clearly defined threat now was not other students but the examinations themselves. And the group seemed to unite against this threat.

· · · · ·

A DYNAMIC VIEW OF FEELINGS AND BEHAVIOR AS EXAMINATIONS APPROACH

As the examinations approached and as student anxiety increased, various changes occurred in behavior. Joking increased, and, while students still sought social support and talked a great deal about examinations, they began specifically to avoid certain people who aroused their anxiety. Stomach-aches, asthma, and a general feeling of weariness became common complaints, and other psychosomatic symptoms appeared. The use of tranquilizers and sleeping pills became more frequent.

For those who had started studying intensively at an early date, exhaustion crept in and they lost their desire and motivation to study.

I just don't seem to be picking up things. You know, like I'll look over stuff and I just don't seem to get it. It's very depressing to spend time and not feel it's doing any good. . . . I just wish they would get them over with. It's just bugging me. . . . I'm getting tired of sitting at that desk. I have all sorts of psychosomatic complaints. My back hurts and so forth. . . . I wish they were over. They're so awful. . . . I was about ready to turn myself into [the psychiatric ward] but now I'm taking antidepressant pills.

A number of other students also complained of an inability to concentrate on their studies:

My minute-to-minute motivation seems to have gone down. When I started, I was a real eager beaver but now it seems, the last week or so, I've had a little trouble. If I have a half hour off, I'll sit in the social room rather than study for that half hour.

Lately I've been feeling depressed. I don't feel that I know anything. I just feel so mentally defective, like what I have done goes into one ear and out the other. . . . Instead of putting in a last-ditch effort, I can't. I'm just sort of tired of the whole business. I'm tired of studying. I'm tired of school. I'm just tired.

While the student feels saturated with study, he still is acutely aware of the short time available for further preparation. Thus he is torn between the feeling that he must study and his inability to concentrate and study effectively, which leads to considerable anxiety, self-doubt, and disgust. As anxiety reaches a high level, students come to agreements not to discuss examinations, but as the saliency of examinations is too great these agreements are rarely maintained. Also, the excessive concern about examinations is reflected in dreams about them. Unreality is another common feeling, the "this isn't happening to me" effect.

As examinations approach, the most common feeling is one of

unpreparedness and impending disaster, although these reports of impending doom usually are disqualified in some way. The student, for example, will predict doom and then declare that he must be pretty stupid to say something as silly as that. Listed below are some of the indications students gave that failure was imminent.

I feel now, rather unrealistically, I think, that I can't remember any names. I can't remember this. I can't remember that. I feel unprepared for this.

I spoke to [student C] . . . about how depressed we were. . . . The main thing he hopes is that they'll let him take them again. He keeps saying this over and over because he's now in one of these stages which I think we all go through, where you just feel that there's no possibility of passing and that you are a failure.

I kept having the feeling like I'm going to fail and that I don't know anything.

When the examinations are nearly upon the student, anxiety is very high, even for those rated as low-anxiety persons, although students do fluctuate between confidence and anxiety. Since studying is difficult, the student questions his motivation, interest, and ability in the field. He reassures himself that he does not care how well he does—that all he really wants out of the process is the Ph.D. degree. Even four weeks prior to examinations 82 per cent of the students reported that they had said to themselves, "All I really want from this process is the Ph.D. degree." They attempted to defend against their feelings by behaving in a silly, manic way, and avoidance joking became very prevalent. Expectation levels were set lower and lower, and many of the students jokingly talked about what they were going to do after they failed or how they were going to prepare for examinations the next time they took them. It appears that for the student supreme confidence at this point was considered not only presumptuous, but sacrilegious. Under these conditions the group became very cohesive and individuals became supportive of one another and exclusive of younger students in the department.

•   •   •   •

19

The Management of Abhorrent Behavior—Survival Period

REX A. LUCAS

This [discussion] is concerned with the way in which men make social adjustments. Specifically, we will examine a situation in which men took action which was abhorrent to them—the drinking of urine. The extreme conditions draw attention to steps in social adjustment and to process and mechanisms that pass unnoticed in day-to-day living.

It hardly need be established that the drinking of urine is a taboo in our society, a taboo so strong that few would even think of consuming it. This is not surprising because during the socialization of the child, the behavior patterns surrounding urination are carefully disassociated from sexual activities and from liquid intake required by the body. Urination is separated spatially and socially from eating, drinking, and other social activities. The widespread prohibition of drinking urine is so strongly held and so remote from everyday life that few entertain the thought of it. Among many, urination is associated with rinsing of hands, which suggests dirt or germs. Urine is usually thought of as a liquid waste from the body; the implications are that urine contains at best impurities and at worst poison.[1]

    •   •   •   •

[1] These statements are valid in a general sense despite a wide range of notable exceptions, even in North American culture. The family physician, for instance, often dipped his finger in a medical urine sample and touched it to his tongue as a quick test for diabetes. Other people recall traditional folk remedies brought from Eastern Europe which incorporated the patient's urine. Despite the taboo, it is probable that many people are able to describe the taste of urine.

During the escape period the men defined their position as one from which escape was highly likely, so their free use of water was appropriate to this definition. No one took seriously a rather tentative warning about the depletion of the water supply. After unsuccessful attempts to make their way to the main shaft, their definition of the situation was modified somewhat—they thought that immediate escape was not too likely. At this point, their concern about water was not great. It was not until the lights failed and further exploration was ruled out, when the men defined their situation as one from which escape was impossible, that they became concerned about the water supply. At this point the men checked the water supply, searched for additional water, and instituted rationing. They shifted their goals and activities from escape to survival.

WATER SUBSTITUTES

[Finally,] the six miners [reached] the point when the last of their water had been used and they sat in the dark, intensely thirsty, and without liquid.

> DICK: There wasn't much we could do but set and wait . . . what we listened for mostly was for the rescue group, and we knew we could last a few days there if the gas didn't get us.

The men, intensely conscious of their need for water, explored possible substitutes and alternatives. They chewed bark, sucked coal, and chewed tobacco in an attempt to keep their mouths and throats moistened. While these alternatives did not provide liquid, they artificially excited the saliva glands, thus modifying the discomfort associated with thirst. Eventually even this comfort was no longer possible:

> FRED: I chewed bark, but I couldn't get no moisture out of it. It was just dry and I spit it out. I tried chewing tobacco, but I couldn't get no juice out of it. See, you don't have any wet in your mouth at all.

The men realized that their new situation was perilous; the use of bark, coal, and tobacco neither contributed moisture nor stimulated the saliva glands. Each man had a dry parched tongue and throat, cracking lips, and an intense thirst. Beyond these discomforts, all six wished to live as long as possible,[2] in case they were found by rescuers. In other words, each man was aware of his own physiological needs, shared a similar definition of the situation, and sought some immediate action. In the words of A. K. Cohen (1955, p. 59), "the crucial condition for the emergence of new cultural forms . . . is the effective interaction with one another of a number of actors with similar problems of adjustment." At this point, the men considered the drinking of urine as a substitute for water.

THE INITIAL GESTURES

The emerging action took place in an extreme context, for the environmental conditions forced the men to consider a course of activity which was unthinkable. In this analysis every word concerned with the phenomenon in the accounts of all six men will be utilized. In this way we can follow the process with some precision and guard against any possible biased selection of material.

The initial gestures were reported in this fashion:

BOB: Our water was all gone, so I said, "Well, boys, we're going to have to drink our pee," and they kind of laughed. Then Ed said, "The more you drink it, the more it'll go through your system, and it will keep us going for a while."

ED: Harry said, "Well, we won't drink it, we will just rinse our mouth out with it."

BOB: So, all at once, I hear somebody up streaming their can, and then after we was all doing it.

This account will be examined sentence by sentence so that we can follow the sequence carefully. Bob made the initial gesture suggest-

---

[2] ". . . thirst depends less on the absolute water content of the body than on its water content *relative* to certain solid constituents, notably salts" (Wolf, 1956, p. 71).

The length of time it is possible for man to survive without water depends upon the heat, humidity, and other environmental conditions. Murray (1960, p. 71) suggests, "Water is one of the essential requirements for human life. . . . Death occurs about four or five days after total water deprivation, depending on other factors such as environmental temperature." Wolf (1956) states: "A rat curiously may survive longer (13 days) with food and no water than with water and no food (8.5 days). This is not true generally of larger animals such as the dog or man. . . . How long one can survive depends on the conditions. . . . It is estimated that a man cannot survive when he has lost water amounting to 20 per cent of his body weight (p. 73). Mariott (1950, p. 13) suggests, "Death occurs when the loss reaches approximately 15 per cent of body weight or 20 to 22 per cent of body water in about 7 to 10 days."

ing a new course of action, "Well, boys, we're going to have to drink our pee." As an innovator, he provided the initial gesture which might elicit responses, suggesting the receptivity of the others. Such an initial gesture often takes the form of a tentative and ambiguous suggestion [3] so as to permit the speaker to retreat, if necessary, to save face; in this case, the gesture was presented, not as a suggestion, but as a tentative statement of future inevitability—"we're going to have to . . ." Thus there was little personal identification with the recommendation of an abhorrent act. But the idea had been made explicit and a potential behavior pattern had been socially born, so to speak.

This initial gesture was motivated by tensions and discomforts common to all the men, so we may well anticipate that the resolution of the problem was carried out through a process of mutual exploration and joint elaboration (Lippett, Watson, & Westley, 1958). Novel social action, and, for that matter, a culture itself, emerges out of social interaction. In this instance, the proposed solution of the miners' problem could not be carried out within the cultural tradition because the suggested action had no embodiment in the miners' action model. For this reason the responses of the other five miners were of prime importance as indicators of the social feasibility of the suggestion. The responses of the five provided the feedback on the acceptability of the suggestion. [4]

The response to the initial gesture was "and they kind of laughed." This response indicated uncertainty rather than amusement. There was no immediate overt acceptance of the idea; on the other hand, there was no outright rejection, no ridicule, no one said "no," nor prophetically, "I'd rather die than drink that stuff." The initial response was merely a "kind of" laughter.

The mutual exploration of the proposed action continued. Ed said, "The more you drink it, the more it'll go through your system, and it will keep us going for a while." In his statement Ed supported the suggestion, expanded and legitimated it. He pointed to the legitimacy of the intake of urine in terms of satisfying biological "needs" of survival, in the Sumner sense, to "keep us going for a while." His statement that drinking urine would sustain life supported the

[3] For a discussion of this process, see Cohen (1955, pp. 60–65).
[4] For a discussion on feedback, see Bales (1951, 1954); Cohen (1955, p. 61); Homans (1950, pp. 153–55, 273–76).

suggestion with strong affect. He also implied that in terms of liquid each man could become a self-contained, self-perpetuating unit— "the more you drink, the more you will have."

THE EXPRESSIVE QUALITIES OF THE ACT

So far, then, we have noted the original exploratory suggestion— uncertainty, laughter, but no rebukes—followed by a statement of approval and further commitment based on the utility of the suggestion.

Next, Harry contributed to the growing social product, "Well, we won't drink it, we will just rinse our mouth [sic] out with it." On the face of it, this statement seems to be most inappropriate—six miners faced death by thirst, yet one man suggested that they do not drink, but merely "rinse our mouth out with it." This requires further analysis.

Until this point we have considered thirst in terms of liquid intake and the drinking of urine in terms of functional requirements of biological or instrumental needs. It is important to remember that the interaction concerns the drinking of *urine*, which is considered repugnant in our society. The proposed social action, as we have seen, was shaped by the men's present situation, their present need, and the present definition of the situation, but it was also affected by preexisting experience. The miners' prior social experience was responsible for their view of urine drinking as abhorrent.

Bales (1951, p. 8), Parsons (1951, pp. 79–88), Hare (1963, p. 12),[5] and others have postulated that analytically every act may be

---

[5] This analytical distinction between instrumental and expressive aspects of behavior is a common one, often appearing as "task-oriented" (instrumental-adaptive) and "emotional-oriented" (expressive-integrative). Hare, for instance, uses the term *task behavior* to include categories of observing, hypothesizing, and formulating action and the term *social-emotional* to include categories of control and affection. The term *expressive*, always polar to *instrumental* or *adaptive* behavior, has a long history in Psychology: see Allport and Vernon (1933), or Wolff (1943). The dichotomy, however named, is a gross one. "Expressive," however, should not be equated with "emotional" because the concept subsumes the expression of the individual idiosyncratic personality in cognitive style, emotional style, motor acts, as well as affect. In a technical sense, "expressive" may be used instead of "feeling," "emotion," or "affect," but certainly, "emotional" cannot be used as a substitute for "expressive." When "expressive" is used in this study, it includes both affect and the idiosyncratic aspects of behavior. The terms *affect, feeling,* and *emotion* are used when there is no doubt that we are considering that aspect of behavior exclusively.

viewed simultaneously as both expressive and instrumental. Acts differ in terms of primacy given to one aspect or the other, but they all involve both. Every word or gesture carries with it at least two kinds of information, task and social-emotional, on at least two kinds of levels, group and individual. First, a gesture has implications for the task of the group in that it affects the decision-making process; second, it has implications for the relative evaluation of members as well as the emotional attachments among members (Hare, 1963, p. 63). Third, on the individual level, every gesture affects individual decision-making and goal achievement, but, fourth, at the same time the gesture affects the internal expressive or social-emotional life of the individual. Again, these four types of implication of any individual act are analytical in nature; in real life it is difficult to distinguish one without talking about the others.

The examination of the interaction leading to urine drinking is important, analytically speaking, because it draws our attention to the expressive aspect of the action. In this instance, the men attached conscious urgency to *both* the instrumental and expressive qualities of the proposed act. The comment of Ed legitimated the instrumental qualities of the act on both an individual and group level: "it will keep us going for a while." On the other hand, Harry made due recognition of and allowance for the expressive qualities. He picked up the cue provided by the laughter which greeted the original gesture. He shared the expressive uneasiness made explicit through this laughter and suggested a preliminary mechanism for the management of sentiments and tensions.

The statement took into account that the emergence of the new instrumentally essential action simultaneously evoked a revulsion in all the men. (When emerging actions do not involve heavily emotion-laden preexisting attitudes, we often forget that the actions constitute innovations or deviant behavior.) As an aid in overcoming this revulsion, Harry stated that if the men could not bring themselves to drink body waste, they would do no harm if they merely rinsed out their mouths to relieve secondary thirst symptoms. The statement suggested that on an individual level the miner would be merely rinsing his mouth and need not face the abhorrence of drinking urine, thus supplying a way of handling individual expressive difficulties. Harry's statement, which went unchallenged, also had expressive implications on a group level. He announced that the individual would not lose face; his prestige would not be affected because he carried out this type of harmless behavior.

At this point, one of the men took an important step, the first preliminary action on the original suggestion. "So all at once, I heard somebody up streaming their can, and then after we was all doing it." "We was all doing it"—once begun, each man took the initial step of saving his urine in his water or lunch can. What had been put forward as a tentative statement by Bob was translated, by this time, into initial action. Step by step each man had become progressively involved, and this was a crucial first physical symbol of action and commitment.

SOCIAL LEGITIMATION OF THE ACT

When the process reached this point, a long discussion and exchange of views occurred—interaction about which we have only suggestions rather than an account. This conversation aided the men in getting used to the idea. It is clear from their accounts that an important factor in this exchange was that one of the miners had heard of or "known fellows who had drunk their own [urine]." Although urine drinking was not within the experience of the miners, this established it as within the realm of human experience. Urine drinking, then, was possible and not unprecedented, although it ran contrary to the workaday mores of the miners themselves:

> ED: When the water ran out, one of the fellows spoke. He said he had known fellows who had drunk their own—that was the argument. Well, each fellow did [drink]. We had our water cans and I had my bottle.
>
> FRED: Bob suggested drinking urine. I never thought of that, you know. Every time we had to go to make our urine, we just saved it in the can.
>
> HARRY: Well, I don't know how we come to mention it. Someone said, "Let's drink our urine." Well, we made up our mind that we should drink it. We was all talking there. We used our own water cans and we used our own urine. I never thought of this before. When we were trapped in the mine explosion [two years previously] we had lots of water.
>
> DICK: My buddy Bob mentioned drinking urine. He hadn't drunk his, but the water was all drunk up and I was so dry. He kept talking about it first.

The citing of the precedent was of great importance because, as the comments clearly document, urine drinking was a novel idea to all but one of the men. Although they all suffered similar discomfort and fear, the particular suggestion put forward by Bob was not concurrently held by the other men. They were not simply waiting for someone to make explicit a shared inward plan of action. The novelty of the suggestion is not surprising considering the lack of a cultural model for such behavior; for five of the miners urine drinking had not been embodied in thought, not to mention action.

The statements of the men indicate that the original suggestion initiated a process of mutual exploration and joint elaboration. The move was not accepted or legitimated on the basis of prestige or status of the person who made the suggestion. The very anonymity of references to Bob, in terms of "one of the fellows," "someone said," supports this contention.

The statements "He said he had known fellows who had drunk their own—that was the argument," [6] "He kept talking about it first," and "We was all talking there" suggest the considerable discussion, justification, and redefinition of the situation that was in progress. The conversation was directed mainly to the expressive aspects of urine drinking. Each miner was contributing to the process of making urine drinking socially permissible.

The six men had come a long way from their first definition that escape was at hand and the copious drinking of water which was appropriate to this assumption. Within three days they defined their situation as one from which escape was impossible, rescue questionable, and they had taken the first action toward drinking urine.

SUMMARY OF MAIN POINTS

The miners became aware of their need for liquid and began to search for alternatives. They sucked and chewed coal, bark, and tobacco. Step by step the next moves were as follows:

1. An initial gesture suggesting urine consumption as a water substitute was put forward.
2. None of the men rejected the suggestion.
3. A response was made approving and enlarging upon the initial gesture, adding legitimation on instrumental grounds.
4. A response was made approving and enlarging upon the initial gesture, adding further legitimation on expressive grounds.

[6] As we shall see, under certain conditions it is preferable to drink someone else's.

5. A social action translated the original suggestion into the first stage of execution. This move initiated action, and through it, reinforced social support for the idea.
6. A long period of discussion characterized by elaboration and justification of the action in expressive terms followed.

This sequence constituted the social legitimation of action which a day previously was unthinkable. Through the sharing of a similar concern, redefinitions of the situation, and a process of mutual conversion, the beginning of a new action pattern emerged on a group level so that, as one miner put it, "we made up our mind that we should drink it." This social decision is an important one for, as Lewin (1947, p. 35) has pointed out, "it is usually easier to change individuals formed into a group than to change any one of them separately."

INDIVIDUAL EMOTIONAL QUALITIES OF THE ACT

At this point we might anticipate the verification of Freud's suggestion that first we discuss it and then we do it. However, despite instrumental urgency and social permissibility, not a single miner was able to drink:

FRED: It gagged me, you know.
DICK: It came up at first.
ED: It was a while before I decided to take mine.
BOB: You've got to go kind of easy because if you don't, you might throw up. I only threw up once.

The involuntary gagging, vomiting, and avoidance were physiological manifestations of strong emotional feeling. These manifestations persisted despite the urgent individual physiological requirements for liquid and the social permissiveness of urine drinking on both instrumental and expressive grounds. The shared abhorrence of urine drinking was so deeply internalized, so much a part of each man's normative system, that each still had to deal *individually* with the emotional nature of the new socially approved behavior. As one man said:

It was just the thought—it was not real water. If somebody had passed it to us in the dark and told us that it was something else, it would have been different, but, of course, we knew what it was. . . .

It is quite apparent that an additional step lies between the achievement of social permissiveness and subsequent individual action. That step involves coming to terms with the expressive aspects of emerging action on an individual basis. Perhaps interracial contact involves similar problems. Although interracial contact may be socially permissible and legally mandatory, to some individuals the implications are so repugnant that personal contact is impossible. Somehow the individual must personally come to terms with the emotional nature of the activity. In the case of the miners, some process or technique was necessary to permit activity, normally repugnant, to become personally acceptable in order to avoid physiological reaction. Each had to overcome his involuntary inability to drink.

All of this is instructive, as it directs our attention to the individual and his relation to emerging action. The emergence of action in a group is usually recognized as an original "need," an innovation, and social acceptance, but the fact that the innovator himself has to come to terms with the innovation is often overlooked. In the case of the miners, this "coming to terms" is clear because of the strong emotional overtones surrounding the nature of the action.

Cohen (1955, p. 61) considers this same process in slightly different terminology:

We may think of this process as one of mutual conversion. The important thing to remember is that we do not first convert ourselves and then others. The acceptability of an idea to oneself depends upon its acceptability to others. Converting the other is part of the process of converting oneself.

This is a neat statement of part of the process under examination. We noted the gestures leading to mutual conversion. But we also saw that, once the drinking of urine became acceptable and group-supported, each individual still had a long way to go before he was able actually to drink. It is clear that social acceptability is an important step toward the emergence of new action, but social acceptability is not individual acceptability. Converting the others is the first part of the process of converting oneself. But once behavior has become socially approved, the next step is the process through which each individual somehow makes this behavior personally acceptable. This is the second part of the process of converting oneself.

TECHNIQUES FOR EXPRESSIVE ADAPTATION

Each man went through behavior routines which permitted him to become "used to the idea." These processes permitted activity normally repugnant to become acceptable in order to reduce the physiological inhibition toward drinking. We now return to the men's accounts:

> BOB: We was all rinsing our mouth out and taking a sup. Your mouth gets so dry and you rinse your mouth out—quite bitter. Well, you just force yourself; you got to take it. You've got to go kind of easy because if you don't you might throw up. I only threw up once. I washed my mouth out once, sometimes twice, before I drank. We saved our own urine.
>
> ED: It was a while before I decided to take mine. Well, at first I would rinse out my mouth. You rinse out your mouth several times first, and then eventually you would take a little swallow, and after a while, it wasn't so bad as you thought it was. Sipping every half hour perhaps, some a little sooner, some a little further away.
>
> FRED: But the first two or three drinks, you know, well, I didn't drink it; it gagged me, you know. I would rinse me mouth out, and then a little would trickle down—but, oh, I would near throw it up. . . . I didn't though.
>
> TOM: After the water ran out, I started to drink urine—my urine. I started wetting my lips and then hold my breath and wash my mouth out.
>
> HARRY: For a day or so I just put a little in my mouth and rinsed my mouth and spit it out. Then we started swallowing a little wee bit.
>
> DICK: Everybody started drinking it. I waited as long as I could, but I had to drink it. I never drank too much all the time I was there, I drank about a glassfull maybe. I started wetting my lips, then washed my mouth out, and I drank about four or five hours later. It came up first.

The six men all used similar techniques to come to terms with the expressive implications of the act. For instance, all the men used internal conversation, in part a continuation of the conversation which had already taken place on an interpersonal level. This involved comments such as, "Well, you just force yourself; you got to take it."

All the men gradually retrained their senses. The men did more than "get used to the idea," they also got used to the reality. Each man removed the secondary thirst symptoms by wetting cracked lips and parched mouth before spitting. In doing so, the miners used a well-recognized social technique of experimenting without irretrievably committing themselves. It will be remembered that, early in the exchange, it was established that just rinsing out the mouth was innocent behavior and did not constitute highly repugnant action. After a span of time manifestly experimenting and latently retraining the senses and emotional reactions, "then we started swallowing a little wee bit," and "after a while, it wasn't as bad as you thought it was."

From this it was not far to a subtle technique. It began with the miner experimenting without irretrievably committing himself. While participating in what he could convince himself was the innocent behavior of mouth rinsing, accidentally on purpose "a little would trickle down." In this technique rather than gradually training the senses, the man was out to deceive his sentiments. By accidentally swallowing a little while he wasn't looking, as it were, he was attempting to bypass the physical manifestations of repugnance.[7] A detailed and systematic discussion of these techniques and mechanisms will be made shortly.

SOCIAL ELABORATION OF THE ACT

Once initial repugnance was overcome, but still a part of this same process of coming to terms with the urine, further social redefinitions and refinements ensued. Joint social elaboration was carried on—the six men literally exchanged recipes. Available flavors were restricted to bark and coal. Two practices began to emerge; the first involved the flavoring of the urine in its container by adding bark or coal, and in the second procedure, the flavor was added in the mouth, by chewing either bark or coal and "juicing it up" by a swallow of urine. But again the men speak for themselves:

BOB: We put bark in it. I think Dick put bark in it, and I put bark in it. We put some coal in it. I said, "Dick, coal is good for our heartburn, why

[7] There is no suggestion in the reports that the men perceived any alternative method of drinking urine other than saving it in containers and then drinking. There is no indication that they knew that urine is sterile while in the body; lone trappers and woodsmen in the North immediately urinate on a cut, using the urine for its sterile qualities before binding the wound. It is only when the urine makes contact with the oxygen in the atmosphere that it immediately begins to decompose and the process of decomposition produces the rank and characteristic odor of urine. The whole problem of gagging from this distasteful stimulus could have been circumvented by drinking urine without allowing it to make contact with the air. This method, however, would have involved the breaking of another set of deeply internalized norms. The revulsion related to urine drinking without the liquid contacting the air was probably even greater than that involved in attempting to drink rank-smelling urine from an open container.

wouldn't it be good to eat?" So we started eating coal. Dick and I did and I think the rest tried it too.

ED: I ground up a little coal, and we had some bark. They would say, "Got a piece of bark there?" and I said, "It is a dry piece," but I chewed it and chewed it and chewed it, and I said, "Boys, you want to do it like that— chew it fine to get the juice." I don't imagine it did any good. Anyway, we would chew it until our mouth got so dry, and once in a while, we would take a swallow of water to juice it up a bit—improvised water.

FRED: We got so dry it was beginning to taste good, you know, I would rinse my mouth out about a couple of times a day, maybe a couple times through the night, I would imagine. Then I got to the stage I could swallow.

HARRY: We chewed some bark, we would take a mouthful of bark and chew that for a while and then take a little drink of water.

BOB: I chewed bark; it was dry getting down, but I took a little bit of my water and I kind of washed it down and I felt better.

Once the problem of drinking had been solved on an individual level, the continuing process returned to the level of interaction for elaboration and refinement. These accounts bring three points to our attention: in the first place, the exchanges of recipes aided individuals in controlling their emotional behavior by pooling techniques. Literally the men are saying, This is how I do it, and it works, so you try it too. In the second place, it was probably helpful to each individual to know that others, by implication at least, were having emotional difficulties in drinking. The very fact that urine drinking itself and the difficulties involved were the subject of long and occasionally bantering exchanges tended to give each man some social support in dealing with his shared, but essentially private problem. In the third place, we should note that through these exchanges a further redefinition emerged. The word "urine" moved from "urine" to "it" to "water," or more delicately, "improvised water."

THE COMPLETION OF THE ACT

. . . Urine was called water, it was being flavored, and once these new patterns were legitimated by the group and each individual in both expressive and instrumental aspects, urine drinking, repugnant under ordinary circumstances, posed few problems. Once the action was firmly established, it became expected and approved behavior within the particular setting:

BOB: I had no trouble at all, once I started to drink.

FRED: I didn't mind the end of it. I was taking gulps of it down, but it would only take that dryness away for maybe five or ten minutes and then you would be just as dry as ever.

TOM: Eventually, I drank as much as I wanted, but I don't think I drank too much. I never felt like vomiting.

HARRY: At the last of it, we were just drinking it. We did worry a bit about it.

DICK: One fellow down there—I thought he was drinking beer. He seemed to be at the can all the time.

Although urine drinking had become a legitimate and accepted action, not all doubts were removed. The comments, "I don't think I drank too much," or "We did worry a bit about it," suggest nagging questions regarding the long-term physiological effects of urine drinking which relate to the notion that urine is harmful if not poisonous. There was some irritation at the inefficiency of the urine because it did not seem to quench the thirst for any great length of time.

The important implication of this urine drinking pattern was that each miner became a self-sustaining, self-priming unit in relation to liquid output and input. Although the new pattern was social in its development, and, once accepted, socially supported, each individual carried on independently.[8]

•   •   •   •   •

[8] Compared with the preoccupation with water and thirst, there were very few comments on food and hunger. Only seven of the eighteen men [these six, plus twelve from another study] mentioned the subject of food in their account of the entrapment. The following comments are typical:

ED: We had very little to eat.

DAN: My stomach never bothered me . . . except for a little gnawing hunger.

This lack of discussion of hunger and food seems to reflect the findings of authorities on the importance of food in relation to water in terms of discomfort and survival. "It is generally agreed that healthy persons can fast for two weeks . . . without undue suffering or adverse physiological effects as long as water is available." (Olsen, 1960, p. 167.) This view is supported by Brown (1947, p. 158), "Food is not very important in a desert emergency nor is it desired by thirsty men." "Thirsty food" was particularly unwelcome by the miners:

FRED: The boys found a chocolate bar. We split that up. Well, I had a piece the first time; well, it made me worse—the chocolate made me thirsty. When it came time around for me to go and get my chocolate, I said, "No. You fellows go ahead. Take it. I don't want it," because it was just making me thirsty.

20

Adaptive Personality Changes

IRVING L. JANIS

STRESS TOLERANCE IN SURGICAL PATIENTS

A series of studies on surgical patients (Janis, 1958) highlights the crucial importance of developing relevant reassurances for coping with stress. Since major surgery involves pain, a profound threat to bodily integrity, and a variety of frustrations, a great deal can be learned on the surgical wards of a general hospital about the processes of normal adjustment to severe stress.

The investigations were designed to help answer some basic questions pertinent to a general theory of stress tolerance: What is the relationship between the intensity of the patient's fear before surgery and the way he reacts to the pains and discomforts of the postoperative period? Is the popular belief true that the more anxious a person becomes when confronted with the threat of impending danger, the poorer he will adjust to the stress when he encounters it? Is a patient better able to cope with postoperative stress if he has been given realistic information beforehand on what is likely to happen?

With these questions in mind, the author carried out a study on the surgical ward of a large community hospital. As a first step, interviews were given to 23 typical patients before and after they underwent major surgery. Each of the patients was facing a highly dangerous and painful operation, such as removal of a lung or part of the stomach. Hospital records, including the physicians' and nurses' daily notes on each patient's behavior, were used to supplement the intensive interviews.

Three general patterns of emotional response were observed:

1. *High anticipatory fear.* These patients were constantly worried

and jittery about suffering acute pain, being mutilated by the surgeon, or dying on the operating table. Openly admitting their *extreme feelings of vulnerability,* they tried to postpone the operation, were unable to sleep without sedation, and continually sought reassurances, even though these gave only momentary relief. After the operation they were *much more likely than others to be anxiety-ridden.* They had stormy emotional outbursts and shrank back in fright when the time came for routine postoperative treatments. Their excessive fears of bodily damage appeared to be based on a chronic sense of personal vulnerability.

2. *Moderate anticipatory fear.* These patients were occasionally worried and tense about specific features of the impending operation, such as the anesthesia. They asked for and received realistic information about what was going to happen to them from the hospital staff. They were able to be reassured, to engage in distracting activities, and to remain outwardly calm during most, though not every minute, of the day before the operation. They felt *somewhat vulnerable,* but their concerns were focused on realistic threats. After the operation they were *much less likely than others to display any emotional disturbance.* They consistently showed high morale and good cooperation with the hospital staff, even when asked to submit to uncomfortable drainage tubes, injections, and other disagreeable postoperative treatments.

3. *Low anticipatory fear.* These patients were constantly cheerful and optimistic about the impending operation. They denied feeling worried, slept well, and were able to read, listen to the radio, and socialize without any observable signs of emotional tension. They appeared to have unrealistic expectations of *almost complete invulnerability.* After the operation, however, they became acutely preoccupied with their vulnerability and were *more likely than others to display anger and resentment toward the staff.* Most of them complained bitterly about being mistreated and sometimes became so negativistic that they tried to refuse even routine postoperative treatments.

Anticipatory Fear and Postoperative Adjustment

The main hypotheses suggested by this series of intensive case studies were supported by a second study, a questionnaire survey conducted among more than 150 male college students who had recently undergone surgical operations. Several measures were used as indicators of each patient's postoperative adjustment. The measures included feelings of anger, complaints against the hospital staff, and current emotional disturbance when recalling the operation. Each of these indicators was examined in relation to what the patient had reported about his fear level before surgery. In each instance a curvilinear relation was found, as shown in Fig. 20.1. The essential feature of this relation is the location of the peak of the curve somewhere in the middle of the fear continuum, rather than at one end or the other.

This outcome clearly contradicts the popular assumption that placid people—those who are least fearful about an impending ordeal—will prove to be less disturbed than others by subsequent stress. One of the main implications of these findings from the surgical studies is this: whenever people are exposed to severe stress, those who had been most calm and most confident about their invulnerability at the outset will tend to become much more upset than those who had been part-time worriers beforehand.

Apparently, a moderate amount of anticipatory fear about realistic threats is necessary for the development of effective inner defenses for coping with subsequent danger and deprivation. The patients who were somewhat fearful before the operation mentally rehearsed various unpleasant occurrences they thought were in store for them. They were motivated to seek and take account of realistic information about the experiences they would be likely to undergo from the time they would awaken from the anesthesia to the end of the period of convalescence. Seldom caught by surprise, these patients felt relatively secure as events proceeded just about as they had expected. Not only were they highly responsive to authoritative reassurances from the hospital staff, but also they could reassure themselves at moments when their fears were strongly aroused. In their postoperative interviews such patients frequently reported instances of self-reassurance; for example, "I knew there might be some bad pains, so when my side started to ache I told myself that this didn't mean anything had gone wrong."

Those who displayed excessively high anxiety before the operation appeared to benefit relatively little from preliminary mental rehearsals of the dangers. In the intensive interviews conducted both

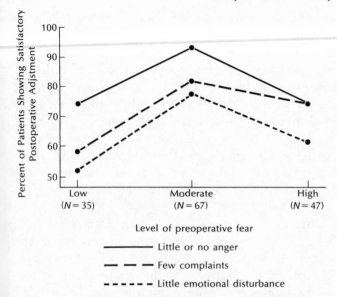

Percent of Patients Showing Satisfactory Postoperative Adjustment

Level of preoperative fear

———————— Little or no anger

— — — Few complaints

- - - - - Little emotional disturbance

Fig. 20.1. Relation between preoperative fear and postoperative adjustment. (Adapted from Janis, 1958, 1968; used with the permission of Irving L. Janis.)

before and after the operation they revealed that they felt highly vulnerable to bodily damage and were unable to develop effective inner defenses for coping with the threat. Most of these patients were found to have a history of neurotic disorder, including past episodes of anxiety attacks. Their postoperative emotional reactions can be regarded as a continuation of their long-standing neuroses and not just a response to the external dangers of surgery.

The patients who were relatively free from anticipatory fears before the operation seem to have remained emotionally calm only by denying or minimizing the possibility of danger and suffering. As soon as the inescapable pains and harassments of normal recovery from a major surgical operation began to plague them, they could no longer maintain their expectations of personal invulnerability and became upset.

As an illustrative example, let us consider the reactions of a 21-year-old woman who had earlier undergone an appendectomy. At that time she had been given realistic information by her physician. Before the operation she had been moderately worried and occasionally asked the nurses for something to calm her nerves, but she showed excellent emotional adjustment throughout her convalescence. About two years later she came to the same hospital for another abdominal operation, the removal of her gall bladder. In the preoperative interview with the investigator she reported that her physician had assured her that "there's really nothing to it; it's a less serious operation than the previous one." This time she remained wholly unconcerned about the operation beforehand, apparently anticipating very little or no suffering. Afterward, experiencing the usual pains and deprivations following a gall bladder operation, she became markedly upset, negativistic, and resentful toward the nursing staff.

Chronic personality predispositions do not seem to account fully for this patient's reactions, since she was capable of showing an entirely different pattern of emotional response, as she had on a previous occasion. The patient's adjustment to the fear-producing situation appeared to be influenced mainly by the insufficient and misleading preparatory communications she was given before the second operation. Since nothing distressing was supposed to happen, she assumed that the hospital staff must be to blame for her postoperative suffering.

In some persons the lack of preoperative fear may be a manifestation of a type of neurotic predisposition that involves using extreme defenses of denial and projection of blame in order to ward off anxiety; probably nothing short of intensive psychotherapy could change this characteristic personality tendency. Most of the patients who showed little or no fear, however, seemed to be clinically normal personalities. Like the patient just described, they never received the type of realistic information that would induce them to face up to the distressing implications of the impending surgery. If they are given clear-cut information by a trustworthy authority, such persons are capable of modifying their defensive attitude and becoming appropriately worried about what they now realize is in store for them. But if they are not given adequate preparatory warnings about postoperative pain and suffering, they will cling to their expectations of personal invulnerability as long as possible, until suffering itself teaches them that they are not invulnerable after all.

THE ROLE OF INFORMATION

As we have just seen, the patients who did not worry beforehand appeared to be much less able to cope with the stresses of surgery than those who had been moderately worried. When the two types of patients were compared on a variety of background factors, the only significant difference turned out to be in the amount of advance information they had obtained. A careful check showed no significant differences as to type of operation, amount of pain, degree of incapacitation, type of anesthesia, or prognosis; nor were there differences between the groups as to age, education, sex, ethnic origin, or the number of prior hospitalizations.

But the two groups did differ on one important factor: the amount of prior information. Patients in the low-fear group had little idea of what to expect, whereas those in the moderate-fear group had been far better informed.

The survey of male surgery cases provided systematic evidence on this point. Illustrative results are shown in Figure 20.2, which compares preoperative fear and postoperative adjustment in the two groups of men who had undergone major surgical operations: 51 men who reported having been informed beforehand about the specific unpleasant experiences in store for them and 26 men who reported having been completely uninformed. The two groups differed in two ways: (1) the well-informed men were more likely to report that they had felt worried or fearful before the operation; and (2) the well-informed men were less likely to report that they had become angry or emotionally upset during the postoperative period of convalescence.

Since these correlational data are based on retrospective reports, they cannot be accepted as conclusive evidence. Nevertheless, they point in the same direction as the observations made in the intensive case studies, suggesting the following hypothesis: if no authoritative warning communications are given and if other circumstances are such that fear is not aroused beforehand, the normal person will lack the motivation to build up effective inner preparation before the onset of the danger, and he will thus have relatively low tolerance for stress when the crisis is actually at hand.

The "Work of Worrying"

The observations and findings from the surgery research suggested a concept of the "work of worrying," a theoretical construct that

278   Janis

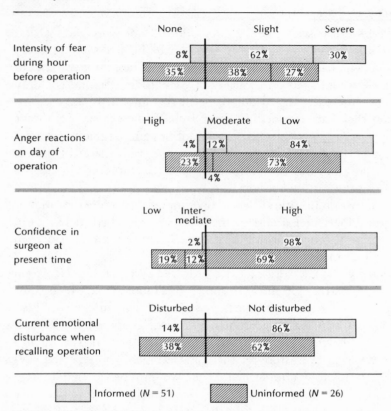

Fig. 20.2. Preoperative fear and postoperative adjustment in informed and uninformed surgical patients. (Adapted from Janis, 1958, 1968; used with the permission of Irving L. Janis.)

emphasizes the potentially positive value of anticipatory fear (Janis, 1958). The "work of worrying" might involve psychological processes similar to the "work of mourning," . . . but there are likely to be some important differences. Freud postulated that the work of mourning begins *after* a blow, such as the death of a loved one, has struck; the work of worrying is assumed to begin *beforehand,* as soon as the individual becomes aware of signs of *impending danger* that might affect him personally.

WHEN THE WORK OF WORRYING IS INCOMPLETE

Sometimes an endangered person remains quite unworried and then finds himself unexpectedly confronted with actual danger stimuli. This is evidently what happens to many surgical patients who are given no explicit warning information that induces them to face up to what is in store for them. They anticipate little or no pain or suffering until the severe stresses of the postoperative period are encountered. Then they are unable to reassure themselves and no longer trust the authorities whose protection they had expected. The patient's failure to worry about the operation in advance seems to set the stage for intense feelings of helplessness as well as resentment toward the members of the staff who, until the moment of crisis, had been counted on to take good care of them, just as good parents would do.

At moments of grave crisis most people are likely to blame the doctors or other authorities for unexpected stress. Many observations of surgical patients and of people exposed to comparable stress situations suggest the following sequence:

Absence of anticipatory fear
↓
Absence of mental rehearsal of the impending danger
↓
Feelings of helplessness when the danger materializes
↓
Increased expectations of vulnerability and disappointment in protective authorities
↓
Intense fear and anger

This sequence can be regarded as the major consequence of *failing to carry out the work of worrying*. Such failures are to be expected whenever a stressful event occurs under any of the following three conditions: (1) if the person is accustomed to suppressing anticipatory fear by means of denial defenses, by overoptimism, and by avoiding warnings that would stimulate the work of worrying; (2) if the stressful event is so sudden that it cannot be prepared for; and (3) if an adequate prior warning is not given, or if strong but false reassurances encourage the person to believe that he is invulnerable.

In order for the work of worrying to be complete, it seems that each source of stress must be anticipated and "worked through" in advance. This necessity is suggested by some outstanding instances of fright and rage observed in surgical patients who had displayed a moderate degree of anticipatory fear.

A young housewife, for example, had been somewhat worried before a lung operation and then, like most others in the moderately fearful group, showed excellent cooperation and little emotional disturbance throughout the postoperative period—except for one brief crisis she had not expected. She knew in advance about the acute incision pains and other unpleasant aspects of the postoperative recovery treatments, since she had undergone a similar operation once before and had asked her physician many pertinent questions about the impending second operation. But on the first postoperative day a physician entered her room and told her she would have to swallow a drainage tube, which she had never heard about before. She became extremely upset, could not relax sufficiently to cooperate, and finally begged the physician to take the tube away and let her alone. During an interview the following day she reported that she began to have extremely unfavorable thoughts about the physician at the time he made the unexpected demand; she suspected that he was withholding information about the seriousness of her condition, that he was unnecessarily imposing a hideous form of treatment on her, and that he was carrying out the treatment "so badly it was practically killing me." At no other time during the long and painful convalescence following the removal of her lung did she have any such doubts about this physician or any other member of the hospital staff; nor did she at any other time display any form of overt resistance. Evidently this was the one stressful event she had not anticipated and for which she had not, therefore, carried out the work of worrying.

This episode might help to explain why other patients who are caught by surprise display so much fright, anger, and uncooperative behavior. Those calm, seemingly stoic patients who do practically none of the work of worrying beforehand would be likely to encounter the same type of disruptive episode many times over during each day of their convalescence.

PREPARATORY COMMUNICATIONS AS A PREREQUISITE FOR
CONSTRUCTIVE WORRYING: SOME FURTHER EVIDENCE

Other studies on the psychological effects of surgical operations, severe illness, community disasters, and combat dangers provide many bits of evidence that are consistent with the foregoing hypotheses derived from the study of surgical patients (Cobb et al., 1954;

Cramond & Aberd, 1954; Grinker et al., 1946; Janis & Leventhal, 1965; Titchner et al., 1957). Like the surgery research, these studies suggest that if a normal person is given accurate prior warning of impending pain and discomfort, together with sufficient reassurances so that fear does not mount to a very high level, he will be less likely to develop acute emotional disturbances than a person who is not warned.

We know that there are exceptions, of course, such as neurotic personalities who are hypersensitive to any threat cues. But this does not preclude the possibility that moderately fear-arousing information about impending dangers and deprivations will function as a kind of emotional inoculation, enabling normal persons to increase their tolerance for stress by developing coping mechanisms and effective defenses. This process is called emotional inoculation because it may be analogous to what happens when antibodies are induced by injections of mildly virulent viruses.

If these inferences are correct, we should find that a group of surgical patients given appropriate preparatory communications before their operations will show better adjustment to the stresses of the postoperative period than an equivalent group of patients given no special preparatory communications other than the information ordinarily available to any hospitalized patient.

This prediction was tested and confirmed in a carefully controlled field experiment with 97 adult surgical patients at the Massachusetts General Hospital (Egbert et al., 1964). The patients, hospitalized for elective abdominal operations, were assigned at random to the experimental and control groups. The two groups were equated on the basis of age, sex, type of operation, and so forth. On the night before his operation each patient was visited by the anesthetist, who gave him routine information about the operation—its time and duration, the nature of the anesthesia, and the fact that he would awaken in the recovery room. The patients in the control group were told nothing more. Those in the experimental group were given four additional types of information intended to help them carry out the work of worrying and to provide some useful coping devices: (1) a description of postoperative pain—where they would feel it, how intense it would be, how long it was likely to last; (2) explicit reassurance that postoperative pain is a normal consequence of an abdominal operation; (3) advice to relax their abdominal muscles in order to reduce the pain, along with special instructions about how to shift from one side to the other without tensing muscles in the sensitive area: and (4) assurance that they would be given pain-killing medication if they could not otherwise achieve a tolerable level of comfort. The information contained in the preparatory communication was repeated to the patients in the experimental group by the anesthetist when he visited them following the operation. Neither the surgeons nor the ward nurses were told about this experiment, to make sure that the experimental (informed) and the control (uninformed) patients would receive equivalent treatment in all other respects.

What difference did the special information make? During the 5 days just after surgery, patients in the experimental group required only half as much sedation as did patients in the control group. Comparisons of the total amounts of morphine administered to the two groups of patients during the postoperative period are shown by the curves in Fig. 20.3. On the day of the operation (day zero in the figure) both groups required about the same amount of narcotics, but on each of the next 5 postoperative days the experimental group required significantly less than the control group.

The investigators tried to rule out the possibility that the well-informed patients might be suffering in silence in order to "please the doctor." They arranged to have the interviews conducted on the first and second postoperative days by an anesthetist whom the patients had never seen before. This independent observer was completely unaware of the type of treatment any of the patients had received, and his "blind" ratings indicated that the patients in the experimental group were in better emotional and physical condition than the controls. Further evidence of the more rapid improvement of the well-informed patients is provided by data on the duration of hospitalization. Completely unaware of the experiment, the surgeons sent the well-informed patients home an average of 2.7 days earlier than the patients who had not been given the special preparatory communication. In line with the earlier correlational findings shown in Fig. 20.2, the investigators also noted that the uninformed controls made many complaints to the staff, such as "Why didn't you tell me it was going to be like this?" Such complaints were rare in the experimental group.

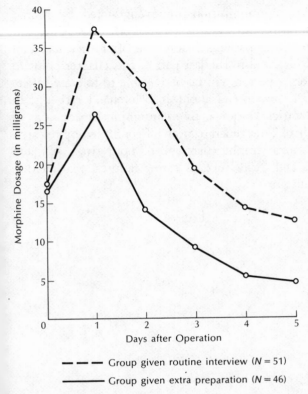

Fig. 20.3. Postoperative narcotic treatment for two groups
of surgical patients—those given a special preparatory
communication and those given a routine interview.
(Adapted from Egbert et al., 1964; reprinted by permission
from the *New England Journal of Medicine* 270:825–27
(1964) and from Irving L. Janis.)

Thus, the experiment provides some systematic evidence concerning the positive value of advance information about postoperative
stress. In this experiment the preoperative information was reiterated
during the first few postoperative days, and this repetition may have
contributed to the effectiveness of the preparatory communication.
Conceivably, the postoperative reassurances alone might have been
responsible for the outcome. There are other possible interpretations
that will have to be checked in subsequent studies. It should be
noted, however, that the results of this study show essentially the
same positive outcome as two similar controlled experiments on the

effects of preparatory communications, one conducted by Moran (1963) with children on pediatric wards and the other by Miller and Treiger (1969) with dental patients before and after they had oral surgery. The studies reviewed in the last part of this chapter point to one general conclusion: a person will be better able to tolerate suffering and deprivation if he worries about it beforehand rather than remaining free from anticipatory fear by maintaining expectations of personal invulnerability. This generalization, if confirmed by research in other stress situations, might turn out to hold true for many nonphysical setbacks and losses such as career failures, marital discord, and bereavement.

21

Dehumanization: A Composite Psychological Defense in Relation to Modern War

VIOLA W. BERNARD, PERRY OTTENBERG,
and
FRITZ REDL

We conceive of dehumanization as a particular type of psychic defense mechanism and consider its increasing prevalence to be a social consequence of the nuclear age. By this growth it contributes, we believe, to heightening the risks of nuclear extermination.

Dehumanization as a defense against painful or overwhelming emotions entails a decrease in a person's sense of his own individuality and in his perception of the humanness of other people. The misperceiving of others ranges from viewing them *en bloc* as "subhuman" or "bad human" (a long-familiar component of group prejudice) to viewing them as "nonhuman," as though they were inanimate items or "dispensable supplies." As such, their maltreatment or even their destruction may be carried out or acquiesced in with relative freedom from the restraints of conscience or feelings of brotherhood.

In our view, dehumanization is not a wholly new mental mechanism, but rather a composite psychological defense which draws selectively on other well-known defenses, including unconscious denial, repression, depersonalization, isolation of affect, and compartmentalization (the elimination of meaning by disconnecting related mental elements and walling them off from each other). Recourse to dehumanization as a defense against stresses of inner conflict and external threat is especially favored by impersonal aspects of modern social organization, along with such special technological features of nuclear weapons as their unprecedented destructive power and the distance between push button and victim.

We recognize that many adaptive, as well as maladaptive,[1] uses of self-protective dehumanization are requisite in multiple areas of contemporary life. As a maladaptive defense in relation to war, however, the freedom from fear which it achieves by apathy or blindness to implications of the threat of nuclear warfare itself increases the actuality of that threat: the masking of its true urgency inactivates motive power for an all-out effort to devise creative alternatives for resolving international conflict. Dehumanization also facilitates the tolerating of mass destruction through bypassing those psychic inhibitions against the taking of human life that have become part of civilized man. Such inhibitions cannot be called into play when those who are to be destroyed have been divested of their humanness. The magnitudes of annihilation that may be perpetrated with indifference would seem to transcend those carried out in hatred and anger. This was demonstrated by the impersonal, mechanized efficiency of extermination at the Nazi death camps.

The complex psychological phenomenon which we call dehumanization includes two distinct but interrelated series of processes: *self-directed dehumanization* relates to self-image, and denotes the diminution of an individual's sense of his own humanness; *object-directed dehumanization* refers to his perceiving others as lacking in those attributes that are considered to be most human. Despite the differences between these two in their origins and intrapsychic relationships within over-all personality development and psychodynamic functioning, both forms of dehumanization, compounded from parts of other defenses, become usable by the individual for emotional self-protection. These two forms of dehumanization are mutually reinforcing: reduction in the fullness of one's feelings for other human beings, whatever the reason for this, impoverishes one's sense of self; any lessening of the humanness of one's self-image limits one's capacity for relating to others.

[1] Adaptive and maladaptive refer to a person's modes of coping with internal and external stress. The distinction hinges on the extent to which such coping is successful with respect to the optimal overall balance of the individual's realistic interests and goals.

It seems to us that the extensive increase of dehumanization today is causally linked to aspects of institutional changes in contemporary society and to the transformed nature of modern war. The mushrooming importance in today's world of technology, automation, urbanization, specialization, various forms of bureaucracy, mass media, and the increased influences of nationalistic, totalitarian, and other ideologies have all been widely discussed by many scholars. The net long-term implications of these processes, whether constructive or destructive, are beyond the scope of this paper, and we do not regard ourselves qualified to evaluate them.

We are concerned here, however, with certain of their more immediate effects on people. It would seem that, for a vast portion of the world's population, elements of these broad social changes contribute to feelings of anonymity, impersonality, separation from the decision-making processes, and a fragmented sense of one's integrated social roles, and also contribute to pressure on the individual to constrict his affective range to some machine-like task at hand. Similarly, the average citizen feels powerless indeed with respect to control over fateful decisions about nuclear attack or its aftermath.

The consequent sense of personal unimportance and relative helplessness, socially and politically, on the part of so many people specifically inclines them to adopt dehumanization as a preferred defense against many kinds of painful, unacceptable, and unbearable feelings referable to their experiences, inclinations, and behavior. *Self-directed dehumanization* empties the individual of human emotions and passions. It is paradoxical that one of its major dynamic purposes is protection against feeling the anxieties, frustrations, and conflicts associated with the "cog-in-a-big-machine" self-image into which people feel themselves pushed by socially induced pressures. Thus, it tends to fulfill the very threat that it seeks to prevent.

These pervasive reactions predispose one even more to regard other people or groups as less than human, or even nonhuman. We distinguish among several different types and gradations of *object-directed dehumanization*. Thus, the failure to recognize in others their full complement of human qualities may be either partial or relatively complete. Partial dehumanization includes the misperceiving of members of "out-groups," *en masse,* as subhuman, bad human, or superhuman; as such, it is related to the psychodynamics of group prejudice. It protects the individual from the guilt and shame he would otherwise feel from primitive or antisocial attitudes, impulses, and actions that he directs—or allows others to direct—toward those he manages to perceive in these categories: if they are subhumans they have not yet reached full human status on the evolutionary ladder and, therefore, do not merit being treated as human; if they are bad humans, their maltreatment is justified, since their defects in human qualities are their own fault. The latter is especially true if they are seen as having superhuman qualities as well, for it is one of the curious paradoxes of prejudice that both superhuman and debased characteristics are ascribed simultaneously to certain groups in order to justify discrimination or aggression against them. The foreigner, for instance, is seen at once as "wicked, untrustworthy, dirty," and "uncanny, powerful, and cunning." Similarly, according to the canons of race prejudice, contradictory qualities of exceptional prowess and extraordinary defect—ascribed to Orientals, Negroes, Jews, or any other group—together make them a menace toward whom customary restraints on behavior do not obtain. The main conscious emotional concomitants of partial dehumanization, as with prejudice, are hostility and fear.

In its more complete form, however, object-directed dehumanization entails a perception of other people as nonhumans—as statistics, commodities, or interchangeable pieces in a vast "numbers game." Its predominant emotional tone is that of indifference, in contrast to the (sometimes strong) feelings of partial dehumanization, together with a sense of *noninvolvement in the actual or foreseeable vicissitudes* of others. Such apathy has crucial psychosocial implications. Among these—perhaps the most important today—is its bearing on how people tolerate the risks of mass destruction by nuclear war.

Although this communication is primarily concerned with the negative and maladaptive aspects of dehumanization, we recognize that it also serves important adaptive purposes in many life situations. In this respect, it resembles other mental mechanisms of defense. Some of the ingredients of dehumanization are required for the effective mastery of many tasks in contemporary society. Thus, in crises such as natural disasters, accidents, or epidemics in which people are injured, sick, or killed, psychic mechanisms are called into play which divest the victims of their human identities, so that feelings of pity, terror, or revulsion can be overcome. Without such selective and transient dehumanization, these emotional reactions would interfere with the efficient and responsible performance of what has to be done, whether it be first aid, surgery, rescue operation, or burial.

Certain occupations in particular require such selectively dehumanized behavior.[2] Examples of these include law enforcement (police, judges, lawyers, prison officials); medicine (physicians, nurses, and ancillary personnel); and, of course, national defense (military leaders, strategists, fighting personnel). Indeed, some degree of adaptive dehumanization seems to be a basic requirement for effective participation in any institutional process. Almost every professional activity has some specific aspect that requires the capacity for appropriate detachment from full emotional responsiveness and the curtailment, at least temporarily, of those everyday human emotional exchanges that are not central to the task at hand, or which might, if present, impede it. The official at the window who stamps the passport may be by nature a warm and friendly man, but in the context of his job, the emigrant's hopes or fears lie outside his emotional vision.

Margaret Bourke-White, the noted photographer, was at Buchenwald at the end of World War II as a correspondent. Her account of herself at that time aptly describes the adaptive use of dehumanization, both self-directed and object-directed: "People often ask me how it is possible to photograph such atrocities . . . I have to work with a veil over my mind. In photographing the murder camps, the protective veil was so tightly drawn that I hardly knew what I had taken until I saw prints of my own photographs. I believe many correspondents worked in the same self-imposed stupor. One has to or it is impossible to stand it" (Bourke-White, 1963).

The only occasions to date on which nuclear bombs have been used in warfare took place when the "baby bombs" were dropped on the civilian populations of Hiroshima and Nagasaki. Lifton (1963) has reported on reactions among the Hiroshima survivors, as well as his own, as investigator. His observations are particularly valuable to us since, as a research psychiatrist, he was especially qualified both to

---

[2] These occupations, therefore, carry the extra risk of their requisite dehumanization becoming maladaptive if it is carried to an extreme or used inappropriately.

elicit and to evaluate psychodynamic data. According to the survivors whom he interviewed, at first one experienced utter horror at the sudden, strange scene of mass deaths, devastation, dreadful burns, and skin stripped from bodies. They could find no words to convey fully these initial feelings. But then each described how, before long, the horror would almost disappear. One would see terrible sights of human beings in extreme agony and yet feel nothing. The load of feeling from empathic responsiveness had become too much to endure; all one could do was to try to survive.

Lifton reports that during the first few such accounts he felt profoundly shocked, shaken, and emotionally spent. These effects gradually lessened, however, so that he became able to experience the interviews as scientific work rather than as repeated occasions of vicarious agony. For both the survivors and the investigator, the "task" provided a focus of concentration and of circumscribed activity as a means of quelling disturbing emotions.

In these instances, the immediate adaptive value of dehumanization as a defense is obvious. It remains open to question, however, whether a further, somewhat related, finding of Lifton's will in the long run prove to be adaptive or maladaptive. He learned that many people in Japan and elsewhere cannot bear to look at pictures of Hiroshima, and even avoid the museum in which they are displayed. There is avoidance and denial of the whole issue which not infrequently leads to hostility toward the A-bomb victims themselves, or toward anyone who expresses concern for these or future victims. May not *this* kind of defense reaction deflect the determination to seek ways of preventing nuclear war?

We believe that the complex mechanism of dehumanization urgently needs to be recognized and studied because its use as a defense has been stepped up so tremendously in recent times, and because of the grave risks it entails as the price for short-term relief. This paper represents only a preliminary delineation, with main attention to its bearing on the nuclear threat.[3]

[3] Because of this primary emphasis, we shall refrain from exploring many important facets of dehumanization which seem less directly relevant to the threat of nuclear warfare. Yet, it permeates so many aspects of modern life that, for clarity in describing it, our discussion must ramify, to some extent, beyond its war-connected context. Still, we have purposely neglected areas of great interest to us, especially with regard to psychopathology, psychotherapy, and community psychiatry, which we think warrant fuller discussion elsewhere.

Many people, by mobilizing this form of ego defense, manage to avoid or to lessen the emotional significance for themselves of today's kind of war. Only a very widespread and deeply rooted defense could ward off the full import of the new reality with which we live: that warfare has been transformed by modern weaponry into something mankind has never experienced before, and that in all-out nuclear war there can be no "victory" for anyone.

The extraordinary complacency with which people manage to shield themselves against fully realizing the threat of nuclear annihilation cannot be adequately explained, we think, by denial and the other well-studied psychological defense mechanisms. This is what has led us to trace out dehumanization as a composite defense, which draws upon a cluster of familiar defenses, magnifying that fraction of each which is most specifically involved with the humanness of one's self-image and the perception of others. It operates against such painful feelings as fear, inadequacy, compassion, revulsion, guilt, and shame. As with other mental mechanisms of defense, its self-protective distortions of realistic perceptions occur, for the most part, outside of awareness.

The extent to which dehumanization takes place consciously or unconsciously, although of considerable interest to us, is not relevant enough to this discussion to warrant elaboration. This also holds true for questions about why dehumanization as such has not hitherto received more attention and study in clinical psychiatry.[4] At least one possible reason might be mentioned, however. Most defense mechanisms were not studied originally in relation to such issues as war and peace, national destiny, or group survival. Instead, they came under scrutiny, during the course of psychotherapy, as part of the idiosyncratic pathology of individual patients. This could have obscured the recognition of their roles in widespread collective reactions.

In order to avoid confusion we should also mention that the term "dehumanization," as we are using it, refers to a concept that is different from and not connected in meaning with the words "humane" and "humanitarian." "Inhumane" cruelty causes suffering; maladaptive dehumanization, as we point out, may also lead to suffering. Yet even these seemingly similar results are reached by very different

[4] No doubt, when the phenomenon is part of a mental disorder, it has been dealt with therapeutically, to some degree, under the names of other defense mechanisms.

routes; to equate them would be a mistake. A surgeon, for example, is treating his patient humanely when, by his dehumanization, he blots out feelings of either sympathy or hostility ʳhat might otherwise interfere with his surgical skill during an operation.

No one, of course, could possibly retain his mental health and carry on the business of life if he remained constantly aware of, and empathically sensitive to, all the misery and injustice that there is in the world. But this very essentiality of dehumanization, as with other defenses, makes for its greatest danger: that the constructive self-protection it achieves will cross the ever-shifting boundaries of adaptiveness and become destructive, to others as well as to the self. In combination with other social factors already mentioned, the perfection of modern techniques for automated killing on a global scale engenders a marked increase in the incidence of dehumanization. Correspondingly, there is intensified risk that this collective reaction will break through the fragile and elusive dividing line that separates healthy ego-supportive dehumanization from the maladaptive callousness and apathy that prevent people from taking those realistic actions which are within their powers to protect human rights and human lives.

A "vicious cycle" relationship would thus seem to obtain between dehumanization as a subjective phenomenon and its objective consequences. Conscience and empathy, as sources of guilt and compassion, pertain to human beings; they can be evaded if the human element in the victims of aggression is first sufficiently obscured. The aggressor is thereby freed from conscience-linked restraints, with injurious objective effects on other individuals, groups, or nations. The victims in turn respond, subjectively, by resorting even more to self-protective dehumanization, as did the Hiroshima survivors whom Lifton interviewed.

One might argue, and with some cogency, that similar conversion of enemies into pins on a military map has been part of war psychology throughout history, so are we not therefore belaboring the obvious? The answer lies in the fundamental changes, both quantitative and qualitative, that nuclear weapons have made in the meaning of war. In fact, the very term "war," with its preatomic connotations, has become something of an outmoded misnomer for the nuclear threat which now confronts us. "Modern war"—before Hiroshima—

reflected, as a social institution, many of the social and technological developments which we have already noted as conducive to increased dehumanization. But with the possibility of instantaneously wiping out the world's population—or a very large section of it—the extent of dehumanization as well as its significance for human survival have both been abruptly and tremendously accelerated.

In part, this seems to be due to the overtaxing of our capacity really to comprehend the sudden changes in amplitudes that have become so salient. In addition to the changed factors of *distance, time,* and *magnitude* in modern technology, there is the push-button nature of today's weaponry and the *indirectness* of releasing a rocket barrage upon sites halfway around the world, all of which lie far outside our range of previous experience. When we look out of an airplane window, the earth below becomes a toy, the hills and valleys reduced to abstractions in our mental canvas; but we do not conceive of ourselves as a minute part of some moving speck in the sky—which is how we appear to people on the ground. Yet it is precisely such reciprocal awareness that is required if we are to maintain a balanced view of our actual size and vulnerability. Otherwise, perceptual confusion introduces a mechanistic and impersonal quality into our reactions.

The thinking and feeling of most people have been unable as yet to come to grips with the sheer expansion of numbers and the frightening shrinkage of space which present means of transportation and communication entail. The news of an animal run over by a car, a child stuck in a well, or the preventable death of one individual evokes an outpouring of sympathetic response and upsets the emotional equanimity of many; yet reports of six million Jews killed in Nazi death camps, or of a hundred thousand Japanese killed in Hiroshima and Nagasaki, may cause but moderate uneasiness. Arthur Koestler (1944) has put it poignantly, "Statistics don't bleed; it is the detail which counts. We are unable to embrace the total process with our awareness; we can only focus on little lumps of reality."

It is this unique combination of psychosocial and situational factors that seems particularly to favor the adoption of the composite defense we have called "dehumanization"—and this in turn acts to generate more and more of the same. The new aspects of time, space magnitude, speed, automation, distance, and irreversibility are not yet "hooked up" in the psychology of man's relationships to his fellow man or to the world he inhabits. Most people feel poorly equipped, conceptually, to restructure their accustomed picture of the world, all of a sudden, in order to make it fit dimensions so alien to their lifelong learning. Anxiety aroused by this threat to one's orientation adds to the inner stress that seeks relief through the defense.

We are confronted with a *lag in our perceptual and intellectual development* so that the enormity of the new reality, with its potential for both destructive and constructive human consequences, becomes blurred in our thinking and feeling. The less elastic our capacity to comprehend meaningfully new significances, the more we cling to dehumanization, unable to challenge its fallacies through knowledge and reason. Correspondingly, the greater our reliance on dehumanization as a mechanism for coping with life, the less readily can the new facts of our existence be integrated into our full psychic functioning, since so many of its vital components, such as empathy, have been shunted aside, stifled, or obscured.

Together, in the writers' opinion, these differently caused but mutually reinforcing cognitive and emotional deficiencies seriously intensify the nuclear risk; latent psychological barriers against the destruction of millions of people remain unmobilized, and hence ineffective, for those who feel detached from the flesh and blood implications of nuclear war. No other mechanism seems to fit so well the requirements of this unprecedented internal and external stress. Dehumanization, with its impairment of our personal involvement, allows us to "play chess with the planets."

Whether it be adaptive or maladaptive, dehumanization brings with it, as we have noted, a temporary feeling of relief, an illusion of problems solved, or at least postponed or evaded. Whatever the ultimate effects of this psychic maneuver on our destiny, however, it would seem to be a wise precaution to try to assess some of its dangerous possibilities.

Several overlapping aspects of maladaptive dehumanization may be outlined briefly and in oversimplified form, as follows:

1. *Increased emotional distance from other human beings.* Under the impact of this defense, one stops identifying with others or seeing them as essentially similar to oneself in basic human qualities. Relationships to others become stereotyped, rigid, and above all, unex-

pressive of mutuality. People in "out-groups" are apt to be reacted to *en bloc;* feelings of concern for them have become anesthetized.

George Orwell (1946) illustrates this aspect of dehumanization in writing of his experience as a patient. His account also serves as an example of the very significant hazard, already mentioned, whereby professionally adaptive uses of this defense (as in medical education and patient care) are in danger of passing that transition point beyond which they become maladaptive and so defeat their original purpose.

Later in the day the tall, solemn, black-bearded doctor made his rounds, with an intern and a troop of students following at his heels, but there were about sixty of us in the ward and it was evident that he had other wards to attend to as well. There were many beds past which he walked day after day, sometimes followed by imploring cries. On the other hand, if you had some disease with which the students wanted to familiarize themselves you got plenty of attention of a kind. I myself, with an exceptionally fine specimen of a bronchial rattle, sometimes had as many as a dozen students queuing up to listen to my chest. It was a very queer feeling—queer, I mean, because of their intense interest in learning their job, together with a seeming lack of any perception that the patients were human beings. It is strange to relate, but sometimes as some young student stepped forward to take his turn at manipulating you, he would be actually tremulous with excitement, like a boy who has at last got his hands on some expensive piece of machinery. And then ear after ear . . . pressed against your back, relays of fingers solemnly but clumsily tapping, and not from any one of them did you get a word of conversation or a look direct in your face. As a non-paying patient, in the uniform nightshirt, you were primarily a *specimen,* a thing I did not resent but could never quite get used to.

2. *Diminished sense of personal responsibility for the consequences of one's actions.* Ordinarily, for most people, the advocacy of or participation in the wholesale slaughter and maiming of their fellow human beings is checked by opposing feelings of guilt, shame, or horror. Immunity from these feelings may be gained, however, by a self-automatizing detachment from a sense of *personal* responsibility for the outcome of such actions, thereby making them easier to carry out. (A dramatic version of the excuse, "I was only carrying out orders," was offered by Eichmann at his trial.)

One "safe" way of dealing with such painful feelings is to focus only on one's fragmented job and ignore its many ramifications. By blocking out the ultimately destructive purpose of a military bombing action, for instance, one's component task therein may become a source of ego-acceptable gratification, as from any successful fulfillment of duty, mastery of a hard problem, or achievement of a dangerous feat. The B-29 airplane that dropped the atomic bomb on Hiroshima was named Enola Gay, after the mother of one of its crew members. This could represent the psychological defense of displacing human qualities from the population to be bombed to the machine.

One of the crew members is reported to have exclaimed: "If people knew what we were doing we could have sold tickets for $100,000!" and another is said to have commented, "Colonel, that was worth the 25¢ ride on the 'Cyclone' at Coney Island" (*Yank, the Army Weekly,* 1947). Such reactions, which may on the surface appear to be shockingly cynical, not only illustrate how cynicism may be used to conceal strong emotions (as seems quite likely in this instance); they also suggest how one may try to use cynicism to bolster one's dehumanization when that defense is not itself strong enough, even with its displacement of responsibility and its focusing on one's fragmented job, to overcome the intensity of one's inner "humanized" emotional protest against carrying out an act of such vast destructiveness.

3. *Increasing involvement with procedural problems to the detriment of human needs.* There is an overconcern with details of procedure, with impersonal deindividualized regulations, and with the formal structure of a practice, all of which result in shrinking the ability or willingness to personalize one's actions in the interests of individual human needs or special differences. This is, of course, the particular danger implicit in the trend toward bureaucracy that accompanies organizational units when they grow larger and larger. The task at hand is then apt to take precedence over the human cost: the individual is seen more as a means to an end than as an end in himself. Society, the Corporation, the Five-Year Plan—these become overriding goals in themselves, and the dehumanized man is turned into a cost item, tool, or energy-factor serving the mass-machine.

Even "scientific" studies of human behavior and development, as well as professional practices based on them, sometimes become dehumanized to a maladaptive extent (Kahne, 1959). Such words as "communicate," "adjust," "identify," "relate," "feel," and even "love" can lose their personal meaningfulness when they are used as mere technical devices instead of being applied to specific human beings in specific life situations.[5] In response to the new hugeness of global problems, patterns of speech have emerged that additionally reflect dehumanized thinking. Segmented-fragmented concepts, such as "fallout problem," "shelter problems," "civil defense," "deterrence," "first strike," "preemptive attack," "overkill," and some aspects of game theory, represent a "move-countermove" type of thinking which tends to treat the potential human victim as a statistic, and to screen out the total catastrophic effect of the contemplated actions upon human lives. The content of strategy takes on an importance that is without any relation to its inevitable *results,* the defense of dehumanization having operated to block out recognition of those awesome consequences that, if they could be seen, would make the strategy unacceptable. The defense, when successful, narcotizes deeper feelings so that nuclear war, as "inevitable," may be more dispassionately contemplated and its tactical permutations assayed. In the course of this, however, almost automatic counteractions of anxiety are frequently expressed through such remarks as: "People have always lived on the brink of disaster," "You can't change human nature; there will have to be wars," and "We all have to die some day."

4. *Inability to oppose dominant group attitudes or pressures.* As the individual comes to feel more and more alienated and lonely in mass society, he finds it more and more difficult to place himself in opposition to the huge pressures of the "Organization." Fears of losing occupational security or of attacks on one's integrity, loyalty, or family are more than most people can bear. Self-directed dehumanization is

[5] Within our own discipline this is all too likely to occur when thousands of sick individuals are converted into "cases" in some of our understaffed and oversized mental hospitals. Bureaucratic hospital structure favors impersonal experience. In an enlightening study, Kahne (1959) points up how this accentuation of automatic and formalized milieu propensities thwarts the specific therapeutic need of psychiatric patients for opportunities to improve their sense of involvement with people.

On another occasion we hope to enlarge on how and why maladaptive uses of dehumanization on the part of professionals, officials, and the general public hamper our collective effort as a community to instill more sensitivity to individual need into patterns of congregate care, not only in mental hospitals but also in general hospitals, children's institutions, welfare and correctional facilities, etc.

resorted to as a defense against such fears and conflicts: by joining the party, organization, or club, and thus feeling himself to be an inconspicuous particle in some large structure, he may find relief from the difficult decisions, uncertainties, and pressures of nonconformity. He may also thereby ward off those feelings of guilt that would arise out of participating in, or failing to protect against, the injustices and cruelties perpetrated by those in power. Thus, during the Nazi regime, many usually kindhearted Germans appear to have silenced their consciences by emphasizing their own insignificance and identifying with the dehumanized values of the dictatorship. This stance permitted the detached, even dutiful, disregard of their fellow citizens, which in turn gave even freer rein to the systematic official conducting of genocide.

5. *Feelings of personal helplessness and estrangement.* The realization of one's relatively impotent position in a large organization engenders anxiety [6] which dehumanization helps to cover over. The internalized perception of the self as small, helpless, and insignificant, coupled with an externalized view of "Society" as huge, powerful, and unopposable, is expressed in such frequently heard comments as: "The government has secret information that we don't have"; or, "They know what's right, who am I to question what they are doing?"; or "What's the use? No one will listen to me. . . ."

The belief that the government or the military is either infallible or impregnable provides a tempting refuge because of its renunciation of one's own critical faculties in the name of those of the powerful and all-knowing leader. Such self-directed dehumanization has a strong appeal to the isolated and alienated citizen as a protective cloak to hide from himself his feelings of weakness, ignorance, and estrangement. This is particularly relevant to the psychological attraction of certain dangerous social movements. The more inwardly frightened, lonely, helpless, and humiliated people become, the greater the susceptibility of many of them to the seductive, prejudiced promises of demagoguery: the award of spurious superiority and privilege achieved by devaluing the full humanness of some other group—racial, religious, ethnic, or political. Furthermore, as an added advantage of the dehumanization "package," self-enhancing

[6] This has been particularly well described in novels by Kafka and Camus.

acts of discrimination and persecution against such victim groups can be carried out without tormenting or deterrent feelings of guilt, since these are absorbed by the "rightness" of the demagogic leader.

In recent decades and in many countries, including our own, we have seen what human toll can be taken by this psychosocial configuration. It has entered into Hitlerism, Stalinism, U.S.A. "lynchmobism." If it is extended to the international arena, against a "dehumanized" enemy instead of an oppressed national minority, atomic weapons will now empower it to inflict immeasurably more human destruction and suffering.

The indifference resulting from that form of dehumanization which causes one to view others as inanimate objects enables one, without conscious malice or selfishness, to write off their misery, injustices, and death as something that "just couldn't be helped." As nonhumans, they are not identified with as beings essentially similar to oneself; "their" annihilation by nuclear warfare is thus not "our" concern, despite the reality that distinctions between "they" and "we" have been rendered all the more meaningless by the mutually suicidal nature of total war.

Although this type of dehumanization is relatively complete, in the sense of perceiving others as not at all human, it may occur in an individual with selective incompleteness under certain special conditions only, while his capacity for other emotional ties is preserved. This may prove socially constructive or destructive, depending on the purposes to which it is put. Thus, we have already noted how "pulling a veil" over her mind helped Bourke-White adaptively in her socially positive job of reporting atrocities. But it was compartmentalized dehumanization that also helped many to commit those very atrocities; they were able to exterminate Jews with assembly-line efficiency as the Nazi "final solution" while still retaining access to their genuine feelings of warmth for family members, friends, and associates.

These contradictory emotional qualities, often appearing side by side in the same person, are also evidenced—in the opposite direction—by outstanding deeds of heroic rescue by those who, under different circumstances, might well exhibit dehumanized behavior. Almost daily, the newspapers carry stories of exceptional altruism; individuals or whole communities devote their entire energies to the rescue of a single child, an animal, or perhaps (in wartime), a wounded enemy soldier. What accounts for the difference between this kind of response to the plight of others, and that of dehumanized callousness? How are the adaptive humanized processes released?

One research approach might consist of the detailed description and comparative analysis of sample situations of both kinds of these collective reactions, which have such opposite social effects. A case history of community apathy which could be compared in such a study with instances of group altruism already on record, was recently provided by A. M. Rosenthal (1964), an editor of *The New York Times.* At first glance, perhaps, his account of dehumanization, involving but one individual and in peacetime, may not seem germane to our discussion about nuclear war. But the macrocosm is reflected in the microcosm. We agree with Mr. Rosenthal that the implications of this episode are linked with certain psychological factors that have helped pave the way for such broad social calamities as Fascism abroad and racial crises in this country, both in the North and South. It does not seem too farfetched, therefore, to relate them to the nuclear threat as well.

For more than half an hour, one night in March 1964, thirty-eight respectable, law-abiding citizens in a quiet middle-class neighborhood in New York City watched a killer stalk and stab a young woman in three separate attacks, close to her home. She was no stranger to these onlookers, her neighbors, who knew her as "Kitty." According to Rosenthal, "Twice the sound of their voices and the sudden glow of their bedroom lights interrupted him and frightened him off. Each time he returned, sought her out and stabbed her again. Not one person telephoned the police during the assault; one witness called after the woman was dead." Later, when these thirty-eight neighbors were asked about their baffling failure to phone for help, even though they were safe in their own homes, "the underlying attitude or explanation seemed to be fear of involvement—any kind of involvement." Their fatal apathy gains in significance precisely because, by ordinary standards, these were decent, moral people—husbands and wives attached to each other and good to their children. This is one of the forms of dehumanization that we have described, in which a reaction of massive indifference—not hostility—leads to grievous cruelty, yet all the while, in another compartment of the self, the same individual's capacity for active caring continues, at least for those within his immediate orbit.

Rosenthal describes his own reaction to this episode as a

peculiar paradoxical feeling that there is in the tale of Catherine Genovese a revelation about the human condition so appalling to contemplate that only good can come from forcing oneself to confront the truth . . . the terrible reality that only under certain situations, and only in response to certain reflexes or certain beliefs, will a man step out of his shell toward his brother. In the back of my mind . . . was the feeling that there was, that there must be some connection between [this story and] the story of the witnesses silent in the face of greater crimes—the degradation of a race, children hungering. . . . It happens from time to time in New York that the life of the city is frozen by an instant of shock. In that instant the people of the city are seized by the paralyzing realization that they are one, that each man is in some way a mirror of every other man. . . . In that instant of shock, the mirror showed quite clearly what was wrong, that the face of mankind was spotted with the disease of apathy—all mankind. But this was too frightening a thought to live with, and soon the beholders began to set boundaries for the illness, to search frantically for causes that were external and to look for the carrier.

As we strive to distinguish more clearly among the complex determinants of adaptive-maladaptive, humanized-dehumanized polarities of behavior, we recognize that stubborn impulses toward individuation are intertwined with the dehumanizing trends on which we have focused. Both humanization and dehumanization are heightened by interpenetrating social and psychological effects of current technological and institutional changes. The progress of the past hundred years has markedly furthered humanization: it has relieved much of human drudgery and strain, and helped to bring about increased leisure and a richer life for a larger part of the world's population. Despite the blurring of personal distinctiveness by excessive bureaucracy, there are now exceptional opportunities, made possible by the same technology that fosters uniformity, for the individual to make rapid contact with, and meaningful contribution to, an almost limitless number of the earth's inhabitants. The same budgets, communication networks, transportation delivery systems, and human organizations that can be used to destroy can also be turned toward the creative fulfillment of great world purposes.

Our situation today favors contradictory attitudes toward how much any individual matters in the scheme of things, both subjectively and from the standpoint of social reality. At one extreme a few individuals in key positions feel—and are generally felt to have—a hugely expanded potential for social impact. Among the vast majority there is, by contrast, an intensified sense of voiceless insignificance in the shaping of events. Objectively, too, there is now among individuals a far greater disparity in their actual power to influence crucial outcomes. More than ever before, the fate of the world depends on the judgment of a handful of heads of state and their advisers, who must make rapid decisions about actions for which there are no precedents. Ideas and events, for better or worse, can have immediate global impact.[7] A push-button can set a holocaust in motion; a transatlantic phone call can prevent one.

In spite of humanizing ingredients in modern life, and the fact that men of good will everywhere are striving ceaselessly toward goals of peace, freedom, and human dignity, we nevertheless place primary emphasis, in this paper, on dehumanization because we feel that the dangers inherent in this phenomenon are particularly pervasive, insidious, and relevant to the risk of nuclear war.

From a broad biological perspective, war may be viewed as a form of aggression between members of the same species, homosapiens. The distinguished naturalist, Lorenz (1963), has recently pointed out a difference, of great relevance to the relationship between dehumanization and nuclear warfare, in the intraspecies behavior of animals who live in two kinds of groups. In the one, the members live together as a crowd of strangers: there are no expressions of mutual aggression, but neither is there any evidence of mutual ties, of relationships of affection, between individuals in the group. On the other hand, some of the fiercest beasts of prey—animals whose bodily weapons are capable of killing their own kind—live in groups in which intense relationships, both *aggressive and affectionate*, exist. Among such animals, says Lorenz, the greater the intraspecies aggression, the stronger the positive mutual attachments as well. These latter develop, through evolution, out of those occasions, such as breeding, when cooperation among these aggressive animals becomes essential to their survival as a species.

[7] The news of President Kennedy's assassination circled the earth with unparalleled speed and evoked a profound worldwide emotional response.

Furthermore—and this is of the utmost importance for survival— the greater the capacity for mutual relationships, the stronger and more reliable are the *innate inhibitions* which prevent them from using the species-specific weapons of predatory aggression, fangs, claws, or whatever, to maim or kill a member of their own species, no matter how strong the hostile urge of one against another. For example, when two wolves fight, according to Lorenz, the potential victor's fangs are powerfully inhibited at what would be the moment of kill, in response to the other's ritualized signal of immobile exposure to his opponent of his vulnerable jugular.

Man's weapons, by contrast, are not part of his body. They are thus not controllable by reflexes fused into his nervous system; control must depend, instead, on psychological inhibitions (which may also function through social controls of his own devising). These psychic barriers to intraspecies aggression—which can lead to our becoming extinct—are rooted in our affiliative tendencies for cooperation and personal attachment. But these are the very tendencies that, as this paper has stressed, dehumanization can so seriously undermine.

Lorenz speaks of a natural balance within a species—essential to its preservation—between the capacity for killing and inhibition. In that sense, perhaps, man jeopardizes his survival by disturbing, with his invention of nuclear bombs, such a balance as has been maintained throughout his long history of periodic "old-style" wars. Such a dire imbalance would be increased by any shift on the part of the "human animal" toward a society essentially devoid of mutual relationships. For this would vitiate the very tendencies toward emotional involvement and cooperation which are the source of our most reliable inhibitions against "overkilling." Therefore, in terms of the parallels suggested by Lorenz, in order to protect ourselves against the doom of extinction as a species, we must encourage and devise every possible means of safeguarding the "family of man" from becoming an uncaring crowd. Not merely the limiting or halting, but the reversing of maladaptive dehumanization emerges as a key to survival.

What can be done to counteract these dangers? Assuredly, there is no single or ready answer. The development of psychic antidotes of rehumanization must involve a multiplicity of variables, levels of discourse and sectors of human activity, commensurate in complexity with the factors that make for *de*humanization. Our attempt in this paper to identify this mental mechanism, and to alert others to its significance, its frequency, and its interrelatedness to nuclear risk, represents in itself a preliminary phase of remedial endeavor. For the very process of recognizing a psychosocial problem such as this, by marshalling, reordering, and interpreting diverse sets of facts to find new significances in them, is a form of social action, and one that is especially appropriate to behavioral scientists. Beyond this initial posing of the problem, however, any chance of effectively grappling with it will require the converging efforts of those in many different professions and walks of life.

Rehumanization as a mode of neutralizing the dangerous effects that we have stressed should not be misconstrued as aiming at the re-establishment of pre-nuclear age psychology—which would be impossible in any case. We cannot set history back nostalgically to "the good old days" prior to automation and the other changes in contemporary society (nor were the conditions of those earlier days really so "good" for the self-realization of a large portion of the population.) On the contrary, the process of rehumanization means to us a way of assimilating and reintegrating, emotionally and intellectually, the profound new meanings that have been brought into our lives by our own advances, so that a much fuller conviction than ever before of our own humanity and interdependence with all mankind becomes intrinsic to our basic frame of reference.

The imperative for speeding up such a universal process of psychological change is rooted in the new and *specific* necessity to insure survival in the face of the awesome irreversibility of nuclear annihilation. The most essential approaches toward achieving this goal, however, lead us into such *general* and only seemingly unrelated issues as the degree of political freedom and social justice; our patterns of child care and child-rearing; and our philosophy of education, as well as the quality of its implementation. For the process of dehumanization, which eventuates in indifference to the suffering implicit in nuclear warfare, has its beginnings in earlier periods and other areas of the individual's life. It is through these areas that influences conducive to rehumanization must be channeled.

We need to learn more, and to make more effective use of what is already known about how to strengthen people's capacity to tolerate irreducible uncertainty, fear, and frustration without having to take refuge in illusions that cripple their potential for realistic behavior. And we urgently need to find ways of galvanizing our powers of imagination (including ways of weakening the hold of the emotionally based mechanisms that imprison it).

Imagination and foresight are among the highest functions of the human brain, from the evolutionary standpoint, and also among the most valuable. They enable us to select and extrapolate from previously accumulated experience and knowledge, in order to create guidelines for coping with situations never before experienced, whose nature is so far unknown.

Other kinds of learning ordinarily serve us well in the complicated process of establishing behavior patterns for meeting new life situations. We are able to learn by trial and error, for example, from our firsthand experiences and from successively testing the value of alternative approaches as similar situations arise. Also, we learn much by vicariously living through the reported experiences of others.

Through imagination, however, a completely new situation can be projected in the mind in its sensate and vivid entirety, so that the lessons it contains for us can be learned without the necessity of going through it in real life. This form of "future-directed" learning, which creative imagination makes possible, is therefore uniquely advantageous in dealing with the problematic issues of thermonuclear war; it permits us to arrive at more rational decisions for preventing it without having to pay the gruesome price of undergoing its actuality.

The fact is that the "once-and-for-all" character of full-scale nuclear war renders the methods of "learning through experience"—our own or others'—not only indefensible (in terms of the human cost) but also utterly unfeasible. The empirical privilege of "profiting" from an experience of that nature would have been denied to most if not all of humanity by the finality of the experience itself.

Accordingly, it would seem that whatever can quicken and extend our capacity for imagination, in both the empathic and conceptual spheres, is a vital form of "civil defense." It requires, to begin with, all the pedagogic ingenuity that we can muster to overcome the lag in our intellectual development that keeps us from fully comprehending the new dimensions of our existence. Yet, our endeavors to develop new modes of thinking can be cancelled out by the constricting and impeding effects of dehumanization. The terrible potential of this subtle mechanism to facilitate the depopulating of the earth lies in its circumventing human restraints against fratricide. We are faced, therefore, with the inescapable necessity of devising ways to increase opportunities for meaningful personal relationships and maximum social participation throughout the entire fabric of our society.

section V
∼∼∼

COPING WITH DEATH AND SEPARATION

Perhaps no topics have enjoyed as much growth of interest among students in recent years as those of death and separation. The mysterious cloak which has traditionally surrounded the concept of death seems to have lifted and we now find ourselves bombarded with an array of books, seminars, and encounter groups all geared to explore this once feared topic. The readings in Section V reflect this new appeal. They are concerned for the most part with how people cope with their own death or the loss of beloved ones. Although much remains to be unraveled, psychiatrists, psychologists, and sociologists interested in "thanatology" (i.e., the study of death) are making progress in our understanding of the psychological aspects of one's own death as well as of coping with the loss of another.

The selections by Becker (1973) and Hackett and Weisman (1964) deal with the "fear of death." In his award-winning and highly challenging book, *The Denial of Death,* Ernest Becker argues that the fear of death is a mainspring of human activity and, in fact, that all human striving is essentially an attempt to deny the "terror of death" and our sense of helplessness and vulnerability about it. Becker finds two basic positions in the literature, namely, the "healthy-minded" argument which says we should not fear death and that our death fear is a culturally acquired pathology, and the "morbidly minded" argument which maintains that even though our fear of death may be reduced it is a natural, appropriate, and universal aspect of life which cannot be eliminated. Becker sides with the latter position but, in another part of his book, states that we can cope effectively with our terror of death, not through denial, but by finding meaning that is seen as continuing beyond the period of one's life.

Hackett and Weisman (1964) observed that patients suffering from myocardial infarction and incurable cancer often deny the threat of imminent death. Yet the effectiveness of the denial process may be undermined by what the authors call "middle knowledge," i.e., the dying patient's dim awareness of his own imminent death. This knowledge is just "below the surface" of the denial, manifesting itself in subtle behavioral signs like slips of the tongue, threatening dreams, etc. Its manifestations vary depending on the dying patient's interpersonal relationships. For example, persons visiting cancer patients tend to withdraw from them psychologically, in a subtle manner, and to feel anxious when the illness, or death, are discussed. As a result, visitors exude optimism seeking to generate a false mood of hope. The patient senses all this, feels alienated and depressed about it, but plays along because to do otherwise would threaten the continuation of these relationships. Thus, he or she not only has to face dying, but also the loss of communication with friends and loved ones along the way. Hackett and Weisman point out, too, how the objective and interpersonal situations differ between the myocardial infarction patient who can maintain hope and the terminal cancer patient who cannot anticipate recovery.

Although these selections provide fascinating suggestions on how people cope with the fear of death, still too little is known which could be serviceable in ameliorating human suffering about dying. Empirical studies in this area are scarce and existing ones rely heavily on measurements of questionable validity, e.g., projective techniques or brief interviews (e.g., Feifel, Freilich, & Hermann, 1973). Nevertheless, progress is being made and, as researchers continue to study the "terror of death" systematically, one can hope for new advances that could enhance both our understanding of the human condition and our ability to help individuals cope effectively with death and dying.

The remaining articles in this section deal primarily with the management of separation, actual and anticipated, with respect to the death of loved ones and the loss of one's home and community. In what is now considered to be a "classic" paper, Lindemann (1944) describes the typical symptoms of grief and argues that the duration of the grief syndrome depends largely upon the success of the "grief work," that is, the psychological process of breaking the old bonds with the deceased and forming new relationships. Lindemann also describes cases of "morbid" reactions requiring professional intervention. Lindemann's observations and generalizations have tended to be limited to cases where the bereaved has no period of anticipation (e.g., relatives of victims of the Cocoanut Grove Fire disaster). When an anticipation period *does* exist prior to the victim's death, the "normal" grief reaction, referred to by Lindemann, may actually be prolonged (e.g., Aldrich, 1974). Despite this limitation, Lindemann's paper remains a landmark in the study of bereavement and the reactions of grief.

Friedman et al. (1963) present a detailed clinical description of the stresses experienced by parents of children dying of leukemia and the characteristic coping devices used by these parents to help them deal with their anticipated loss. The reader will be struck by the seemingly endless and often contradictory pressures felt by the parents and the numerous coping mechanisms (such as intellectualization and denial) used to handle their distress as well as to manage their dying child. Friedman et al. remind us again (see also, for example, Bernard, Ottenberg, & Redl, 1965; Hackett & Weisman, 1964; Lucas, 1969) that social factors can have considerable impact on stress and its resolution. For example, Friedman et al. note that relatives, typically the grandparents, frequently displayed more denial than the parents, thus often making it more difficult for the parents to fully accept the reality of the child's condition. Social forces, however, seemed also to help the parents in that many learned how to cope with their distress by observing other parents in the study successfully go through similar experiences. In short, the observations provided by Friedman et al. offer crucial insights into various psychological and sociological processes often inherent in the struggle to survive and manage the anticipated loss of a beloved one from a terminal illness.

In today's modern city, forced dislocation and relocation are common phenomena, yet their psychological impact on individuals is little understood. In a compassionate article, Fried (1963) presents interview data strongly suggesting that many people who undergo forced relocation view it as a major form of stress and actually react to it very much as to the loss of a loved one: that is, they display patterns of grief and mourning for "a lost home." Fried documents these grieving reactions with a number of case studies and discusses possible determinants of their intensity and duration. With "urban renewal" being a commonplace occurrence, Fried's observations and comments deserve serious consideration.

22

〜〜〜〜〜〜〜〜〜〜〜〜〜〜〜〜〜〜〜〜〜〜〜〜〜〜〜〜〜〜〜〜〜〜〜〜

The Terror of Death

ERNEST BECKER

The first thing we have to do with heroism is to lay bare its underside, show what gives human heroics its specific nature and impetus. Here we introduce directly one of the great rediscoveries of modern thought: that of all things that move man, one of the principal ones is his terror of death. After Darwin the problem of death as an evolutionary one came to the fore, and many thinkers immediately saw that it was a major psychological problem for man (cf., for example, Cochrane, 1934; Hall, 1915). They also very quickly saw what real heroism was about, as Shaler (1900) wrote just at the turn of the century: heroism is first and foremost a reflex of the terror of death. We admire most the courage to face death; we give such valor our highest and most constant adoration; it moves us deeply in our hearts because we have doubts about how brave we ourselves would be. When we see a man bravely facing his own extinction we rehearse the greatest victory we can imagine. And so the hero has been the center of human honor and acclaim since probably the beginning of specifically human evolution. But even before that our primate ancestors deferred to others who were extrapowerful and courageous and ignored those who were cowardly. Man has elevated animal courage into a cult.

Anthropological and historical research also began, in the nineteenth century, to put together a picture of the heroic since primitive and ancient times. The hero was the man who could go into the spirit world, the world of the dead, and return alive. He had his descendants in the mystery cults of the Eastern Mediterranean, which were cults of death and resurrection. The divine hero of each of these cults was one who had come back from the dead. And as we know today from the research into ancient myths and rituals, Christianity itself was a competitor with the mystery cults and won out—among other reasons—because it, too, featured a healer with supernatural powers who had risen from the dead. The great triumph of Easter is the joyful shout "Christ has risen!"—an echo of the same joy that the devotees of the mystery cults enacted at their ceremonies of the victory over death. These cults, as G. Stanley Hall (1915, p. 562) so aptly put it, were an attempt to attain "an immunity bath" from the greatest evil: death and the dread of it. All historical religions addressed themselves to this same problem of how to bear the end of life. Religions like Hinduism and Buddhism performed the ingenious trick of pretending not to want to be reborn, which is a sort of negative magic: claiming not to want what you really want most (cf. Harrington, 1969, p. 82). When philosophy took over from religion it also took over religion's central problem, and death became the real "muse of philosophy" from its beginnings in Greece right through Heidegger and modern existentialism.[1]

We already have volumes of work and thought on the subject, from religion and philosophy and—since Darwin—from science itself. The problem is how to make sense out of it; the accumulation of research and opinion on the fear of death is already too large to be dealt with and summarized in any simple way. The revival of interest in death, in the last few decades, has alone already piled up a formidable literature, and this literature does not point in any single direction.

THE "HEALTHY-MINDED" ARGUMENT

There are "healthy-minded" persons who maintain that fear of death is not a natural thing for man, that we are not born with it. An increasing number of careful studies on how the actual fear of death develops in the child (see Feifel, 1959, Chapter 6; Rochlin, 1967, p. 67) agree fairly well that the child has no knowledge of death until about the age of three to five. How could he? It is too abstract an idea, too removed from his experience. He lives in a world

---

[1] See Choron's (1963) excellent study.

that is full of living, acting things, responding to him, amusing him, feeding him. He doesn't know what it means for life to disappear forever, nor theorize where it would go. Only gradually does he recognize that there is a thing called death that takes some people away forever; very reluctantly he comes to admit that it sooner or later takes everyone away, but this gradual realization of the inevitability of death can take up until the ninth or tenth year.

If the child has no knowledge of an abstract idea like absolute negation, he does have his own anxieties. He is absolutely dependent on the mother, experiences loneliness when she is absent, frustration when he is deprived of gratification, irritation at hunger and discomfort, and so on. If he were abandoned to himself his world would drop away, and his organism must sense this at some level; we call this the anxiety of object-loss. Isn't this anxiety, then, a natural, organismic fear of annihilation? Again, there are many who look at this as a very relative matter. They believe that if the mother has done her job in a warm and dependable way, the child's natural anxieties and guilts will develop in a moderate way, and he will be able to place them firmly under the control of his developing personality (Bowlby, 1952, p. 11). The child who has good maternal experiences will develop a sense of basic security and will not be subject to morbid fears of losing support, of being annihilated, or the like (cf. Tietz, 1970). As he grows up to understand death rationally by the age of nine or ten, he will accept it as part of his world view, but the idea will not poison his self-confident attitude toward life. The psychiatrist Rheingold (1967) says categorically that annihilation anxiety is not part of the child's natural experience but is engendered in him by bad experiences with a depriving mother. This theory puts the whole burden of anxiety onto the child's nurture and not his nature. Another psychiatrist, in a less extreme vein, sees the fear of death as greatly heightened by the child's experiences with his parents, by their hostile denial of his life impulses, and, more generally, by the antagonism of society to human freedom and self-expansiveness (Levin, 1951).

As we will see later on, this view is very popular today in the widespread movement toward unrepressed living, the urge to a new freedom for natural biological urges, a new attitude of pride and joy in the body, the abandonment of shame, guilt, and self-hatred. From this point of view, fear of death is something that society creates and at the same time uses against the person to keep him in submission; the psychiatrist Moloney (1949, p. 217) talked about it as a "culture mechanism," and Marcuse (1959) as an "ideology." Norman O. Brown (1959, p. 270) in a vastly influential book [*Life Against Death*], went so far as to say that there could be a birth and development of the child in a "second innocence" that would be free of the fear of death because it would not deny natural vitality and would leave the child fully open to physical living.

It is easy to see that, from this point of view, those who have bad early experiences will be most morbidly fixated on the anxiety of death; and if by chance they grow up to be philosophers they will probably make the idea a central dictum of their thought—as did Schopenhauer, who both hated his mother and went on to pronounce death the "muse of philosophy." If you have a "sour" character structure or especially tragic experiences, then you are bound to be pessimistic. One psychologist remarked to me that the whole idea of the fear of death was an import by existentialists and Protestant theologians who had been scarred by their European experiences or who carried around the extra weight of a Calvinist and Lutheran heritage of life-denial. Even the distinguished psychologist Gardner Murphy (1959, p. 320) seems to lean to this school and urges us to study *the person* who exhibits the fear of death, who places anxiety in the center of his thought; and Murphy asks why the living of life in love and joy cannot also be regarded as real and basic.

THE "MORBIDLY MINDED" ARGUMENT

The "healthy-minded" argument just discussed is one side of the picture of the accumulated research and opinion on the problem of the fear of death, but there is another side. A large body of people would agree with these observations on early experience and would admit that experiences may heighten natural anxieties and later fears, but these people would also claim very strongly that nevertheless the fear of death is natural and is present in everyone, that it is the basic fear that influences all others, a fear from which no one is immune, no matter how disguised it may be. William James (1902) spoke very early for this school, and with his usual colorful realism he called death "the worm at the core" of man's pretensions to happiness. No less a student of human nature than Max Scheler thought that all men must have some kind of certain intuition of this "worm at the core," whether they admitted it or not (Choron, 1963, p. 17). Countless other authorities—some of whom we shall parade in the following pages—belong to this school: students of the stature of Freud, many of his close circle, and serious researchers who are not psychoanalysts. What are we to make of a dispute in which there are two distinct camps, both studded with distinguished authorities? Jacques Choron (1963, p. 272) goes so far as to say that it is questionable whether it will ever be possible to decide whether the fear of death is or is not the basic anxiety. In matters like this, then, the most that one can do is to take sides, to give an opinion based on the authorities that seem to him most compelling, and to present some of the compelling arguments.

I frankly side with this second school—in fact, [the book from which this article was excerpted] is a network of arguments based on the universality of the fear of death, or "terror" as I prefer to call it, in order to convey how all-consuming it is when we look it full in the face. The first document that I want to present and linger on is a paper written by the noted psychoanalyst Gregory Zilboorg (1943); it is an especially penetrating essay that—for succinctness and scope—has not been much improved upon, even though it appeared several decades ago.[2] Zilboorg says that most people think death fear is absent because it rarely shows its true face; but he argues that underneath all appearances fear of death is universally present:

For behind the sense of insecurity in the face of danger, behind the sense of discouragement and depression, there always lurks the basic fear of death, a fear which undergoes most complex elaborations and manifests itself in many indirect ways. . . . No one is free of the fear of death. . . . The anxiety neuroses, the various phobic states, even a considerable number of depressive suicidal states and many schizophrenias amply demonstrate the ever-present fear of death which becomes woven into the major conflicts of the given psychopathological conditions. . . . We may take for granted that the fear of death is always present in our mental functioning. (1943, pp. 465–67)

[2] See Eissler's (1955, p. 277) nice technical distinction between the anxiety of death and the terror of it, in his book of essays loaded with subtle discussion.

Hadn't James said the same thing earlier, in his own way?

Let sanguine healthy-mindedness do its best with its strange power of living in the moment and ignoring and forgetting, still the evil background is really there to be thought of, and the skull will grin in at the banquet. (1902, p. 121)

The difference in these two statements is not so much in the imagery and style as in the fact that Zilboorg's comes almost a half-century later and is based on that much more real clinical work, not only on philosophical speculation or personal intuition. But it also continues the straight line of development from James and the post-Darwinians who saw the fear of death as a biological and evolutionary problem. Here I think he is on very sound ground, and I especially like the way he puts the case. Zilboorg points out that this fear is actually an expression of the instinct of self-preservation, which functions as a constant drive to maintain life and to master the dangers that threaten life:

Such constant expenditure of psychological energy on the business of preserving life would be impossible if the fear of death were not as constant. The very term "self-preservation" implies an effort against some force of disintegration; the affective aspect of this is fear, fear of death. (1943, p. 467) [3]

In other words, the fear of death must be present behind all our normal functioning, in order for the organism to be armed toward self-preservation. But the fear of death cannot be present constantly in one's mental functioning, else the organism could not function. Zilboorg continues:

If this fear were constantly conscious, we should be unable to function normally. It must be properly repressed to keep us living with any modicum of comfort. We know very well that to repress means more than to put away and to forget that which was put away and the place where we put it. It means also to maintain a constant psychological effort to keep the lid on and inwardly never relax our watchfulness. (1943, p. 467)

And so we can understand what seems like an impossible paradox: the ever-present fear of death in the normal biological functioning of

---

[3] Or, we might more precisely say, with Eissler, fear of annihilation, which is extended by the ego into the consciousness of death. See Eissler (1955, p. 267).

our instinct of self-preservation, as well as our utter obliviousness to this fear in our conscious life:

Therefore in normal times we move about actually without ever believing in our own death, as if we fully believed in our own corporeal immortality. We are intent on mastering death. . . . A man will say, of course, that he knows he will die some day, but he does not really care. He is having a good time with living, and he does not think about death and does not care to bother about it—but this is a purely intellectual, verbal admission. The affect of fear is repressed.(1943, pp. 468–71)

The argument from biology and evolution is basic and has to be taken seriously; I don't see how it can be left out of any discussion. Animals in order to survive have had to be protected by fear-responses, in relation not only to other animals but to nature itself. They had to see the real relationship of their limited powers to the dangerous world in which they were immersed. Reality and fear go together naturally. As the human infant is in an even more exposed and helpless situation, it is foolish to assume that the fear response of animals would have disappeared in such a weak and highly sensitive species. It is more reasonable to think that it was instead heightened, as some of the early Darwinians thought: early men who were most afraid were those who were most realistic about their situation in nature, and they passed on to their offspring a realism that had a high survival value (cf. Shaler, 1900). The result was the emergence of man as we know him: a hyperanxious animal who constantly invents reasons for anxiety even where there are none.

The argument from psychoanalysis is less speculative and has to be taken even more seriously. It showed us something about the child's inner world that we had never realized: namely, that it was more filled with terror, the more the child was different from other animals. We could say that fear is programmed into the lower animals by ready-made instincts; but an animal who has no instincts has no programmed fears. Man's fears are fashioned out of the ways in which he perceives the world. Now, what is unique about the child's perception of the world? For one thing, the extreme confusion of cause-and-effect relationships; for another, extreme unreality about the limits of his own powers. The child lives in a situation of utter dependence; and when his needs are met it must seem to him that he has magical powers, real omnipotence. If he experiences pain, hunger, or discomfort, all he has to do is to scream and he is relieved and lulled by gentle, loving sounds. He is a magician and a telepath who has only to mumble and to imagine and the world turns to his desires.

But now the penalty for such perceptions. In a magical world where things cause other things to happen just by a mere thought or a look of displeasure, anything can happen to anyone. When the child experiences inevitable and real frustrations from his parents, he directs hate and destructive feelings toward them; and he has no way of knowing that malevolent feelings cannot be fulfilled by the same magic as were his other wishes. Psychoanalysts believe that this confusion is a main cause of guilt and helplessness in the child. In his very fine essay Wahl summed up this paradox:

> The socialization processes for all children are painful and frustrating, and hence no child escapes forming hostile death wishes toward his socializers. Therefore, none escape the fear of personal death in either direct or symbolic form. Repression is usually . . . immediate and effective. . . . (1959, pp. 24–25)

The child is too weak to take responsibility for all this destructive feeling, and he can't control the magical execution of his desires. This is what we mean by an immature ego: the child doesn't have the sure ability to organize his perceptions and his relationship to the world; he can't control his own activity; and he doesn't have sure command over the acts of others. He thus has no real control over the magical cause-and-effect that he senses, either inside himself or outside in nature and in others: his destructive wishes could explode, his parents' wishes likewise. The forces of nature are confused, externally and internally; and for a weak ego this fact makes for quantities of exaggerated potential power and added terror. The result is that the child—at least some of the time—lives with an inner sense of chaos that other animals are immune to (cf. Moloney, 1949, p. 117).

Ironically, even when the child makes out real cause-and-effect relationships they become a burden to him because he overgeneralizes them. One such generalization is what the psychoanalysts call the "talion principle." The child crushes insects, sees the cat eat a mouse and make it vanish, joins with the family to make a pet rabbit disappear into their interiors, and so on. He comes to know something about the power relations of the world but can't give them relative value: the parents could eat him and make him vanish, and he could likewise eat them; when the father gets a fierce glow in his eyes as he clubs a rat, the watching child might also expect to be clubbed—especially if he has been thinking bad magical thoughts.

I don't want to seem to make an exact picture of processes that are still unclear to us or to make out that all children live in the same world and have the same problems; also, I wouldn't want to make the child's world seem more lurid than it really is most of the time; but I think it is important to show the painful contradictions that must be present in it at least some of the time and to show how fantastic a world it surely is for the first few years of the child's life. Perhaps then we could understand better why Zilboorg said that the fear of death "undergoes most complex elaborations and manifests itself in many indirect ways." Or, as Wahl so perfectly put it, death is a *complex symbol* and not any particular, sharply defined thing to the child:

The child's concept of death is not a single thing, but it is rather a composite of mutually contradictory paradoxes . . . death itself is not only a state, but a complex symbol, the significance of which will vary from one person to another and from one culture to another. (1959, pp. 25–26)

We could understand, too, why children have their recurrent nightmares, their universal phobias of insects and mean dogs. In their tortured interiors radiate complex symbols of many inadmissible realities—terror of the world, the horror of one's own wishes, the fear of vengeance by the parents, the disappearance of things, one's lack of control over anything, really. It is too much for any animal to take, but the child has to take it, and so he wakes up screaming with almost punctual regularity during the period when his weak ego is in the process of consolidating things.

THE "DISAPPEARANCE" OF THE FEAR OF DEATH

Yet, the nightmares become more and more widely spaced, and some children have more than others: we are back again to the beginning of our discussion, to those who do not believe that the fear of death is normal, who think that it is a neurotic exaggeration that draws on bad early experiences. Otherwise, they say, how explain that so many people—the vast majority—seem to survive the flurry of childhood nightmares and go on to live a healthy, more-or-less optimistic life, untroubled by death? As Montaigne (in Choron, 1963, p. 100) said, the peasant has a profound indifference and a patience toward death and the sinister side of life; and if we say that this is because of his stupidity, then "let's all learn from stupidity." Today, when we know more than Montaigne, we would say "let's all learn from repression"—but the moral would have just as much weight: repression takes care of the complex symbol of death for most people.

But its disappearance doesn't mean that the fear was never there. The argument of those who believe in the universality of the innate terror of death rests its case mostly on what we know about how effective repression is. The argument can probably never be cleanly decided: if you claim that a concept is not present because it is repressed, you can't lose; it is not a fair game, intellectually, because you always hold the trump card. This type of argument makes psychoanalysis seem unscientific to many people, the fact that its proponents can claim that someone denies one of their concepts because he represses his consciousness of its truth.

But repression is not a magical word for winning arguments; it is a real phenomenon, and we have been able to study many of its workings. This study gives it legitimacy as a scientific concept and makes it a more or less dependable ally in our argument. For one thing, there is a growing body of research trying to get at the consciousness of death denied by repression that uses psychological tests such as measuring galvanic skin responses; it strongly suggests that underneath the most bland exterior lurks the universal anxiety, the "worm at the core" (cf., for example, Alexander, Colley, & Adlerstein, 1957; Golding, Atwood, & Goodman, 1966; Greenberg & Alexander, 1962).

For another thing, there is nothing like shocks in the real world to jar loose repressions. Recently psychiatrists reported an increase in anxiety neuroses in children as a result of the earth tremors in Southern California. For these children the discovery that life really includes cataclysmic danger was too much for their still-imperfect denial systems—hence open outbursts of anxiety. With adults we see this manifestation of anxiety in the face of impending catastrophe where it takes the form of panic. Recently several people suffered broken limbs and other injuries after forcing open their airplane's safety door during take-off and jumping from the wing to the ground; the incident was triggered by the backfire of an engine. Obviously underneath these harmless noises other things are rumbling in the creature.

But even more important is how repression works: it is not simply a negative force opposing life energies; it lives on life energies and uses them creatively. I mean that fears are naturally absorbed by expansive organismic striving. Nature seems to have built into organisms an innate healthy-mindedness; it expresses itself in self-delight, in the pleasure of unfolding one's capacities into the world, in the incorporation of things in that world, and in feeding on its limitless experiences. This is a lot of very positive experience, and when a powerful organism moves with it, it gives contentment. As Santayana once put it: a lion must feel more secure that God is on his side than a gazelle. On the most elemental level the organism works actively against its own fragility by seeking to expand and perpetuate itself in living experience; instead of shrinking, it moves toward more life. Also, it does one thing at a time, avoiding needless distractions from all-absorbing activity; in this way, it would seem, fear of death can be carefully ignored or actually absorbed in the life-expanding processes. Occasionally we seem to see such a vital organism on the human level: I am thinking of the portrait of *Zorba the Greek* drawn by Nikos Kazantzakis. Zorba was an ideal of the nonchalant victory of all-absorbing daily passion over timidity and death, and he purged others in his life-affirming flame. But Kazantzakis himself was no Zorba—which is partly why the character of Zorba rang a bit false—nor are most other men. Still, everyone enjoys a working amount of basic narcissism, even though it is not a lion's. The child who is well nourished and loved develops, as we said, a sense of magical omnipotence, a sense of his own indestructibility, a feeling of proven power and secure support. He can imagine himself, deep down, to be eternal. We might say that his repression of the idea of his own death is made easy for him because he is fortified against it in his very narcissistic vitality. This type of character probably helped Freud to say that the unconscious does not know death. Anyway, we know that basic narcissism is increased when one's child-hood experiences have been securely lifesupporting and warmly en-hancing to the sense of self, to the feeling of being really special, truly Number One in creation. The result is that some people have more of what the psychoanalyst Leon J. Saul (1970) has aptly called "Inner Sustainment." It is a sense of bodily confidence in the face of experience that sees the person more easily through severe life crises and even sharp personality changes; it almost seems to take the place of the directive instincts of lower animals. One can't help thinking of Freud again, who had more inner sustainment than most men, thanks to his mother and favorable early environment; he knew the confidence and courage that it gave to a man, and he himself faced up to life and to a fatal cancer with a Stoic heroism. Again we have evidence that the complex symbol of fear of death would be very vari-able in its intensity; it would be, as Wahl (1959, p. 26) concluded, "profoundly dependent upon the nature and the vicissitudes of the developmental process."

But I want to be careful not to make too much of natural vitality and inner sustainment. . . . Even the unusually favored Freud suf-fered his whole life from phobias and from death-anxiety; and he came to fully perceive the world under the aspect of natural terror. I don't believe that the complex symbol of death is ever absent, no matter how much vitality and inner sustainment a person has. Even more, if we say that these powers make repression easy and natural, we are only saying the half of it. Actually, they get their very power from repression. Psychiatrists argue that the fear of death varies in intensity depending on the developmental process, and I think that one important reason for this variability is that the fear is transmuted in that process. If the child has had a very favorable upbringing, it only serves all the better to hide the fear of death. After all, repres-sion is made possible by the natural identification of the child with the powers of his parents. If he has been well cared for, identification comes easily and solidly, and his parents' powerful triumph over death automatically becomes his. What is more natural to banish one's fears than to live on delegated powers? And what does the whole growing-up period signify, if not the giving over of one's life-project? . . . What we will see is that man cuts out for himself a manageable world: he throws himself into action uncritically, unthinkingly. He accepts the cultural programming that turns his nose where he is supposed to look; he doesn't bite the world off in one piece as a giant would, but in small manageable pieces, as a beaver does. He uses all kinds of techniques, which we call the "character defenses": he learns not to expose himself, not to stand out; he learns to embed himself in other-power, both of concrete persons and of things and cultural commands; the result is that he comes to exist in the imagined infallibility of the world around him. He doesn't have to have fears when his feet are solidly mired and his life mapped out in a ready-made maze. All he has to do is to plunge ahead in a compulsive style of drivenness in the "ways of the world" that the child learns and in which he lives later as a kind of grim equanimity—the "strange power of living in the moment and ignoring and forgetting"—as James put it. This is the deeper reason that Montaigne's peasant isn't troubled until the very end, when the Angel of Death, who has always been sitting on his shoulder, extends his wing. Or at least until he is prematurely startled into dumb awareness, like the "Husbands" in John Cassavetes' fine film. At times like this, when the awareness dawns that has always been blotted out by frenetic, ready-made activity, we see the transmutation of repression redistilled, so to speak, and the fear of death emerges in pure essence. This is why people have psychotic breaks when repression no longer works, when the forward momentum of activity is no longer possible. Besides, the peasant mentality is far less romantic than Montaigne would have us believe. The peasant's equanimity is usually immersed in a style of life that has elements of real madness, and so it protects him: an undercurrent of constant hate and bitterness expressed in feuding, bullying, bickering and family quarrels, the petty mentality, the self-deprecation, the superstition, the obsessive control of daily life by a strict authoritarianism, and so on. As the title of a recent essay by Joseph Lopreato has it: "How would you like to be a peasant?"

[There is] another large dimension in which the complex symbol of death is transmuted and transcended by man—belief in immortality, the extension of one's being into eternity. Right now we can conclude that there are many ways that repression works to calm the anxious human animal, so that he need not be anxious at all.

I think we have reconciled our two divergent positions on the fear of death. The "environmental" and the "innate" positions are both part of the same picture; they merge naturally into one another; it all depends from which angle you approach the picture: from the side of the disguises and transmutations of the fear of death or from the side of its apparent absence. I admit with a sense of scientific uneasiness that whatever angle you use, you don't get at the actual fear of death; and so I reluctantly agree with Choron that the argument can probably never be cleanly "won." Nevertheless something very important emerges: there are different images of man that he can draw and choose from.

On the one hand, we see a human animal who is partly dead to the world, who is most "dignified" when he shows a certain obliviousness to his fate, when he allows himself to be driven through life; who is most "free" when he lives in secure dependency on powers around him, when he is least in possession of himself. On the other hand, we get an image of a human animal who is overly sensitive to the world, who cannot shut it out, who is thrown back on his own meagre powers, and who seems least free to move and act, least in possession of himself, and most undignified. Whichever image we choose to identify with depends in large part upon ourselves. . . .

23

Reactions to the Imminence of Death

THOMAS P. HACKETT
and
AVERY D. WEISMAN

In a large general hospital, where numerous deaths occur in the course of a day, it is almost impossible to find a dying patient who is allowed to respond to the imminence of death in his own way. By the time he reaches his deathbed, the attitudes and fixed opinions of physicians and relatives have been thrust upon him. With the "best interest" of the patient at heart they encourage and offer hope even before the patient expresses a desire for such reassurance. The healthy human being assumes that the threat of death eclipses all other fears and does not realize that the dying patient may not share this point of view. Although the prospect of death is awesome and fearful to those about to die, it does not necessarily exclude other concerns.

This presentation deals with two groups of people: (1) terminal cancer patients who are facing certain death, and (2) patients with severe myocardial disease who have a chance of survival, but who are threatened with the possibility of imminent death. It will be shown that both groups react to the death threat by denying it in various ways, some effective and some not. The effectiveness of this denial (Engel, 1962; Freud, 1937; Lewin, 1950), we feel, depends to a large extent upon the way in which it is handled by those who care for the patient. We define denial as the repudiation of part or all of the available meaning of an event for the purpose of minimizing fear and anxiety.

The importance of the attitudes of others and their influence on the way in which a patient reacts to the threat of his death became apparent to us a few years ago when we began to investigate the emotional responses of 28 patients in the terminal stages of cancer (Hackett and Weisman, 1962; Weisman and Hackett, 1962). Each was seen approximately four times a week until he died. Relatives were interviewed when possible, and close communication existed between the psychiatrist and the surgeon or internist in charge of the case. All these patients had been told they had cancer, but none had been informed that he would die within a short time.

From our interviews with patients, families, nurses, and physicians we found two seemingly incongruous patterns. Relatives, nurses, and doctors substantiated what most of us believe to be true of the dying patient—that he is an expert at denying that he is dying. On the other hand, when the tape recordings of these interviews were examined in detail, we found quite obvious references to impending death. Threatening dreams, nightmares, slips of the tongue, references to loneliness and grief, and the tendency to recount stories of fatal illnesses they had witnessed in friends or relatives documented our suspicion that these patients were deeply concerned about the true nature of their disease. Hesitant and indirect questions about what could be expected of the future offered the investigators the opportunity to share the fears of their patients. Such inquiries were generally so unobtrusive that the physician could easily disregard them if he chose. Not all 28 patients disclosed their fears to the same degree. Some directed their concern to continuing symptoms, especially to physical pain, rather than to death itself; but all revealed more about themselves as a result of having a receptive listener.

Because the attitude of the visitor so often determined the type of communication, it was possible for two people to come away from separate visits to a sickroom, each maintaining an opposite point of view. The first might say the patient was untroubled and confident, the other that the patient was deeply concerned about his immediate fate. More often than not, the visitor, intent on encouraging optimism, heard only what he wanted to hear. The fear of death was not openly expressed. Instead, the patient would complain of symptoms without inquiring about the reasons for their persistence. He would often speak tentatively about the distant future when he would be well. Such a remark offered an ideal chance for the optimist to join in the planning. If this were done, the patient appeared to be animated and pleased. Should the visitor refrain, the patient usually became silent and somber. All of the 28 patients were aware of false optimism. Yet, at the same time, they gave every appearance of being susceptible, grasping and clinging to the flimsiest of hopes. It was as though their ability to deal consistently with the reality of their illness was determined in large part by the attitude of their visitors.

It is difficult for most people to succeed in deceiving those who know them well. The husband of a patient in the terminal phase of carcinoma of the cervix said, "I couldn't tell her with a straight face she'd get better. She'd see right through me." With this man deception would impose a telltale strain. His wife might be heartened to receive good news, but would, at the same time, be aware of the way it was imparted. The doctor faces a similar scrutiny, even though he may be a stranger to the patient. Often, it is not what he says, but the manner in which he expresses it, that alerts the patient. Sixteen of the 28 patients complained that their doctors told them too little and tended to generalize in the answers they did give. On the other hand, the patient's questions were usually asked in such a way that a generalization would supply a seemingly adequate reply. In only one instance did a patient ask her doctor whether she was going to die soon. The direct question is more often put to individuals who are not in a position to answer it, such as ward attendants and student nurses, whose discomfiture adds to the patient's sense of alarm.

ATTITUDES OF THE PATIENT

As a result of a change in the attitudes of those around him, a change based largely upon the desire to generate false hope, the patient comes to know that he is dying. It is a peculiar kind of knowledge because it seems to violate everything he most wants to believe or everything that people think he wants to believe. We have used the term "middle knowledge" (Hackett and Weisman, 1962; Weis man and Hackett, 1961, 1962) to describe the dying patient's awareness of his imminent death. He is between knowing that what his body tells him means death and what those around him deny is death. He yields to their encouragement because to do otherwise would risk the loss of human contact—a loss as genuinely threatening as death itself. His ability to reject selectively the significance of symptoms increases at times so that he can actually experience transient hope. But always underneath is the gnawing fear that a hoax is being perpetrated on him. He is truly in the middle of knowing and not knowing. Hinton (1963), in his study of 102 dying patients, observed that "at least three-quarters of the patients here studied became aware that they were probably dying." He goes on to say, "If a patient sincerely wanted to know his possible fate, and was met by prevarication or empty reassurance, he felt lonely and mistrustful."

The most agonizing and intolerable threat to the dying is loneliness—the feeling of being apart from the lives of others. The loneliness is compounded by a perceptible change which occurs in those who care for them. The living tend to draw away from the dying. Sometimes it is an obvious withdrawal, more often a subtle sense of growing estrangement. Anyone who has been through a deathwatch appreciates the difficulty of being a helpless observer when someone's life is dwindling away. Much of this hardship can be alleviated for the visitor if he encourages the patient to think about an eventual recovery and a return to health. This type of myth-making is largely for the benefit of the visitor. The patient soon comes to find that when he does hint at wanting to know more and when he is skeptical of what the doctors tell him, his inquiries are met with awkward silences, scoldings about losing faith, or broad blandishments of hope. He learns that to pursue his doubts by asking questions seldom yields more than uneasiness between himself and those upon whom he depends for companionship. Therefore he stops asking and becomes a player in the deathbed drama in which optimism is the theme. For the terminal patient the effectiveness of denial is sharply undercut by "middle knowledge," which is the product of both the patient's ability to assess the reality of the facts of his illness and his capacity for gauging the honesty of others.

Since the treatment of the terminal patient is not the major concern of this paper, the reader is referred to the principal contributors in this field (Eissler, 1955; Feifel, 1959; Worcester, 1940). The most controversial issue in therapy always revolves about the amount of information the patient should be given. Those who believe that the patient should be encouraged to deny focus their therapy on ways of judiciously supplementing the patient's use of denial. The others, who feel that many patients have less capacity to use denial than is commonly thought, direct their attention toward minimizing those factors, among which denial is a frequent offender, which augment the feeling of isolation and loneliness in the dying. They believe that being the victim of a silent conspiracy between doctors and relatives imposes as much pain upon the patient as the facts of his illness. If there is a way of preparing the dying for death, it will have as its foundation the affirmation of warmth and affection between the patient and those who are about to be bereft.

In contrast to the person dying of cancer, the patient who has sustained a myocardial infarction appears to derive more benefit from denial. Our work with the cardiac patient began with an investigation of 23 patients placed on the monitor cardiac pacemaker (Browne and Hackett, unpublished data). This group was chosen because it consisted of people facing a death threat in a setting which we felt might accentuate fear. As a rule, one of every two patients requiring pacemaker assistance succumbs. The appearance of the instrument was not designed to comfort the patient. It consists of an oscillograph which makes a continuous recording of the patient's EKG and an audible bleep which accompanies the pulse. The bleep, which sounds like the nagging peep of a newly hatched chick, alerts the nurse to cardiac irregularities. Should the heart stop, an alarm bell rings and an automatic shocking device sends jolts of electricity to stimulate the myocardium. This device is at the patient's bedside. We predicted that our patients would prefer having the apparatus out of their rooms, monitored at some central point where they could not hear the bleep or see the tracing. This was not the case—another reflection of how often the healthy fail in their attempts to empathize with the sick and dying.

Of the 23 patients, 4 were in semicoma, 5 were delirious and 14 were alert and responsive. Only one of the 14 was frightened by the machine. The remaining 13 patients regarded it as a friendly protector. This attitude was enhanced by the nurse who admitted them to the ward. She, with providential wisdom, introduced the pacemaker as a "mechanical guardian angel" without, of course, mentioning that its capacity for salvaging failing hearts was limited (Craffey, 1960). Even those patients who experienced the painful shocks did not mind having the pacemaker in the room. Instead of being apprehensive at having to listen to the bleep which accompanied every heartbeat, 12 patients interpreted the sound as a reassurance that everything was all right. One patient was annoyed by the sound but wanted the machine in his room despite it. The most common fantasy was that as long as they were attached to the machine their hearts could not stop. It was not unusual for these patients to experience anxiety when being weaned from the pacemaker. The majority chose to regard the machine as an ally and to reject the recognition that it also vividly presented evidence of their precarious condition.

Along with concentrating on the salutary aspects of the pacemaker, these same 13 patients consistently denied that their hearts were severely damaged and that they feared death. This type of denial can be separated into two groups which we may call major and partial denial. The group of major deniers consisted of 7 males, all of whom denied having any fear or worry about their illness. Each believed that too much attention was being given his heart. Even though 3 of them had suffered from previous coronaries, and 2 others had been shocked by the pacemaker, they denied concern about the possibility of dying or even of being unable to return to their old manner of life and work. Their life histories were filled with situations in which the death stress was met with denial. For example, one who had been the victim of a bandit had charged the gunman, was wounded three times, and afterwards asserted that he had never considered the possibility of being killed before, during, or after this incident. Another had spent three weeks on a life raft in the Pacific, never doubting that he would be rescued. All had histories of anginal pain for which help was never sought. Characteristically, when the symptoms of the myocardial infarction began, these patients ignored them until others noticed their distress and insisted on their seeking hospital attention. Illness they considered a weakness, and those who allowed themselves to acknowledge it, weaklings. They all shared what could best be described as an exaggerated Victorian concept of manly behavior. They believed that a true man did not feel fear or if he felt it, never admitted that he did.

The 6 patients in the category of partial deniers were similar to the major deniers, except that, upon closer questioning, they admitted having experienced fear as a reaction to their illness even while they tended to minimize it. Their pasts were not as florid with examples of stoicism in the face of adversity as were the others'. They tended to rationalize the symptoms of their heart attacks as "indigestion" or "muscle strain" rather than to attempt to ignore the symptoms altogether. One patient, a man in his late twenties with an extensive family history of coronary disease, experienced severe precordial pain following his participation in a wrestling match. He immediately thought that he was having a heart attack but felt that his age was against it. In order to decide the issue he determined to run up five flights of stairs to his apartment, thinking that if it was his heart he would die; if not, he would live. He made the effort, almost perishing on the way, and fell into bed gasping, but happy in the knowledge that his distress was not "coronary trouble." Even after he had been admitted to the hospital and diagnosed as having a massive myocardial infarction, he tended to doubt the diagnosis as the result of his experiment with the stairs. Nevertheless, he submitted to the restrictions placed upon him and behaved as though he fully believed what he had been told by his doctor. Like all other patients in the category of partial deniers, he spoke of the future as though it would in no way be altered by his illness.

Both the major and the partial deniers displayed emotions entirely consistent with what they said. Anxiety and depression were not in evidence. No patient required tranquillizers. However, as we analyzed the tape recorded interviews, there were inconsistencies, contradictions, and slips of the tongue which readily demonstrated the presence of "middle knowledge." It was not, however, as undermining or as minatory as the "middle knowledge" of the cancer patient. One reason for the difference, we feel, is that the cardiac patient's tendency to minimize or deny was honestly augmented by the attitude of those who attended him. There was no silent conspiracy between doctor and relatives because everyone was in agreement that hope was of paramount importance. The cardiac patient did not have to be deceived. The encouragement offered him stemmed from the knowledge that legitimate hope existed. He could indeed pull through this episode and live out a considerable span of years. Death, although a genuine possibility, was not an imminent certainty. Relatives, as well as hospital personnel, did not have to pretend or act out an optimism which had no basis in fact. Although the cardiac patient was more concerned about his heart and future than he would directly admit, he did not suffer the alien and lonely fear of being deceived. While it is true that he selectively denied many grim aspects of his illness and converted the pacemaker into an ally without recognizing its more sinister meaning, the cardiac patient's denial could honestly be bolstered by those who were responsible for his health.

Whereas the terminal cancer patient often has a legitimate basis for complaining that he has been deserted by his doctors and nurses, the critical cardiac patient was constantly looked after. None spoke of being lonely. On the contrary, their most frequent complaint was of receiving too much attention for what they considered a minor condition. Their denial was never challenged directly or inadvertently. The close attention they received was in marked contrast to the situation of the patient dying from a malignancy. When the latter is pronounced incurable, the physician often asks the chaplain to make regular visits and concomitantly withdraws his presence. At the same time that he substitutes the chaplain's visits for his own, the doctor frequently increases the amount of narcotics administered to the patient who has been declared terminal. This is especially obvious when the doctor has judiciously limited the narcotic intake over long periods against the patient's will. When this change is abrupt and unexplained, the patient invariably interprets it as a sign that nothing more can be done for him.

The tendency of the human being exposed to the threat of death to negate or alter the meaning of the threat along less stressful lines is further illustrated in another study of cardiac patients (Olin and Hackett, unpublished data). Thirty-two randomly selected cases of acute myocardial infarction were interviewed very shortly after admission to the hospital. None appeared anxious or overly concerned about his condition. Reassurance about prognosis and the future was not requested. All denied being frightened. The initial symptom in each case was chest pain, which was severe in 27 cases. The average duration of the pain from its onset to the time active measures were taken to obtain medical help was 5.2 hours. This delay in seeking help is explained by the patient's attempts to rationalize the cause of his discomfort. Fifteen patients believed they had severe indigestion and sought relief through antacids and other self-administered medications. Four thought they were coming down with a lung condition such as pneumonia. Nine diagnosed themselves as possibly having heart trouble and the remaining 4 attributed the pain respectively to cancer, a cold, an ulcer, and fatigue. The 9 who correctly diagnosed their condition as "coronary" delayed obtaining medical help an average of 10.3 hours (twice that of the others), indicating that suspecting a diagnosis does not always result in appropriate action. In fact, the longest period of delay in the group (60 hours) was endured by one of these 9. All 32 patients responded to the pain as though they were determined to avoid, at all costs, acknowledging its true significance. This came to light as the data revealed that 24 patients were familiar with coronary disease either through having had anginal attacks, a previous myocardial infarction, or through witnessing it in a relative or close friend. Thirteen of the 24 patients had histories of anginal attacks and of these, 4 had been hospitalized with previous myocardial infarctions. Obtaining a past history of symptoms suggesting coronary disease in either the patient or his relatives was not always a simple matter. Four patients in this series denied having had anginal attacks and 6 others gave a negative family history. Whereas subsequent interviews with relatives tended to substantiate the patient's account of his present illness, they also revealed alarming gaps in memory for significant past events. The wife of one man said that he had been troubled by severe attacks of precordial pain for a number of years before his present admission. Upon being confronted by this he minimized these spells as "acute indigestion." "They always went away when I burped or took sodium bicarb." When he was told that the "spells," as described by his wife, often occurred when he was working vigorously, he replied, "Yeah, that's why you sweat, to get the acid out. It builds up in your stomach and you get pain. My father had the same thing." It turned out that his father, who he said had died of a "shock" had complained for years of "indigestion" and then dropped dead suddenly. A check with the family doctor disclosed that the patient's father had been taking nitroglycerine tablets regularly, not antacids as the patient had remembered. In taking the history of the coronary patient, one must remember to verify the absence of symptoms with a relative.

For the groups of patients studied, denial was the common response to the stress of imminent death. The defense of denial is always accompanied by a "middle knowledge" which indicates underlying doubts antipathetic to the goal of denial. The power or extent of the "middle knowledge" depends in large part upon the patient's interpersonal relationships. Its effectiveness depends in large part on the way it is dealt with in an interpersonal setting. If the other party honestly endorses the optimism he offers the patient, which seems to be so with our cardiac cases, "middle knowledge" does not undermine the effectiveness of denial. When, however, the other party cannot genuinely reciprocate hopefulness and must rely upon myth-making to create an aura of optimism, the flaws of the deception do not escape the terminal cancer patient. "Middle knowledge" undercuts the usefulness of their denial whether it is experienced as open doubt or as vague uneasiness. In treating any critically ill patient one must always assume that he harbors many unspoken questions. The physician should not offer unsolicited answers for these questions but should develop a relationship in which the patient is free to raise whatever issues he chooses.

24

Symptomatology and Management of Acute Grief

INTRODUCTION

At first glance, acute grief would not seem to be a medical or psychiatric disorder in the strict sense of the word but rather a normal reaction to a distressing situation. However, the understanding of reactions to traumatic experiences whether or not they represent clear-cut neuroses has become of ever-increasing importance to the psychiatrist. Bereavement or the sudden cessation of social interaction seems to be of special interest because it is often cited among the alleged psychogenic factors in psychosomatic disorders. The enormous increase in grief reactions due to war casualties, furthermore, demands an evaluation of their probable effect on the mental and physical health of our population.

The points to be made in this paper are as follows:

1. Acute grief is a definite syndrome with psychological and somatic symptomatology.

2. This syndrome may appear immediately after a crisis; it may be delayed; it may be exaggerated or apparently absent.

3. In place of the typical syndrome there may appear distorted pictures, each of which represents one special aspect of the grief syndrome.

4. By the appropriate techniques these distorted pictures can be

Read at the Centenary Meeting of The American Psychiatric Association, Philadelphia, Pa., May 15–18, 1944.

successfully transformed into a normal grief reaction with resolution. Our observations comprise 101 patients. Included are (1) psychoneurotic patients who lost a relative during the course of treatment, (2) relatives of patients who died in the hospital, (3) bereaved disaster victims (Cocoanut Grove Fire) and their close relatives, (4) relatives of members of the armed forces.

The investigation consisted of a series of psychiatric interviews. Both the timing and the content of the discussions were recorded. These records were subsequently analysed in terms of the symptoms reported and of the changes in mental status observed progressively through a series of interviews. The psychiatrist avoided all suggestions and interpretations until the picture of symptomatology and spontaneous reaction tendencies of the patients had become clear from the records. The somatic complaints offered important leads for objective study. Careful laboratory work on spirograms, g.-i. functions, and metabolic studies are in progress and will be reported separately. At present we wish to present only our psychological observations.

SYMPTOMATOLOGY OF NORMAL GRIEF

The picture shown by persons in acute grief is remarkably uniform. Common to all is the following syndrome: sensations of somatic distress occurring in waves lasting from twenty minutes to an hour at a time, a feeling of tightness in the throat, choking with shortness of breath, need for sighing, and an empty feeling in the abdomen, lack of muscular power, and an intense subjective distress described as tension or mental pain. The patient soon learns that these waves of discomfort can be precipitated by visits, by mentioning the deceased, and by receiving sympathy. There is a tendency to avoid the syndrome at any cost, to refuse visits lest they should precipitate the reaction, and to keep deliberately from thought all references to the deceased.

The striking features are (1) the marked tendency to sighing respiration; this respiratory disturbance was most conspicuous when the patient was made to discuss his grief. (2) The complaint about lack of strength and exhaustion is universal and is described as follows: "It is almost impossible to climb up a stairway." "Everything I lift seems so heavy." "The slightest effort makes me feel exhausted." "I can't walk to the corner without feeling exhausted." (3) Digestive symptoms are described as follows: "The food tastes like sand." "I have no appetite at all." "I stuff the food down because I have to eat." "My saliva won't flow." "My abdomen feels hollow." "Everything seems slowed up in my stomach."

The sensorium is generally somewhat altered. There is commonly a slight sense of unreality, a feeling of increased emotional distance from other people (sometimes they appear shadowy or small), and there is intense preoccupation with the image of the deceased. A patient who lost his daughter in the Cocoanut Grove disaster visualized his girl in the telephone booth calling for him and was much troubled by the loudness with which his name was called by her and was so vividly preoccupied with the scene that he became oblivious to his surroundings. A young navy pilot lost a close friend; he remained a vivid part of his imagery, not in terms of a religious survival but in terms of an imaginary companion. He ate with him and talked over problems with him, for instance, discussing with him his plan of joining the Air Corps. Up to the time of the study, six months later, he denied the fact that the boy was no longer with him. Some patients are much concerned about this aspect of their grief reaction because they feel it indicates approaching insanity.

Another strong preoccupation is with feelings of guilt. The bereaved searches the time before the death for evidence of failure to do right by the lost one. He accuses himself of negligence and exaggerates minor omissions. After the fire disaster the central topic of discussion for a young married woman was the fact that her husband died after he left her following a quarrel, and a young man whose wife died was preoccupied with having fainted too soon to save her.

In addition, there is often disconcerting loss of warmth in relationship to other people, a tendency to respond with irritability and anger, a wish not to be bothered by others at a time when friends and relatives make a special effort to keep up friendly relationships.

These feelings of hostility, surprising and quite inexplicable to the patients, disturbed them and again were often taken as signs of approaching insanity. Great efforts are made to handle them, and the result is often a formalized, stiff manner of social interaction.

The activity throughout the day of the severely bereaved person shows remarkable changes. There is no retardation of action and speech; quite the contrary, there is a push of speech, especially when talking about the deceased. There is restlessness, inability to sit still, moving about in an aimless fashion, continually searching for something to do. There is, however, at the same time, a painful lack of capacity to initiate and maintain organized patterns of activity. What is done is done with lack of zest, as though one were going through the motions. The bereaved clings to the daily routine of prescribed activities: but these activities do not proceed in the automatic, self-sustaining fashion which characterizes normal work but have to be carried on with effort, as though each fragment of the activity became a special task. The bereaved is surprised to find how large a part of his customary activity was done in some meaningful relationship to the deceased and has now lost its significance. Especially the habits of social interaction—meeting friends, making conversation, sharing enterprises with others—seem to have been lost. This loss leads to a strong dependency on anyone who will stimulate the bereaved to activity and serve as the initiating agent.

These five points—(1) somatic distress, (2) preoccupation with the image of the deceased, (3) guilt, (4) hostile reactions, and (5) loss of patterns of conduct—seem to be pathognomonic for grief. There may be added a sixth characteristic, shown by patients who border on pathological reactions, which is not so conspicuous as the others but nevertheless often striking enough to color the whole picture. This is the appearance of traits of the deceased in the behavior of the bereaved, especially symptoms shown during the last illness, or behavior which may have been shown at the time of the tragedy. A bereaved person is observed or finds himself walking in the manner of his deceased father. He looks in the mirror and believes that his face appears just like that of the deceased. He may show a change of interests in the direction of the former activities of the deceased and may start enterprises entirely different from his former pursuits. A wife who lost her husband, an insurance agent, found herself writing to many insurance companies offering her services with somewhat exaggerated schemes. It seemed a regular observation in these patients that the painful preoccupation with the image of the deceased described above was transformed into preoccupation with symptoms or personality traits of the lost person, but now displaced to their own bodies and activities by identification.

COURSE OF NORMAL GRIEF REACTIONS

The duration of a grief reaction seems to depend upon the success with which a person does the *grief work,* namely emancipation from the bondage to the deceased, readjustment to the environment in which the deceased is missing, and the formation of new relationships. One of the big obstacles to this work seems to be the fact that many patients try to avoid the intense distress connected with the grief experience and to avoid the expression of emotion necessary for it. The men victims after the Cocoanut Grove fire appeared in the early psychiatric interviews to be in a state of tension with tightened facial musculature, unable to relax for fear they might "break down." It required considerable persuasion to yield to the grief process before they were willing to accept the discomfort of bereavement. One assumed a hostile attitude toward the psychiatrist, refusing to allow any references to the deceased and rather rudely asking him to leave. This attitude remained throughout his stay on the ward, and the prognosis for his condition is not good in the light of other observations. Hostility of this sort was encountered on only occasional visits with the other patients. They became willing to accept the grief process and to embark on a program of dealing in memory with the deceased person. As soon as this became possible there seemed to be a rapid relief of tension and the subsequent interviews were rather animated conversations in which the deceased was idealized and in which misgivings about the future adjustment were worked through.

Examples of the psychiatrist's role in assisting patients in their readjustment after bereavement are contained in the following case histories. The first shows a very successful readjustment.

A woman, aged 40, lost her husband in the fire. She had a history of good adjustment previously. One child, ten years old. When she heard about her husband's death she was extremely depressed, cried bitterly did not want to live, and for three days showed a state of utter dejection.

When seen by the psychiatrist, she was glad to have assistance and described her painful preoccupation with memories of her husband and her fear that she might lose her mind. She had a vivid visual image of his presence, picturing him as going to work in the morning and herself as work dering whether he would return in the evening, whether she could stand his not returning, then, describing to herself how he does return, plays with the dog, receives his child, and gradually she tries to accept the fact that he is not there any more. It was only after ten days that she succeeded in accepting his loss and then only after having described in detail the remarkable qualities of her husband, the tragedy of his having to stop his activities at the pinnacle of his success, and his deep devotion to her.

In the subsequent interviews she explained with some distress that she had become very much attached to the examiner and that she waited for the hour of his coming. This reaction she considered disloyal to her husband but at the same time she could accept the fact that it was a hopeful sign of her ability to fill the gap he had left in her life. She then showed a marked drive for activity, making plans for supporting herself and her little girl, mapping out the preliminary steps for resuming her old profession as secretary, and making efforts to secure help from the occupational therapy department in reviewing her knowledge of French.

Her convalescence, both emotional and somatic, progressed smoothly, and she made a good adjustment immediately on her return home.

A man of 52, successful in business, lost his wife, with whom he had lived in happy marriage. The information given him about his wife's death confirmed his suspicions of several days. He responded with a severe grief reaction, with which he was unable to cope. He did not want to see visitors, was ashamed of breaking down, and asked to be permitted to stay in the hospital on the psychiatric service, when his physical condition would have permitted his discharge, because he wanted further assistance. Any mention of his wife produced a severe wave of depressive reaction, but with psychiatric assistance he gradually became willing to go through this painful process, and after three days on the psychiatric service he seemed well enough to go home.

He showed a high rate of verbal activity, was restless, needed to be occupied continually, and felt that the experience had whipped him into a state of restless overactivity.

As soon as he returned home he took an active part in his business, assuming a post in which he had a great many telephone calls. He also took over the role of amateur psychiatrist to another bereaved person, spending time with him and comforting him for his loss. In his eagerness to start anew, he developed a plan to sell all his former holdings, including his house, his furniture, and giving away anything which could remind him of his wife. Only after considerable discussion was he able to see that this would mean avoiding immediate grief at the price of an act of poor judgment. Again he had to be encouraged to deal with his grief reactions in a more direct manner. He has made a good adjustment.

With eight to ten interviews in which the psychiatrist shares the grief work, and with a period of from four to six weeks, it was ordinarily possible to settle an uncomplicated and undistorted grief reaction. This was the case in all but one of the 13 Cocoanut Grove fire victims.

Morbid grief reactions represent distortions of normal grief. The conditions mentioned here were transformed into "normal reactions" and then found their resolution.

a. *Delay of Reaction.* The most striking and most frequent reaction of this sort is *delay* or *postponement.* If the bereavement occurs at a time when the patient is confronted with important tasks and when there is necessity for maintaining the morale of others, he may show little or no reaction for weeks or even much longer. A brief delay is described in the following example.

> A girl of 17 lost both parents and her boy friend in the fire and was herself burned severely, with marked involvement of the lungs. Throughout her stay in the hospital her attitude was that of cheerful acceptance without any sign of adequate distress. When she was discharged at the end of three weeks she appeared cheerful, talked rapidly, with a considerable flow of ideas, seemed eager to return home and to assume the role of parent for her two younger siblings. Except for slight feelings of "lonesomeness" she complained of no distress.
>
> This period of griefless acceptance continued for the next two months, even when the household was dispersed and her younger siblings were placed in other homes. Not until the end of the tenth week did she begin to show a true state of grief with marked feelings of depression, intestinal emptiness, tightness in her throat, frequent crying, and vivid preoccupation with her deceased parents.

That this delay may involve years became obvious first by the fact that patients in acute bereavement about a recent death may soon upon exploration be found preoccupied with grief about a person who died many years ago. In this manner a woman of 38, whose mother had died recently and who had responded to the mother's death with a surprisingly severe reaction, was found to be but mildly concerned with her mother's death but deeply engrossed with unhappy and perplexing fantasies concerning the death of her brother, who died twenty years ago under dramatic circumstances from metastasizing carcinoma after amputation of his arm had been postponed too long

he discovery that a former unresolved grief reaction may be precipi-
ated in the course of the discussion of another recent event was soon
emonstrated in psychiatric interviews by patients who showed all
ne traits of a true grief reaction when the topic of a former loss
ose.

The precipitating factor for the delayed reaction may be a deliber-
te recall of circumstances surrounding the death or may be a sponta-
eous occurrence in the patient's life. A peculiar form of this is the
ircumstance that a patient develops the grief reaction at the time
rhen he himself is as old as the person who died. For instance, a
uilroad worker, aged 42, appeared in the psychiatric clinic with a
icture which was undoubtedly a grief reaction for which he had no
xplanation. It turned out that when he was 22, his mother, then
2, had committed suicide.

b. *Distorted Reactions.* The delayed reactions may occur after an in-
erval which was not marked by any abnormal behavior or distress,
ut in which there developed an *alteration* in the patient's *conduct*
erhaps not conspicuous or serious enough to lead him to a psychia-
rist. These alterations may be considered as the surface manifesta-
ions of an unresolved grief reaction, which may respond to fairly
imple and quick psychiatric management if recognized. They may
e classified as follows: (1) *overactivity without a sense of loss,* rather
rith a sense of wellbeing and zest, the activities being of an expan-
ive and adventurous nature and bearing semblance to the activities
ormerly carried out by the deceased, as described above; (2) *the
cquisition of symptoms belonging to the last illness of the deceased.* This
ype of patient appears in medical clinics and is often labelled hypo-
hondriasis or hysteria. To what extent actual alterations of physio-
ogical functions occur under these circumstances will have to be a
ield of further careful inquiry. I owe to Dr. Chester Jones a report
bout a patient whose electrocardiogram showed a definite change
uring a period of three weeks, which started two weeks after the
ime her father died of heart disease.

While this sort of symptom formation "by identification" may still
e considered as conversion symptoms such as we know from hyste-
ia, there is another type of disorder doubtlessly presenting (3) a
ecognized *medical disease,* namely, a group of psychosomatic condi-
ions, predominantly ulcerative colitis, rheumatoid arthritis, and

asthma. Extensive studies in ulcerative colitis have produced evidence that 33 out of 41 patients with ulcerative colitis developed their disease in close time relationship to the loss of an important person. Indeed, it was this observation which first gave the impetus for the present detailed study of grief. Two of the patients developed bloody diarrhea at funerals. In the others it developed within a few weeks after the loss. The course of the ulcerative colitis was strikingly benefited when this grief reaction was resolved by psychiatric technique.

At the level of social adjustment there often occurs a conspicuous (4) *alteration in relationship to friends and relatives.* The patient feels irritable, does not want to be bothered, avoids former social activities, and is afraid he might antagonize his friends by his lack of interest and his critical attitudes. Progressive social isolation follows, and the patient needs considerable encouragement in re-establishing his social relationships.

While overflowing hostility appears to be spread out over all relationships, it may also occur as (5) *furious hostility against specific persons;* the doctor or the surgeon are accused bitterly for neglect of duty and the patient may assume that foul play has led to the death. It is characteristic that while patients talk a good deal about their suspicions and their bitter feelings, they are not likely to take any action against the accused, as a truly paranoid person might do.

Many bereaved persons struggle with much effort against these feelings of hostility, which to them seem absurd, representing a vicious change in their characters. [They want these feelings] to be hidden as much as possible. Some patients succeed in hiding their hostility but become wooden and formal, with (6) affectivity and conduct *resembling schizophrenic pictures.* A typical report is this, "I go through all the motions of living. I look after my children. I do my errands. I go to social functions, but it is like being in a play; it doesn't really concern me. I can't have any warm feelings. If I were to have any feelings at all I would be angry with everybody." This patient's reaction to therapy was characterized by growing hostility against the therapist, and it required considerable skill to make her continue interviews in spite of the disconcerting hostility which she had been fighting so much. The absence of emotional display in this patient's face and actions was quite striking. Her face had a masklike appearance, her movements were formal, stilted, robot-like, without the fine play of emotional expression.

Closely related to this picture is (7) a *lasting loss of patterns of social interaction.* The patient cannot initiate any activity, is full of eagerness to be active—restless, can't sleep—but throughout the day he will not start any activity unless "primed" by somebody else. He will be grateful at sharing activities with others but will not be able to make up his mind to do anything alone. The picture is one of lack of decision and initiative. Organized activities along social lines occur only if a friend takes the patient along and shares the activity with him. Nothing seems to promise reward; only the ordinary activities of the day are carried on, and these in a routine manner, falling apart into small steps, each of which has to be carried out with much effort and without zest.

There is, in addition, a picture in which a patient is active but in which most of his activities attain a coloring which is (8) *detrimental to his own social and economic existence.* Such patients, with uncalled for generosity, give away their belongings, are easily lured into foolish economic dealings, lose their friends and professional standing by a series of "stupid acts," and find themselves finally without family, friends, social status, or money. This protracted self-punitive behavior seems to take place without any awareness of excessive feelings of guilt. It is a particularly distressing grief picture because it is likely to hurt other members of the family and drag down friends and business associates.

This leads finally to the picture in which the grief reaction takes the form of a straight (9) *agitated depression* with tension, agitation, insomnia, feelings of worthlessness, bitter self-accusation, and obvious need for punishment. Such patients may be dangerously suicidal.

A young man aged 32 had received only minor burns and left the hospital apparently well on the road to recovery just before the psychiatric survey of the disaster victims took place. On the fifth day he had learned that his wife had died. He seemed somewhat relieved of his worry about her fate [and] impressed the surgeon as being unusually well-controlled during the following short period of his stay in the hospital.

On January 1st he was returned to the hospital by his family. Shortly after his return home he had become restless, did not want to stay at home, had taken a trip to relatives trying to find rest, had not succeeded, and had returned home in a state of marked agitation, appearing preoccupied, frightened, and unable to concentrate on any organized activity. The mental status presented a somewhat unusual picture. He was restless, could not sit still or participate in any activity on the ward. He would try to read, drop it after a few minutes, or try to play pingpong, give it up after a short time. He would try to start conversations, break them off abruptly, and then fall into repeated murmured utterances: "Nobody can help me. When is it going to happen? I am doomed, am I not?" With great effort it was possible to establish enough rapport to carry on interviews. He complained about his feeling of extreme tension, inability to breathe, generalized weakness and exhaustion, and his frantic fear that something terrible was going to happen. "I'm destined to live in insanity or I must die. I know that it is God's will. I have this awful feeling of guilt." With intense morbid guilt feelings, he reviewed incessantly the events of the fire. His wife had stayed behind. When he tried to pull her out, he had fainted and was shoved out by the crowd. She was burned while he was saved. "I should have saved her or I should have died too." He complained about being filled with an incredible violence and did not know what to do about it. The rapport established with him lasted for only brief periods of time. He then would fall back into his state of intense agitation and muttering. He slept poorly even with large sedation. In the course of four days he became somewhat more composed, had longer periods of contact with the psychiatrist, and seemed to feel that he was being understood and might be able to cope with his morbid feelings of guilt and violent impulses. On the sixth day of his hospital stay, however, after skillfully distracting the attention of his special nurse, he jumped through a closed window to a violent death.

If the patient is not conspicuously suicidal, it may nevertheless be true that he has a strong desire for painful experiences, and such patients are likely to desire shock treatment of some sort, which they picture as a cruel experience, such as electrocution might be.

A 28-year-old woman, whose 20-month-old son was accidentally smothered developed a state of severe agitated depression with self-accusation, inability to enjoy anything, hopelessness about the future, overflow of hostility against the husband and his parents, also with excessive hostility against the psychiatrist. She insisted upon electric-shock treatment and was finally referred to another physician who treated her. She responded to the shock treatments very well and felt relieved of her sense of guilt.

It is remarkable that agitated depressions of this sort represent only a small fraction of the pictures of grief in our series.

Our observations indicate that to a certain extent the type and severity of the grief reaction can be predicted. Patients with obsessive personality make-up and with a history of former depressions are likely to develop an agitated depression. Severe reactions seem to occur in mothers who have lost young children. The intensity of interaction with the deceased before his death seems to be significant. It is important to realize that such interaction does not have to be of the affectionate type; on the contrary, the death of a person who invited much hostility, especially hostility which could not well be expressed because of his status and claim to loyalty, may be followed by a severe grief reaction in which hostile impulses are the most conspicuous feature. Not infrequently the person who passed away represented a key person in a social system, his death being followed by disintegration of this social system and by a profound alteration of the living and social conditions for the bereaved. In such cases readjustment presents a severe task quite apart from the reaction to the loss incurred. All these factors seem to be more important than a tendency to react with neurotic symptoms in previous life. In this way the most conspicuous forms of morbid identification were found in persons who had no former history of a tendency to psychoneurotic reactions.

MANAGEMENT

Proper psychiatric management of grief reactions may prevent prolonged and serious alterations in the patient's social adjustment, as well as potential disease. The essential task facing the psychiatrist is that of sharing the patient's grief work, namely, his efforts at extricating himself from the bondage to the deceased and at finding new patterns of rewarding interaction. It is of the greatest importance to notice that not only overreaction but underreaction of the bereaved must be given attention, because delayed responses may occur at unpredictable moments and the dangerous distortions of the grief reaction, not conspicuous at first, may be quite destructive later, and these may be prevented.

Religious agencies have led in dealing with the bereaved. They have provided comfort by giving the backing of dogma to the patient's wish for continued interaction with the deceased, have developed rituals which maintain the patient's interaction with others, and have counteracted the morbid guilt feelings of the patient by Divine Grace and by promising an opportunity for "making up" to the deceased at the time of a later reunion. While these measures have helped countless mourners, comfort alone does not provide adequate assistance in the patient's grief work. He has to accept the pain of the bereavement. He has to review his relationships with the deceased, and has to become acquainted with the alterations in his own modes of emotional reaction. His fear of insanity, his fear of accepting the surprising changes in his feelings, especially the overflow of hostility, have to be worked through. He will have to express his sorrow and sense of loss. He will have to find an acceptable formulation of his future relationship to the deceased. He will have to verbalize his feelings of guilt, and he will have to find persons around him whom he can use as "primers" for the acquisition of new patterns of conduct. All this can be done in eight to ten interviews.

Special techniques are needed if hostility is the most marked feature of the grief reaction. The hostility may be directed against the psychiatrist, and the patient will have such guilt over his hostility that he will avoid further interviews. The help of a social worker or a minister, or if these are not available, a member of the family, to urge the patient to continue coming to see the psychiatrist may be indispensable. If the tension and the depressive features are too great, a combination of benzedrine sulphate, 5–10 mgm. b.i.d., and sodium amytal, 3 gr. before retiring, may be useful in first reducing emotional distress to a tolerable degree. Severe agitated depressive reactions may defy all efforts of psychotherapy and may respond well to shock treatment.

Since it is obvious that not all bereaved persons, especially those suffering because of war casualties, can have the benefit of expert psychiatric help, much of this knowledge will have to be passed on to auxiliary workers. Social workers and ministers will have to be on the look-out for the more ominous pictures, referring these to the psychiatrist while assisting the more normal reactions themselves.

ANTICIPATORY GRIEF REACTIONS

While our studies were at first limited to reactions to actual death, it must be understood that grief reactions are just one form of separation reactions. Separation by death is characterized by its irreversibility and finality. Separation may, of course, occur for other reasons. We were at first surprised to find genuine grief reactions in patients who had not experienced a bereavement but who had experienced separation, for instance with the departure of a member of the family into the armed forces. Separation in this case is not due to death but is under the threat of death. A common picture hitherto not appreciated is a syndrome which we have designated *anticipatory grief*. The patient is so concerned with her adjustment after the potential death of father or son that she goes through all the phases of grief—depression, heightened preoccupation with the departed, a review of all the forms of death which might befall him, and anticipation of the modes of readjustment which might be necessitated by it. While this reaction may well form a safeguard against the impact of a sudden death notice, it can turn out to be of a disadvantage at the occasion of reunion. Several instances of this sort came to our attention when a soldier just returned from the battlefront complained that his wife did not love him anymore and demanded immediate divorce. In such situations apparently the grief work has been done so effectively that the patient has emancipated herself and the readjustment must now be directed towards new interaction. It is important to know this because many family disasters of this sort may be avoided through prophylactic measures.

BIBLIOGRAPHICAL NOTE

Many of the observations are, of course, not entirely new. Delayed reactions were described by Helene Deutsch (1937). Shock treatment in agitated depressions due to bereavement has recently been advocated by Myerson (1944). Morbid identification has been stressed at many points in the psychoanalytic literature and recently by H. A. Murray (1937). The relation of mourning and depressive psychoses has been discussed by Freud (1917), Melanie Klein (1940), and Abraham (1924). Bereavement reactions in war time were discussed by Wilson (1941). The reactions after the Cocoanut Grove fire were described in some detail in a chapter of the monograph on this civilian disaster (Cobb & Lindemann, 1943). The effect of wartime separations was reported by Rosenbaum (1944). The incidence of grief re-actions among the psychogenic factors in asthma and rheumatoid arthritis has been mentioned by Cobb, *et al.* (Cobb, Bauer, & Whitey, 1939; McDermott & Cobb, 1939).

25

Behavioral Observations on Parents Anticipating the Death of a Child

STANFORD B. FRIEDMAN, PAUL CHODOFF, JOHN W. MASON,
and
DAVID A. HAMBURG

There are few tasks in the practice of medicine as difficult as trying to help the parents of a child afflicted with a disease which is invariably fatal. Since the physician cannot change the reality of the tragic situation, he frequently feels totally unable to lessen the parental suffering. However, understanding the nature of the stress as experienced by the parents and appreciating that there are characteristic ways in which they cope with the situation should enable the physician to offer helpful support in a majority of cases.

Forty-six parents of children with neo-plastic disease were involved at the National Institutes of Health (NIH) in a study of the adrenal cortical response under conditions of chronic psychological stress, and this work has been reported elsewhere (Friedman, Mason, & Hamburg, 1963). The present paper is concerned with the clinical impressions gained over a 2-year period while this study was in progress and the implication of these findings to physicians caring for children with similar diseases, adding to what is presently in the literature (Bierman, 1956; Bozeman, Orbach, & Sutherland, 1955; Greene & Miller, 1958; Knudson & Natterson, 1960; Natterson & Knudson, 1960; Orbach, Sutherland, & Bozeman, 1955; Richmond & Waisman, 1955).

SUBJECTS AND GENERAL METHOD OF STUDY

The 46 subjects represented one or both parents of 27 children, all of whom had been referred for treatment with chemotherapeutic agents to the Medicine Branch of the National Cancer Institute. In all cases, the child had previously been hospitalized elsewhere for clinical evaluation, and the suggestion for referral was most frequently made by a physician at the time he communicated the diagnosis to the parents. In a minority of cases, the matter of referral was initiated at a time later in the child's clinical course. Within 24 hours of each child's admission to NIH, the parents were informed of this study by the principal investigator and invited to participate. During a 10-month period in 1960–61, a total of 36 children (including 2 siblings) were admitted for the first time to the pediatric ward of the National Cancer Institute. Of these, the parents of one child did not wish to participate in the study, while the parents of seven other children were unavailable for formal inclusion, though most could be interviewed occasionally.

The median age of the 26 mothers was 33 years, and that of the 20 fathers, 35 years. As seen in Table 25.1, there was broad representation of socioeconomic level, though the majority of parents were high school graduates and from families where the estimated annual income was $4,500 or more. Approximately two-thirds of the parents lived in an urban or suburban environment, and a majority professed the Protestant faith. One mother and three fathers were married for the second time.

Nineteen of the 27 children, including the two who were siblings, had acute lymphocytic leukemia, one had acute myelogenous leukemia, 6 had metastatic "solid" tumors, and one child was found to have a benign lesion following an erroneous referral diagnosis of leukemia. The median time from when the parents learned the child's diagnosis from the referring physician and admission to the National Cancer Institute was 2 and 5 weeks for the children with leukemia and "solid" tumors, respectively. The group of children with leukemia appeared to experience a clinical course consistent with a recent review of this disease by Freireich *et al.* (1961), though somewhat modified by the constant development of new therapeutic techniques. All the children with "solid" tumors had widely metasta-

Table 25.1. *Descriptive Data on the 26 Mothers and 20 Fathers*

	Mothers		Fathers	
Data	No.	%	No.	%
Age				
Range	23–49	—	25–49	—
Mean	33.4	—	36.0	—
Median	33.0	—	35.3	—
Education				
<High school	8	31	7	35
High school	12	46	7	35
>High school	6	23	6	30
Income (est.)				
<$4,500	6	23	5	25
$4,500–$7,500	16	62	12	60
>$7,500	4	15	3	15
Environment				
Urban	15	58	13	65
Suburban	3	12	1	5
Rural	8	31	6	30
Religion				
Protestant	23	88	17	85
Catholic	3	12	3	15

tic lesions and were referred for systemic chemotherapy. The sex distribution, age at the time admitted, and the average number of siblings for this group of children is shown in Table 25.2.

Thirty-five parents, 20 mothers and 15 fathers, lived some distance from NIH and were admitted to a ward of the National Institute of Mental Health, where they resided during all or a portion of the time their children were hospitalized. Eleven parents, 6 mothers and 5 fathers, who lived in the immediate vicinity of NIH were available for study to a lesser extent and were seen on what we have considered an "outpatient" basis.

The period of observation for the parents living on the ward ranged from approximately 1 week to 8 months; 2 months was the median time for the mothers and 1 month for the fathers. The parents spending a total of 4 to 8 months on this ward had their stay interspersed with periods at home when their children were ambulatory.

The ward for the parents was two stories above the children's ward and was designated as a "normal volunteer" floor. There were gener-

Table 25.2. *Descriptive Data on the 27 Children*

	Diagnostic Group			
Data	Leukemia (N = 20)	"Solid" Tumor (N = 6)	Benign Lesion (N = 1)	All Groups (N = 27)
Sex				
Male	12	2	—	14
Female	8	4	1	13
Age (in years)				
Range	1.5–16.0	2.0–7.5	—	1.5–16.0
Mean	7.0	5.0	—	6.5
Median	5.3	4.5	4.0	5.0
Siblings				
Average number	2.4 *	1.7 †	—	2.2
Patient only child	1	—	—	1
Patient oldest child	4	2	—	6
Patient youngest child	9	3	1	13

* Includes three stepchildren in one family; two in a second family.
† Patient and sibling adopted in one family.

ally 6 to 8 parents staying on this ward at any given time, and the floor was arranged so that each couple, or two mothers, could have a single room with an adjoining bathroom. The parents were usually on the pediatric floor with their children during visiting hours (11 A.M. to 1 P.M., and 3 P.M. to 8 P.M.), but spent most of the remaining hours on their own "normal volunteer" ward, though they were entirely free to leave the Clinical Center at any time.

The parents studied in the ward setting were interviewed by one of the investigators (S.B.F.) in his office at least once a week and were seen on the ward almost daily. In addition to these interviews and observational notes, the nurses on the "normal volunteer" ward made and recorded observations, and each morning the parents filled out a brief questionnaire regarding their activities during the previous 24 hours. The parents seen on an "outpatient" basis were interviewed approximately once every 2 weeks when their children were hospitalized, and there was the additional opportunity to see these parents during periods when their children were in remission and living at home. All parents were also observed interacting with their children on the pediatric ward, though no systematic attempt was made to study the children.

The interviews were primarily concerned with each parent's perception of his child's illness and clinical course, the defenses utilized by the parent to protect him from the impact of the stressful situation and the threatened loss, and the individual's ways of dealing with the many problems that arise when caring for a seriously ill child. Further information was obtained at weekly group sessions open to all the parents and led by one of the investigators (S.B.F.); this investigator was also in frequent contact with the ward physicians,[1] the nurses caring for the children, and with the social worker assigned to the pediatric ward.

Although the parents of the children with leukemia and metastatic tumors faced many of the same problems and shared similar experiences, this paper will primarily discuss the parents of the children with leukemia. An attempt will be made to generalize from our observations, with an emphasis on the findings that are most relevant to the problems of clinical management. No claim is made that the psychodynamics underlying the observed behavior have been fully described; data regarding the specific symbolic meaning of the threatened and actual loss for each of the parents were generally not available.

In cases where we contrast our findings with those of others, we would like to emphasize that differences probably existed in the populations under study and the unique setting in which our study was conducted. However, though the parents living on the "normal volunteer" ward were in a somewhat artificial setting, the general applicability of our findings is supported by the similarity of behavior observed both in the parents studied on the ward and in those studied while they continued to live at home.

EARLY REACTIONS OF PARENTS

Learning the Diagnosis

In general, the parents stated that they had some prior knowledge about leukemia and therefore suspected their child might have this disease before actually hearing it from a doctor, and, in this sense,

---

[1] The ward physicians at the National Cancer Institute have the title of Clinical Associate, having completed internship and at least one year of residency prior to their NIH experience. During each year of this study, there were three ward physicians assigned to the children's floor, each spending 9 months on this and an adult service.

they somewhat anticipated the news. However, without exception, the parents recalled a feeling of "shock" or of being "stunned" when hearing the definitive diagnosis. Only an occasional parent reported a concomitant feeling of disbelief, though in retrospect most parents feel that it took some days before the meaning of the diagnosis "sank in." Thus, in this study, the majority of parents appeared to intellectually accept the diagnosis and its implication, rather than to manifest the degree of disbelief (Knudson & Natterson, 1960; Natterson & Knudson, 1960) and marked denial (Bozeman, Orbach, & Sutherland, 1955) described by others. Only later did they consciously begin to hope that the diagnosis might be in error.

In cases where the referring doctor discussed leukemia and its clinical course in detail, the parents later realized that little of this general information was comprehended at the time. Certain immediate decisions had to be made, particularly whether the child was to be referred to NIH, and only that information which aided the parents in handling this immediate situation appeared meaningful. The fathers generally took the major responsibility for such decisions at this time, and also tended to offer emotional support to their wives.

Upon arrival at NIH, there was a tendency to be overwhelmingly impressed, and this was associated with revived hope, expressed by statements such as: "If any place can save my child, it will be here." During the period of this study, this reaction was anticipated by the ward physicians who pointed out shortly after the child's admission the realistic aspects of the situation and the present limitations of the chemothearpy.

These statements by the ward physician that NIH was not omnipotent often invoked an immediate reaction of hostility, sometimes expressed by saying that "only God could decide" their child's future. However, after a period of a few days to a few weeks, all but a minority of the parents then praised the ward physician for having taken this approach. They felt that they had "now heard the worst," and no longer had to contend with the dread that there was some unknown, even more devastating news, yet to come. Our impression was that this direct approach gave the parents confidence in their ability to master subsequent developments, and tended to discourage unrealistic and maladaptive behavior patterns.

Three fathers, two of whom were not formally included in this study, reported a marked hostile component during their early reaction to learning the diagnosis. One confessed to an immediate urge to "blow up the world," another overtly threatened to attack his child's physicians, and a third partially succumbed to the impulse to injure others by deliberate recklessness while driving. All three of these fathers had a history of significant psychiatric problems, two in the form of overt paranoid behavior. Though it was not unusual for a parent to show evidence of hostility directed towards others, the open frank expression of such thoughts and impulses always reflected psychopathology in our experience.

Guilt

Once the diagnosis of leukemia was made, the parents would, almost without exception, initially blame themselves for not having paid more attention to the early nonspecific manifestations of the disease. They wondered whether the child would not have had a better chance of responding to therapy if the diagnosis had been made sooner. Although such reactions of guilt were extremely common, and the deep emotional basis of such feelings has been emphasized by others (Richmond & Waisman, 1955), most parents in this study readily accepted assurance from the physician that they had not neglected their child. Particularly reassuring to the parents was the information that the long-term prognosis in most cases of childhood leukemia is essentially the same no matter when the diagnosis is made.

Thus, in the majority of parents, guilt was not manifested by prolonged and exaggerated feelings of wrong-doing, but was more characteristically a transient phenomenon. The various etiologic possibilities which were considered included genetic and controllable environmental factors, but most parents did not dwell on their own possible contribution to the development of the disease and were able to minimize their feelings of guilt. However, we are aware that the degree of guilt reported in a study such as this is dependent upon the intensity with which each subject is studied, the depth of interpretation by the investigator, and the definition of the term itself.

Notwithstanding the above qualifications, a minority of parents did display obvious indications of guilt that were more than transient, and which appeared as persistent self-blame for the child's illness. As one mother said, "It is God's way of punishing me for my sins." More often, a parent would blame himself for not having been more appreciative of the child before his illness. Things had not been done together, the buying of toys had been postponed, or perhaps the child had been disciplined too severely. This attitude frequently led to over-indulging and over-protecting the now ill child, with no limits put on his behavior. The ward physician would sometimes comment on such extreme practices, but this parental pattern, to the extent that it was generated by underlying guilt, was exceedingly resistant to change.

Seeking Information

The ward physician had at least one lengthy interview with the parents shortly after each child was admitted and, later, periodically discussed the child's condition with the parents and was readily available to answer any further questions. The parents were generally aware of and appreciative of these efforts, but there remained what appeared to be an insatiable need to know *everything* about the disease. For many weeks, there was, characteristically, an extensive search for additional information, especially about therapeutic developments.

This search took many forms, but most noticeable, at least to the medical and nursing staffs, was the exchange of information among parents on the floor solarium which served as a waiting room for the parents between the morning and afternoon visiting hours. Here the "new" parents would glean information from the group, not only about leukemia and its therapy, but also regarding hospital policies and organization. Information from the three ward physicians and the nurses would be pooled and minutely evaluated for consistency. However, it was inevitable that a parent would not be completely objective in relaying information, and an individual's fears, defenses, neurotic tendencies, and lack of a general medical background would not infrequently lead to misinterpretations and overgeneralizations; limitations that most parents recognized in this mutual sharing of information.

Friends and relatives served as an abundant source of "information" about leukemia, often given with the intent of cheering up the parents. For instance, a parent might be told of a patient who lived for years with leukemia, the informant failing to say that the patient had been an elderly man with a chronic type of the disease. This kind of "information" was of little practical use to the parents and contributed to their tendency to deny the disease, a point which will be discussed later.

Newspaper and magazine articles were read many times if they were even remotely related to leukemia or childhood cancer, and relatives, friends, and acquaintances from all parts of the country would send such clippings. Furthermore, particular attention was paid to *where* the reported work had been done, with parents openly inquiring whether the doctors at NIH were aware of a "latest development." There were repeated requests for written authoritative information about leukemia, as it was recognized by the parents, particularly the mothers who usually had the responsibility of keeping their husbands informed, that there was a limitation on how much could be accurately retained after talking with a doctor.

It was noted that parents would become confused and anxious whenever they perceived divergent "facts" or opinions regarding their child's condition, even if the differences were negligible or imaginary. For instance, one couple became quite agitated when a doctor said their child had a bacteremia and then a second physician referred to the same process as septicemia. Similarly, the parents would perceive minor or major variations in degrees of pessimism or optimism at any given time among the doctors.

The seeking of information can be understood partly as a realistic attempt to learn as much as possible about leukemia in order to better master the situation and care for the ill child. However, the process of learning about leukemia appeared constructive only up to a point, and a sudden upsurge of parental questions often reflected increased anxiety or conflict, which could not be resolved by the acquisition of more detailed information about the disease.

PSYCHOLOGICAL MANAGEMENT OF THE ILL CHILD

The Hospitalized Child

An almost universal concern of the parents was the question of how much the children knew, or should know, regarding their diagnosis. Anxiety about this problem was considerable, although obviously influenced by the particular parents involved, the age of the child, and the help received in this area from the physician. The majority of parents, even those who realistically accepted the nature of the tragedy, shielded their children from ever hearing the word "leukemia," though in the hospital setting this was at times all but impossible. Our impression is that *some* acknowledgement of the illness is often helpful, especially in the older child, in preventing the child from feeling isolated, from believing that others are not aware of what he is experiencing, or from feeling that his disease is "too awful" to talk about. Unfortunately we have no data which clearly help answer the question of how best to inform children of their illness, but others (Dameshek & Gunz, 1958; Hoerr, 1963; Rothenberg, 1961) have suggested approaches, though primarily applicable to the adult with a fatal disease, and Marmor (1963) further comments on the difficulty of the physician's task in deciding what to tell the cancer patient and his family.

Another common problem was that the younger children with leukemia frequently openly rejected their parents, making such statements as, "I hate you and I don't ever want to see you again," with the result that the parents would feel that they had, in some way, failed their child. This pattern of behavior appeared most commonly after the children had been ill for some time, and seemed in part related to the parents' inability to prevent painful procedures and prolonged hospitalization with consequent damage to the usual childhood faith in parental omnipotence. Furthermore, we have speculated that the children sensed their dependence on the medical and nursing staff and were therefore fearful of expressing hostility directly toward these individuals.

This ability of even young children to perceive the transfer of authority from their parents to the professional staff manifested itself in many ways. Within a remarkably short time, the children would, for instance, directly ask the nurses and doctors for permission to deviate from their diet or to partake in various recreational activities. The parents were accordingly bypassed and would often feel that they were no longer important to their children. Even when the children developed symptoms at home, they might ask the parents to call "my doctor," again reflecting their awareness that the parents' ability to help them was limited.

Diagnostic and therapeutic procedures were painful to the parents as well as to the children. Parents differed on whether or not they desired to be with their children during such procedures, although they usually would not express their wishes unless explicitly asked. Some parents were markedly relieved when they were not expected to be present at such times; others became less anxious if they were allowed to stay with their children and comfort them.

Parents of the younger children often mentioned the difficulty they experienced each evening when they had to leave a child crying in protest or despair. The parents would generally make an effort to continue the usual routine of putting their child to bed, usually with the help of a favorite toy or doll, and within a week or two most children accepted the fact that the parents had to leave each evening. However, a minority of children and parents never appeared to tolerate this daily separation.

The Child in Remission

Parents would eagerly look forward to the time that their child would go into remission and be discharged from the hospital, but their pleasurable anticipation of this event was frequently tempered by considerable concern regarding the necessity of again assuming the major responsibility for the child's care. They feared that without warning some acute medical problem would arise, and any past feelings of inadequacy associated with failure to recognize the original symptoms were reawakened.

Discipline was a common problem when the child returned home, especially if the parents hesitated to set reasonable limits on the child's behavior. The over-indulged child would increase his demands on the family until rather belated disciplinary measures had to be instituted, sometimes only after the other children in the family had grown openly resentful of the special favors received by their apparently well sibling.

Over-protection usually accompanied the over-indulgence, with activities such as swimming and bicycle riding being prohibited as they might "tire" the child. Ecchymoses resulting from normal activities created anxiety in the parents who associated the bruises with leukemia, and in many cases, this anxiety may have unconsciously led to unnecessary curtailment of the child's physical activity. Furthermore, the fear that the child might overhear his diagnosis sometimes led to discouraging attendance at school and other activities. Thus, returning home for some children meant living a rather isolated and restricted life, and the added strain for the parents led a few of them to be aware of longing for the relative security of the hospital.

DEFENSE PATTERNS AND COPING MECHANISMS

Coping Behavior

Coping behavior is a term that has been used (Hamburg, Hamburg, & deGoza, 1953; Visotsky et al., 1961) to denote all of the mechanisms utilized by an individual to meet a significant threat to his psychological stability and to enable him to function effectively. Such behavior would consist of the responses to environmental factors that help the individual master the situation, as well as the intrapsychic processes which contribute to the successful adaptation to a psychologic stress. The stressful episode in this study, evoking such adaptive and defensive reactions, has been defined as the totality of events associated with being the parent of a child with a fatal disease, and includes both the external events and the associated inner conflicts, impulses, and guilt.

The success or failure of this coping behavior may be evaluated in at least two ways. The observer may judge whether the behavior allows the individual to carry out certain personal and socially defined goals. In the setting of this study, one frame of reference was the relative ability of the parent to participate in the care of the ill child and fulfill other family responsibilities. Though value judgments on the part of the observer are constantly invoked when using such criteria, this area is certainly of major concern to the physician caring for the child with leukemia.

The effectiveness of coping behavior may also be evaluated in terms of the individual parent's ability to tolerate the stressful situation without disruptive anxiety or depression, regardless of whether the behavior is socially desirable. Such judgments were made in studying the parents' hormonal response (Friedman, Mason, & Hamburg, 1963; Wolff et al., 1963), where it was found that pathological as well as socially desirable coping patterns were associated with stable 17-hydroxycorticosteroid excretion rates, *if* such behavior was effective in protecting the individual from anxiety and depression. Optimally then, coping behavior not only enables the parent to deal effectively with the reality situation, but also serves the protective function of keeping anxiety and other emotional distress within tolerable limits.

The "shock" of learning the diagnosis and the associated lack of emotional experience has already been mentioned, and this may conveniently be classified as an extreme degree of isolation of affect, a mechanism by which the apparent intellectual recognition of a painful event is not associated with a concomitant intolerable emotional response. Only after a few hours or days was there profound emotional feeling and expression associated with the intellectual awareness of what had happened, this usually occurring only after the necessary arrangements had been made for the child's immediate treatment. This lack of affective experience continued to be a conspicuous defense, and enabled parents to talk realistically about their children's condition and prognosis with relatively little evidence of emotional involvement. Thus, the parents were frequently described by the medical and nursing staffs as being "strong," though occasionally this behavior was interpreted as reflecting a "coldness" or lack of sincere concern. The parents were also often aware of this paucity of emotional feeling, frequently explaining it on the grounds that they "could not break down" in the presence of the children or their physicians. However, that there was some uneasiness about their apparent lack of emotional expression was suggested by the fact that parents would occasionally verbalize their confusion and even guilt over not feeling worse.

In an occasional parent, the process of intellectualization was extreme, as if the parent was trying to master the situation through complete understanding. Here, there was not only the usual desire for medical knowledge, but a persistent tendency to discuss leukemia in a detached and highly intellectualized manner, at times clearly identifying with the physicians. For instance, the parent might wish to examine a peripheral blood smear, since he "always wondered how our body works."

Over a period of time the parents became increasingly knowledgeable about leukemia, and would often request rather detailed information regarding their child's condition, especially about laboratory results. Inquiries about a hemoglobin level or leukocyte count were common, and in addition, occasionally such data would spontaneously be given by a doctor in order to help explain the more general situation. This led to attempts, generally unsuccessful, on the part of some parents to predict what therapy their child should receive next, with confusion and suspicion when their "medical judgement" disagreed with that of the physician. Having once received such detailed information, the parents tended to expect a daily briefing, and would exhibit at first disappointment, then anger, when this routine was interrupted. Such concern over details did serve a defense function by allowing the parents, as well as the doctors, to avoid the more general, but also the more tragic and threatening aspects of the case. However, our impression was that, over-all, more anxiety was generated than dissipated by this practice.

Another defense, less ubiquitous than isolation of affect, but also generally present in greater or lesser degree, was the mechanism of denial, by which is meant the intellectual disclaiming of a painful event or feeling. A few parents openly denied the seriousness of the illness and prognosis; in these individuals there was always a history of a similar defense pattern during past episodes of stress. Such parents did not seem to "understand" the importance of various procedures and therapeutic plans, and were therefore prone to direct hostility towards the physicians.

Motor activity also appeared to often serve a coping function, the parent usually being partially aware of the motivation behind such activity. Thus, one mother realized that when her child was acutely ill, she would markedly increase the amount of time she spent sewing and knitting. This intermittent activity served to physically remove this mother from the threatening situation and to give her "something else to do and think about."

The mothers readily participated in the overall care of their children, and the importance of such activity to the parents, such as allaying existing guilt, has been emphasized by others (Bierman, 1956; Knudson & Natterson, 1960; Orbach, Sutherland, & Bozeman, 1955; Richmond & Waisman, 1955). This type of activity appeared most supportive to the mothers who, in contrast to their spouses, found the nursing role consistent with their past experiences and self-image.

It should be emphasized that defensive activity does not always, by any means, interfere with adequate and effective behavior. Rather, there appears to be an optimal range of defending or "buffering" oneself from the impact of having a child with a fatal disease. Deviation from this range in one direction, by denying reality, interferes with optimal participation in the care of the child by not allowing the parent to fully meet the responsibilities and demands associated with the situation. On the other hand, when a parent lacks adequate defense patterns applicable to these circumstances, his ability to care effectively for his child is also significantly hampered. This latter situation was vividly illustrated by one father who wanted to stay by his boy's bedside, but found it intolerable to do so because he would be preoccupied with thoughts of the boy ultimately dying. The only way this father could decrease his own anxiety was to stay away from the Children's Ward, leaving his boy alone for relatively long periods of time.

Social Influences

As has been discussed, the adjustment seen in most of the parents characteristically included a relatively high degree of intellectual acceptance of the diagnosis and prognosis. Realistic arrangements, including those directly related to the care of the ill child, were therefore facilitated. However, this acceptance was not easy to achieve and came about only after a good deal of emotional struggle, expressed as "We had to convince ourselves of the diagnosis." It is therefore pertinent that relatives and friends did not usually help in this process, but rather, were more likely to hinder the realization of the child's condition.

Typically, the children's grandparents tended to be less accepting of the diagnosis than the parents, with more distant relatives and friends challenging reality even more frequently. The tendency for the degree of reality-distortion to increase with the remoteness of its source from the immediate family almost made it appear that some of the parents were surrounded by "concentric circles of disbelief." Friends and relatives would question the parents as to whether the doctors were *sure* of the diagnosis and prognosis, and might suggest that the parents seek additional medical opinion. Comments would be made that the ill child, especially if he was in remission, could not possibly have leukemia as he looked too well or did not have the "right symptoms." Individuals cured of "leukemia" would be cited, and in a few cases, faith healers and pseudomedical practitioners were recommended.

Although parents generally perceived most of these statements and suggestions as attempts to "cheer us up and give us hope," they found themselves in the uncomfortable position of having to "defend" their child's diagnosis and prognosis, sometimes experiencing the feeling that others thought they were therefore "condemning" their own child. Thus, the parents were not allowed to express any feelings of hopelessness, yet, as will be discussed later, they were paradoxically expected to appear grief-stricken.

Grandparents not only displayed more denial than the parents, but often appeared more vulnerable to the threatened loss of the loved child. Therefore, many of the parents felt that they had to give emotional support to the grandparents, at a time when it was most difficult for them to assume this supportive role. Our impression is that this marked degree of emotional involvement on the part of the grandparents helps explain the observations of Bozeman, Orbach, and Sutherland (1955), who noted that the mothers in their study did not often turn to their own mothers for support or guidance. In spite of this, grandparents generally were informed of the diagnosis almost immediately, though parents would occasionally first tell "people we hardly knew . . . just to make sure that we could get through it."

Though society did not allow the parents to give up the hope that their children might survive, it also assumed that they would be grief-stricken. Therefore, the parents were not expected to take part in normal social activities, or be interested in any form of entertainment. The relatively long course of leukemia made this expectation not only unrealistic, but also undesirable in that some diversion appears necessary in allowing the parents to function effectively in the care of the ill child. Illustrative of this area of conflict was the experience of one mother, whose child had had leukemia for one year. She gave a birthday party for one of her other children and was immediately challenged by relatives who "could not understand how my family could have a party *at a time like this.*" Such remarks often produced anxiety, guilt, or confusion in a parent, leading this same mother to remark "that being a parent of a leukemic child is hard, but not as hard as other people make it."

An additional problem was that friends and relatives often besieged the parents with requests for information about their child. Parents would have to repeatedly describe each new development, listening by the hour to repetitive expressions of encouragement and sympathy, and occasionally having to reassure others that the disease was not contagious. This arduous task was ameliorated in the cases where a semiformal system evolved where some one individual, often a close friend or a minister, would be kept up to date so that he in turn could answer the multitude of questions.

Although it was clear that friends and relatives sometimes aggravated the parents' distress, they also provided significant emotional support in the form of tactful and sympathetic listening and by offering to be of service, as has been described in detail by Bozeman, Orbach, and Sutherland (1955). The major source of emotional support for most parents during the period of hospitalization appeared to be the other parents of similarly afflicted children, with the feeling that "we are all in it together" and with concern for the distress experienced by the other parents, a mode of adjustment discussed in detail by Greene (1958). The parents learned from each other, and could profit by observing the coping behavior manifested by others in the group. Thus, the common fear of "going to pieces" when their child would become terminally ill was greatly alleviated by watching others successfully, albeit painfully, go through the experience.

Search For Meaning

The parents generally found it intolerable to think of their child's leukemia as a "chance" or meaningless event. Therefore, they tried to construct an explanation for it, displaying a certain amount of urgency until one appropriate to their particular frame of reference could be accepted.

A few parents were content with what might be termed a "deferred explanation"; that is, they accepted and appeared satisfied with the knowledge that it would be some years before a scientifically accurate answer was available to tell them why *their* child had acquired leukemia. Parents in this category were all relatively well-educated and were able to evaluate the current thoughts regarding the etiology of leukemia, coming to the *conclusion* that definitive proof of causation was still lacking. However, this did not constitute an acceptance of leukemia as a "chance" phenomenon, but rather implied an ability to wait for the accumulation of more knowledge regarding the etiology of the disease.

A greater number of parents appeared to need a more immediate and definite answer. They would eagerly and unconditionally accept one of the more recent theories concerning the etiology of leukemia, such as the "viral theory," with some additional explanation as to why it was *this* particular child, rather than some other child, who developed the disease. Most parents constructed an explanation which was a composite of scientific facts, elements from the parent's past experiences, and fantasies. Though in the majority of cases their concept of etiology served to partially resolve any feelings of being responsible for the child's illness, the synthesis sometimes appeared to reflect parental self-blame. In these instances the guilt appeared to be less anxiety-provoking than the total lack of a suitable cause for the leukemia, and therefore guilt may at times be thought of as serving a defense function for the individual (Chodoff, 1959).

Religion

The attempt of parents to attribute meaning to the fact that their child developed leukemia was inseparable from their religious beliefs and orientation. Most parents expressed the sentiment that religion was of comfort to them, occasionally making such statements as "It helps us be more accepting" and "At least we know he will be in Heaven and not suffering." These statements seemed to be sincere reflections of the help that the parents received from their religious beliefs, though these same parents did not characteristically discuss the child's prognosis in religious terms, nor were topics of religion often brought up spontaneously in the interview situation. In contrast, a few individuals primarily thought about their child's illness in a religious context, with statements made that "This is the Lord's way of protecting him from an even worse fate." In these parents there was a tendency to accept the illness as God's will, with the acknowledgement that one could not expect to fully understand His ways.

Although a strong religious orientation made the illness more un derstandable for some parents, having a child with leukemia caused other parents to doubt their previously unquestioned religious faith and these doubts sometimes led to transient expressions of guilt. However, to our knowledge no parent actually renounced his religion as a result of this experience. In fact, it was common for a parent to report an eventual "return to religion," and express sympathy for any of the other parents who did not have sufficient religious faith to help them in this time of need.

Hope and Anticipatory Grief

The element of hope as it refers to a favorable alteration of the expected sequence of events, though hard to evaluate, is of general clinical importance (Marmor, 1963; Menninger, 1959), and was universally emphasized by the parents. Comments would be made such as "Without hope I could never keep going . . . though I know deep down nothing really can be done." Unlike massive denial, hope did not appear to interfere with effective behavior and was entirely compatible with an intellectual acceptance of reality. That the persistence of hope for a more favorable outcome does not require the need to intellectually deny the child's prognosis is of clinical significance, as it differentiates hope from defense patterns that potentially may greatly distort reality. Hope actually helped the parents accept "bad news" in that the ward physician would often couple discouraging news with some hopeful comment.

As the disease progressed in the children, there was usually a corresponding curtailment of hope in the parents. Whereas at first they might hope for the development of a curative drug, as the child became increasingly ill, the hope might be only for one further remission. Parents would note that they no longer were making any long-range plans and that they were living on a day-to-day basis. The hopes regarding their children would tend to be so short-term and limited that parents would find themselves preoccupied with a question such as whether their child would be well enough that evening to attend a movie, rather than think about his ultimate fate. This gradual dissipation and narrowing of hope appeared inversely related to the increasing presence of what has been called anticipatory grief (Lindemann, 1944).

The amount of grieving in anticipation of the forthcoming loss varied greatly in the individual parents, and in a few, never was obvious at any time during the child's clinical course. However, in most, as noted by others (Natterson & Knudson, 1960), the grief process was usually quite apparent by the fourth month of the child's illness, frequently being precipitated by the first acute critical episode in the child's disease. Grieving then gradually evolved as the disease progressed and any death on the ward often had a potentiating effect.

The signs and symptoms of this anticipatory mourning process were not as well defined as in an acute grief reaction. However, it was common for parents to complain of somatic symptoms, apathy, weakness, and preoccupation with thoughts of the ill child. Sighing was frequently observed, and many parents would occasionally cry at night and appear depressed. At other times there seemed to be an increase in motor activity and a tendency to talk for hours about the ill child, an observation consistent with the findings of Lindemann (1944).

The process of resigning oneself to the inevitable outcome was frequently accompanied by statements of wishing "it was all over with." The narrowing of hope and the completion of much of the grief work was described by one mother who stated: "I still love my boy, want to take care of him and be with him as much as possible . . . but still feel sort of detached from him." In spite of feeling "detached" from her child, this mother continued to be most effective in caring for and comforting her child, with no evidence of physical abandonment. Richmond and Waisman (1955) have commented on the usefulness of this anticipatory mourning in stepwise preparing the parent for the eventual loss, and the few parents in our study who did not display such behavior experienced a more prolonged and distressing reaction after the child actually died.

TERMINAL PHASE

Terminal Episode and Death

The parents realized that the clinical condition was much more serious when all of the established chemotherapeutic agents had been exhausted, this event marking what might be considered the beginning of the terminal phase of the illness. Characterisically at the time, there was an acceleration of the grief-work or the actual precipitation of mourning in those few individuals who previously had denied the prognosis, and to the staff, the parents often appeared resigned to the fact that their child would die. Often, as previously described (Richmond & Waisman, 1955), parents would become increasingly involved in the care of other children on the ward, and occasionally a parent would openly express the desire to resume a more normal life and return to the other children at home. Though these feelings prevailed, there still were residuals of hope, if only that the child might "just smile once more" or "have one more good day." During this terminal period, the knowledge that the doctor "who knows the case best" would be in daily seemed of particular importance. However, in spite of this appreciative attitude, the parents were also less understanding and easily became annoyed when even minor things did not go exactly according to plan. There were apt to be frequent, though brief, expressions of irritation or anger, often followed by spontaneous denial of such feelings. These transient manifestations of hostility might have been related to the direct challenging of an underlying, unrecognized belief in the omnipotent nature of the doctors and the hospital, or in some cases, a displacement of unconscious resentment and ambivalence from the ill child to the medical staff.

In this setting, the child's death was generally taken calmly, but with the appropriate expression of affect. Outbursts of uncontrollable grief or open expressions of self-blame were the exception, and usually there was some indication of relief that the child was no longer suffering. There were arrangements, telephone calls, and decisions to be made, and characteristically the father again assumed the more dominant and supportive role, just as he had shortly after the diagnosis had first been made.

The death of the child therefore did not appear to be a severe superimposed stressful situation, but rather an anticipated loss at the end of a long sequence of events. This was also reflected in the 17-hydroxycorticosteroid excretion rates (Friedman, Mason, & Hamburg, 1963), in that there was not one parent who showed a marked rise during the last day of urine collection, which frequently included the time the child had actually died, nor were plasma corticosteroid elevations observed several hours after the child's death (Friedman,

Mason & Hamburg, unpublished data). These findings might in part be due to the parents not yet experiencing the emotion, as many of them remarked that they "just cannot believe that it's all over . . . it just hasn't hit yet."

Follow-up Observations

The parents of the children who died relatively early in our study were invited to return to NIH for a 3-day period. Twenty-three parents were thus approached; 18, including 8 couples, accepted and were seen 3 to 8 months after the end of their children's illness. In addition, three parents who lived in the immediate vicinity of NIH were also available for study during a comparable period.

The grief reactions following the actual loss of the children, as related by these parents, were very similar to, though in some cases not as intense as, those following a sudden loss (Lindemann, 1944), and the mourning usually became much less pronounced after 3 to 6 weeks. There was a tendency for feelings of guilt and self-blame to be verbalized, often for the first time, and as others (Solnit & Green, 1959) have noted, repeated reassurance from the doctor was frequently quite comforting during this period. One might speculate that in some cases an unconscious or barely conscious wish for relief of tension through the child's death during the terminal phase provided the motivation for such expressions of guilt during the mourning period.

Of the 18 parents who returned to NIH after their child's death, 16 felt that the return had been a helpful experience. Some of these parents believed that they "would have been drawn back," even if they had not been invited to again participate in the study. This feeling existed in the face of a "dread about returning," sometimes accompanied by a tendency to think of their child as still a patient at the hospital. In these parents, there was a feeling of relief soon after arrival at NIH, expressed as "It wasn't anywhere near as hard as thought it would be," followed by statements to the effect that returning to NIH "has put a period on the whole affair . . . it now seems more real that Jimmy is not with us." In our opinion, this suggests that an unconscious remnant of denial persisted in many parents, reflecting a previous denial process that was not always readily apparent when the child was still alive. This apparent acceleration in the termination of the grief process was not reported by two parents who did not appear to have accepted their loss to any significant degree, though approximately 6 months had elapsed since the death of their children.

Though our follow-up observations are still limited and confined to 24 couples, it is known that five mothers became pregnant either during or immediately following their child's illness. There is not sufficient data in three cases to judge whether the pregnancy was planned, but in the other two there was a deliberate effort to conceive. One additional couple attempted to adopt a child approximately 4 months after their own child had died, and in one other family, the mother is attempting to become pregnant some 6 months after their youngest child died.

None of the parents who have thus far participated in our follow-up study have reported an increased incidence of somatic complaints or minor illnesses, nor have any of the parents developed any acute medical problems requiring hospitalization subsequent to the actual loss of their child. However, it is recognized that the follow-up period has been of inadequate length to make any statements regarding the possible relationship of unresolvable object loss and the grief reaction to the development of disease, as has been suggested by Schmale (1958) and Engel (1961).

IMPLICATION FOR PHYSICIANS AND CONCLUSIONS

Each parent of a child with a fatal disease reacts to the tragedy in a unique manner, consistent with his particular personality structure, past experiences, and the individualized meaning and specific circumstances associated with the threatened loss. In general, optimal medical management depends on the physician's awareness and evaluation of certain aspects of this specific background information. However, the parents of children with leukemia do share many similar problems that are inherent in the situation, and certain modes of adjustment commonly occur in a characteristic sequence. The parental behavior, though not stereotyped, is therefore predictable to some degree.

Characteristically, most parents are unable to incorporate detailed information regarding the disease and its clinical course during the first days after learning the diagnosis. The physician should therefore concentrate on explaining the child's acute condition and keep his guidance relevant to the immediate problem, helping the parents with whatever decisions must be made. Sufficient time and privacy should be available to allow the parents to ask their questions, repetitiously at times, since this is one of the processes by which they come to accept the tragic diagnosis. If referral to a larger medical center is contemplated, the parents should be led to have realistic expectations, neither anticipating a "cure" nor frightened by statements that "nothing can be done."

After the child's medical management has been decided and the immediate problems subside, the parents should be furnished with sufficient information about leukemia [2] to allow them to realistically help in the care and handling of their child. Such information also aids them in resolving any feelings of guilt or sense of responsibility for their child's illness. However, requests for detailed medical information, such as the daily laboratory findings, should be discouraged and evaluated in terms of what underlying needs the parents are attempting to fulfill. The physician should appreciate the frequent attempts of parents to find some "meaning" or "cause" for their child's illness, and unrealistic etiologic explanations should only gradually be questioned. In order to avoid unnecessary confusion and anxiety, all medical information should, whenever possible, be communicated to the parents by the same physician.

The physician should be alert to the problems of the hospitalized child, and parents should be informed, when indicated, that overt manifestations of apathy, depression and hostility are often the natural consequence of prolonged illness and hospitalization in children Apparent by-passing of parental authority, or even open rejection o: the parents by the child, may precipitate episodes of anxiety anc guilt in the parents, and every attempt should be made not to furthe undermine the parental role. During the child's hospitalization nurses can be particularly helpful in guiding parents, especially fa thers, in effective participation in their child's care. At the time c discharge, parents should be instructed about the physical and emc

[2] A publication entitled "Childhood Leukemia: A Pamphlet for Parents" is available physicians for distribution to parents from the Information and Publications Office, N tional Cancer Institute, Bethesda, Maryland.

tional care of their child, reassured regarding their adequacy to meet the demands of the situation, and advised of the availability of prompt medical help during this period. Special emphasis should be paid to discussing what activities are reasonable for the child, with the aim of preventing undue restrictions and over-protection.

Coping mechanisms observed in parents should be viewed in terms of how such behavior contributes, or interferes, with meeting the needs of the ill child and other family members, yet not neglecting to appreciate the protective function such behavior has in keeping anxiety and depression within tolerable limits for the individual parent. There are many appropriate ways for parents to master the situation and advice should be consistent with the individual's particular coping pattern, with attention paid to the expectations and demands that may be made by friends and relatives. An acceptance and understanding of anticipatory grief can further enable the physician to help parents adjust to their inevitable and painful loss, though the child's physician should not modify his course of treatment because of this anticipatory mourning experienced by the parents. Expressions of guilt or hostility should not be considered abnormal unless they are extreme and persistent; in these cases further evaluation, and perhaps psychiatric consultation, is indicated.

The physician should not underestimate the importance of his mere presence, to both the child and the parents. Parents particularly need his support when their child first becomes seriously ill, even though in reality a remission is likely to follow. Though the physician must keep somewhat "emotionally distant" from the family he is treating in order to maintain his own effectiveness and objectivity, his empathy and understanding are vitally important in caring for the child with a fatal disease and the child's family.

ACKNOWLEDGMENT

The authors are deeply indebted to the parents who participated in this project, and to the Clinical Associates who cared for their children on Ward 2-East. Dr. Myron Karon of the Medicine Branch of the National Cancer Institute offered his continuous support and facilitated many aspects of this study. We also gratefully acknowledge the encouragement and support given by Drs. C. Gordon Zubrod, Emil Frei, III, and Emil J. Freireich of the National Cancer Institute. Mr. Paul C. Hartsough tabulated much of the data, and Mrs. Joanna Kieffer, Miss Susan Rusinow, and Mrs. Martha Mantel were responsible for the office and secretarial work. The authors are also indebted to Mrs. Mary Miller and her nursing staff on the "normal volunteer" ward and to Mr. Lawrence Burke of the Social Service Department. Drs. George Engel, Arthur Schmale, and Gilbert Forbes were kind enough to critically review the manuscript.

26

Grieving for a Lost Home

MARC FRIED

INTRODUCTION

For some time we have known that the forced dislocation from an urban slum is a highly disruptive and disturbing experience. This is implicit in the strong, positive attachments to the former slum residential area—in the case of this study the West End of Boston—and in the continued attachment to the area among those who left before any imminent danger of eviction. Since we were observing people in the midst of a crisis, we were all too ready to modify our impressions and to conclude that these were likely to be transitory reactions. But the postrelocation experiences of a great many people have borne out their most pessimistic prerelocation expectations. There are wide variations in the success of postrelocation adjustment and considerable variability in the depth and quality of the loss experience. But for the majority it seems quite precise to speak of their reactions as expressions of *grief*. These are manifest in the feelings of painful loss, the continued longing, the general depressive tone, frequent symptoms of psychological or social or somatic distress, the active work required in adapting to the altered situation, the sense of helplessness, the occasional expressions of both direct and displaced anger, and tendencies to idealize the lost place (Abraham, 1911, 1924; Bibring, 1953; Bowlby, 1961; Freud, 1917; Hoggart, 1957; Klein, 1940; Lindemann, 1944; Marris, 1958; Rochlin, 1961; Volkart, 1957).

At their most extreme, these reactions of grief are intense, deeply felt, and at times overwhelming. In response to a series of questions concerning the feelings of sadness and depression which people experienced *after* moving, many replies were unambiguous: "I felt as though I had lost everything," "I felt like my heart was taken out of me," "I felt like taking the gaspipe," "I lost all the friends I knew," "I always felt I had to go home to the West End and even now I feel like crying when I pass by," "Something of me went with the West End," "I felt cheated," "What's the use of thinking about it," "I threw up a lot," "I had a nervous breakdown." Certainly, some people were overjoyed with the change and many felt no sense of loss. Among 250 women, however, 26 per cent report that they still feel sad or depressed two years later, and another 20 per cent report a long period (six months to two years) of sadness or depression. Altogether, therefore, at least 46 per cent give evidence of a fairly severe grief reaction or worse. And among 316 men, the data show only a slightly smaller percentage (38 per cent) with long-term grief reactions. The true proportion of depressive reactions is undoubtedly higher since many women and men who report no feelings of sadness or depression indicate clearly depressive responses to other questions.

In answer to another question, "How did you feel when you saw or heard that the building you had lived in was torn down?" a similar finding emerges. As in the previous instance, the responses are often quite extreme and most frequently quite pathetic. They range from those who replied: "I was glad because the building had rats," to moderate responses such as "The building was bad but I felt sorry," and "I didn't want to see it go," to the most frequent group comprising such reactions as "It was like a piece being taken from me," "I felt terrible," "I used to stare at the spot where the building stood," "I was sick to my stomach." This question in particular, by its evocative quality, seemed to stir up sad memories even among many people who denied any feeling of sadness or depression. The difference from the previous result is indicated by the fact that 54 per cent of the women and 46 per cent of the men report severely depressed or disturbed reactions; 19 per cent of the women and about 31 per cent of the men report satisfaction or indifference; and 27 per cent of the women and 23 per cent of the men report moderately depressed or ambivalent feelings. Thus it is clear that, for the majority of those who were displaced from the West End, leaving their residential area involved a moderate or extreme sense of loss and an accompanying affective reaction of grief.

While these figures go beyond any expectation which we had or which is clearly implied in other studies, the realization that relocation was a crisis with potential danger to mental health for many people was one of the motivating factors for this investigation.[1] In studying the impact of relocation on the lives of a working-class population through a comparison of prerelocation and postrelocation interview data, a number of issues arise concerning the psychology of urban living which have received little systematic attention. Yet, if we are to understand the effects of relocation and the significance of the loss of a residential environment, it is essential that we have a deeper appreciation of the psychological implications of both physical and social aspects of residential experience. Thus we are led to formulations which deal with the functions and meanings of the residential area in the lives of working-class people.

.   .   .   .

THE NATURE OF THE LOSS IN RELOCATION: CASE ANALYSES

The dependence of the sense of continuity on external resources in the working class, particularly on the availability and local presence of familiar places which have the character of "home," and of familiar people whose patterns of behavior and response are relatively predictable, does not account for all of the reaction of grief to dislocation. In addition to these factors, which may be accentuated by depressive predispositions, it is quite evident that the realities of *post*relocation experience are bound to affect the perpetuation, quality, and depth of grief. And, in fact, our data show that there is a strong association between positive or negative experiences in the postrelocation situation and the proportions who show severe grief. But this issue is complicated by two factors: (1) the extent to which potentially meaningful postrelocation circumstances can be a satisfying experience is *affected* by the degree and tenaciousness of previous commitments to the West End, and (2) the postrelocation "reality" is, in part, *selected* by the people who move and thus is a function of many personality factors, including the ability to anticipate needs, demands, and environmental opportunities.

[1] This is implicit in the prior work on "crisis" and situational predicaments by Dr. Erich Lindemann, under whose initiative the current work was undertaken and carried out.

In trying to understand the effects of prerelocation orientations and postrelocation experiences of grief, we must bear in mind that the grief reactions we have described and analyzed are based on responses given approximately two years after relocation. Most people manage to achieve some adaptation to their experiences of loss and grief, and learn to deal with new situations and new experiences on their own terms. A wide variety of adaptive methods can be employed to salvage fragments of the sense of continuity, or to try to reestablish it on new grounds. Nonetheless, it is the tenaciousness of the imagery and affect of grief, despite these efforts at dealing with the altered reality, which is so strikingly similar to mourning for a lost person.

In coping with the sense of loss, some families try to remain physically close to the area they know, even though most of their close interpersonal relationships remain disrupted; and by this method, they appear often to have modified their feelings of grief. Other families try to move among relatives and maintain a sense of continuity through some degree of constancy in the external bases for their group identity. Yet others respond to the loss of place and people by accentuating the importance of those role relationships which remain. Thus, a number of women report increased closeness to their husbands, which they often explicitly relate to the decrease in the availability of other social relationships for both partners and which, in turn, modifies the severity of grief. In order to clarify some of the complexities of prerelocation orientations and of postrelocation adjustments most concretely, a review of several cases may prove to be instructive.

It is evident that a very strong positive prerelocation orientation to the West End is relatively infrequently associated with a complete absence of grief; and that, likewise, a negative prerelocation orientation to the area is infrequently associated with a strong grief response. The two types which are numerically dominant are, in terms of rational expectations, consistent: those with strong positive feelings about the West End and severe grief; and those with negative feelings about the West End and minimal or moderate grief. The two "deviant" types, by the same token, are both numerically smaller and inconsistent: those with strong positive prerelocation orientations and little grief; and those with negative prerelocation orientations and severe grief. A closer examination of those "deviant" cases with strong prerelocation commitment to the West End and minimal postrelocation grief often reveals either important reservations in their prior involvement with the West End or, more frequently, the denial or rejection of feelings of grief rather than their total absence. And the association of minimal prerelocation commitment to the West End with a severe grief response often proves on closer examination to be a function of a deep involvement in the West End which is modified by markedly ambivalent statements; or, more generally, the grief reaction itself is quite modest and tenuous or is even a pseudogrief which masks the primacy of dissatisfaction with the current area.

GRIEF PATTERNS: CASE EXAMPLES

In turning to case analysis, we shall concentrate on the specific factors which operate in families of all four types, those representing the two dominant and those representing the two deviant patterns.

1. The Figella family exemplifies the association of strong, positive prerelocation attachments to the West End and a severe grief reaction. This is the most frequent of all patterns and, although the Figella family is only one "type" among those who show this pattern, they are prototypical of a familiar West End constellation.

Both Mr. and Mrs. Figella are second-generation Americans who were born and brought up in the West End. In her prerelocation interview, Mrs. Figella described her feelings about living in the West End unambiguously: "It's a wonderful place, the people are friendly." She "loves everything about it" and anticipates missing her relatives above all. She is satisfied with her dwelling: "It's comfortable, clean, and warm." And the marriage appears to be deeply satisfying for both husband and wife. They share many household activities and have a warm family life with their three children.

Both Mr. and Mrs. Figella feel that their lives have changed a great deal since relocation. They are clearly referring, however, to the pattern and conditions of their relationships with other people. Their home life has changed little except that Mr. Figella is home more. He continues to work at the same job as a manual laborer with a modest but sufficient income. While they have many economic insecurities, the relocation has not produced any serious financial difficulty for them.

In relocating, the Figella family bought a house. Both husband and wife are quite satisfied with the physical arrangements but, all in all, they are dissatisfied with the move. When asked what she dislikes about her present dwelling, Mrs. Figella replied simply and pathetically: "It's in Arlington and I want to be in the West End." Both Mr. and Mrs. Figella are outgoing, friendly people with a very wide circle of social contacts. Although they still see their relatives often, they both feel isolated from them and they regret the loss of their friends. As Mr. Figella puts it: "I come home from work and that's it. I just plant myself in the house."

The Figella family is, in many respects, typical of a well-adjusted working-class family. They have relatively few ambitions for themselves or for their children. They continue in close contact with many people; but they no longer have the same extensiveness of mutual cooperation in household activities, they cannot "drop in" as casually as before, they do not have the sense of being surrounded by a familiar area and familiar people. Thus, while their objective situation is not dramatically altered, the changes do involve important elements of stability and continuity in their lives. They manifest the importance of externally available resources for an integral sense of spatial and group identity. However, they have always maintained a very close marital relationship, and their family provides a substantial basis for a sense of continuity. They can evidently cope with difficulties on the strength of their many internal and external resources. Nonetheless, they have suffered from the move, and find it extremely difficult to reorganize their lives completely in adapting to a new geographical situation and new patterns of social affiliation. Their grief for a lost home seems to be one form of maintaining continuity on the basis of memories. While it prevents a more wholehearted adjustment to their altered lives, such adjustments would imply forsaking the remaining fragments of a continuity which was central to their conceptions of themselves and of the world.

2. There are many similarities between the Figella family and the Giuliano family. But Mrs. Giuliano shows relatively little prerelocation commitment to the West End and little postrelocation grief. Mr. Giuliano was somewhat more deeply involved in the West End

and, although satisfied with the change, feels that relocation was "like having the rug pulled out from under you." Mr. and Mrs. Giuliano are also second-generation Americans, of similar background to the Figellas. But Mrs. Giuliano only moved to the West End at her marriage. Mrs. Giuliano had many objections to the area: "For me it is too congested. I never did care for it . . . too many barrooms, on every corner, too many families in one building. . . . The sidewalks are too narrow and the kids can't play outside." But she does expect to miss the stores and many favorite places. Her housing ambitions go beyond West End standards and she wants more space inside and outside. She had no blood relatives in the West End but was close to her husband's family and had friends nearby.

Mr. Giuliano was born in the West End and he had many relatives in the area. He has a relatively high status manual job but only a modest income. His wife does not complain about this although she is only moderately satisfied with the marriage. In part she objected to the fact that they went out so little and that he spent too much time on the corner with his friends. His social networks in the West End were more extensive and involved than were Mrs. Giuliano's. And he missed the West End more than she did after the relocation. But even Mr. Giuliano says that, all in all, he is satisfied with the change.

Mrs. Giuliano feels the change is "wonderful." She missed her friends but got over it. And a few of Mr. Giuliano's group live close by so they can continue to hang together. Both are satisfied with the house they bought although Mrs. Giuliano's ambitions have now gone beyond this. The postrelocation situation has led to an improved marital relationship: Mr. Giuliano is home more and they go out more together.

Mr. and Mrs. Giuliano exemplify a pattern which seems most likely to be associated with a beneficial experience from relocation. Unlike Mr. and Mrs. Figella, who completely accept their working-class status and are embedded in the social and cultural patterns of the working class, Mr. and Mrs. Giuliano show many evidences of social mobility. Mr. Giuliano's present job is, properly speaking, outside the working-class category because of its relatively high status and he himself does not "work with his hands." And Mrs.

Giuliano's housing ambitions, preferences in social relationships, orientation to the class structure, and attitudes toward a variety of matters from shopping to child rearing are indications of a readiness to achieve middle-class status. Mr. Giuliano is prepared for and Mrs. Giuliano clearly desires "discontinuity" with some of the central bases for their former identity. Their present situation is, in fact, a transitional one which allows them to reintegrate their lives at a new and higher status level without too precipitate a change. And their marital relationship seems sufficiently meaningful to provide a significant core of continuity in the process of change in their patterns of social and cultural experience. The lack of grief in this case is quite understandable and appropriate to their patterns of social orientation and expectation.

3. Yet another pattern is introduced by the Borowski family, who had an intense prerelocation commitment to the West End and relatively little postrelocation grief. The Borowski's are both second-generation and have four children.

Mrs. Borowski was brought up in the West End but her husband had lived there only since the marriage (fifteen years before). Her feelings about living in the West End were clear: "I love it—it's the only home I've ever known." She had reservations about the dirt in the area but loved the people, the places, and the convenience, and maintained an extremely wide circle of friends. They had some relatives nearby but were primarily oriented towards friends, both within and outside the West End. Mr. Borowski, a highly skilled manual worker with a moderately high income, was as deeply attached to the West End as his wife.

Mr. Borowski missed the West End very much but was quite satisfied with their new situation and could anticipate feeling thoroughly at home in the new neighborhood. Mrs. Borowski proclaims that "home is where you hang your hat; it's up to you to make the adjustments." But she also says, "If I knew the people were coming back to the West End, I would pick up this little house and put it back on my corner." She claims she was not sad after relocation but, when asked how she felt when the building she lived in was torn down, a strangely morbid association is aroused: "It's just like a plant . . . when you tear up its roots, it dies! I didn't die but I felt kind of bad. It was home. . . . Don't look back, try to go ahead."

Despite evidences of underlying grief, both Mr. and Mrs. Borowski have already adjusted to the change with remarkable alacrity. They bought a one-family house and have many friends in the new area. They do not feel as close to their new neighbors as they did to their West End friends, and they still maintain extensive contact with the latter. They are comfortable and happy in their new surroundings and maintain the close, warm, and mutually appreciative marital relationship they formerly had.

Mr. and Mrs. Borowski, and particularly Mrs. Borowski, reveal a sense of loss which is largely submerged beneath active efforts to deal with the present. It was possible for them to do this both because of personality factors (that is, the ability to deny the intense affective meaning of the change and to detach themselves from highly "cathected" objects with relative ease) and because of prior social patterns and orientations. Not only is Mr. Borowski, by occupation, in the highest group of working-class status, but this family has been "transitional" for some time. Remaining in the West End was clearly a matter of preference for them. They could have moved out quite easily on the basis of income, and many of their friends were scattered throughout metropolitan Boston. But while they are less self-consciously mobile than the Giuliano's, they had already shifted to many patterns more typical of the middle class before leaving the West End. These ranged from their joint weekly shopping expeditions to their recreational patterns, which included such sports as boating and such regular plans as yearly vacations. They experienced a disruption in continuity by virtue of their former spatial and group identity. But the bases for maintaining this identity had undergone many changes over the years; and they had already established a feeling for places and people, for a potential redefinition of "home" which was less contingent on the immediate and local availability of familiar spaces and familiar friends. Despite their preparedness for the move by virtue of cultural orientation, social experience, and personal disposition, the change was considerably wrenching for them. But, to the extent that they can be categorized as "over-adjusters," the residue of their lives in the West End is primarily a matter of painful memories which are only occasionally reawakened.

4. The alternate deviant pattern, minimal prerelocation commitment associated with severe postrelocation grief, is manifested by

Mr. and Mrs. Pagliuca. As in the previous case, this classification applies more fully to Mrs. Pagliuca, since Mr. Pagliuca appears to have had stronger ties to the West End. Mr. Pagliuca is a second-generation American, but Mrs. Pagliuca is first-generation, from an urban European background. For both of them, however, there is some evidence that the sadness and regret about the loss of the West End should perhaps be designated as pseudogrief.

Mrs. Pagliuca had a difficult time in the West End. But she also had a difficult time before that. She moved into the West End when she got married. And she complained bitterly about her marriage, her husband's relatives, West Enders in general. She said of the West End: "I don't like it. The people . . . the buildings are full of rats. There are no places to play for the children." She liked the apartment but complained about the lady downstairs, the dirt, the repairs required, and the coldness during the winter. She also complained a great deal about lack of money. Her husband's wages were not too low but he seemed to have periods of unemployment and often drank his money away.

Mr. Pagliuca was attached to some of his friends and to the bars in the West End. But he didn't like his housing situation there. And his reaction tended to be one of bitterness ("a rotten deal") rather than of sadness. Both Mr. and Mrs. Pagliuca are quite satisfied with their postrelocation apartment but are thoroughly dissatisfied with the area. They have had considerable difficulty with neighbors: ". . . . I don't like this; people are mean here; my children get blamed for anything and everything; and there's no transportation near here." She now idealizes the West End and claims that she misses everything about it.

Mr. Pagliuca is an unskilled manual laborer. Financial problems create a constant focus for difficulty and arguments. But both Mr. and Mrs. Pagliuca appear more satisfied with one another than before relocation. They have four children, some of whom are in legal difficulty. There is also some evidence of past cruelty toward the children, at least on Mrs. Pagliuca's part.

It is evident from this summary that the Pagliuca family is deviant in a social as well as in a statistical sense. They show few signs of adjusting to the move or, for that matter, of any basic potential for successful adjustment to further moves (which they are now planning). It may be that families with such initial difficulties, with such a tenuous basis for maintaining a sense of continuity under any circumstances, suffer most acutely from disruption of these minimal ties. The Pagliuca family has few inner resources and, having lost the minimal external resources signified by a gross sense of belonging, of being tolerated if not accepted, they appear to be hopelessly at sea. Although we refer to their grief as "pseudogrief" on the basis of the shift from prerelocation to postrelocation statements, there is a sense in which it is quite real. Within the postrelocation interviews their responses are quite consistent; and a review of all the data suggests that, although their ties were quite modest, their current difficulties have revealed the importance of these meager involvements and the problems of reestablishing anew an equivalent basis for identity formation. Thus, even for Mr. and Mrs. Pagliuca, we can speak of the disruption in the sense of continuity, although this continuity was based on a very fragile experience of minimal comfort, with familiar places and relatively tolerant people. Their grief reaction, pseudo or real, may further influence (and be influenced by) dissatisfactions with any new residential situation. The fact that it is based on an idealized past accentuates rather than minimizes its effect on current expectations and behavior.

CONCLUSIONS

Grieving for a lost home is evidently a widespread and serious social phenomenon following in the wake of urban dislocation. It is likely to increase social and psychological "pathology" in a limited number of instances; and it is also likely to create new opportunities for some, and to increase the rate of social mobility for others. For the greatest number, dislocation is unlikely to have either effect but does lead to intense personal suffering despite moderately successful adaptation to the total situation of relocation. Under these circumstances, it becomes most critical that we face the realities of the effects of relocation on working-class residents of slums and, on the basis of knowledge and understanding, that we learn to deal more effectively with the problems engendered.

In evaluating these data on the effect of prerelocation experiences on postrelocation reactions of grief, we have arrived at a number of conclusions:

1. The affective reaction to the loss of the West End can be quite

precisely described as a grief response showing most of the characteristics of grief and mourning for a lost person.

2. One of the important components of the grief reaction is the
fragmentation of the sense of spatial identity. This is manifest, not
only in the prerelocation experience of the spatial area as an expanded
"home," but in the varying degrees of grief following relocation,
arising from variations in the prerelocation orientation to and use of
local spatial regions.

3. Another component, of equal importance, is the dependence of
the sense of group identity on stable, social networks. Dislocation
necessarily led to the fragmentation of this group identity which was
based, to such a large extent, on the external availability and overt
contact with familiar groups of people.

4. Associated with these "cognitive" components, described as the
sense of spatial identity and the sense of group identity, are strong
affective qualities. We have not tried to delineate them but they appear to fall into the realm of a feeling of security in and commitment
to the external spatial and group patterns which are the tangible, visible aspects of these identity components. However, a predisposition
to depressive reactions also markedly affects the depth of grief reaction.

5. Theoretically, we can speak of spatial and group identity as
critical foci of the sense of continuity. This sense of continuity is not
necessarily contingent on the external stability of place, people, and
security or support. But for the working class these concrete, external
resources and the experience of stability, availability, and familiarity
which they provide are essential for a meaningful sense of continuity.
Thus, dislocation and the loss of the residential area represent a fragmentation of some of the essential components of the sense of continuity in the working class.

It is in the light of these observations and conclusions that we
must consider problems of social planning which are associated with
the changes induced by physical planning for relocation. Urban planning cannot be limited to "bricks and mortar." While these data tell
us little about the importance of housing or the aspects of housing
which are important, they indicate that considerations of a nonhous-
ing nature are critical. There is evidence, for example, that the
frequency of the grief response is not affected by such housing factors

as increase or decrease in apartment size or home ownership. But physical factors may be of great importance when related to the subjective significance of different spatial and physical arrangements, or to their capacity for gratifying different sociocultural groups. For the present, we can only stress the importance of local areas as *spatial and social* arrangements which are central to the lives of working-class people. And, in view of the enormous importance of such local areas, we are led to consider the convergence of familiar people and familiar places as a focal consideration in formulating planning decisions.

We can learn to deal with these problems only through research, through exploratory and imaginative service programs, and through a more careful consideration of the place of residential stability in salvaging the precarious thread of continuity. The outcomes of crises are always manifold and, just as there is an increase in strain and difficulty, so also there is an increase in opportunities for adapting at a more satisfying level of functioning. The judicious use of minimal resources of counseling and assistance may permit many working-class people to reorganize and integrate a meaningful sense of spatial and group identity under the challenge of social change. Only a relatively small group of those whose functioning has always been marginal and who cannot cope with the added strain of adjusting to wholly new problems are likely to require major forms of intervention.

In general, our results would imply the necessity for providing increased opportunities for maintaining a sense of continuity for those people, mainly from the working class, whose residential areas are being renewed. This may involve several factors: (1) diminishing the amount of drastic redevelopment and the consequent mass demolition of property and mass dislocation from homes; (2) providing more frequently for people to move within their former residential areas during and after the renewal; and (3) when dislocation and relocation are unavoidable, planning the relocation possibilities in order to provide new areas which can be assimilated to old objectives. A closer examination of slum areas may even provide some concrete information regarding specific physical variables, the physical and spatial arrangements typical of slum areas and slum housing, which offer considerable gratification to the residents. These may often be translated into effective modern architectural and areal design. And, in conjunction with planning decisions which take more careful account of the human consequences of urban physical change, it is possible to utilize social, psychological, and psychiatric services. The use of highly skilled resources, including opportunities for the education of professional and even lay personnel in largely unfamiliar problems and methods, can minimize some of the more destructive and widespread effects of relocation; and, for some families, can offer constructive experiences in dealing with new adaptational possibilities. The problem is large. But only by assuring the integrity of some of the external bases for the sense of continuity in the working class, and by maximizing the opportunities for meaningful adaptation, can we accomplish planned urban change without serious hazard to human welfare.

[*Bibliographical note:* see studies by Erikson (1946; 1956) and Firey (1947).]

The following works, *not previously cited* in this book, should be of particular concern to individuals wishing additional readings on stress and coping:

Arnold, M. (ed.). 1970. *Feelings and Emotions*. New York, Academic Press.

Averill, J. R. 1968. Grief: Its nature and significance. *Psychological Bulletin* 70:721–48.

—— 1973. Personal control over aversive stimuli and its relationship to stress. *Psychological Bulletin* 80:286–303.

Baker, G. W. and D. W. Chapman (eds.). 1962. *Man and Society in Disaster*. New York, Basic Books.

Beck, A. T. 1967. *Depression*. New York, Harper and Row.

Benedict, R. 1946. *The Chrysanthemum and the Sword*. Boston, Houghton Mifflin.

Bettelheim, B. 1960. *The Informed Heart*. New York, The Free Press of Glencoe.

Bourne, P. G., R. M. Rose, and J. W. Mason. 1967. Urinary 17-OHCS levels. *Archives of General Psychiatry* 17:104–10.

Bowlby, J. 1973. *Separation: Anxiety and Anger*. Attachment and Loss series. Vol. 2. New York, Basic Books.

Coelho, G. V., D. A. Hamburg, R. Moos, and P. Randolph (eds.). 1970. *Coping and Adaptation: A Behavioral Sciences Bibliography*. Chevy Chase, Maryland, National Institute of Mental Health.

Ekman, P., and W. V. Friesen. 1975. *Unmasking the Face*. Englewood Cliffs, Prentice-Hall.

Glass, D. C. (ed.). 1967. *Neurophysiology and Emotion*. New York, The Rockefeller University Press and Russell Sage Foundation.

Izard, C. E. 1971. *The Face of Emotion*. New York, Appleton-Century-Crofts.

Klausner, S. Z. (ed.). 1968. *Why Man Takes Chances: Studies in Stress-Seeking*. New York, Anchor Books.

Kubler-Ross, E. 1969. *On Death and Dying*. New York, Macmillan.

Lazarus, R. S. 1976. *Patterns of Adjustment*. New York, McGraw-Hill.

Lewis, O. 1966. The culture of poverty. *Scientific American* 215:19–25.

Lifton, R. J. 1967. *Death in Life*. New York, Random House.

Mason, J. W. 1970. Strategy in psychosomatic research. *Psychosomatic Medicine* 32:427–39.

May, R. 1950. *The Meaning of Anxiety*. New York, The Ronald Press.

Neugarten, B. L. (ed.). 1968. *Middle Age and Aging: A Reader in Social Psychology*. Chicago, University of Chicago Press.

Opton, E. M., Jr. 1971. It never happened and besides they deserved it. In N. Sanford and C. Comstock (eds.), *Sanctions for Evil.* San Francisco, Jossey-Bass, pp. 49–70.

Parkes, C. M. 1972. *Bereavement.* New York, International Universities Press.

Sarason, I. G., and C. D. Spielberger (eds.). 1975. *Stress and Anxiety.* Vol. 2. Washington, D.C., Hemisphere Publishing Corporation.

Schwartz, G. E. 1973. Biofeedback as therapy: Some theoretical and practical issues. *American Psychologist* 28:666–73.

Seligman, M. E. P. 1975. *Helplessness: On Depression, Development, and Death.* San Francisco, W. H. Freeman and Company.

Selye, H. 1974. *Stress Without Distress.* Philadelphia, New York, J. B. Lippincott Co.

—— 1975. Confusion and controversy in the stress field. *Journal of Human Stress* 1:37–44.

Shneidman, E. S. 1973. Suicide notes reconsidered. *Psychiatry* 36:379–94.

Sjoback, H. 1973. *The Psychoanalytic Theory of Defensive Processes.* New York, John Wiley and Sons.

Spielberger, C. D., and I. G. Sarason (eds.). 1975. *Stress and Anxiety.* Vol. 1. Washington, D.C., Hemisphere Publishing Corporation.

Tanner, O., and the editors of Time-Life Books. 1976. *Stress.* New York, Time-Life Books.

Weisman, A. D. 1972. *On Dying and Denying.* New York, Behavioral Publications, Inc.

Weiss, J. M. 1968. Effects of coping response on stress. *Journal of Comparative and Physiological Psychology* 65:251–60.

Zubek, J. P. (ed.). 1969. *Sensory Deprivation: Fifteen Years of Research.* New York, Appleton-Century-Crofts.

REFERENCES

Abraham, K. 1911. Notes on the psychoanalytical investigation and treatment of manic-depressive insanity and allied conditions. In *Selected Papers of Karl Abraham*. Vol. 1. New York, Basic Books (1953), pp. 137–56.

—— 1924. A short study of the development of the libido, viewed in the light of mental disorders. In *Selected Papers of Karl Abraham*. Vol. 1. New York, Basic Books (1953), pp. 418–501.

Abram, H. S. 1965. Adaptation to open heart surgery: A psychiatric study of responses to the threat of death. *American Journal of Psychiatry* 122:659–67.

Ainsworth, H. 1958. Rigidity, insecurity, and stress. *Journal of Abnormal and Social Psychology* 56:67–74.

Aldrich, C. K. 1974. Some dynamics of anticipatory grief. In B. Schoenberg, A. C. Carr, A. H. Kutscher, D. Peretz, and I. K. Goldberg (eds.), *Anticipatory Grief*. New York, Columbia University Press, pp. 3–9.

Alexander, I. E., R. S. Colley, and M. Adlerstein. 1957. Is death a matter of indifference? *Journal of Psychology* 43:277–83.

Allee, W. C. 1951. *Cooperation Among Animals*. New York, Henry Schuman.

Allport, G. W., and P. E. Vernon. 1933. *Studies in Expressive Movement*. New York, Macmillan.

Anastasi, A. 1964. *Fields of Applied Psychology*. New York, McGraw-Hill.

Anderson, N. H. 1970. *Toward a Quieter City*. New York, A Report of the Mayor's Task Force on Noise Control (January).

Andreasen, N. J. C., A. S. Norris, and C. E. Hartford. 1971. Incidence of long-term psychiatric complications in severely burned adults. *Annals of Surgery* 174:785–93.

Andreasen, N. J. C., R. Noyes, Jr., and C. E. Hartford. 1972. Factors influencing adjustment of burn patients during hospitalization. *Psychosomatic Medicine* 34:517–25.

Andreasen, N. J. C., R. Noyes, Jr., C. E. Hartford, G. Brodland, and S. Proctor. 1972. Management of emotional reactions in seriously burned adults. *New England Journal of Medicine* 286:65–69.

Appley, M. H. 1962. Motivation, threat perception, and the induction of psychological stress. *Proceedings of the Sixteenth International Congress of Psychology*, Bonn, 1960. Amsterdam, North Holland Publishers, pp. 880–81 (Abstract).

Appley, M. H., and R. Trumbull. 1967a. On the concept of psychological stress. In M. H. Appley and R. Trumbull (eds.), *Psychological Stress*. New York, Appleton-Century-Crofts, pp. 1–13.

Appley, M. H., and R. Trumbull (eds.). 1967b. *Psychological Stress*. New York, Appleton-Century-Crofts.

Arnold, M. B. 1960. *Emotion and Personality.* Vols. 1 and 2. New York, Columbia University Press.

Atthowe, J. M., Jr. 1960. Types of conflict and their resolution: A reinterpretation. *Journal of Experimental Psychology* 59:1–9.

―――― 1961. Interpersonal decision making: The resolution of a dyadic conflict. *Journal of Abnormal and Social Psychology* 62:114–19.

Averill, J. R., and E. M. Opton, Jr. 1968. Psychophysiological assessment: Rationale and problems. In P. McReynolds (ed.), *Advances in Psychological Assessment.* Vol. 1. Palo Alto, California, Science and Behavior Books, pp. 265–88.

Averill, J. R., and M. Rosenn. 1972. Vigilant and nonvigilant coping strategies and psychophysiological stress reactions during the anticipation of electric shock. *Journal of Personality and Social Psychology* 23:128–41.

Axline, V. 1971. *Dibs—In Search of Self.* Harmondsworth, England, Penguin Books (reprint of 1964 publication).

Azrin, N. H. 1958. Some effects of noise on human behavior. *Journal of Experimental Analysis of Behavior* 1:183–200.

Bailey, A. 1969. Noise is a slow agent of death. *New York Times Magazine* 46 (November 23):131–35.

Bales, R. F. 1951. *Interaction Process Analysis: A Method for the Study of Small Groups.* Reading, Massachusetts, Addison-Wesley Press.

―――― 1954. In conference. *Harvard Business Review* 32:44–50.

Barber, T. X. 1961. Death by suggestion: A critical note. *Psychosomatic Medicine* 23:153–55.

Bard, P. 1928. A diencephalic mechanism for the expression of rage with special reference to the sympathetic nervous system. *American Journal of Physiology* 84:490–513.

Barnett, S. A. 1960. Social behaviour among tame rats and among wild-white hybrids. *Proceedings of the Zoological Society of London* 134:611–21.

―――― 1963. *The Rat: A Study in Behaviour.* Chicago, Aldine.

―――― 1964. Social stress. In J. D. Carthy and C. L. Duddington (eds.), *Viewpoints in Biology.* Vol. 3. London, England, Butterworths, pp. 170–218.

Barrow, J. H., Jr. 1955. Social behavior in fresh-water fish and its effect on resistance to trypanosomes. *Proceedings of the National Academy of Science* 41:676–79.

Basedow, H. 1925. *The Australian Aboriginal.* Adelaide, F. W. Preece and Sons.

Basowitz, H., H. Persky, S. J. Korchin, and R. R. Grinker. 1955. *Anxiety and Stress.* New York, McGraw-Hill.

Beam, J. C. 1955. Serial learning and conditioning under real-life stress. *Journal of Abnormal and Social Psychology* 51:543–52.

Becker, E. 1973. *The Denial of Death.* New York, The Free Press.

Beecher, H. K. 1952. Experimental pharmacology and measurement of the subjective response. *Science* 116:157–62.

Bem, J., M. A. Wallach, and N. Kogan. 1965. Group decision making under risk of aversive consequences. *Journal of Personality and Social Psychology* 1:453–60.

Benoit, J., I. Assenmacher, and E. Brard. 1955. Evolution testiculaire du canard domestique maintenu à l'obscurité totale pendant une longue durée. *Comptes-Rendus Academie des Sciences* 241 (Paris):251–53.

—— 1956. Etude de l'évolution testiculaire du canard domestique soumis très jeune à un éclairement artificiel permanent pendant deux ans. *Comptes-Rendus Academie des Sciences* 242 (Paris):3113–15.

Berkeley, A. W. 1952. Level of aspiration in relation to adrenal cortical activity and the concept of stress. *Journal of Comparative and Physiological Psychology* 45:443–49.

Berkun, M. M., H. M. Bialek, R. P. Kern, and K. Yagi. 1962. Experimental studies of psychological stress in man. *Psychological Monographs* 76:Whole No. 534.

Berlyne, D. E. 1957. Conflict and choice time. *British Journal of Psychology* 48:106–18.

—— 1960. *Conflict, Arousal, and Curiosity.* New York, McGraw-Hill.

Bernard, V. W., P. Ottenberg, and F. Redl. 1965. Dehumanization: A composite psychological defense in relation to modern war. In M. Schwebel (ed.), *Behavioral Science and Human Survival.* Palo Alto, California, Science and Behavior Books, pp. 64–82.

Bernardis, L., and F. Skelton. 1963. Effect of crowding on hypertension and growth in rats bearing regenerating adrenals; *and* Effect of gentling on development of adrenal regeneration hypertension in immature female rats. *Proceedings of the Society for Experimental Biology and Medicine* 113:952–57.

Berrien, F. K. 1946. The effects of noise. *Psychological Bulletin* 43:141–61.

Bettelheim, B. 1967. *The Empty Fortress: Infantile Autism and the Birth of Self.* London, Collier-Macmillan.

Bibring, E. 1953. The mechanism of depression. In P. Greenacre (ed.), *Affective Disorders.* New York, International Universities Press, pp. 13–48.

Bierman, H. R. 1956. Parent participation program in pediatric oncology: A preliminary report. *Journal of Chronic Diseases* 3:632–39.

Birnbaum, R. M. 1964. Autonomic reaction to threat and confrontation conditions of psychological stress. University of California, Berkeley, unpublished doctoral dissertation.

Bishop, L. F., and P. Reichert. 1969. The psychological impact of the coronary care unit. *Psychosomatics* 10:189–92.

Block, C. H. 1964. Interrelations of stress and anxiety in determining problem-solving performance. *Dissertation Abstracts* 25:1316.

Blum, S. 1967. Noise: How much more can we take? *McCall's* 49 (January):113–16.

Boggs, D. H., and J. R. Simon. 1968. Differential effects of noise on tasks of varying complexity. *Journal of Applied Psychology* 52:148–53.

Boklage, M. G. 1970. ICU training program. *Hospitals* 44:78–80.

Bourke-White, M. 1963. *Portrait of Myself.* New York, Simon and Schuster.

Bowlby, J. 1952. *Maternal Care and Mental Health.* Geneva, World Health Organization.

—— 1961. Processes of mourning. *International Journal of Psychoanalysis* 42:317–40.

Bozeman, M. F., C. E. Orbach, and A. M. Sutherland. 1955. Psychological impact of cancer and its treatment, III. The adaptation of mothers to the threatened loss of their children through leukemia: Part I. *Cancer* 8:1–19.

Brehm, M. L., K. W. Back, and M. D. Bogdonoff. 1964. A physiological effect of cognitive dissonance under stress and deprivation. *Journal of Abnormal and Social Psychology* 69:303–10.

Broadbent, D. E. 1954. Some effects of noise on visual performance. *Quarterly Journal of Experimental Psychology* 6:1–5.

—— 1957. Effects of noise on behavior. In C. M. Harris (ed.). *Handbook of Noise Control.* New York, McGraw-Hill, pp. 10/1–10/34.

—— 1958. *Perception and Communication.* London, Pergamon.

Bronson, F. H., and B. E. Eleftheriou. 1965a. Adrenal response to fighting in mice: Separation of physical and psychological causes. *Science* 147:627–28.

—— 1965b. Relative effects of fighting on bound and unbound corticosterone in mice. *Proceedings of the Society for Experimental Biology and Medicine* 118:146–49.

Brown, A. H. 1947. Water shortage in the desert. In E. F. Adolph (ed.), *Physiology of Man in the Desert.* New York, Interscience Publishers, pp. 136–59.

Brown, C. C. (ed.). 1967. *Methods in Psychophysiology.* Baltimore, Maryland, Williams and Wilkins.

Brown, N. O. 1959. *Life Against Death: The Psychoanalytical Meaning of History.* New York, Viking Books.

Brown, W. 1845. *New Zealand and Its Aborigines.* London, Smith, Elder, and Company.

Browne, I., and T. Hackett. Unpublished data.

Burns, W. 1968. *Noise and Man.* London, John Murray.

Buss, A. H. 1966. *Psychopathology.* New York, John Wiley and Sons.

Byrne, D. 1964. Repression-sensitization as a dimension of personality. In B. A. Maher (ed.), *Progress in Experimental Personality Research.* Vol. 1. New York, Academic Press, pp. 169–220.

Calhoun, J. B. 1949. A method for self-control of population growth among mammals living in the wild. *Science* 109:333–35.

—— 1962. Population density and social pathology. *Scientific American* 206:139–48.

Cannon, W. B. 1923. *Traumatic Shock.* New York, D. Appleton and Company.

—— 1929. *Bodily Changes in Pain, Hunger, Fear, and Rage.* Boston, C. T. Branford Company.

—— 1942. "Voodoo" death. *American Anthropologist* 44:169–81.

Cannon, W. B., J. Fraser, and A. N. Hooper. 1917. *Report No. 2 of the Special Investigation Committee on Surgical Shock and Allied Conditions, Medical Research Committee, on Some Alterations in the Distribution and Character of the Blood in Wound Conditions.* London, Great Britain, Special Report Series, Medical Research Committee.

Capretta, P. J., and M. M. Berkun. 1962. Validity and reliability of certain measures of psychological stress. *Psychological Reports* 10:875–76.

Carlson, J. G., and R. D. Wood. 1974. Need the final solution be justified? University of Hawaii, unpublished manuscript.

Carpenter, C. R. 1958. Territoriality: A review of concepts and problems. In A. Roe and G. G. Simpson (eds.), *Behavior and Evolution.* New Haven, Yale University Press, pp. 224–50.

Castaneda, A., and D. S. Palermo. 1955. Psychomotor performance as a function of amount of training and stress. *Journal of Experimental Psychology* 50:175–79.

Chess, S. 1971. Autism in children with congenital rubella. *Journal of Autism and Childhood Schizophrenia* 1:33–47.

Chitty, D. 1958. Self-regulation of numbers through changes in viability. *Cold Spring Harbor Symposium of Quantitative Biology* 22:277–80.

Chodoff, P. 1959. Adjustment to disability: Some observations on patients with multiple sclerosis. *Journal of Chronic Diseases* 9:653–70.

Choron, J. 1963. *Death and Western Thought.* New York, Collier Books.

Christian, J. J., and D. E. Davis. 1956. The relationship between adrenal weight and population status of urban Norway rats. *Journal of Mammalogy* 37:475–86.

Christian, J. J., V. Flyger, and D. E. Davis. 1960. Factors in mass mortality of a herd of Sika deer (*Cervus nippon*). *Chesapeake Science* 1:79–95.

Christian, J. J., and H. O. Williamson. 1958. Effect of crowding on experimental granuloma formation in mice. *Proceedings of the Society for Experimental Biology and Medicine* 99:385–87.

Clancy, H., and G. McBride. 1969. The autistic process and its treatment. *Journal of Child Psychology and Psychiatry and Allied Disciplines* 10:233–44.

Cleland, J. B. 1928. Disease amongst the Australian aborigines. Part IV. *Journal of Tropical Medicine and Hygiene* 31:232–35.

Cobb, B. C., R. L. Clark, Jr., C. McGuire, and C. D. Howe. 1954. Patient-responsible delay of treatment of cancer: A social psychological study. *Cancer* 7:920–26.

Cobb, S., W. Bauer, and I. Whitney. 1939. Environmental factors in rheumatoid arthritis. *Journal of the American Medical Association* 113:668–70.

Cobb, S., and E. Lindemann. 1943. Neuropsychiatric observations after the Cocoanut Grove fire. *Annals of Surgery* 117:814–24.

Cochrane, A. L. 1934. Elie Metschnikoff and his theory of an *"Instinct de la mort." International Journal of Psychoanalysis* 15:265–70.

Coelho, G. V., D. A. Hamburg, and J. E. Adams (eds.). 1974. *Coping and Adaptation.* New York, Basic Books.

Cofer, C. N., and M. H. Appley. 1964. *Motivation: Theory and Research.* New York, John Wiley and Sons.

Cohen, A. 1969. Effects of noise on psychological state. In W. D. Ward and J. E. Frick (eds.), *Noise as a Public Health Hazard: Proceedings of the Conference.* ASHA Reports 4. Washington, D.C., The American Speech and Hearing Association (February), pp. 74–88.

Cohen, A. K. 1955. *Delinquent Boys.* Glencoe, Illinois, The Free Press.

Cohen, F. 1975. Psychological preparation, coping, and recovery from surgery. University of California, Berkeley, unpublished doctoral dissertation.

Cohen, F., and R. S. Lazarus. 1973. Active coping processes, coping dispositions, and recovery from surgery. *Psychosomatic Medicine* 35:375–89.

Coleman, J. C. 1976. *Abnormal Psychology and Modern Life.* 5th ed. Glenview, Illinois; Scott, Foresman and Company.

Copeland, J., and J. Hodges. 1973. *For the Love of Ann.* London, Arrow Original.

Corso, J. F. 1952. The effects of noise on human behavior. Report WADC-No. 53-81. Wright-Patterson Air Force Base, Ohio, Wright Air Development Center.

Coser, R. L. 1959. Some social functions of laughter. *Human Relations* 12:171–82.

Cowen, E. L. 1952. The influence of varying degrees of psychological stress on problem-solving rigidity. *Journal of Abnormal and Social Psychology* 47:512–19.

Craffey, R. 1960. The cardiac pacemaker. *Massachusetts General Hospital Nursing Alumnae Quarterly* 1:8–11.

Cramond, W., and D. Aberd. 1954. Psychological aspects of uterine disfunction. *Lancet* 2:1241–45.

Creak, M. 1961. Schizophrenic syndrome in childhood: Progress report of a working party. *British Medical Journal* 2:889–90.

Croog, S. H. 1961. Ethnic origins, educational level, and responses to a health questionnaire. *Human Organization* 20:65–69.

Curry-Lindahl, K. 1963. New theory on a fabled exodus. *Natural History* 122:46–53.

D'Amato, M. E., and W. E. Gumenik. 1960. Some effects of immediate versus randomly delayed shock on an instrumental response and cognitive processes. *Journal of Abnormal and Social Psychology* 60:64–67.

d'Ambrosio, R. 1971. *No Language but a Cry.* London, Cassell.

Dameshek, W., and F. Gunz. 1958. *Leukemia.* New York, Grune and Stratton.

Darley, M. M. 1966. Fear and social comparison as determinants of conformity behavior. *Journal of Personality and Social Psychology* 4:73–78.

Darwin, C. 1872. *The Expression of the Emotions in Man and the Animals.* London, John Murray.

Davis, D. E., and C. P. Read. 1958. Effect of behavior on development of resistance in trichinosis. *Proceedings of the Society for Experimental Biology and Medicine* 99:269–72.

Davis, J. M., W. F. McCourt, J. Courtney, and P. Solomon. 1961. Sensory deprivation: The role of social isolation. *Archives of General Psychiatry* 5:85–90.

Davis, R. C., and T. Berry. 1964. Gastrointestinal reactions to response-contingent stimulation. *Psychological Reports* 15:95–113.

Davis, R. C., A. M. Buchwald, and R. Frankmann. 1959. Autonomic and muscular responses and their relation to simple stimuli. *Psychological Monographs* 69:Whole No. 405.

Davis, S. W. 1956. Stress in combat. *Scientific American* 194:31–35.

Deevey, E. S. 1960. The hare and the haruspex: A cautionary tale. *American Scientist* 48:415–29.

DeMeyer, J. 1967. The environment of the intensive care unit. *Nursing Forum* 6:262–72.

Deutsch, H. 1937. Absence of grief. *Psychoanalytic Quarterly* 6:12–22.

Dey, F. L. 1970. Auditory fatigue and predicted permanent hearing defects from rock-and-roll music. *New England Journal of Medicine* 282:467–69.

Dittes, J. E. 1961. Impulsive closure as a reaction to failure induced threat. *Journal of Abnormal and Social Psychology* 63:562–69.

Dohrenwend, B. S., and B. P. Dohrenwend. 1966a. Stress situations, birth order, and psychological symptoms. Part 1. *Journal of Abnormal Psychology* 71:215–23.

—— 1966b. Stress situations, birth order and psychological symptoms. Part 2. *Journal of Abnormal Psychology* 71:215–23.

Dohrenwend, B. S., and B. P. Dohrenwend (eds.). 1974. *Stressful Life Events: Their Nature and Effects*. New York, John Wiley and Sons.

Dubos, R. 1965. *Man Adapting*. New Haven, Yale University Press.

Eckerman, W. C. 1964. The relationship of need achievement to production, job satisfaction, and psychological stress. *Dissertation Abstracts* 24:3446.

Efron, D., and J. P. Foley. 1937. A comparative investigation of gestural behavior patterns in Italian and Jewish groups living under different as well as similar environmental conditions. *Zeitschrift Fuer Sozialforschung* 6:151–59.

Egbert, L., G. Battit, C. Welch, and M. Bartlett. 1964. Reduction of postoperative pain by encouragement and instruction of patients. *New England Journal of Medicine* 270:825–27.

Eilbert, L. 1960. *Indoctrination Procedures for Personnel Assigned to Arctic Sites*. Final Report (January), Pittsburgh, Penn., American Institute for Research, Contract AF 41 (657) -241. Ladd AFB, Alaska, Arctic Aeromedical Lab.

Eissler, K. R. 1955. *The Psychiatrist and the Dying Patient*. New York, International Universities Press.

Ellenberger, H. F. 1970. *The Discovery of the Unconscious.* New York, Basic Books, Inc.

Elliott, R. 1965. Reaction time and heart rate as functions of magnitude of incentive and probability of success. *Journal of Personality and Social Psychology* 2:604–9.

——— 1966. Effects of uncertainty about the nature and advent of a noxious stimulus (shock) upon heart rate. *Journal of Personality and Social Psychology* 3:353–57.

Ellis, P. E., and J. B. Free. 1964. Social organization of animal communities. *Nature* 201:861–63.

Elton, C. S. 1958. *The Ecology of Invasions by Animals and Plants.* New York, John Wiley and Sons.

Engel, G. L. 1961. Is grief a disease?: A challenge for medical research. *Psychosomatic Medicine* 23:18–22.

——— 1962. *Psychological Development in Health and Disease.* Philadelphia, W. B. Saunders.

Engel, G. L., and J. Romano. 1959. Delirium: A syndrome of cerebral insufficiency. *Journal of Chronic Diseases* 9:260–77.

Epstein, S. 1967. Toward a unified theory of anxiety. In B. A. Maher (ed.), *Progress in Experimental Personality Research.* Vol. 4. New York, Academic Press, pp. 1–89.

Eriksen, C. W., R. S. Lazarus, and J. R. Strange. 1952. Psychological stress and its personality correlates. *Journal of Personality* 20:277–86.

Erikson, E. 1946. Ego development and historical change. *Psychoanalytic Study of the Child* 2:359–96.

——— 1956. The problem of ego identity. *Journal of the American Psychoanalytic Association* 4:56–121.

Etkin, W. 1964. *Social Behavior and Organization Among Vertebrates.* Chicago, University of Chicago Press.

Farber, I. E., and K. W. Spence. 1956. Effects of anxiety, stress, and task variables on reaction time. *Journal of Personality* 25:1–18.

Feather, N. T. 1965. The relationship of expectation of success to need achievement and test anxiety. *Journal of Personality and Social Psychology* 1:118–26.

——— 1966. Effects of prior success and failure on expectations of success and subsequent performance. *Journal of Personality and Social Psychology* 3:237–99.

Feifel, H. (ed.). 1959. *The Meaning of Death.* New York, McGraw-Hill.

Feifel, H., J. Freilich, and L. J. Hermann. 1973. Death fear in dying heart and cancer patients. *Journal of Psychosomatic Research* 17:161–66.

Feldman, S. E., and J. K. Rice. 1965. Tolerance for unambiguous feedback. *Journal of Personality and Social Psychology* 2:341–47.

Fenichel, O. 1945. *The Psychoanalytic Theory of Neurosis.* New York, Norton.

Fenz, W. D. 1964. Conflict and stress as related to physiological activation and sensory perceptual and cognitive functioning. *Psychological Monographs: General and Applied* 78:Whole No. 585.

Festinger, L. A. 1957. *A Theory of Cognitive Dissonance.* Evanston; Row, Peterson and Company.

Finney, J. M. T. 1934. Discussion of papers on shock. *Annals of Surgery* 100:746.

Firey, W. 1947. *Land Use in Central Boston.* Cambridge, Harvard University Press.

Fischer, H. K., B. Dlin, W. Winters, S. Hagner, and E. Weiss. 1962. Time patterns and emotional factors related to the onset of coronary occlusion. Presented to the Annual Meeting of the American Psychosomatic Society.

Flickinger, G., and H. Ratcliffe. 1961. The effect of grouping on the adrenals and gonads of chickens. *Proceedings of the Federation of American Societies for Experimental Biology* 20:176.

Fox, R. 1959. *Experiment Perilous.* New York, The Free Press of Glencoe.

Frank, J. D. 1961. *Persuasion and Healing: A Comparative Study of Psychotherapy.* New York, Schocken Books.

Freeman, J. J. 1958. *Principles of Noise.* New York, John Wiley and Sons.

Freeman, N. E. 1933. Decrease in blood volume after prolonged hyperactivity of the sympathetic nervous system. *American Journal of Physiology* 103:185–202.

Freeman, N. E., H. Freedman, and C. C. Miller. 1941. The production of shock by the prolonged continuous injection of adrenalin in unanesthetized dogs. *American Journal of Physiology* 131:545–53.

Freeman, N. E., R. S. Morison, and M. E. MacK. Sawyer. 1933. The effect of dehydration on adrenal secretion and its relation to shock. *American Journal of Physiology* 104:628–35.

Freireich, E. J., E. A. Gehan, D. Sulman, D. R. Boggs, and E. Frei, III. 1961. The effect of chemotherapy on acute leukemia in the human. *Journal of Chronic Diseases* 14:593–608.

Freud, A. 1937. *The Ego and the Mechanisms of Defense.* New York, International Universities Press.

Freud, S. 1917. Mourning and melancholia. In *Collected Papers.* Vol. 4. New York, Basic Books (1959), pp. 152–70.

—— 1936. *The Problem of Anxiety.* New York, Norton (also published as *Inhibitions, Symptoms and Anxiety*).

Fried, M. 1963. Grieving for a lost home. In L. J. Duhl (ed.), *The Urban Condition.* New York, Basic Books, pp. 151–71.

Friedman, M., and R. H. Rosenman. 1974. *Type A Behavior and Your Heart.* New York, Alfred Knopf.

Friedman, S. B., P. Chodoff, J. W. Mason, and D. A. Hamburg. 1963. Behavioral observations on parents anticipating the death of a child. *Pediatrics* 32:610–25.

Friedman, S. B., J. W. Mason, and D. A. Hamburg. 1963. Urinary 17-hydroxycorticosteroid levels in parents of children with neoplastic disease: A study of chronic psychological stress. *Psychosomatic Medicine* 25:364–76.

—— Unpublished data.

Fritz, C. E. 1957. Disasters compared in six American communities. *Human Organization* 16:6–9.

Fritz, C. E., and E. S. Marks. 1954. The NORC studies of human behavior in disaster. *Journal of Social Issues* 10:26–41.

Fukushima, D. K., H. L. Bradlow, L. Hellman, and T. F. Gallagher. 1968. On cortisol production rate. *Journal of Clinical Endocrinology and Metabolism* 28:1618–22.

—— 1969. Further studies of cortisol production rate. *Journal of Clinical Endocrinology and Metabolism* 29:1042–44.

Gal, R. 1973. Coping processes under seasickness conditions. Unpublished manuscript.

Gardam, J. F. 1969. Nursing stresses in the intensive care unit. *Journal of the American Medical Association* 208:2337–38 (Letters to the editor).

Gifford, S., and B. Murewski. 1964. Minimal sleep deprivation alone and in small groups: Effects on ego-functioning and 24 hour body temperature and adreno-cortical patterns. *Symposium on Medical Aspects of Stress in the Military Climate*. Washington, D. C., Walter Reed Army Institute of Research, Walter Reed Army Medical Center.

Glass, D. C., and J. E. Singer. 1972. *Urban Stress*. New York, Academic Press.

Glorig, A. 1958. *Noise and Your Ear*. New York, Grune and Stratton.

Goldberger, L. 1966. Cognitive test performance under LSD-25, placebo and isolation. *Journal of Nervous Mental Disorders* 142:4–9.

Golding, S. I., G. A. Atwood, and R. A. Goodman. 1966. Anxiety and two cognitive forms of resistance to the idea of death. *Psychological Reports* 18:359–64

Goldstein, K., and M. Scheerer. 1941. Abstract and concrete behavior: An experimental study with special tests. *Psychological Monographs* 53: Whole No. 2.

Goldstein, M. J. 1959. Relationship between coping and avoiding behavior an response to fear-arousing propaganda. *Journal of Abnormal and Social Psycholog* 58:247–52.

—— 1973. Individual differences in response to stress. *American Journal of Community Psychology* 2:113–37.

Gore, S. 1973. The influence of social support in ameliorating the consequenc of job loss. University of Michigan, Ann Arbor. Unpublished doctoral dissertatic

Graham, D. T., and I. Stevenson. 1963. Disease as response to life stress. In I. Lief, V. F. Lief, and N. R. Lief (eds.), *The Psychological Basis of Medical Practi* New York, Harper and Row, pp. 115–36.

Gray, S. J., C. S. Ramsey, R. Villarreal, and L. J. Krakaner. 1956. Adrenal influences upon the stomach and the gastric response to stress. In H. Selye and G. Hansen (eds.), *Fifth Annual Report on Stress*. (1955–56.) New York, MD Publications, Inc., p. 138.

Greenberg, I. M., and I. E. Alexander. 1962. Some correlates of thoughts and feelings concerning death. *Hillside Hospital Journal* 2:120–26.

Greene, W. A., Jr. 1958. Role of a vicarious object in the adaptation to object loss: I. Use of a vicarious object as a means of adjustment to separation from a significant person. *Psychosomatic Medicine* 20:344–50.

Greene, W. A., Jr., and G. Miller. 1958. Psychological factors and reticuloendothelial disease: IV. Observations on a group of children and adolescents with leukemia: An interpretation of disease development in terms of the mother-child unit. *Psychosomatic Medicine* 20:124–44.

Greenwood, M. 1935. *Epidemics and Crowd-Diseases*. London, Williams and Norgate.

Grinker, R. R., and J. P. Spiegel. 1945. *Men Under Stress*. Philadelphia, Blakiston.

Grinker, R. R., B. Willerman, A. Bradley, and A. Fastovsky. 1946. A study of psychological predisposition to the development of operational fatigue. Parts 1 and 2. *American Journal of Orthopsychiatry* 16:191–214.

Guetzkow, H., and J. Gyr. 1954. An analysis of conflict in decision-making groups. *Human Relations* 7:367–82.

Gullahorn, J. T. 1956. Measuring role conflict. *American Journal of Sociology* 61:299–303.

Haan, N. 1969. A tripartite model of ego functioning: Values and clinical research applications. *Journal of Nervous and Mental Diseases* 148:14–30.

Hackett, T. P., and N. H. Cassem. 1975. Psychological management of the myocardial infarction patient. *Journal of Human Stress* 1:25–38.

Hackett, T. P., N. H. Cassem, and H. Wishnie. 1969. Detection and treatment of anxiety in the coronary care unit. *American Heart Journal* 78:727–30.

Hackett, T. P., and A. D. Weisman. 1962. The treatment of the dying. *Current Psychiatric Therapies* 2:121–26.

—— 1964. Reactions to the imminence of death. In G. H. Grosser, H. Wechsler, and M. Greenblatt (eds.), *The Threat of Impending Disaster*. Cambridge, Mass., M. I. T. Press, pp. 300–11.

Haggard, E. A. 1949. Psychologial causes and results of stress. In Committee a Undersea Warfare (ed.), *Human Factors in Undersea Warfare*. Washington, .C., National Research Council, pp. 441–61.

Hall, E. T. 1959. *The Silent Language*. New York, Doubleday.

—— 1964. Silent assumptions in social communication. In D. Rioch and E. A. einstein (eds.), *Disorders of Communication*. Baltimore, Williams and Wilkins, . 41–55.

Hall, G. S. 1915. Thanatophobia and immortality. *American Journal of Psychology* 26:550–613.

Hamblin, R. L. 1958. Group integration during a crisis. *Human Relations* 11:67–77.

Hamburg, D. A., and J. E. Adams. 1967. A perspective on coping behavior: Seeking and utilizing information in major transitions. *Archives of General Psychiatry* 17:277–84.

Hamburg, D. A., C. P. Artz, E. Reiss, W. H. Amspacher, and R. E. Chambers. 1953. Clinical importance of emotional problems in the care of burn patients. *New England Journal of Medicine* 248:355–59.

Hamburg, D. A., G. V. Coelho, and J. E. Adams. 1974. Coping and adaptation: Steps toward a synthesis of biological and social perspectives. In G. V. Coelho, D. A. Hamburg, and J. E. Adams (eds.), *Coping and Adaptation.* New York, Basic Books, pp. 403–40.

Hamburg, D. A., B. Hamburg, and S. deGoza. 1953. Adaptive problems and mechanisms in severely burned patients. *Psychiatry* 16:1–20.

Hardy, J. D., H. G. Wolff, and H. Goodell. 1952. *Pain Sensations and Reactions.* Baltimore, Williams and Wilkins.

Hare, A. P. 1963. *Handbook of Small Group Research.* Glencoe, Illinois, The Free Press.

Harleston, B. W. 1962. Test anxiety and performance in problem-solving situations. *Journal of Personality* 30:557–73.

Harrington, A. 1969. *The Immortalist. New York, Random House.*

Harris, F. G., J. Mayer, and H. A. Becker. 1955. *Experiences in the Study of Combat in the Korean Theater.* I. *Report on Psychiatric and Psychological Data.* WRAIR-43-55 (November). Washington, D.C., Walter Reed Army Institute of Research, Walter Reed Army Medical Center.

Harris, W., R. R. Mackie, and C. L. Wilson. 1956. *Performance Under Stress: A Review and Critique of Recent Studies.* Tech. Rep. VI. ASTIA AD No. 10377Ϛ (July). Los Angeles, California, Human Factors Research Corporation.

Hay, D., and D. Oken. 1972. The psychological stresses of intensive care uni nursing. *Psychosomatic Medicine* 34:109–18.

Hediger, H. 1950. *Wild Animals in Captivity.* London, Butterworths.

Hill, R., and D. A. Hansen. 1962. Families in disaster. In G. W. Baker an E. W. Chapman (eds.), *Man and Society in Disaster.* New York, Basic Books, pp 185–221.

Hinde, R. A. 1960. An ethological approach. In J. M. Tanner (ed.), *Stress ar Psychiatric Disorder.* Oxford, Blackwell, pp. 49–58.

—— 1970. *Animal Behavior.* New York, McGraw-Hill.

Hinkle, L. E., Jr. 1974. The effect of exposure to culture change, social chang and changes in interpersonal relationships on health. In B. S. Dohrenwend a

B. P. Dohrenwend (eds.), *Stressful Life Events: Their Nature and Effects.* New York, John Wiley and Sons, pp. 9–44.

Hinton, J. M. 1963. The physical and mental distress of dying. *Quarterly Journal of Medicine* 32 (January, New series):1–21.

Hodges, W. F., and C. D. Spielberger. 1966. The effects of threat of shock on heart rate for subjects who differ in manifest anxiety and fear of shock. *Psychophysiology* 2:287–94.

Hoerr, S. O. 1963. Thoughts on what to tell the patient with cancer. *Cleveland Clinic Quarterly* 30:11–16.

Hofer, M. A., C. T. Wolff, S. B. Friedman, and J. W. Mason. 1972. A psychoendocrine study of bereavement: Part I. 17-hydroxycorticosteroid excretion rates of parents following death of their children from leukemia. *Psychosomatic Medicine* 34:481–91.

Hoggart, R. 1957. *The Uses of Literacy: Changing Patterns in English Mass Culture.* New York, Oxford University Press.

Hokanson, J. E., and M. Burgess. 1962. The effects of status, type of frustration and aggression on vascular processes. *Journal of Abnormal and Social Psychology* 65:232–37.

Holmes, T. H., and M. Masuda. 1974. Life change and illness susceptibility. In B. S. Dohrenwend and B. P. Dohrenwend (eds.), *Stressful Life Events: Their Nature and Effects.* New York, John Wiley and Sons, pp. 45–72.

Holmes, T. H., and R. H. Rahe. 1967. The social readjustment rating scale. *Journal of Psychosomatic Research* 11:213–18.

Homans, G. C. 1950. *The Human Group.* New York, Harcourt, Brace.

Hundley, J. M. 1973. *The Small Outsider.* Sydney, Angus and Robertson (reprint of 1971 publication).

Hutt, C., S. J. Hutt, D. Lee, and C. Ounsted. 1964. Arousal and childhood autism. *Nature* (London) 204:908–9.

Hutt, M. L. 1947. A clinical study of "consecutive" and "adaptive" testing with the revised Stanford-Binet. *Journal of Consulting Psychology* 11:93–103.

Hutt, S. J., and C. Hutt (eds.). 1970a. *Behaviour Studies in Psychiatry.* Oxford, England, Pargamon Press.

Hutt, S. J. and C. Hutt. 1970b. *Direct Observation and Measurement of Behavior.* Springfield, Illinois, Charles C. Thomas.

Irle, M., and B. Rohrmann. 1968. Gesamtbericht über die Hamburger Voruntersuchung zum DFG-projekt Fluglarmforschung. Mannheim und Hamburg, West Germany, unpublished manuscript (April).

Jackson, C. W., and J. C. Pollard. 1962. Sensory deprivation and suggestion: theoretical approach. *Behavioral Science* 7:332–42.

James, W. 1902. *Varieties of Religious Experience: A Study in Human Nature.* New York, Mentor Edition (1958).

—— 1905. *The Principles of Psychology.* Vol. 1. New York, Henry Holt and Company.

Janis, I. L. 1958. *Psychological Stress.* New York, John Wiley and Sons.

—— 1968. When fear is healthy. *Psychology Today* 1:46–49, 60–61.

—— 1974. *Psychological Stress: Psychoanalytic and Behavioral Studies of Surgical Patients.* New York, Academic Press.

Janis, I. L., and H. Leventhal. 1965. Psychological aspects of physical illness and hospital care. In B. Wolman (ed.), *Handbook of Clinical Psychology.* New York, McGraw-Hill, pp. 1360–77.

Janis, I. L., G. F. Mahl, J. Kagan, and R. R. Holt. 1969. *Personality.* New York; Harcourt, Brace, and World.

Jansen, G. 1961. Adverse effects of noise on iron and steel workers. *Stahl und Eisen* 81:217–20. (As cited in Kryter, 1970.)

—— 1969. Effects of noise on physiological state. In W. D. Ward and J. E. Frick (eds.), *Noise as a Public Health Hazard: Proceedings of the Conference.* ASHA Reports 4. Washington, D.C., The American Speech and Hearing Association (February), pp. 89–98.

Jerison, H. J., and S. Wing. 1957. Effects of noise and fatigue on a complex vigilance task. Report WADC-TR-57-14. Wright-Patterson Air Force Base, Ohio, Wright Air Development Center.

Jones, N. G. Blurton (ed.). 1972. *Ethological Studies of Infant Behaviour.* London, Cambridge University Press.

Jonsson, E., A. Kajland, B. Paccaguella, and S. Sorensen. 1969. Annoyance reactions to traffic noise in Italy and Sweden. *Archives of Environmental Health* 19:692–99.

Kahne, M. J. 1959. Bureaucratic structure and impersonal experience in mental hospitals. *Psychiatry* 22:363–75.

Kalish, H., N. Garmezy, E. Rodnick, and R. Bleke. 1958. The effects of anxiety and experimentally induced stress on verbal learning. *Journal of General Psychology* 59:87–95.

Kamano, D. K. 1963. Relationship of ego disjunction and manifest anxiety to conflict resolution. *Journal of Abnormal and Social Psychology* 66:281–84.

Kamp, L. N. J. 1964. Autistic syndrome in one of a pair of monozygotic twins. *Psychiatria, Neurologia, Neurochirurgia* 67:143–47.

Kanner, L. 1943. Autistic disturbances of affective contact. *The Nervous Child* 2:217–50.

—— 1973. *Childhood Psychosis.* Washington, D.C., Winston (distributed b Wiley).

Katchmar, L. T. 1953. *Indicators of Behavior Decrement: 22. The Effects of Stres Anxiety, and Ego Involvement on "Shift" Task Performance.* Project DA-49-007-MI 222, Technical Report 22. College Park, Maryland, University of Maryland, Arn Medical Research and Development Building.

Katchmar, L. T., S. Ross, and T. G. Andrews. 1958. Effects of stress and anxiety on performance of a complex verbal coding task. *Journal of Experimental Psychology* 55:559–64.

Katkin, E. S. 1965. Relationship between manifest anxiety and two indices of autonomic response to stress. *Journal of Personality and Social Psychology* 2:324–33.

Katz, J. L., P. Ackman, Y. Rothwax, E. J. Sachar, H. Weiner, L. Hellman, and T. F. Gallagher. 1970a. Psychoendocrine aspects of cancer of the breast. *Psychosomatic Medicine* 32:1–18.

Katz, J. L., H. Weiner, T. G. Gallagher, and L. Hellman. 1970b. Stress, distress, and ego defenses. *Archives of General Psychiatry* 23:131–42.

Keeley, K. 1962. Prenatal influence on behavior of offspring of crowded mice. *Science* 135:44–45.

Kelley, H. H., J. C. Condry, Jr., A. E. Dahlke, and A. H. Hill. 1965. Collective behavior in a simulated panic situation. *Journal of Experimental Social Psychology* 1:20–54.

Kissel, S. 1965. Stress-reducing properties of social stimuli. *Journal of Personality and Social Psychology* 2:378–84.

Klein, M. 1940. Mourning and its relations to manic-depressive states. *International Journal of Psychoanalysis* 21:125–53.

Knudson, A. G., Jr., and J. M. Natterson. 1960. Participation of parents in the hospital care of fatally ill children. *Pediatrics* 26:482–90.

Koestler, A. 1944. On disbelieving atrocities. In A. Koestler, *The Yogi and the Commissar and Other Essays.* London, Hutchinson, pp. 89–93 (1965).

Koford, C. B. 1963. Rank of mothers and sons in bands of rhesus monkeys. *Science* 141:356–57.

Koriat, A., R. Melkman, J. R. Averill, and R. S. Lazarus. 1972. The self-control of emotional reactions to a stressful film. *Journal of Personality* 40:601–19.

Kornfeld, D. S. 1969a. Psychiatric aspects of patient care in the operating suite and special areas. *Anesthesiology* 31:166–71.

—— 1969b. Psychiatric view of the intensive care unit. *British Medical Journal* :108–10.

Kryter, K. D. 1950. The effects of noise on man. *Journal of Speech and Hearing Disorders* 1:Monograph Supplement I.

—— 1968. An example of "engineering psychology": The aircraft noise problem. *American Psychologist* 23:240–44.

—— 1970. *The Effects of Noise on Man.* New York, Academic Press.

Kryter, K. D., N. D. Ward, J. D. Miller, and D. H. Eldredge. 1966. Hazardous exposure to intermittent and steady-state noise. *Journal of the Acoustical Society America* 39:451–64.

Lacey, J. I., J. Kagan, B. C. Lacey, and H. A. Moss. 1963. The visceral level: situational determinants and behavioral correlates of autonomic response patterns.

In P. H. Knapp (ed.), *Expression of the Emotions in Man.* New York, International Universities Press, pp. 161–96.

Lasagna, L. 1962. Some explored and unexplored psychological variables in therapeutics. *Proceedings of the Royal Society of Medicine* (London) 55:773–76.

Lazarus, R. S. 1966. *Psychological Stress and the Coping Process.* New York, McGraw-Hill.

—— 1973. The self-regulation of emotion. Paper given at symposium entitled Parameters of Emotion, Stockholm, Sweden (June 4–6).

—— 1974a. Cognitive and coping processes in emotion. In B. Weiner (ed.), *Cognitive Views of Human Motivation.* New York, Academic Press, pp. 21–32.

—— 1974b. Psychological stress and coping in adaptation and illness. *International Journal of Psychiatry in Medicine* 5:321–33.

—— 1975. A cognitively oriented psychologist looks at biofeedback. *American Psychologist* 30:553–61.

Lazarus, R. S., and E. Alfert. 1964. The short-circuiting of threat. *Journal of Abnormal and Social Psychology* 69:195–205.

Lazarus, R. S., J. R. Averill, and E. M. Opton, Jr. 1970. Towards a cognitive theory of emotion. In M. B. Arnold (ed.), *Feelings and Emotions.* New York, Academic Press, pp. 207–32.

—— 1974. The psychology of coping: Issues of research and assessment. In G. V. Coelho, D. A. Hamburg, and J. E. Adams (eds.), *Coping and Adaptation.* New York, Basic Books, pp. 249–315.

Lazarus, R. S., R. W. Baker, D. M. Broverman, and J. Mayer. 1957. Personality and psychological stress. *Journal of Personality* 25:559–77.

Lazarus, R. S., J. Deese, and S. Osler. 1951. *Review of Research on Effects of Psychological Stress Upon Performance.* Research Bulletin 51-28 (December). San Antonio, Texas, Human Resources Research Center, ATC, Lackland AFB.

—— 1952. The effects of psychological stress upon performance. *Psychological Bulletin* 49:293–317.

Leonard, A. G. 1906. *The Lower Niger and Its Tribes.* London, Macmillan and Company.

Levi, L. (ed.). 1971. *Society, Stress, and Disease: The Psychosocial Environment and Psychosomatic Diseases.* Vol. 1. London, Oxford University Press.

Levin, A. J. 1951. The fiction of the death instinct. *Psychiatric Quarterly* 25:257–81.

Levine, S., and N. A. Scotch (eds.). 1970. *Social Stress.* Chicago, Aldine.

Lewin, B. 1950. *The Psychoanalysis of Elation.* New York, W. W. Norton, Inc.

Lewin, K. 1947. Frontiers in group dynamics: Concept, method and reality in social science; social equilibria and social change. *Human Relations* 1:5–41.

Lief, H. I., and R. S. Fox. 1963. Training for "detached concern" in medical students. In H. I. Lief, V. F. Lief, and N. R. Lief (eds.), *The Psychological Basis Medical Practice.* New York, Harper and Row, pp. 12–35.

Lifton, R. 1963. Psychological effects of the atomic bomb in Hiroshima: The theme of death. *Daedalus* 92 (Summer):462–97.

Lindemann, E. 1944. Symptomatology and management of acute grief. *American Journal of Psychiatry* 101:141–48.

Lipowski, Z. J. 1967. Delirium: Clouding of consciousness and confusion. *Journal of Nervous and Mental Disease* 154:227–55.

Lippett, R., J. Watson, and B. Westley. 1958. *The Dynamics of Planned Change: A Comparative Study of Principles and Techniques.* New York, Harcourt, Brace.

Lofchie, S. H. 1955. The performance of adults under distraction stress: A developmental approach. *Journal of Psychology* 39:109–16.

Lorenz, K. 1963. *Das Sogenannte Böse—Zur Naturgeschichte der Aggression.* Vienna, Dr. G. Borotha-Schoeler Verlag.

Luby, E. D., J. L. Grisell, C. E. Frohman, H. Lees, B. D. Cohen, and J. S. Gottlieb. 1962. Biochemical, psychological, and behavioral responses to sleep deprivation. *Annals of the New York Academy of Science* 96:71–79.

Lucas, R. A. 1969. *Men in Crisis.* New York, Basic Books.

Mackintosh, J. H. 1962. Effect of strain and group size on the response of mice to "seconal" anaesthesia. *Nature* 194:1304.

Malmo, R. B., A. A. Smith, and W. A. Kohlmeyer. 1956. Motor manifestation of conflict in interview: A case study. *Journal of Abnormal and Social Psychology* 52:268–71.

Manning, A. 1972. *An Introduction to Animal Behaviour.* London, Arnold.

Mansson, H. H. 1972. Justifying the final solution. *Omega* 3:79–87.

Marcuse, H. 1959. The ideology of death. In H. Feifel (ed.), *The Meaning of Death.* New York, McGraw-Hill, pp. 64–76.

Margolis, G. J. 1967. Postoperative psychosis on the intensive care unit. *Comprehensive Psychiatry* 8:227–32.

Mariott, H. I. 1950. *Water and Salt Depletion.* Springfield, Illinois, Charles C. Thomas.

Marmor, J. 1963. The cancer patient and his family. In H. I. Lief, V. F. Lief, and N. R. Lief (eds.), *The Psychological Basis of Medical Practice.* New York, Harper and Row, pp. 309–17.

Marris, P. 1958. *Widows and Their Families.* London, Routledge and Kegan Paul.

Mason, J. W. 1959. Psychological influences on the pituitary-adrenal cortical system. *Recent Progress in Hormone Research* 15:345–89.

—— 1968. A review of psychoendocrine research on the pituitary-adrenal cortical system. *Psychosomatic Medicine* 30:576–607.

—— 1971. A re-evaluation of the concept of "non-specificity" in stress theory. *Journal of Psychiatric Research* 8:323–33.

—— 1975a. A historical view of the stress field. Part 1. *Journal of Human Stress* 1:6–12.

Mason, J. W. 1975b. A historical view of the stress field. Part 2. *Journal of Human Stress* 1:22–36.

Masuda, M., and T. H. Holmes. 1967. The social readjustment rating scale: A cross-cultural study of Japanese and Americans. *Journal of Psychosomatic Research* 11:227–37.

Matarazzo, R. G., and J. D. Matarazzo. 1956. Anxiety level and pursuitmeter performance. *Journal of Consulting Psychology* 20:70.

McDermott, N. T., and S. Cobb. 1939. Psychiatric survey of 50 cases of bronchial asthma. *Psychosomatic Medicine* 1:203–44.

McDonald, D. G., J. Stern, and W. Hahn. 1963. Effects of differential housing and stress on diet selection, water intake, and body weight in the rat. *Journal of Applied Physiology* 18:937–42.

McGrath, J. E. 1970a. Settings, measures, and themes: An integrative review of some research on social-psychological factors in stress. In J. E. McGrath (ed.), *Social and Psychological Factors in Stress.* New York; Holt, Rinehart, and Winston, pp. 58–96.

McGrath, J. E. (ed.). 1970b. *Social and Psychological Factors in Stress.* New York; Holt, Rinehart, and Winston.

McGrath, J. J., and J. F. Hatcher. 1961. Irrelevant stimulation and vigilance under fast and slow stimulus. *ASW Technical Report No. 7.* Los Angeles, California; Human Factors, Research.

McKennell, A. C., and E. A. Hunt. 1966. *Noise Annoyance in Central London.* London, The Government Social Survey, SS/332 (March).

McKissick, G. E., G. L. Flickinger, Jr., and H. L. Ratcliffe. 1961. Coronary arteriosclerosis in isolated, paired, and grouped chickens. *Proceedings of the Federation of American Societies for Experimental Biology* 20:91.

Mechanic, D. 1962. *Students Under Stress.* New York, The Free Press of Glencoe.

—— 1963. Religion, religiosity, and illness behavior: The special case of the Jews. *Human Organization* 22:202–8.

—— 1974. Discussion of research programs on relations between stressful life events and episodes of physical illness. In B. S. Dohrenwend and B. P. Dohrenwend (eds.), *Stressful Life Events: Their Nature and Effects.* New York, John Wiley and Sons, pp. 87–97.

Mecklin, J. M. 1969. It's time to turn down all that noise. *Fortune* (October): 130–33, 188, 190, 195.

Medawar, P. B. 1967. *The Art of the Soluble.* London, Methuen.

Melzack, R. 1973. *The Puzzle of Pain.* New York, Basic Books.

Menninger, K. A. 1954. Regulatory devices of the ego under major stress. *International Journal of Psychoanalysis* 35:412–20.

—— 1959. Hope. *American Journal of Psychiatry* 116:481–91.

—— 1963. *The Vital Balance.* New York, Viking Press.

Milburn, T. W. 1961. Space crews, psychology, and American society. *Journal of Social Issues* 17:24–28.

Milgram, S. 1965. Some conditions of obedience and disobedience to authority. *Human Relations* 18:57–76.

—— 1970. The experience of living in cities. *Science* 13:1461–68.

Miller, D. 1959. A brief review of salient specific findings on morale and human behavior of young men living under the isolation and relative deprivation of radar base habitability. Working Paper. Washington, D.C., Disaster Research Group, Division of Anthropology and Psychology, National Academy of Sciences—National Research Council.

Miller, G. A. 1969. Psychology as a means of promoting human welfare. *American Psychologist* 24:1063–75.

Miller, J. C., and N. Treiger. 1969. Management of dependency under preoperative stress. Mimeographed prepublication report.

Miller, J. G., L. Bouthilet, and C. Eldridge. 1953. *A Bibliography for the Development of Experimental Stress-Sensitive Tests for Predicting Performance in Military Tasks.* PRB Technical Report 1079, Research Note 22. Washington, D.C., Psychological Research Associates.

Miller, L. H., and B. M. Shmavonian. 1965. Replicability of two GSR indices as function of stress and cognitive activity. *Journal of Personality and Social Psychology* 2:753–56.

Mira, E. 1939. Psychiatric experience in the Spanish war. *British Medical Journal* 1:1217–20.

Mischel, W. 1968. *Personality and Assessment.* New York, John Wiley and Sons.

Moloney, J. C. 1949. *The Magic Cloak: A Contribution to the Psychology of Authoritarianism.* Wakefield, Mass., Montrose Press.

Monat, A., J. R. Averill, and R. S. Lazarus. 1972. Anticipatory stress and coping reactions under various conditions of uncertainty. *Journal of Personality and Social Psychology* 24:237–53.

Moos, R. H. (ed.). 1976. *Human Adaptation: Coping with Life Crises.* Lexington, Mass., D. C. Heath and Company.

Moran, P. A. 1963. An experimental study of pediatric admission. New Haven, Yale University School of Nursing, unpublished master's thesis.

Murphy, G. 1959. Discussion. In H. Feifel (ed.), *The Meaning of Death.* New York, McGraw-Hill, pp. 317–40.

Murphy, L. B. 1962. *The Widening World of Childhood.* New York, Basic Books.

—— 1974. Coping, vulnerability, and resilience in childhood. In G. V. Coelho, D. A. Hamburg, and J. E. Adams (eds.), *Coping and Adaptation.* New York, Basic Books, pp. 69–100.

Murphy, R. E. 1959. Effects of threat of shock, distraction, and task design on performance. *Journal of Experimental Psychology* 58:1134–41.

Murray, E. J. 1960. Adjustment to environmental stress in fallout shelters. In G. W. Baker and J. H. Rohrer (eds.), *Symposium on Human Problems in the Utilization of Fallout Shelters*. Disaster Study No. 12. Washington, D.C., National Academy of Sciences—National Research Council, pp. 67–77.

Murray, E. J., E. H. Schein, K. T. Erikson, W. F. Hill, and M. Cohen. In press. The effects of sleep deprivation on social behavior. (Experiment No. 2) *Journal of Social Psychology*.

Murray, H. A. 1937. Visual manifestations of personality. *Journal of Abnormal and Social Psychology* 32:161–84.

Myerson, A. 1944. Prolonged cases of grief reaction treated by electric shock. *New England Journal of Medicine* 230:255–56.

Natterson, J. M., and A. G. Knudson. 1960. Observations concerning fear of death in fatally ill children and their mothers. *Psychosomatic Medicine* 22:456–65.

Nomikos, M. S., E. M. Opton, Jr., J. R. Averill, and R. S. Lazarus. 1968. Surprise versus suspense in the production of stress reaction. *Journal of Personality and Social Psychology* 8:204–8.

O'Gorman, G. 1970. *The Nature of Childhood Autism*. London, Butterworth.

Olin, H., and T. Hackett. Unpublished data.

Olsen, R. L. 1960. The implications of food acceptability for shelter occupancy. In G. W. Baker and J. H. Rohrer (eds.), *Symposium on Human Problems in the Utilization of Fallout Shelters*. Disaster Study No. 12. Washington, D. C., National Academy of Sciences—National Research Council, pp. 167–79.

Orbach, C. E., A. M. Sutherland, and M. F. Bozeman. 1955. Psychological impact of cancer and its treatment, III. The adaptation of mothers to the threatened loss of their children through leukemia: Part 2. *Cancer* 8:20–33.

Ornitz, E. M. 1973. Childhood autism—A review of the clinical and experimental literature. *California Medicine* 118:21–47.

Orr, D. B. 1964. Research behavior impairment due to stress: An experiment in long-term performance. *Journal of Experimental Psychology* 68:94–102.

Orwell, G. 1946. How the poor die. In G. Orwell, *Shooting an Elephant, and Other Essays*. New York, Harcourt, Brace (1950), pp. 19–31.

Osler, S. F. 1954. Intellectual performance as a function of two types of psychological stress. *Journal of Experimental Psychology* 47:115–21.

Page, J. D. 1975. *Psychopathology: The Science of Understanding Deviance*. Chicago, Aldine.

Palermo, D. S. 1957. Proactive interference and facilitation as a function of amount of training and stress. *Journal of Experimental Psychology* 53:293–96.

Park, C. C. 1972. *The Siege*. Harmondsworth, England, Penguin Books (reprint of 1967 publication).

Parkes, E. H. 1963. The effect of situational stress, set-strength, and trait anxiety on problem-solving rigidity. *Dissertation Abstracts* 24:385.

Parsons, H. M. 1966. STAVE: STress AVoidance/Escape. SP-2459. Santa Monica, California, System Developmental Corporation (August).

Parsons, T. 1951. *The Social System.* Glencoe, Illinois, The Free Press.

Pascal, G. R. 1951. Psychological deficit as a function of stress and constitution. *Journal of Personality* 20:175–87.

Pepinsky, P., H. Pepinsky, and W. Pavlik. 1960. The effects of task complexity and time pressure upon team productivity. *Journal of Applied Psychology* 44:34–38.

Pervin, L. A. 1963. The need to predict and control under conditions of threat. *Journal of Personality* 31:570–85.

Pinkerton, J. (ed.). 1814. *A General Collection of the Best and Most Interesting Voyages and Travels in All Parts of the World.* Vol. 16. London; Longman, Hurst, Rees, and Orine.

Plag, J. A., and J. M. Goffman. 1966a. A formula for predicting effectiveness in the Navy from characteristics of high school students. *Psychology in the Schools* 3:216–21.

——— 1966b. The prediction of four-year military effectiveness from characteristics of naval recruits. *Military Medicine* 131:729–35.

Plutchik, R. 1959. The effects of high-intensity intermittent sound on performance, feeling, and physiology. *Psychological Bulletin* 56:133–51.

Porteus, S. D. Personal Communication.

Postman, L., and D. Brown. 1952. Perceptual consequences of success and failure. *Journal of Abnormal and Social Psychology* 47:213–21.

Pronko, N. E., and W. R. Leith. 1956. Behavior under stress: A study of its disintegration. *Psychological Reports* 2:205–22 (Monograph Supplement 5).

Rahe, R. H. 1972. Subjects' recent changes and their near-future illness susceptibility. *Advances in Psychosomatic Medicine* 8:2–19.

——— 1974. The pathway between subjects' recent life changes and their near-future illness reports: Representative results and methodological issues. In B. S. Dohrenwend and B. P. Dohrenwend (eds.), *Stressful Life Events: Their Nature and Effects.* New York, John Wiley and Sons, pp. 73–86.

——— In press. Life crisis and major health change. In The American College of Neuropharmacology (ed.), *Prediction.* Vol. 2. Charles C. Thomas.

Rahe, R. H., and R. J. Arthur. 1968. Life-change patterns surrounding illness experience. *Journal of Psychosomatic Research* 11:341–45.

Rahe, R. H., and A. E. Christ. 1966. An unusual cardiac (ventricular) arrhythmia in a child: Psychiatric and psychophysiologic aspects. *Psychosomatic Medicine* 28:181–88.

Rahe, R. H., and T. H. Holmes. 1965. Social, psychologic, and psychophysiologic aspects of inguinal hernia. *Journal of Psychosomatic Research* 8:486–91.

Rahe, R. H., J. D. McKean, and R. J. Arthur. 1967. A longitudinal study of life-change and illness patterns. *Journal of Psychosomatic Research* 10:355–66.

Rahe, R. H., M. Meyer, M. Smith, G. Kajer, and T. H. Holmes. 1964. Social stress and illness onset. *Journal of Psychosomatic Research* 8:35–44.

Reich, W. 1933. *Character Analysis.* New York, Orgone Institute Press (1949).

Reid, D. 1948. Sickness and stress in operational flying. *British Journal of Social Medicine* 2:123–31.

Rheingold, J. C. 1967. *The Mother, Anxiety, and Death: The Catastrophic Death Complex.* Boston; Little, Brown.

Richmond, J. B., and H. A. Waisman. 1955. Psychologic aspects of management of children with malignant diseases. *American Journal of Diseases of Children* 89:42–47.

Rimland, B. 1971. The differentiation of childhood psychoses: An analysis of checklists for 2,218 psychotic children. *Journal of Autism and Childhood Schizophrenia* 1:161–74.

Rochlin, G. 1961. The dread of abandonment: A contribution to the etiology of the loss complex and to depression. *The Psychoanalytic Study of the Child* 16:451–70.

—— 1967. *Griefs and Discontents.* Boston; Little, Brown.

Rodda, M. 1967. *Noise in Society.* London, Oliver and Boyd.

Rohrer, J. H. 1959. Studies of human adjustment to polar isolation and implications of those studies for living in fallout shelters. Working Paper. Washington, D.C., Disaster Research Group, Division of Anthropology and Psychology, National Academy of Sciences—National Research Council.

Romano, J., and G. L. Engel. 1944a. Delirium: I. Electroencephalographic data. *A.M.A. Archives of Neurology and Psychiatry* 51:356–77.

—— 1944b. Physiologic and psychologic considerations of delirium. *Medical Clinics of North America* 28:629–38.

Rome, H. 1969. The irony of the ICU. *Psychiatry Digest* 30:10–14.

Rosen, S. 1970. Noise, hearing, and cardiovascular function. In B. L. Welch and A. S. Welch (eds.), *Physiological Effects of Noise.* New York, Plenum Press, pp. 57–66.

Rosenbaum, M. 1944. Emotional aspects of wartime separations. *Family* 24:337–41.

Rosenberg, L. 1961. Group size, prior experience, and conformity. *Journal of Abnormal and Social Psychology* 63:436–37.

Rosenthal, A. M. 1964. *Thirty-Eight Witnesses.* New York, McGraw-Hill.

Ross, B. M., J. W. Rupel, and D. A. Grant. 1952. Effects of personal, impersonal, and physical stress upon cognitive behavior in a card sorting problem. *Journal of Abnormal and Social Psychology* 47:546–51.

Roth, W. E. 1897. *Ethnological Studies among the North-West-Central Queensland Aborigines.* Brisbane and London, E. Gregory. Government Printer.

Rothenberg, A. 1961. Psychological problems in terminal cancer management. *Cancer* 14:1063–73.

Rutter, M. 1965. *Infantile Autism.* London, Methuen.

Rutter, M., L. Bartak, and S. Newman. 1971. Autism—A central disorder of cognition and language? In M. Rutter (ed.), *Infantile Autism: Concepts, Characteristics, and Treatment.* London, Churchill Livingstone, pp. 148–71.

Sachar, E. J., J. R. Fishman, and J. W. Mason. 1965. Influence of the hypnotic trance on plasma 17-hydroxycorticosteroid concentration. *Psychosomatic Medicine* 27:330–41.

Salter, M. 1970. Nursing in an intensive therapy unit. *Nursing Times* 66:486–87.

Sanders, A. F. 1961. The influence of noise on two discrimination tasks. *Ergonomics* 4:253–58.

Sanua, V. 1960. Sociocultural factors in responses to stressful life situations: The behavior of aged amputees as an example. *Journal of Health and Human Behavior* 1:17–24.

Sarason, I. G., C. de Monchaux, and T. Hunt. 1975. Methodological issues in the assessment of life stress. In L. Levi (ed.), *Emotions: Their Parameters and Measurement.* New York, Raven Press, pp. 499–509.

Saul, L. J. 1970. Inner sustainment. *Psychoanalytic Quarterly* 39:215–22.

Schachtel, E. G. 1959. *Metamorphosis.* New York, Basic Books.

Schachter, S., and J. E. Singer. 1962. Cognitive, social, and physiological determinants of emotional state. *Psychological Review* 69:379–99.

Schachter, S., T. A. Williams, R. Rowe, J. S. Schachter, and J. Jameson. 1965. Personality correlates of physiological reactivity to stress: A study of forty-six college males. *American Journal of Psychiatry* 121:12–22.

Schmale, A. H., Jr. 1958. Relationship of separation and depression to disease: I. A report on a hospitalized medical population. *Psychosomatic Medicine* 20:259–77.

—— 1964. Object loss; "giving up" and disease onset: An overview of research in progress. In *Symposium on Medical Aspects of Stress in the Military Climate.* Washington, D.C., Walter Reed Army Institute of Research, Walter Reed Army Medical Center.

Selye, H. 1952. *The Story of the Adaptation Syndrome.* Montreal, Acta, Inc.

—— 1956. *The Stress of Life.* New York, McGraw-Hill.

Shaler, N. S. 1900. *The Individual: A Study of Life and Death.* New York, Appleton-Century-Crofts.

Shannon, T. X., and G. M. Isbell. 1963. Stress in dental patients: Effect of local anesthetic procedures. Technical Report No. SAM-TDR-63-29. Brooks Air Force Base, Texas, United States Air Force School of Aerospace Medicine.

Shapiro, D. 1965. *Neurotic Styles.* New York, Basic Books.

Siegal, H. S. 1959. The relation between crowding and weight of adrenal glands in chickens. *Ecology* 40:495–98.

Silverman, R. E., and B. Blitz. 1956. Learning and two kinds of anxiety. *Journal of Abnormal and Social Psychology* 52:301–3.

Skinner, B. F. 1953. *Science and Human Behavior.* New York, Macmillan.

Smelser, N. J. 1963. *Theory of Collective Behavior.* New York, The Free Press of Glencoe.

Smith, E. E. 1959. Individual versus group goal conflict. *Journal of Abnormal and Social Psychology* 58:134–37.

Smith, K. R. 1951. Intermittent loud noise and mental performance. *Science* 114:132–33.

Smith, M. B. 1961. "Mental health" reconsidered: A special case of the problem of values in psychology. *American Psychologist* 16:299–306.

Smock, C. D. 1955a. The influence of psychological stress on the "intolerance of ambiguity." *Journal of Abnormal and Social Psychology* 50:177–82.

—— 1955b. The influence of stress on the perception of incongruity. *Journal of Abnormal and Social Psychology* 50:354–56.

Soares de Sousa, G. 1879. *Tratado Descriptivo do Brasil em 1587.* Rio de Janeiro, Typographia Universal de Laemmert.

Solnit, A. J., and M. Green. 1959. Psychologic considerations in the management of deaths on pediatric hospital services: I. The doctor and the child's family. *Pediatrics* 24:106–12.

Speisman, J. C., R. S. Lazarus, A. Mordkoff, and L. Davison. 1964. Experimental reduction of stress based on ego defense theory. *Journal of Abnormal and Social Psychology* 68:367–80.

Spielberger, C. D. (ed.). 1972. *Anxiety: Current Trends in Theory and Research.* Vols. 1 and 2. New York, Academic Press.

Spiro, M. E. 1965. Religious systems as culturally constituted defense mechanisms. In M. E. Spiro (ed.), *Context and Meaning in Cultural Anthropology.* New York, The Free Press, pp. 100–13.

Steele, J. 1963. A preliminary analysis of the Burmese Rorschachs. Unpublished manuscript.

Sternbach, R. A. 1966. *Principles of Psychophysiology.* New York, Academic Press.

Sternbach, R. A., and B. Tursky. 1965. Ethnic differences among housewives in psychophysical and skin potential responses to electric shock. *Psychophysiology* 1:241–46.

Stewart, W. H. 1969. Keynote address. In W. D. Ward and J. E. Frick (eds.), *Noise as a Public Health Hazard: Proceedings of the Conference.* ASHA Reports 4. Washington, D.C., The American Speech and Hearing Association (February), pp. 7–11.

Stokols, D. 1972. On the distinction between density and crowding: Some implications for future research. *Psychological Review* 79:275–77.

Stopol, M. S. 1954. The consistency of stress tolerance. *Journal of Personality* 23:13–29.

Stroh, G., and D. Buick. 1970. The effect of relative sensory isolation on the behaviour of two autistic children. In S. J. Hutt and C. Hutt (eds.), *Behaviour Studies in Psychiatry*. Oxford, Pergamon Press, pp. 161–74.

Suchman, E. A. 1964. Sociomedical variations among ethnic groups. *American Journal of Sociology* 70:319–31.

——— 1965. Social patterns of illness and medical care. *Journal of Health and Human Behavior* 6:2–16.

Sutcliffe, J. P., and M. Hoberman. 1956. Factors influencing choice in role conflict situations. *American Sociological Review* 21:695–703.

Symington, T., A. R. Currie, R. S. Curran, and J. N. Davidson. 1955. The reaction of the adrenal cortex in conditions of stress. In *Ciba Foundations Colloquia on Endocrinology*. Vol. 8. *The Human Adrenal Cortex*. Boston, Mass.; Little, Brown and Company, pp. 70–91.

Teichner, W. H., E. Arees, and R. Reilley. 1963. Noise and human performance, a psychophysiological approach. *Ergonomics* 6:83–97.

Thieme, G. 1971. *Leben mit Unserem Autistischen Kind*. Lüdenscheid, West Germany, Hilfe für das Autistische Kind e.V.

Thiessen, D. D. 1963. Varying sensitivity of $C_{57}BL/Crgl$ mice to grouping. *Science* 141:827–28.

Tietz, W. 1970. School phobia and the fear of death. *Mental Hygiene* 54:565–68.

Tinbergen, E. A., and N. Tinbergen. 1972. Early childhood autism: An ethological approach. *Fortschritte der Verhaltensforschung (Advances in Ethology)*: Whole Vol. 10. Berlin and Hamburg, Verlag Paul Parey.

Tinbergen, N. 1953. *Social Behaviour in Animals*. London, Methuen.

——— 1974. Ethology and stress diseases. *Science* 185:20–27.

Titchner, J., I. Zweling, L. Gottschalk, M. Levine, H. Silver, A. Cowett, S. Cohen, and W. Colbertson. 1957. Consequences of surgical illness and treatment: Interaction of emotions, personality and surgical illness, and treatment, convalescence. *A.M.A. Archives of Neurology and Psychiatry* 77:623–34.

Toffler, A. 1970. *Future Shock*. New York, Bantam.

Torrance, E. P. 1954. The behavior of small groups under the stress conditions of "survival." *American Sociological Review* 19:751–55.

Tregear, E. 1890. The Maoris of New Zealand. *Journal of the Anthropological Institute of Great Britain and Ireland* 19:97–123.

Tursky, B., and R. A. Sternbach. 1967. Further physiological correlates of ethnic differences in responses to shock. *Psychophysiology* 1:151–62.

Ulrich, C. 1957. Measurement of stress evidenced by college women in situations involving competition. *Research Quarterly, American Association of Health and Physical Education* 25:160–92.

Vaillant, G. E. 1963. Twins discordant for early infantile autism. *Archives of General Psychiatry* 9:163–67.

Varnhagen, F. A. 1875. *Historia Geral do Brasil.* Vol. 1. Rio de Janeiro, E. & H. Laemmert.

Venables, P. H., and I. Martin (eds.). *A Manual of Psychophysiological Methods.* Amsterdam, North-Holland Publishing Company.

Visotsky, H. M., D. A. Hamburg, M. E. Goss, and B. A. Lebovitz. 1961. Coping behavior under extreme stress: Observations of patients with severe poliomyelitis. *Archives of General Psychiatry* 5:423–48.

Vogel, W. R., S. Raymond, and R. S. Lazarus. 1959. Intrinsic motivation and psychological stress. *Journal of Abnormal and Social Psychology* 58:225–33.

Volkart, E. H., with S. T. Michael. 1957. Bereavement and mental health. In A. H. Leighton, J. A. Clausen, and R. N. Wilson (eds.), *Explorations in Social Psychiatry.* New York, Basic Books, pp. 281–307.

Vreeland, R., and G. Ellis. 1969. Stresses on the nurse in an intensive-care unit. *Journal of the American Medical Association* 208:332–34.

Wadeson, R. W., J. W. Mason, D. A. Hamburg, and J. H. Handlon. 1963. Plasma and urinary 17-OHCS responses to motion pictures. *Archives of General Psychiatry* 9:146–56.

Wahl, C. W. 1959. The fear of death. In H. Feifel (ed.), *The Meaning of Death.* New York, McGraw-Hill, pp. 16–29.

Wallace, Sir Cuthbert. 1919. *Introduction to Report No. 26 to Medical Research Committee, on Traumatic Toxaemia as a Factor in Shock.* London, Great Britain, Medical Research Committee.

Warner, W. L. 1941. *A Black Civilization; A Social Study of an Australian Tribe.* New York and London, Harper and Brothers.

Washburn, S. L., and L. Devore. 1961. The social life of baboons. *Scientific American* 204:62–71.

Weiner, B. 1966. Role of success and failure in the learning of easy and complex tasks. *Journal of Personality and Social Psychology* 3:339–44.

Weinstein, J., J. R. Averill, E. M. Opton, Jr., and R. S. Lazarus. 1968. Defensive style and discrepancy between self-report and physiological indexes of stress. *Journal of Personality and Social Psychology* 10:406–13.

Weisman, A. D., and T. Hackett. 1961. Predilection to death: Death and dying as a psychiatric problem. *Psychosomatic Medicine* 23:232–56.

—— 1962. The dying patient. *Forest Hospital Publication* 1:16–20.

Weiss, E., and O. S. English. 1957. *Psychosomatic Medicine.* Philadelphia, W. B. Saunders.

Weitz, J. 1970. Psychological research needs on the problems of human stress. In J. E. McGrath (ed.), *Social and Psychological Factors in Stress.* New York; Holt, Rinehart, and Winston, pp. 124–33.

Weller, L. 1963. The effects of anxiety on cohesiveness and rejection. *Human Relations* 16:189–97.

Welty, C. 1957. The geography of birds. *Scientific American* 197:118–28.

Wexler, S. S. 1971. *The Story of Sandy.* New York, Signet (reprint of 1955 publication).

Weybrew, B. B. 1967. Patterns of psychophysiological response to military stress. In M. H. Appley and R. Trumbull (eds.), *Psychological Stress.* New York, Appleton-Century-Crofts, pp. 324–62.

White, R. W. 1974. Strategies of adaptation: An attempt at systematic description. In G. V. Coelho, D. A. Hamburg, and J. E. Adams (eds.), *Coping and Adaptation.* New York, Basic Books, pp. 47–68.

Whitehorn, J. C. 1953. Introduction and survey of the problems of stress. In *Symposium on Stress.* Washington, D.C., Walter Reed Army Medical Center, Army Medical Service Graduate School, pp. 2–7.

Wilkinson, R. 1969. Some factors influencing the effect of environmental stressors upon performance. *Psychological Bulletin* 72:260–72.

Wilson, A. T. M. 1941. Reactive emotional disorders. *Practitioner* 146:254–58.

Wing, L. 1970. The syndrome of early childhood autism. *British Journal of Hospital Medicine* 4:381–92.

—— 1971. *Autistic Children.* London, Constable.

Wolf, A. V. 1956. Thirst. *Scientific American* 194:70–76.

Wolff, C. T., S. B. Friedman, M. A. Hofer, and J. W. Mason. 1964. Relationship between psychological defenses and mean urinary 17-hydroxycorticosteroid excretion rates. I. A predictive study of parents of fatally ill children. *Psychosomatic Medicine* 26:576–91.

Wolff, C. T., M. A. Hofer, and J. W. Mason. 1964. Relationship between psychological defenses and mean urinary 17-hydroxycorticosteroid excretion rates. II. Methodologic and theoretical considerations. *Psychosomatic Medicine* 26:592–609.

Wolff, C. T., J. W. Mason, S. B. Friedman, and M. A. Hofer. 1963. The relationship between ego defenses and the adrenal response to the prolonged threat of loss: A predictive study. Atlantic City, New Jersey, Presented at the Annual Meeting of the American Psychosomatic Society.

Wolff, H. G. 1953. *Stress and Disease.* Springfield, Illinois, Charles C. Thomas.

Wolff, W. 1943. *The Expression of Personality: Experimental Depth Psychology.* New York, Harper and Brothers.

Woodhead, M. M. 1959. Effect of brief loud noise on decision making. *Journal of the Acoustical Society of America* 31:1329–31.

Worcester, A. 1940. *The Care of the Aged, the Dying and the Dead.* 2nd ed. Springfield, Illinois, Charles C. Thomas.

Wrightsman, L. S., Jr. 1960. Effects of waiting with others on changes in level of felt anxiety. *Journal of Abnormal and Social Psychology* 61:216–22.

Yank, the Army Weekly. 1947. New York; Duell, Sloan and Pearce.

Zax, M., and E. L. Cowen. 1972. *Abnormal Psychology: Changing Conceptions.* New York; Holt, Rinehart and Winston.

Zborowski, M. 1952. Cultural components in response to pain. *Journal of Social Issues* 8:16–30.

—— 1969. *People in Pain.* San Francisco, Jossey-Bass.

Zeuner, F. E. 1963. *A History of Domesticated Animals.* London, Hutchinson.

Zilboorg, G. 1943. Fear of death. *Psychoanalytic Quarterly* 12:465–75.

Zuckerman, M., and M. M. Haber. 1965. Need for stimulation as a source of stress response to perceptual isolation. *Journal of Abnormal and Social Psychology* 70:371–77.

Authors whose works are not quoted or discussed in detail are excluded from this index. For complete bibliographical information, see References and Supplementary Readings.